INSIDERS' GUIDE® TO

THE OREGON COAST

FOURTH EDITION

LIZANN DUNEGAN

INSIDERS' GUIDE

GUILFORD, CONNECTICUT
AN IMPRINT OF GLOBE PEQUOT PRESS

All the information in this guidebook is subject to change. We recommend that you call ahead to obtain current information before traveling.

INSIDERS' GUIDE®

Copyright © 2004, 2007, 2009 Morris Book Publishing, LLC
Previously published in 2000 by Falcon Publishing, Inc.

Interior design: Sheryl Kober
Maps: XNR Productions, Inc. © Morris Book Publishing, LLC
Layout Artist: Maggie Peterson

ISSN 1545-1402
ISBN 978-0-7627-4872-3

Printed in the United States of America
10 9 8 7 6 5 4 3 2 1

CONTENTS

Directory of Maps

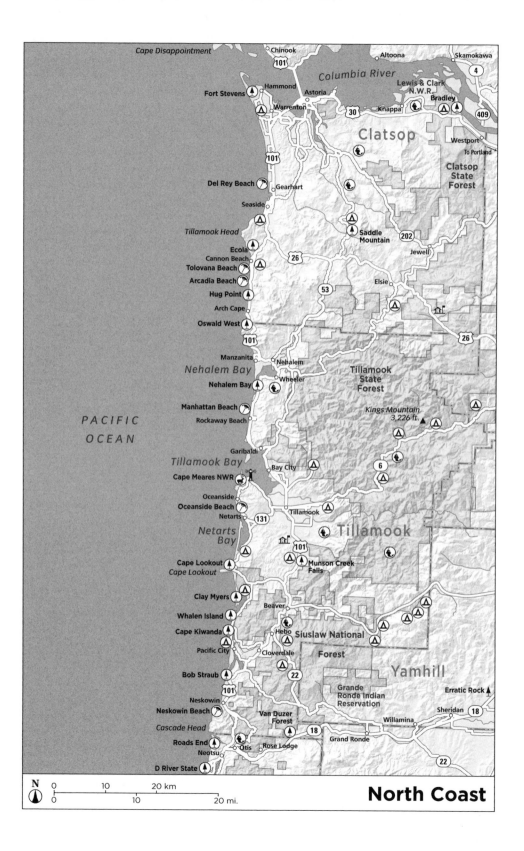

Cape Disappointment
Chinook
Altoona
Skamokawa
Columbia River
4
Fort Stevens
Hammond
Astoria
Lewis & Clark
N.W.R.
Bradley
Warrenton
Knappa
409
30
101
Clatsop
Westport
To Portland
101
Clatsop
State
Forest
Del Rey Beach
Gearhart
Seaside
Saddle
Mountain
202
Tillamook Head
Jewell
Ecola
26
Cannon Beach
Tolovana Beach
Arcadia Beach
Elsie
Hug Point
53
Arch Cape
Oswald West
26
101
Manzanita
Nehalem
Nehalem Bay
Wheeler
Tillamook
State
Forest
Nehalem Bay
Manhattan Beach
Kings Mountain
3,226 ft.
Rockaway Beach
PACIFIC
OCEAN
Garibaldi
Tillamook Bay
Bay City
6
Cape Meares NWR
Oceanside
Oceanside Beach
Tillamook
Netarts
131
Netarts
Bay
Tillamook
Cape Lookout
Cape Lookout
101
Munson Creek
Falls
Clay Myers
Beaver
Whalen Island
Siuslaw National
Cape Kiwanda
Hebo
Pacific City
Forest
Cloverdale
Yamhill
Bob Straub
22
Grande
Ronde Indian
Reservation
Erratic Rock
101
Neskowin
Sheridan
Neskowin Beach
18
Cascade Head
Van Duzer
Forest
18
Willamina
Roads End
Otis
Rose Lodge
Grand Ronde
Neotsu
22
D River State

N
0   10   20 km
0   10   20 mi.

North Coast

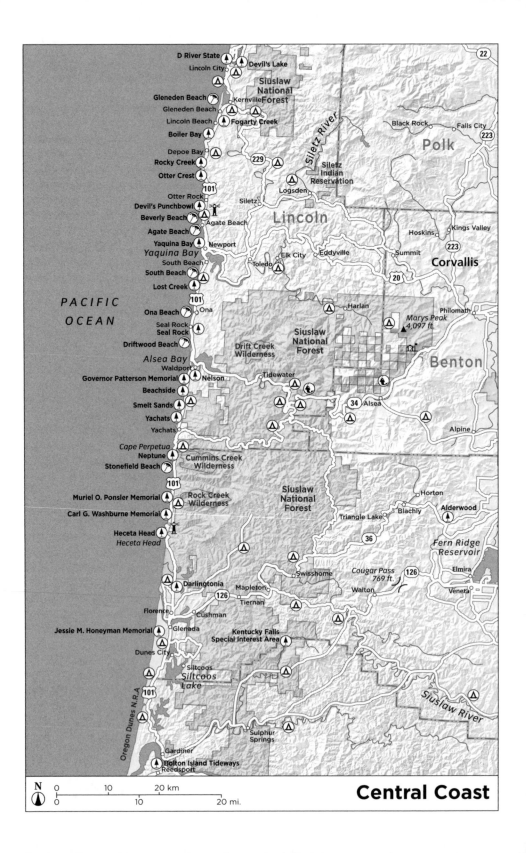

Central Coast

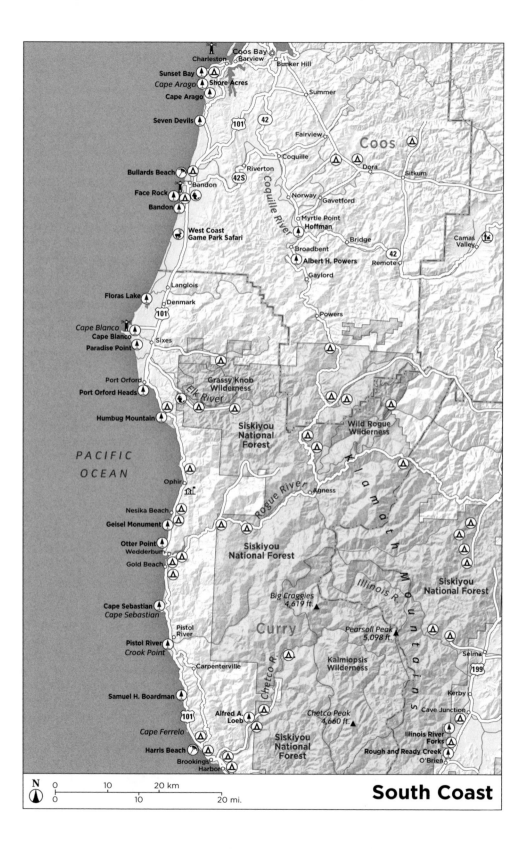

South Coast

Coos Bay
Charleston · Barview
Bunker Hill
Sunset Bay
Cape Arago · Shore Acres
Cape Arago
Summer
Seven Devils
Coos
Fairview
Coquille
Dora
Sitkum
Riverton
Bullards Beach
Bandon
Face Rock
Bandon
Norway
Gavetford
Myrtle Point
Hoffman
Bridge
West Coast
Game Park Safari
Broadbent
Albert H. Powers
Remote
Camas Valley
Gaylord
Langlois
Floras Lake
Denmark
Powers
Cape Blanco
Cape Blanco
Paradise Point
Sixes
Grassy Knob
Wilderness
Port Orford
Port Orford Heads
Elk River
Siskiyou
National
Forest
Wild Rogue
Wilderness
Humbug Mountain
PACIFIC
OCEAN
Klamath
Rogue River
Ophir
Agness
Nesika Beach
Geisel Monument
Otter Point
Wedderburn
Gold Beach
Siskiyou
National Forest
Illinois R.
Siskiyou
National Forest
Big Craggies
4,619 ft.
Cape Sebastian
Cape Sebastian
Pearsoll Peak
5,098 ft.
Curry
Selma
Pistol River
Crook Point
Pistol River
Carpenterville
Kalmiopsis
Wilderness
Mountains
Kerby
Cave Junction
Samuel H. Boardman
Chetco R.
Chetco Peak
4,660 ft.
Cape Ferrelo
Alfred A.
Loeb
Illinois River
Forks
Rough and Ready Creek
O'Brien
Harris Beach
Brookings
Harbor
Siskiyou
National
Forest

N
0   10   20 km
0   10   20 mi.

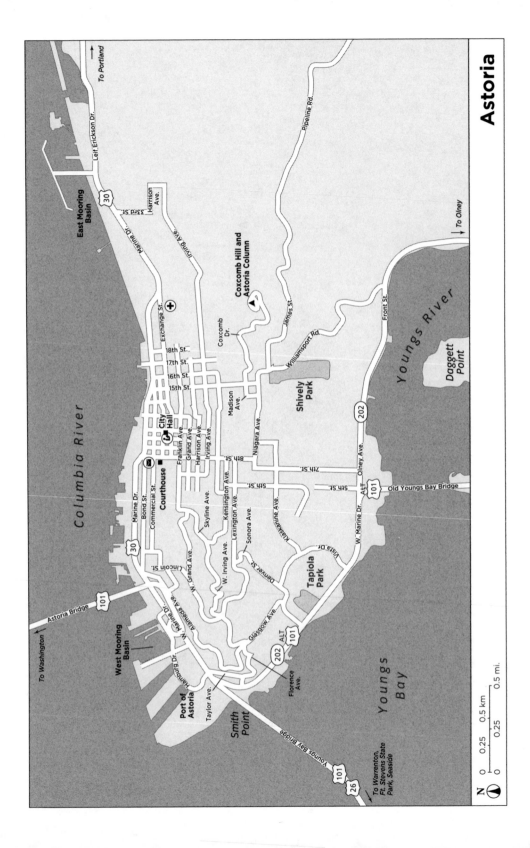

Astoria

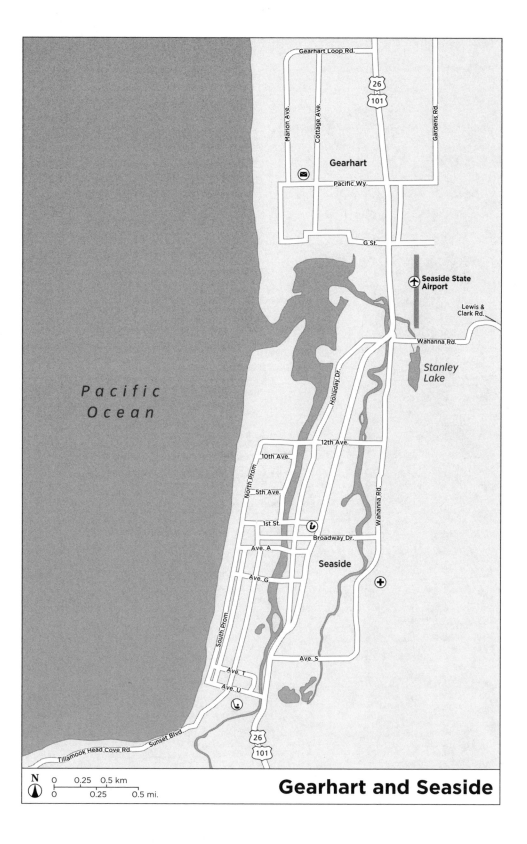

Gearhart and Seaside

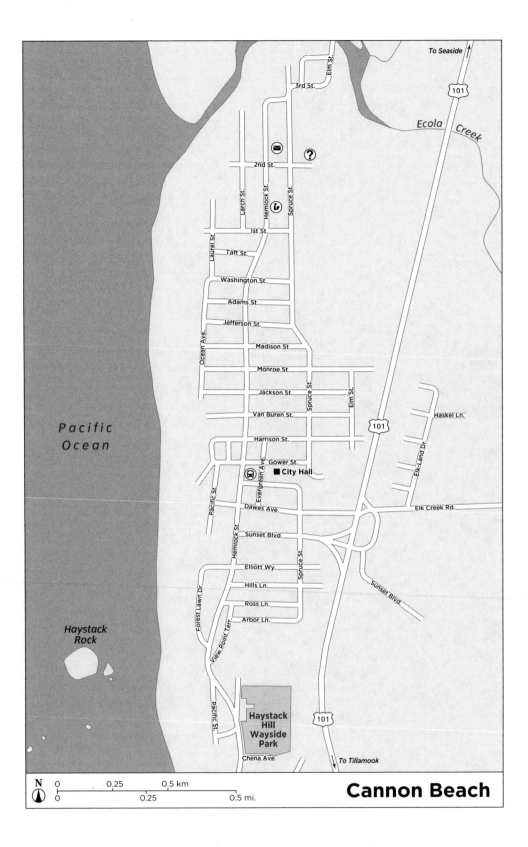

To Seaside

101

Ecola Creek

3rd St.

Elm St.

2nd St.

Larch St.
Hemlock St.
Spruce St.

1st St.

Laurel St.

Taft St.

Washington St.

Adams St.

Jefferson St.

Ocean Ave.

Madison St.

Monroe St.

Jackson St.

Spruce St.

Elm St.

Van Buren St.

101

Haskel Ln.

Harrison St.

Elk-Land Dr.

Gower St.

Evergreen Ave.

■ City Hall

Pacific St.

Pacific Ocean

Dawes Ave.

Elk Creek Rd.

Hemlock St.

Sunset Blvd.

Spruce St.

Elliott Wy.

Sunset Blvd.

Hills Ln.

Forest Lawn Dr.

Ross Ln.

View Point Terr.

Arbor Ln.

Haystack Rock

Pacific St.

Haystack Hill Wayside Park

101

Chena Ave.

To Tillamook

N

0   0.25   0.5 km
0   0.25   0.5 mi.

Cannon Beach

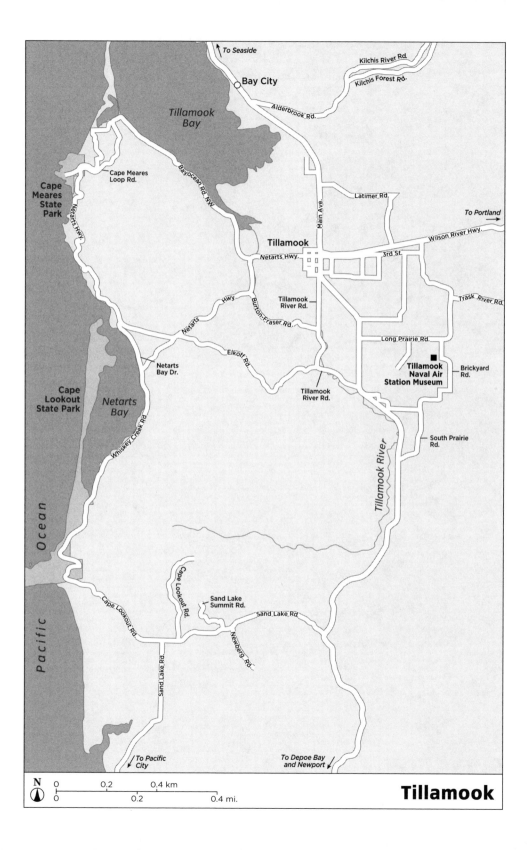

Tillamook

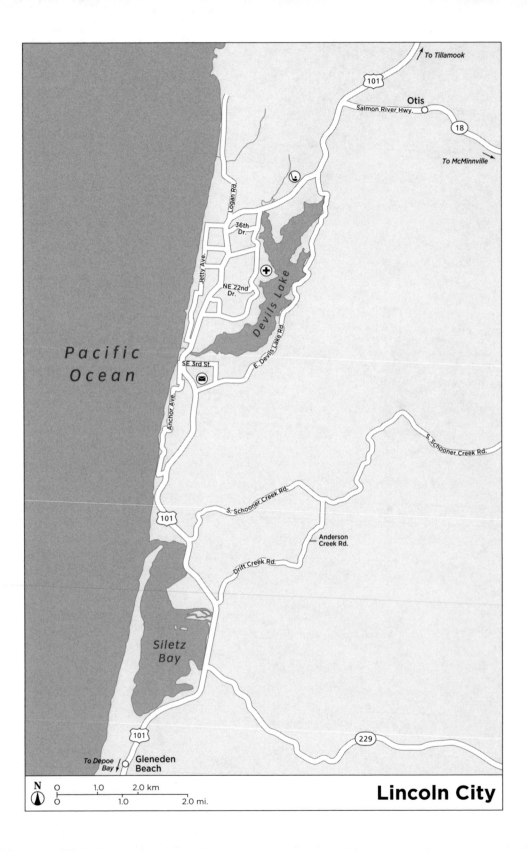

To Tillamook

101

Otis

Salmon River Hwy.

18

To McMinnville

Logan Rd.

36th Dr.

Jetty Ave.

NE 22nd Dr.

Devils Lake

E. Devils Lake Rd.

Pacific Ocean

SE 3rd St.

Anchor Ave.

S. Schooner Creek Rd.

101

S. Schooner Creek Rd.

Anderson Creek Rd.

Drift Creek Rd.

Siletz Bay

101

229

To Depoe Bay

Gleneden Beach

N

0   1.0   2.0 km
0   1.0   2.0 mi.

Lincoln City

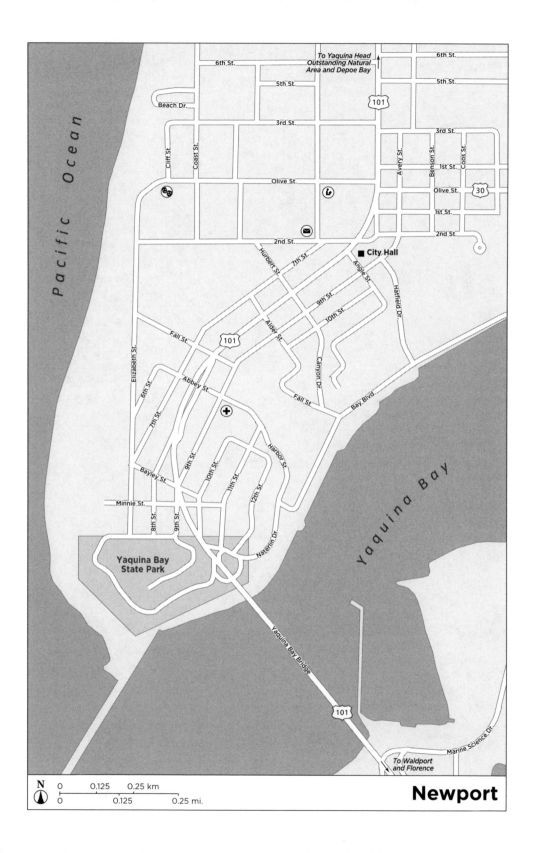

Pacific Ocean

To Yaquina Head
Outstanding Natural
Area and Depoe Bay

6th St.
6th St.
5th St.
5th St.
Beach Dr.
3rd St.
101
3rd St.
Cliff St.
Coast St.
Avery St.
Benson St.
Coos St.
1st St.
Olive St.
Olive St.
30
1st St.
2nd St.
2nd St.
Hurbert St.
7th St.
City Hall
Angle St.
Hatfield Dr.
9th St.
10th St.
Fall St.
Alder St.
101
Canyon Dr.
Elizabeth St.
Abbey St.
Fall St.
Bay Blvd.
6th St.
7th St.
9th St.
Harbor St.
Bayley St.
10th St.
11th St.
12th St.
Minnie St.
8th St.
9th St.
Naterlin Dr.

Yaquina Bay
State Park

Yaquina Bay

Yaquina Bay Bridge

101

Marine Science Dr.

To Waldport
and Florence

N

| 0 | 0.125 | 0.25 km |
| 0 | 0.125 | 0.25 mi. |

Newport

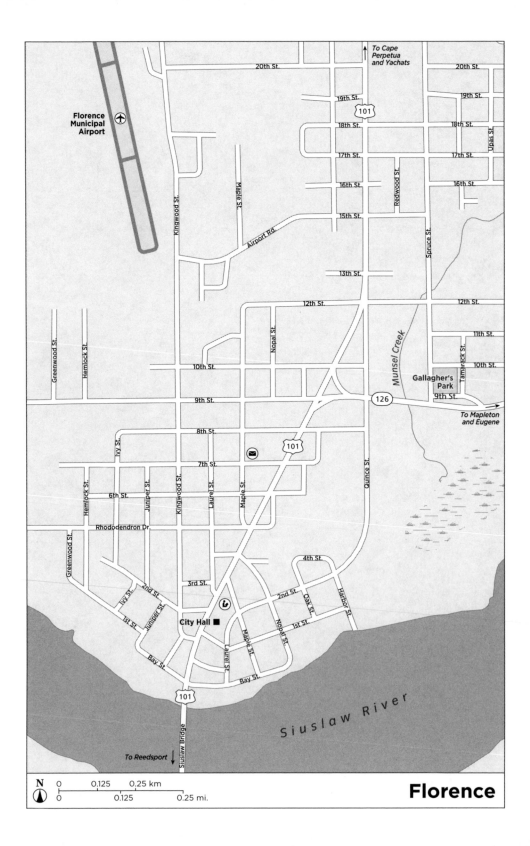

Florence

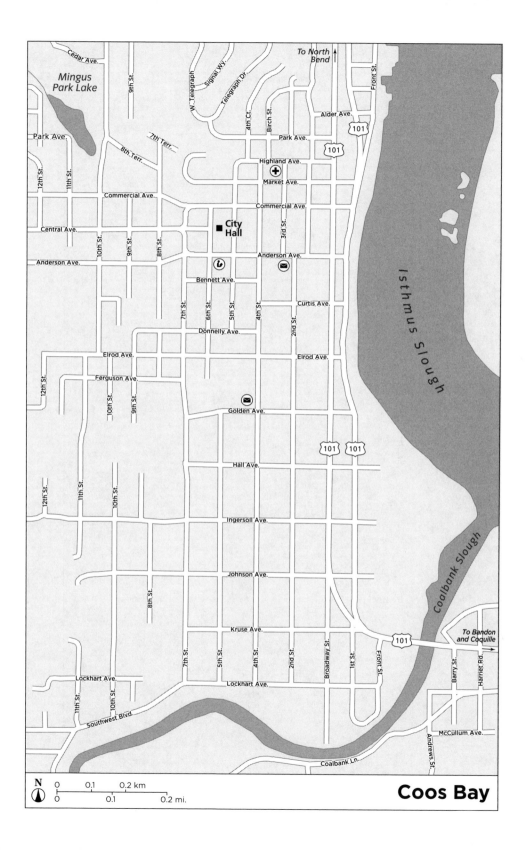

Coos Bay

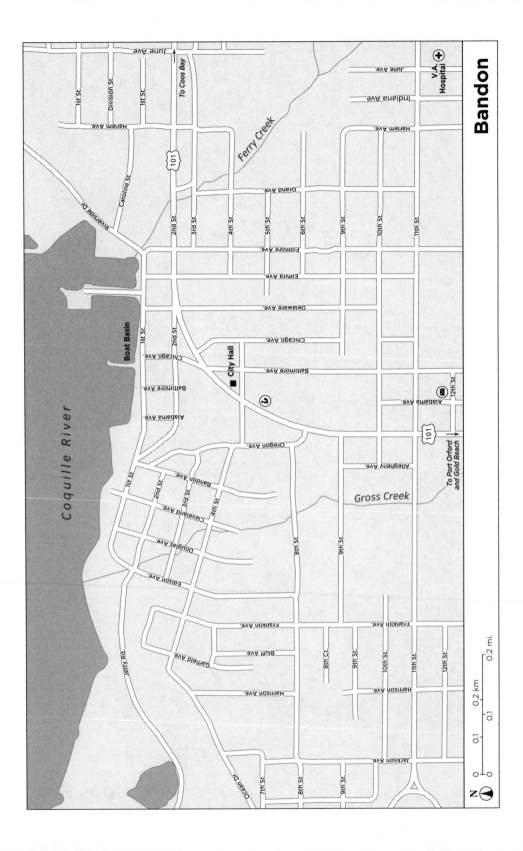

Bandon

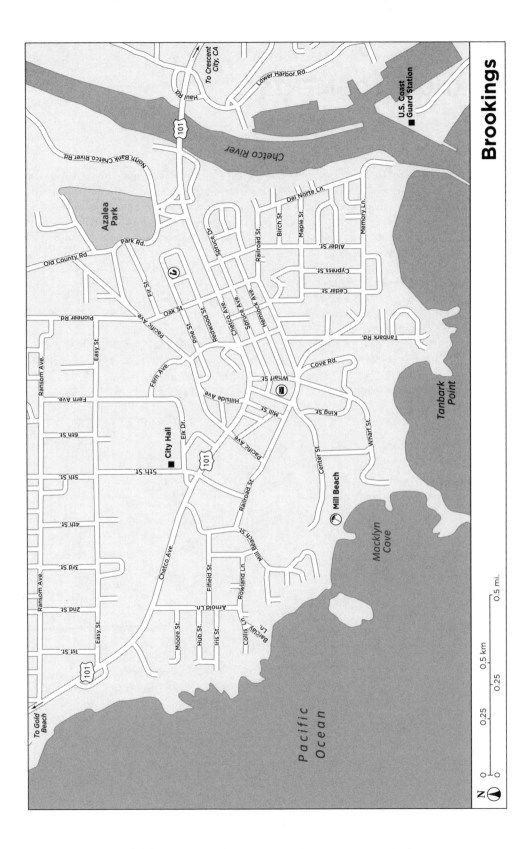

Brookings

ACKNOWLEDGMENTS

The pleasure of writing is never more apparent than when you have the opportunity to talk with people who love where they live and are enthusiastic to share their experiences and knowledge. In my research for this book, I talked to hundreds of Insiders who were happy to spend time with me and tell me about their own unique part of the Oregon Coast. I would like to express my appreciation to the staff at the chambers of commerce and visitor centers in each coastal community who took the time to talk with me and to send me research material.

I want to thank my husband Ken Skeen who was always there to support me and give me advice when I was working under tight deadlines and burning the midnight oil at my computer. He has always supported me in all my writing endeavors and is always happy to accompany me on research trips. Special thanks also to my family and friends who put up with my frequent absences from social activities as I stayed at home holed up in my office or was out of town on research trips.

In researching and writing this book, I have been very fortunate to get a closer look at the Oregon Coast—its scenic beaches, its forests and mountains, and its diverse communities and friendly people. Thank you for selecting the *Insiders' Guide to the Oregon Coast*. It is my sincere wish that as you read and use this book you, too, will enjoy its scenic beauty, diverse communities, and extraordinary people.

HOW TO USE THIS BOOK

The Oregon Coast, like all shorelines, is a place defined by change. The beach never looks the same from one day to the next. The sands shift and scatter, driftwood sets sail to explore new coves, the tide brings new treasures and wreckage twice each day, and then takes them away again. The Coast is thrilling because it is beautiful and fruitful and barren and deadly. Modern existence, which is all abstraction and hurry, presents us with few chances to behold the course of life in its entirety, but here we see it every day. The forces of change work constantly everywhere, but here we see them hourly.

In such a landscape it is useful to have a companion who is familiar with the terrain, someone who can show you where to go, what to do, and what is different about the shoreline of Oregon. This book is designed to help you navigate the Oregon Coast so you can see for yourself what all the fuss is about.

This guide is organized both thematically and geographically in order to help you get the most out of your visit. In the thematic chapters, we explain general information about activities of interest for visitors and locals alike. We'll tell you about the pleasures of nature and of civilization, the beaches and the golf courses, the fishing and the festivals. We'll also tell you about what to expect if you decide to move to the Oregon Coast, how to find the radio station that carries what you want to hear, and short trips you can take to sample the pleasures of inland Oregon. Most of the information within each chapter follows a north-to-south pattern.

The first three chapters—Area Overview, History, and Getting Here, Getting Around—are designed to help you get to the Coast and to orient you to the basic layout of this long, narrow region and the means of negotiating it. These chapters will let you know what to expect in terms of road conditions and weather, geography and industry.

When you want to know how, or at least where, to spend your nights, the next three chapters on hotels and motels, bed-and-breakfasts, and camping will be useful. Ideas on where to eat, go out on the town, and shop are listed in the next three chapters.

The next several chapters feature the stimuli for most visits to the Oregon Coast—its beauty and all the industry and recreation that has sprung up because of it. These are the chapters to read when you want to know how to spend your days on the Coast; you'll find detailed listings on kid-friendly destinations, annual events and festivals, art galleries and theaters, must-see attractions, parks to visit, and detailed listings on a wealth of activities you can participate in.

The final three chapters return to a thematic organization—they cover day trips, relocation, and media. Just over the mountains a variety of activities beckon the adventuresome, from cave exploration and wine tasting to big-city shopping in Portland. The Day Trips chapter tells you how to get there. And if, upon coming back, you decide that you never want to leave the Coast again (it has been known to happen), the next chapter, Relocation, will tell you how to find a place to settle to suit your manner of living. And the final chapter, Media, will give relocators and anyone else the news about the news. Also throughout you'll find special tidbits of Insiders' knowledge (look for the **i**).

Naturally, we think of our book as only a place to start, ever bearing in mind that the forces of change that work on the shoreline also apply to businesses, attractions, recreation, and highways. Let us know if you find changes that ought to be reported in future editions. All true Insiders explore for themselves. If, as you travel, you find you have something to tell us, please send your comments and suggestions to editorial@GlobePequot.com.

AREA OVERVIEW

The gorgeous Oregon Coast is a mix of basalt headlands, more than a dozen rivers flowing to the Pacific, a number of estuarine sanctuaries, and some of the world's largest continuous sand dunes, backed by a cordillera of low-slung mountains that rose to heights of 2,000 to 5,500 feet above sea level between 20 and 50 million years ago.

About 25 million years ago, the Oregon Coast began to rise from the sea as sediment deposit, and ever since that geologic action, the Pacific Ocean floor has been sliding under the shoreline, causing it to rise a minute amount every year. Every 300 to 400 years a major earthquake along with a tsunami, or huge tidal wave, strikes the Oregon Coast, further shaping its landscape. The last recorded quake of this magnitude was in the early 1700s, but since that cataclysm there was a 10-foot wave that smashed into the Oregon Coast on March 27 and 28, 1964, as a result of an earthquake in Alaska.

In this extraordinary region, roughly equidistant from the equator and the North Pole, the weather is typified by wet winters and reasonably dry summers with mild temperatures year-round.

One meteorological event uncovered a few marvels on the Oregon Coast. In 1998 winter storms churned up sturdy tidal activity that abraded roughly 10 feet of sand from Moolack Beach near Newport, revealing semi-petrified stumps and root systems of a 4,000-year-old forest. The surprise surfacing of these remnants of ancient trees was not only a treat for geologists but also a telling metaphor for fans of the Beaver State's 362-mile stretch of sand dunes, headlands, beaches, fishing villages, bays, streams, and inlets.

For visitors to the Oregon Coast, there is always more to discover: adventures just around the next windswept promontory, intriguing salty critters lurking in tide pools, or tasty hot clam chowder awaiting worn-out, hungry beachcombers. Travelers can leisurely cruise down U.S. 101 or use I-5 and one of nine routes over the coastal range to get to specific destinations. They can find that slice of shoreline just right for kite-flying or take a weeklong respite at one of the state's many coastal campgrounds; they can tour the haunted lighthouses at Tillamook, Heceta Head, or Yaquina Bay; or watch from a storm-thrashed bluff near Bandon as gray whales head home to Alaska.

Thanks to Oregon governor Oswald West, who declared the state's beaches public property in 1913 as a way of designating the beaches and headlands as transportation routes, and a legislature that confirmed that decision in the 1960s, the Oregon coastline is not wall-to-wall condos and posh resorts reserved for Club Med types. There are plenty of amenities, yet the abundance of salt air, sand dunes, and not-so-gentle breezes retains the area's wildness.

To introduce you to this linear wonder of a tourist destination for all ages and income brackets, here's a brief profile that will help you decide where to go and what to do, as well as deliver some history and cultural clues. We'll start a verbal motorcade at the Astoria Bridge across the Columbia River from Washington and meander down US 101 past some incredible viewpoints, along sinuous stretches of shops, restaurants, museums, and novelty spots to Brookings at the gateway to California.

ASTORIA

Completed in 1966, Astoria Bridge, which carries US 101 over the Columbia River, brings you to the west end of the downtown waterfront of one of the oldest American cities west of the Missouri River. Near the newly renovated waterfront, this all-American burg sprawls up high hills with dozens of charming Victorian homes, bed-and-breakfasts, and hotels.

But don't expect to find the locals overly sentimental about their town. A popular bumper sticker—"We Ain't Quaint"—expresses their sense of pride and a refusal to get too cute.

Named after fur-trader mogul John Jacob Astor, who claimed the stretch of habitable beach in 1811 with the landing of his vessel, the *Tonquin,* Astoria was the shipping point for Astor's thousands of beaver and otter pelts from the Pacific Northwest. His claim gave the United States a shaky sovereignty over the North Pacific realm. After a territorial squabble that ensued during the War of 1812, the town was temporarily named Fort George under British rule, and then returned to the United States in 1818. It then settled down into serving as a major pioneer destination.

Starting in 1866 as gold miners in Oregon and California eagerly gobbled canned salmon, a surge of salmon fishing and canning at the mouth of the Columbia turned Astoria into Oregon's second-largest city. Using small fishing boats and huge drift nets hauled ashore by teams of horses, Astorians caught, processed, and sold the tasty chinooks to diners worldwide. But that changed after World War II as fishing, lumber, and exports waned. Now, tourism beckons as the newest industry for this cheerful little town that gets more than its share of rain.

Astoria points of interest include the Columbia River Maritime Museum with its maritime artifacts; the Flavel House, a well-preserved mansion built by Oregon's first steamship captain; and the Astoria Column, a tall structure on top of Coxcomb Hill east of town. On the outside of this 125-foot tower modeled on Trajan's Column in Rome is a spiral of graphics celebrating the vivid history of Oregon including the arrival of the Lewis and Clark Expedition in 1805. Astoria also features a two-mile river walk along the scenic Columbia River and the historic Astoria Trolley that runs from Memorial Day through Labor Day.

SEASIDE

Seaside, just north of Tillamook Head, is a lively tourist town hosting thousands of visitors from the north Willamette Valley every year, including a traditional migration of college and high school students during spring break. Established in the 1870s as a resort and as a way to sell railroad tickets, Seaside still has lots of fun for everyone. In 1873 Seaside constructed a turn-around officially designated as the end of the Lewis and Clark Trail that remains the symbolic center of Oregon's oldest coastal resort (the explorers journeyed down the coast to seek salt). Seaside features a 1.5-mile-long Promenade that goes through the heart of town and gives you access to shops, arcades, and restaurants and is popular with locals and visitors alike.

CANNON BEACH

Cannon Beach, christened after a cannon that washed ashore from a fighting vessel in 1846, is a more sophisticated coastal village with dozens of art galleries on Hemlock Street—a long, thin strip of town tightly pressed between the beach and the cliffs where US 101 sits. You might even miss it if you're not careful, yet few people do. You'll often find Cannon Beach stuffed to the gills with folks and their cars. On a fair-weather weekend, you may not really be "getting away from it all," as it—the traffic jams and the throngs—may have come right along with you. In the warmer seasons, the outdoor cafes and bar patios lend this town a European flavor you can't normally find in Oregon. It's at once rustic, metropolitan, and trendy, and firmly entrenched in small-town America. There are myriad colorful and unusual shops up and down this striking little town, everything from wildly decorated kite shops and galleries to unusual specialty stores and a hopping arts and theater scene. And the vast majority of the buildings here are built in a charming, rustic kind of architecture usually composed of sturdy, dark, and unadorned wood, which obviously is made to take the weather around here.

Cannon Beach is also known for its natural wonders. Haystack Rock—the monolithic sea stack on the beach—is the biggest natural wonder around here, measuring in as the tallest one in the world. At lower tides, the base of it is accessible, and parts of this are endlessly fun to climb around or on for viewing the tide pools. You're not allowed to climb on all of it, however, because much of it is a wildlife refuge. Ecola State Park is another notable site along Cannon Beach, as is Indian Beach on the park's north end. Spectacular views of Cannon Beach, Tillamook Head Lighthouse, and a nice mix of cliffs and sandy and rocky beaches create a tempting expedition package. The trails going through Tillamook Head (and that lead to Seaside) begin just above Indian Beach.

According to local legend, a Spanish pirate ship ran aground near Neahkanie Mountain, just south of Cannon Beach, prompting its captain to bury a shipment of gold and beeswax there. For hundreds of years, many people have tried to find it without luck. While chances of finding this hidden wealth are slim, a visual treasure awaits those who venture to the top of the mountain.

Cannon Beach is also known for its rich celebration of the arts and is filled with art galleries featuring watercolor landscapes to shops that specialize in hand blown glass.

TILLAMOOK

A chain of fishing villages and resort communities—Manzanita, Nehalem, Rockaway Beach, and Garibaldi—leads to Tillamook, known for scrumptious cheese and ice cream produced at the Tillamook Cheese Factory and huge blimp hangars used in the 1993 *Teenage Mutant Ninja Turtles* movie. The blimp hangars are reportedly the largest wooden buildings in the world.

East of Tillamook, in August 1933, a 290,000-acre forest fire known as The Tillamook Burn wiped out a half a billion feet of timber. Now almost fully reforested, the area is a tribute to tree planting by volunteers.

South of Tillamook and north of Neskowin on US 101, the Three Capes Loop takes travelers on a 35-mile jaunt worth the detour. The first promontory, Cape Meares, has a state park, wildlife refuge, and a contorted spruce called the Octopus Tree. Cape Lookout is just that. Take a 2.5-mile hike out to the far edge of this 500-foot cliff for a spectacular view and an excellent whale-watching perch. The third cape is Kiwanda, a low, sandy peninsula that is a favorite launch for hang gliders. Below this sandstone escarpment is a beach where fishermen launch dories into the pounding surf.

NESKOWIN

Back on US 101, the next stop is Neskowin, a pleasant little resort with horseback riding, beachcombing, and, if you're in the mood, a stroll out to Proposal Rock. Two miles south of Neskowin, 1,800-foot Cascade Head offers more ambitious hikers a trek through a rain forest to grassy slopes overlooking a glittering sea.

i Oregon's beaches owe much of their character to two governors: Oswald West and Tom McCall. Oswald West passed legislation in 1913 that designated the coast's entire wet sand shoreline a public thoroughfare. In 1967 Tom McCall persuaded the legislature to strengthen the law to include the dry sand, too.

LINCOLN CITY

Next down the highway is Lincoln City, a long stretch of salty-dog boutiques, each with a flock of ceramic seagulls rivaling plastic flamingos in Florida. A recommended stop: the Otis Cafe on Highway 18 north of town. This Oregon institution serves outrageous hash browns and molasses bread. Another marvel is the 440-foot D River, listed in the *Guinness Book of World Records* as the world's shortest river.

DEPOE BAY

Depoe Bay, a fishing town turned tourist stop, has its own spectacle worth a look—the Spouting Horns—50-foot geysers that shoot through a sea cave at high tide. Along this slice of the Oregon Coast there are also lots of great waysides, beaches, and parks with colorful names like Otter Crest, Cape Foulweather, and Devils Punchbowl.

NEWPORT

After braving brisk northerly winds, gleaning wet sand for agates, and watching sea anemones wave back at you, stop by the Oregon Coast Aquarium in Newport, one of the nation's top aquariums.

Newport has two distinct districts shaped by its vivid history—a bayfront with working docks, pubs, chowder palaces, and gift shops; and Nye Beach, once a fashionable vacation spot that still charms visitors with nostalgic hotels, cafes, bookshops, and cozy gift emporiums.

It started in the 1890s when the "summer people" began to flock to Newport from the Willamette Valley simmering with stifling heat. The only way to get there in those days was on a train that left Corvallis, Oregon, to traverse the Coast Range to Yaquina City, a roughhewn harbor 5 miles up the Yaquina River from Newport. Families toting rattan picnic baskets and steamer trunks full of woolen bathing suits then boarded ferryboats that transported them down to the bayfront. At this point, some folks would climb aboard wagons that would deliver them to hotels and others hoofed it from the bay to Fall Street, a wood-planked route that descended its muddy way down to the beach. This treacherous avenue was appended in 1893 with more streets between Front Street (for a while the Roosevelt Highway, a precursor to US 101) and the beach.

Once in sight of the awesome and surfy splash of the Pacific, the summer people had the option of staying in posh hotel rooms, renting rustic cottages, or pitching tents on designated parcels of flat sand. Local vendors rented these canvas summer homes, cast-iron stoves, pots and pans, and utensils for those who vacationed throughout the summer. Husbands and fathers, taking advantage of three-day excursion discounts, would work during the week and then join their families on weekends.

OYSTERVILLE

Located 1 mile above Yaquina City on the south bank of the Yaquina River, which reaches the sea just south of Newport, is the town site of Oysterville. It was here that a huge cache of these bivalves was discovered in 1861. For many years these oysters were shipped to San Francisco, New York, and other major global cities until they were virtually fished out. Yet, today, the oyster culture is back and doing well.

WALDPORT

South of this oyster cache, gold miners found lots of gold dust in the beach sand from 1879 to 1880. The town established nearby combined the German word for forest (wald) with the English word port. Today, Waldport has an interpretive center with a history of its charming old bridge, which was replaced by a streamlined span.

i Oregon Online, the Web site for the State of Oregon, is a comprehensive resource for information on everything from tourist attractions to tax rates. You can find it at www.oregon.gov.

YACHATS

Yachats (that's ya-hots), a curve of homes and shops along the base of Cape Perpetua, is a singularly lively town and is worth a stop. Once a Native American reservation, the village evolved into a tourist stop with its first streets paved with shells from the middens left by the Native Americans forced out of their homes. Now, lots of retirees live here, as well as artists and writers seeking sanctuary for their craft. Just south is a drive up to the top of Cape Perpetua for a fantastic view of the ocean and often, particularly December through May, of the gray whales that cavort as they migrate south to Baja and north to Alaska.

The next spectacular view is the lighthouse at Heceta. According to an account in Mike Helms' *Oregon Ghosts and Monsters*, it is inhabited by a ghost named Rue—an elderly lady in pioneer garb who floats a few inches above the floor, screams in the night, and rattles dishes. Some say she is the wife of an early lighthouse keeper whose child died and was buried nearby. There are no tours of Heceta Lighthouse.

Not as spooky, but just as noisy, are the Sea Lion Caves 10 miles north of Florence on US 101, where you can take an elevator down into the caves to observe these sleek beasts lolling on a slick rock while taking a break or raising a resounding ruckus.

FLORENCE

Florence is located south of Yachats and just north of the Oregon Dunes National Recreation Area on US 101 and is a mix of old and new. Commercial buildings and bland malls line US 101 but the real character of Florence can be found in Old Town located along the Siuslaw River. Unique shops, very good seafood restaurants, and coffeehouses fill this section of town. If you want to learn more about the history of this area, visit the Siuslaw Pioneer Museum (278 Maple St.; 541-997-7884). It provides an inside look at the life of the Siuslaw tribe that lived along the river and contains interesting facts about the area's pioneer past.

OREGON DUNES NATIONAL RECREATION AREA

After a wander through Old Town Florence near the mouth of the Siuslaw River, head on to the Oregon Dunes National Recreation Area, the largest ocean-fronted dune area in the world, with 32,150 acres of dunes and just over 38 miles of ocean beachfront. Some of the dunes reach heights of 300 feet. The headquarters for the Oregon Dunes National Recreation Area is located in Reedsport at the north end of town on US 101 (855 Hwy. 101; 503-271-3611). Writer Frank Herbert reported that, after a visit to this 47-mile Sahara, he was inspired to pen his classic science-fiction novel, *Dune*.

REEDSPORT

Although Reedsport is trying to encourage tourism, it has a way to go. A good start is a visit to the Umpqua Discovery Center located at 409 Riverfront Way in Reedsport (541-271-4816, www .umpquadiscoverycenter.com). This center features many interactive cultural history exhibits that center around ocean tides and Oregon coast ecology. Four miles west of Reedsport, Winchester Bay harbors the largest sport charter fishing fleet on the Oregon Coast. Twenty miles south of this marina, the highway rises dramatically as the elegant span of McCullough Bridge crosses Coos Bay, the deepest harbor between San Francisco and Puget Sound. It was here that lumber baron Asa Simpson established what would eventually be the largest lumber port in the world. Follow signs to three must-visit sites: Sunset Bay State Park, a protected swimming and picnic spot; Shore Acres State Park, a surprisingly exquisite mix of English and Asian gardens built by Simpson; and rugged Cape Arago State Park, with its wind-bent shore pines and colonies of sea lions.

COOS BAY

Another good hiking opportunity is Millicoma Marsh. As any hiker who has conquered the icy flanks of a glacier to return with the graceful memory of a single mountain lily is quite aware, it is often a modest wonder that makes a journey worth the while. A short distance from Coos Bay is a near-perfect example called Millicoma Marsh.

Located at the south end of Coos Bay (the bay, not the timber town), the marsh is the wet tip of a broad peninsula between Isthmus Slough, with its log-booms and cattails, and Coos River, an unassuming stream draining dozens of creeks out of the southern Coast Range. It's also home to osprey, kites, egrets, herons, ducks, geese, and bashful coots.

A mile-and-a-half hike through their marshy turf takes off from the sports field of Millicoma Middle School, between the scoreboard and a roofed picnic site. A raised trail, often choked into a tight path by blackberry vines, loops out into the marsh past meadows and ponds to the edge of the bay and back to the sports field across a shell midden that was once an outdoor kitchen for local Native Americans.

Not only a stroll for avid bird-watchers, this easily accessible walk is an excellent opportunity for anyone of any age to spend time in a natural setting. There are sheltered benches and interpretive plaques and, at an obvious intersection, a side trail that continues east to an observation deck. Watch out for banana and chocolate slugs. You don't want to serve up a banana split with your boot.

Down on the northern edge of Oregon's banana belt (Coos Bay to Port Orford), after a windy summer slides into traditionally sloppy September, days actually get warmer, and the sun busts up clouds to command a bright blue sky and the wind gentles down to a sweet breeze.

A jaunt along the Coast before the onslaught of relentlessly overcast days has other advantages: There are fewer folks to elbow through to get to the sites and sounds; RV caravans have dwindled; baggy shorts, dangling Leicas, and pastel flip-flops are in short supply; and scenic-knockout picnic spots are both available and bountiful.

BANDON

Twenty-five miles south of Coos Bay, Bandon sits on the southern bank of the Coquille River. Easily the liveliest spot on the South Coast year-round, Bandon is particularly engaging during its autumnal days when brisk seaside siroccos lighten up for a while.

A historic resort town that survived devastating fires in 1914 and 1936 to emerge phoenixlike with flashy new feathers, Bandon has Old Town, a picturesque boat basin, a famous cheese plant, a cranberry sweet shop, and a historical museum that tells the remarkable tale of this fishing village that was enticing tourists as early as the 1920s.

A jaunt to this charming little burg at the mouth of the Coquille River should start with a visit to the lighthouse on the north jetty. This 47-foot austere Italianate tower no longer beams its warning seaward but remains as Bandon's official icon. A drive through Bullards Beach State Park just north of the bridge across the Coquille leads to the lighthouse. It's open only during summer but worth a visit to wander about its base at any time of year to get a splashy feel for the rough history of timber schooners, sternwheelers, and fishing boats that challenged the most dangerous bar on the Oregon Coast.

After a vigorous stroll on Bullards Beach or across the river to the sand reaches south of the Coquille (check out Elephant Rock, Face Rock, and a host of sea pinnacles and offshore islands), you can take your fresh hunger down to the docks along First Street. Here, you can rent a crab pot from Bandon Bait and Tackle (110 First St., 541-347-3905) and catch your own dinner complete with pincers or have the best fish and chips in the county casually served at the Bandon Fish Market (249 First St., 541-347-4282).

After lunch its fun to walk along the bouncing docks in Bandon's boat basin, where a small fishing fleet sustains a local maritime tradition. Between the docks and a bluff are dozens of crafts and gift shops, chic boutiques, bookstores, and a half-dozen robust eateries. Of particular note are the Bandon Card and Gift Shoppe (265 Second St., 541-347-9214), a rambunctiously visual treat and The Cobbler's Bench in the old Masonic Hall at 110 Second St., in which a real cobbler repairs footwear on antique equipment. A renovated Old Town, combined with postcard-perfect beaches nearby, makes Bandon a premier destination.

Oregon's South Coast in autumn is a little-known place and time. The stormy weather of September and most of October eases for a while and honest-to-raingod balmy days bring coastfolk a short break before the gray settles in for the winter. This second summer also offers travelers a chance to savor an off-season, low-key adventure they needn't share with mobs of tourists jamming the salty boulevards.

LANGLOIS TO THE ELK RIVER

One good bet is the reasonably untrammeled, often stunning terrain of North Curry County. After US 101 leaves Coos County a few miles north of Langlois, there is a shift in the flavor of the territory. It's a bit more mystic, perceptibly more distant from the "Valley" and its throb and clamor of civilized pursuits. The little town of Langlois (Francophiles, forget the correct pronunciation—it's Lang-LOYSE) has minimal amenities but a couple of neat antiques stores.

Perhaps of more interest is Floras Creek, a fairy-tale stream tumbling down from the Coast Range. According to folklore and enthused newspaper accounts, a blustery storm in 1893 toppled an oak tree on a Floras Creek farm to reveal an ancient wall that was obviously not the work of indigenous peoples or Europeans. Amateur archeologists and historians ventured a guess that the discovery was a remnant of the Lost City of Quivira sought in vain by the conquistadors. Uh, maybe it's the air down there.

After Floras Creek, the road swoops down into lowland with a village in the middle aptly called Denmark. A glance to the west to catch a distant view of the Pacific explains why Scandinavian settlers felt at home.

Don't expect a lot of roadside attractions along the stretch between Langlois and Port Orford. You'll not find a single T-shirt or homey painting on a crosscut saw for sale. But there are reasons to turn off US 101. A good choice is the Sixes River, easily recognized by a sign and a grocery store that's been around for awhile. As you start upstream you'll pass the ghostly remains of the town of Sixes. This small town was once the hangout for miners and loggers with a post office, store, blacksmith shop, and hotel. The Sixes River is obviously a hot spot for trout and salmon fisherfolk. As opposed to the Elk and Chetco Rivers, the fish spawning up the Sixes are prized natives, not hatchery stock. The locals celebrate their stream's celebrity status. You'll drive by mailboxes in the shape of a lunging chinook and other domestic pescatory motifs.

For a few miles the Sixes runs wide and gravelly with evidence of old and more recent mining claims seen on ledges and bars. Four miles upriver you'll come to Edson Creek Boat Launch and County Park. This Curry County facility is tucked in a narrow, pleasant meadow along the banks of Edson Creek. Lots of grass and tables with grills make it a great picnic spot.

Eleven miles from US 101, where the north and south forks of the Sixes join, the Bureau of Land Management operates the Sixes River Campground. Units are spread out in a forested area with lots of room for campers.

Beyond the forks, the river gets wilder as the road climbs into a bedrock canyon. Unless you are a reckless adventurer with an all-road rig, this is a good place to turn around and head back.

The next turn is another river road up the celebrated Elk River. A designated Wild and Scenic River, the Elk flows into the ocean just south of the Sixes. Seven miles upstream, a fish hatchery open to the public gives stoppers-by a chance to learn how steelhead and salmon are raised for release in local rivers. Then you'll climb into one of the most scenic river canyons in the Pacific Northwest. Fir and hemlock line the riverbank, cedar and madrone rise along hillsides, and, for a short while, a lovely arbor of white alders frames the road. And down in the green, white, and blue splash and flow, there are gravel bars of speckled granite, carved channels of striated white quartz, moss-thick boulders with bracken, licorice, and maidenhair fern.

Sunshine Bar at 12 miles up, and Butler Bar 3 miles farther, are agreeable little campsites, but the gem in this setting is Laird Lake Campground 10 miles beyond Butler Bar. Not as developed as the other two, Laird Lake has two wood-sorrel carpeted campsites installed along a jump-across creek.

After a meander up the Elk or Sixes River, it's just about 7 miles south on US 101 to Port Orford, where visitors can enjoy the sight of fishing boats lifted to a dock or lowered into the sea with cranes. Beyond this historic fishing village, Humbug Mountain rises 1,756 feet right out of the ocean! A winding trail leads to the top and a view of this magical seascape. On the route out to Blanco just north of Port Orford there's a right turn that will take you down to the Hughes House, a Victorian home built in 1898 for rancher and county commissioner Patrick Hughes. It's open as a museum from May 1 to September 30, but it's worth a side trip for a quick look even if it's closed. While you're down on the coastal flat, reconnect with the Sixes River in a picnic area between the Hughes House and the river's last mile to the sea.

A nighttime tour of the lantern room in the 1870 Cape Blanco Lighthouse offers visitors a chance to climb 67 steps back into history. The guided tour starts in Port Orford where lighthouse buffs are shuttled out to Cape Blanco, a 186-foot headland that is reportedly the most westerly point in the contiguous United States. Here, at the tip of this rugged promontory, visitors will enter

The exception to all Oregon Coast weather is Brookings, where it is possible to enjoy 70-degree days in January.

the oldest and highest lighthouse in continuous use in Oregon. Rather than a brisk walk-through, the visit is a two-and-a-half-hour program of living history with a costumed tour guide playing the role of the lighthouse keeper and his wife telling stories of local historical context.

The evening visit is available throughout the year unless gusts (ever present even during second summer) start blowing over 70 miles per hour. There's a free daytime tour of the lighthouse that doesn't include a hike up to the lantern room.

After trekking up a couple of rivers and beachcombing along the Coast that Sir Francis Drake dubbed New Albion, it might be time to get a bite or shop a bit in Port Orford or "Port Awford" as the longtime locals say. This seaport offers visitors the historic and, to some, the disconcerting sight of offshore Battle Rock upon which explorers held off attacks by irate Native Americans. Another scene to check out is the dock where fishing boats are lifted or lowered into the sea with cranes.

GOLD BEACH AND BROOKINGS

Gold Beach, the next village south of Port Orford, serves as the outfitting center for jet boaters and hikers heading up the Rogue River. Then south of Gold Beach, Brookings is the jump off for the Chetco River and the remote, virtually unexplored Kalmiopsis Wilderness. The last good camping spot before the border is Harris Beach State Park just north of Brookings.

HISTORY

The history of the Oregon Coast is one of mystery, adventure, discovery, perseverance, intolerance, and economic prosperity. Before we start the parade of gold-hungry buccaneers, courageous explorers, and stalwart pioneers, here's a quick look at the land.

Largely made up of headlands, cliffs of black basaltic rock, long stretches of beach, and towering cones of sand dunes, the coastline was the ending spot of long masses of lava flowing westward from earthquakes and volcanoes. A good example is Tillamook Head, the final point of a 400-mile-long flow of lava coming all the way from Idaho about 15 million years ago.

Since then, erosion and storms have whittled away at the coast, but essentially it's the same as it has been for a million years—a special, wondrous strip where the massive Pacific Ocean meets the final northwest edge of the country.

PRE-EUROPEAN HISTORY

Before the European explorers arrived on the Oregon Coast in the mid-16th century, the Native American population numbered roughly 45,000. As with all the aboriginal peoples of North and South America, the Oregon tribes are assumed to have arrived from the far eastern plains of Siberia 8,000 to 10,000 years ago, following game animals as they crossed the frozen Bering Straits.

Their population shrank at the beginning of the 19th century: Smallpox and other diseases, combined with conflicts generated by the incursion of farmers, miners, and other settlers, decimated the tribes. Below we give a quick sketch of tribes that once roamed along the coast.

Salish

The Salish are a large tribal group that occupied a coastal zone stretching from the Strait of Georgia in British Columbia to the Puget Sound area of Washington state. Their territories skirted the proud, ferocious Chinook at the mouth of the Columbia River, but then continued along the coast as far south as the Siletz River in Oregon. The tribe lived in wood-plank houses with intricate wood carvings, including totem poles, and subsisted primarily on fresh, dried, or jerked salmon. Known for their generous ritual of distributing wealth at "potlatches," the Salish held parties at which they celebrated their wealth by giving much of it away.

Tillamook

The Tillamook, Nehalem, and Nestucca, living along the Salmon and Nehalem Rivers, were numbered at over 2,000 by Lewis and Clark during their visit in 1805. By 1970 this clan grouping had been reduced to 139.

Siletz

The southernmost Salish tribe once lived on the river that bears its name. There are still a few Siletz on the Siletz Reservation upriver in the rural portion of Lincoln County. The Siletz still sell canned salmon and Native American memorabilia in shops along the Coast.

Alsean/Yakonan/Siuslaw

The Alsean on the Alsea River at present-day Waldport, the Yakonan on the Yaquina River near Newport, the Siuslaw on the Siuslaw River near Florence, and the Lower Umpqua on the lower Umpqua River near Reedsport are all linguistically related river-estuarine tribes. These Native hunters and gatherers gleaned shellfish and seined for salmon; hunted seals and elk; and gathered and traded for dentalia shells—a collectively recognized coin of the realm stretching from the far north to mid-California.

It was estimated in 1780 that these tribes numbered 5,000. After the arrival of land-hungry Europeans and the frictions that sparked the hostilities of the 1850s, most of these tribespeople were relocated to the Siletz Reservation on that part known as the Southern or Alsea Reservation. Currently, the combination of these tribal clans, with the exception of the Siuslaw, is the Confederated Siletz tribe.

In 1916 a small number of surviving Siuslaws joined the Hanis and Miluk Coos to form an extension of the Coos.

Kusan Tribe

Two tribes that coexisted along the coast between the Coos and Coquille Rivers are the Hanis and Kusan. The northern division was the Hanis, or Coos proper, who lived around the bay and river that bear their name. The southern division was the Miluk on the lower Coquille near its estuary. The two tribes, numbering roughly 2,000 in 1780, harvested crabs, clams, and mussels from the sea and journeyed upriver to hunt the animal that is now known as Roosevelt elk.

After being moved to the Yachats agency of the Siletz Reservation and eventually returning to Coos Bay to reclaim their identity, the Coos, now about 300 strong are currently working toward economic independence via a proposed gambling casino and other projects.

Coquille

This string of clans that for centuries camped along southern Oregon's Coquille River has historically been plagued by hostile neighbors and racist newcomers. Now, vigilant stewards of our diminishing wild forests are concerned that the "Kokwell" won't appropriately care for their ancestral forest.

This tale, a good example of how history has treated these migrants from Siberia, begins when these particular nomads arrived in the 800,000-acre territory fed by the west-flowing river that now bears their name. Here, they lived peacefully as gatherers of an estuarine bounty, as hunters who trapped elk in deep pits in mountain meadows, as fisher-folk who caught slippery salmon in willow weirs and who smoked lamprey eels over alder fires, and as harvesters who dug and toasted white camas bulbs.

To celebrate their harvests, they danced with woodpecker and puffin beaks clacking around their ankles. To spruce up, they plucked whiskers out of their cheeks with clamshells. To supplement their diet in spare times, they spiced their meager meals with skunk cabbage leaves. When someone passed on, they solemnly placed dentalia shells in the mouth of the dead for spending money in the hereafter.

The *Mishi Kwut inetunne* camped along the four forks of the upper Coquille and spoke an Athapascan tongue similar to Navajo and Aztec. Downriver, the Na-So-Mah and other Penutian speakers such as the Miluk or Lower Coos shared their native voice with the Hopi and Zuni. In time, clans on both the lower and upper river were lumped together as the Coquilles by late-coming, note-taking Euro-Americans.

The tribal families along the Coquille River were first mentioned by Hudson's Bay Company trapper Alexander McLeod, who ambled by in 1826. He concluded that the locals were honest, if canny, traders. The Coquilles then got a taste of Anglo arrogance on July 3, 1828, when explorer Jedediah Smith and his party tore down riverside homes near the mouth of the Coquille, lashing the stolen planks into rafts to cross the river.

After gold was discovered in 1852 at Whiskey Creek, 10 miles north of the Coquille, tension between downriver Coquilles and oft-drunken miners escalated. In January 1854, a gang of 40 miners went .50-caliber ballistic, killing 16 and wounding dozens more. Then a year after this massacre, a few Coquille warriors participated in the 1855–56 Rogue River Indian War, storming out of the upper Coquille to burn cabins and cause retributive mayhem. By 1856, all but a handful of Coquille were either killed off, had intermarried, or traveled a trail of tears to Fort Umpqua or Yaquina Bay.

Those who were left were astonished when Grandmother Rock, a huge pillar jutting up from a bluff overlooking the Pacific near Bandon, was blown up in 1881 and its blue schist debris used to build a jetty, which was completed in 1900. The destruction of this sacred pillar, once used for shamanic ceremonies, was a formidable symbol of the disintegration of the Coquille, but it took an official act on August 13, 1956, to conclude over a century of insults suffered by the tribe.

On that date, the Termination Act, signed by President Eisenhower, announced that the Coquilles and 42 other bands of Native Americans west of the Cascades no longer existed. After a long struggle that lasted into the politically charged '80s, the 600-strong tribe was reinstated in 1989. Part of the agreement was the submission of an economic self-sufficiency plan. The Coquille purchased a huge plywood mill along U.S. 101 and turned it into the Mill Casino, a popular haunt for locals as well as tourists. With timberland returned to the tribe by the Bureau of Land Management, an assisted living facility, and other holdings, the tribe has dramatically bolstered its fiscal health.

PIRATES AND EXPLORERS

Although many think that the first explorers along the Oregon Coast were Europeans who made the arduous trip around the tip of Tierra del Fuego, there are records of earlier explorations. A fifth-century Chinese journal gives an account of a Buddhist priest's travels to a strange land he called Fu-Sang. The details of Hwui Shan's travelogue suggest that he sailed down the west coast of America, and legends among the Native Americans describe boats that might have been classic Chinese junks.

Definitely on record are the adventures of Sir Francis Drake. In 1579, this legendary English explorer and buccaneer sailed his *Golden Hinde* up the Pacific coastline past the promontories at Cape Blanco and Cape Arago to be the first European to venture north of California. It is unknown and fiercely debated where he actually set foot. What is known is that he named the region New Albion because of the similarity of the headlands at Cape Blanco to the White Cliffs of Dover in his homeland.

What lured him up the coastline was not only the thrill of discovery but the opportunities to raid the Spanish vessels laden with gold from the looting of the Aztec and Incan territories. After marauding his way north, Drake decided to search out a passage that would bring him safely east to England. This hope was virtually universal among nations that wanted the riches of the far Orient delivered as quickly as possible to their national coffers. The search for the Northwest Passage would dominate exploration of the North Pacific for centuries. But Drake had challenges, among them the "vile, thicke, and stinking fogges," and was forced to eventually give up his quest and sail west past Asia and Africa and back home to London.

In 1592, in response to the smashing success of the English pirate, the Spanish commissioned Greek captain Juan de Fuca to head north up the coast in search of new claims and more gold. De Fuca returned jubilantly, claiming that he had discovered the Northwest Passage. Although he was as wrong as all the other searchers for the elusive shortcut home, he did get a great stretch of water named after him (the Strait of Juan de Fuca in Washington).

Another Spanish sea captain, Sebastian Viscaino returned from his exploration with the news that the Oregon shoreline was empty of navigable harbors or usable inlets.

But that grim news didn't stop the explorers and seekers of wealth. New players on the scene were the Russian fur traders who ventured across the Bering Strait and down Alaska to northern

California in the mid-1700s. Now the Natives were bartering with, selling furs to, and pestering the English, Spanish, and Russians, who all claimed the new land for their own. With the high prices paid for fur pelts, there was a frenzy of trade: 200,000 pelts were delivered to China and Europe before the sea otters were virtually eliminated along the Oregon Coast.

In 1776 English Captain James Cook, a hero for his circumnavigation of the globe (1769–71), was appointed commander of an expedition to explore the Northwest coast in search of the Northwest Passage. His motivation was heightened by a promised reward of 20,000 pounds if he discovered that route. Leaving England with two vessels, the *Discovery* and *Resolution,* Cook ventured along the Oregon Coast. The first prominent headland Cook sighted was Cape Foulweather, just north of Yaquina Bay. Reversing his course, he sighted another headland just south of Coos Bay, which he named Cape Gregory, later given the name Cape Arago. Eventually Cook traveled to Hawaii where he was slain by Natives.

By 1776, when Americans declared their independence from England, the Spanish had established a permanent settlement at San Francisco Bay. A year earlier, the Spanish sea captains Bruno de Heceta, Juan Perez, and Juan Francisco de la Bodega y Quadra sailed north from San Blas, stopped briefly near the California-Oregon border, and then made it as far north as Vancouver Island. Heceta Head, the scenic headland north of Florence, was named after Heceta.

English Captain John Meares discovered Cape Lookout and Tillamook Bay in 1778, dubbing it "Quicksand Bay." Meares sailed past the Columbia River but failed to identify it as a major river.

In 1788 Robert Gray's ship, *Lady Washington,* sailed up the Oregon Coast anchoring in Tillamook Bay, where he traded and quarreled with local Native Americans. The first known contact with South Coast Indians came three years later in 1791, when Captain James Baker's *Jenny* arrived at Winchester Bay at the mouth of the Umpqua River.

In 1792 English Captain George Vancouver, commanding the warships *Discovery* and *Chatham,* sailed up the Northwest coast, claiming all of it for England. On April 24, 1792, he anchored his ships just south of Cape Blanco at present-day Port Orford, naming the spot after a colleague, George, the Earl of Orford. Perhaps the most significant discovery on the part of the British was the crossing of the Columbia River bar by Captain Gray's *Columbia Redivivia* on May 11, 1792. Gray journeyed about 14 miles upriver, planting the U.S. flag and claiming the grand River of the West for the United States.

So it was a high time for adventure, trade, piracy, and discovery along the West Coast. All of this set the stage for the grandest tale of all—the overland trek of the Corps of Discovery led by Meriwether Lewis and William Clark. After visionary President Thomas Jefferson acquired the massive territory west of the Mississippi River in the Louisiana Purchase, he commissioned his young secretary, Lewis, to assemble a team to map out what Jefferson hoped would be a trade route from St. Louis, Missouri, to the Pacific. He was wrong, but the maps drawn, specimens taken, Native tribespeople interviewed, and the brave endurance of the Lewis and Clark band made remarkable history. Leaving Missouri in 1803, they journeyed across the northern plains, across the Rocky Mountains, and down the Snake and Columbia Rivers to that day, November 7, 1805, when Clark wrote in his journal: "Great joy in camp we are in View of the Ocian, this great Pacific Octean which we been So long anxious to See. And the roreing or noise made by the waves brakeing on the rockey Shores (as I suppose) may be heard distinctly." Actually, it wasn't really the Pacific but the lower Columbia's estuary. After eight more days of floating westward, they climbed Cape Disappointment to see the sparkling Pacific. The lads wintered near Astoria, hiked down the coast to gather salt and a few chunks of blubber from a beached 100-foot whale, and then, grousing about grey clouds and constant drizzle as do all Pacific Northwesterners, they reversed their journey and headed home to a tumultuous welcome.

One last historic narrative is well known on the southern Oregon Coast—the Skirmish at Battle Rock. In 1851, Captain William Tichenor decided to establish a seaport in the tranquil cove that is now Port Orford. Tichenor's plan was to construct a headquarters for the shipment of huge masses of gold yet to be gleaned from northwest gold rush sites. He hired a crew to camp on a large rock in the center of the cove, left supplies and a four-pound cannon for defense, and said he would be back in two weeks with more supplies. The 400-foot-long promontory was quickly assaulted, and 17 Natives died in the conflict, mostly from cannon fire. The Europeans managed to escape the rock and straggle north to the nearest settlement.

We can only imagine the ghostly shapes of the ancient sailing ships wending up the coast to unknown territory; we can only surmise how it felt to find a "New England," a land rich with furs to take home to Russia, and more riches for the royal court of Spain. But driving past Port Orford on US 101, it's hard to miss Battle Rock, with its sparse growth of wind-battered spruce and fir trees and the echo of that four-pound cannon.

EUROPEAN SETTLEMENT

After the close of the buccaneering and exploring era, settlers flocked to the Oregon Coast to search for gold in the black sand of the beaches, to establish commercial fishing plants, to mine for coal and ship lumber down to booming San Francisco, and to begin constructing a chain of resort/destination villages that now dot the Coast. Here are a few short tales of towns settled by those who pioneered the Coast, endured howling winds, thunderous rainstorms, and lonely isolation.

Lakeport

Let's start with a grandiose mistake. At the turn of the 20th century, a group of investors attempted to create a resort town south of Bandon. Their plan was to build a town called Lakeport around a man-made lake fed by local streams. A canal would be dug a few miles to the ocean. Boats would sail up the canal laden with rich tourists, thus creating "The Venice of the West." The lake was dug, a hotel built, and then, as the canal was about to be dug as well, an embarrassed engineer informed the investors that their property was below sea level. So much for the scheme of Lakeport.

Newport's Fashionable Seasons

A brief history of the settling of Newport is a capsule sampling of how villages along the Oregon Coast grew from rough camps into present-day tourist meccas—all without canals that would send the Pacific cascading into their shops, hotels, and restaurants.

Those were stylish days at the beach as Newport turned from the quaint 1800s to the faster-paced 20th century. A remarkable moment captured by local merchant and photographer A. L. Thomas shows a crowd of vacationers and locals in their fashionable best, promenading along the jellyfish-sprinkled plaza beneath the bluffs at Nye Beach. Instead of contemporary down vests and padded parkas, the women wear long dark skirts, white puff-sleeved blouses, and Sunday gone-to-meetin' hats while they hold parasols against the high sun. The men stand about in impeccable bowler hats and three-piece suits. Down closer to the surf, not-so-stiff youngsters cavort in saltwater-soggy, neck-to-ankle swimming togs.

In 1904 Thomas published *Glimpses of the Sea Shore at Newport, Ore.* The selection of photos included his famous shot of "Jumpoff Joe," a huge sandstone arch north of Nye Beach that has since washed away. As these alluring photos and word of Newport's tourist amenities spread throughout the country, more facilities and activities emerged at this booming resort. Along with horse rides north to visit Yaquina Head Lighthouse and meanders to browse curio shops for agate-adorned lamps and shell-speckled crockery, to sample cookies at Polly Anna Bake Shop or taffy at the Cozy Corner Confectionery, there was the inevitable visit to The Natatorium.

"The Nat," as it was fondly nicknamed, was a large wooden building that held a swimming pool of salt water and a dance floor. Built in 1912, this recreational wonder was also the site of a miniature golf course, roller skating, movies, boxing matches, and concerts by those big bands that motored between engagements in snub-nosed busses.

The Nat burned to the ground in 1921, but was quickly rebuilt to once again become the center of the Nye Beach social scene. It was torn down in 1967, and little evidence of The Nat remains—only photos, fond memories, and fragments of its foundation in a vacant lot behind the Yaquina Art Center, once a clothes-changing station for swimmers.

Another long-gone amenity was Dr. Minthorn's Hot Sea Baths, a three-story building just south of The Nat. In the late 1890s and early 1900s, hot seawater was piped into porcelain tubs for folks seeking a soothing way to recuperate from various ailments. A popular feature of this sanitorium was a veranda enclosed in glass where a bather could enjoy the sun and avoid the wind.

The most notable remnant of Nye Beach's heyday is the Sylvia Beach Hotel (267 N.W. Cliff, 888-795-8422, www.sylviabeachhotel.com) a charmingly renovated historic landmark built between 1910 and 1913. Originally named The New Cliffhouse, it became the Hotel Gilmore in 1921 when Peter and Cecile Gilmore traded their chicken ranch for the hostelry. It later fell into disrepair until it was reopened in 1987 by Sally Ford and Goody Cable. The two owners renamed the hotel in honor of Sylvia Beach, who operated the Shakespeare & Co. Bookstore in Paris during the 1920s and '30s. Now a resting and reading retreat for book lovers, it offers 20 guest rooms, all named after and decorated in honor of various scribblers. Lodgers can stay in the Agatha Christie, Robert Louis Stevenson, Jane Austen, or Mark Twain Rooms. Or if one is bold, there's the Edgar Allan Poe Room, a gothic little chamber with an ornament a bit more foreboding than a dangling participle.

Seaside

Railroad mogul Ben Holladay built this first coastal tourist mecca, an attraction for tourists since the early 1870s. His key service was a train that ran from Portland to Seaside. Since then, the town has continued to flourish as a tourist haven, particularly during spring break, when thousands of college and high school students come to visit and blow off some steam.

Lily Bulbs

A special industry, the growing and shipping of lily bulbs in the Chetco Valley, took off during World War II when the Japanese bulb growers stopped exporting their products to the United States. Now only 10 farms exist but they produce 95 percent of the Easter lily bulbs for the world market.

Fire Bombs

In World War II, the Japanese also had an influence on the Oregon Coast when their planes dropped incendiary bombs on Coast Range forests—reportedly the first bombs of any sort dropped on the American mainland. The plan was to start huge forest fires, thus distracting the western coastal defenses so that the Japanese could attack. The problem was that the bombs landed in forests soaking wet from constant torrential downpours. The fires were extinguished by this inclement weather.

Hume's Salmon Canneries

Robert D. Hume, deservedly know as the "Salmon King," started the first West Coast salmon-canning plant on the Sacramento River in 1864. He then built another cannery at Astoria and in 1876 started a salmon cannery on the south bank of the Rogue River at Gold Beach. The cannery at Gold Beach turned out three-quarters of a million cans annually between 1880 and 1900.

Bandon

Founded by Irish baron George Bennett, who named it after his home in Ireland, Bandon soon became an important port on the South Coast with exports of lumber, fish, woolen goods, and dairy products. After the completion of a jetty in 1912, the maritime traffic across the wicked Coquille River Bar was safer and increased dramatically. The town also grew into a rip-snorting resort burg with horseracing, a swimming natatorium, gambling parlors, and a number of dance halls. But a fire in 1914 along the waterfront, and another in 1936 throughout the town caused by the spread of flames by oily grease, made headlines throughout the nation. Now, rebuilt and prospering, Bandon is a popular stopping point for many travelers. The sea stacks and other scenic off-shore rocks, long driftwood-littered beaches, and numerous restaurants and shops have returned this town to the days when it was *the place* to head for to cool off when the hot days of the Willamette Valley became unbearable.

CONTEMPORARY DAYS

In recent years the history of the Oregon Coast has been relatively calm compared to its tempestuous older days but there are a few notable events worth mentioning.

The Bonfire of the Sentries

Portland-based freelance writer and environmental activist Phillip Johnson created an answer to his frustrations with hit-and-miss efforts to protect the Oregon Coast. His vision was an unbroken chain of dedicated guardians keeping watch over the state's shoreline.

In 1992 The Oregon Shores Conservation Coalition (OSCC), founded in 1971 in support of Governor Tom McCall's beach bill, was suffering setbacks due in part to underfunding and not enough help to cover meetings and hearings and crucial circumstances affecting the environmental health of the Coast.

Then, while looking out to sea from a bluff overlooking the Pacific, an idea occurred to Johnson, a history graduate with a degree in medieval European studies. During medieval times, sentinels stood by woodpiles spaced along coastal headlands. If attackers came by sea, the guards would set bonfires to alert the locals. Johnson imagined a similar network of citizen experts, a cadre of Paul Reveres in windbreakers from the Astoria Bridge to the California line—one person taking responsibility for each of Oregon's coastal miles.

He launched his idea in November 1993 with a small grant from the McKenzie River Gathering, a statewide funding organization that provides seed money for projects and programs. The Coast was divided into 311 segments based on accessibility and topography such as river mouths and jutting capes. More than 170 miles are now cared for but more remain.

The Exploding Whale

Whales have always drifted in from the briny depths to beach as confused yet alive creatures or dead masses of blubber. For Native Americans, a beached whale was cause for great celebration—a grand example of their motto that when "the tide comes in, the table is set." For contemporary Euro-Americans, it was a different matter in November 1970. After a whale had washed up on a beach near Florence and was beginning to perfume the air, the Oregon Highway Department decided to clean it up by blowing it up with half a ton of dynamite. The plan was to break the carcass into little bits that would be nibbles for gulls, crabs, and other scavengers. But the plan went awry when the dynamite exploded the whale into huge chunks that rained down upon the startled crowd and smashed a nearby car.

Two Unsolved Mysteries
Port Orford Meteorite

Geologist Dr. John Evans was a wandering scientist/adventurer who collected hundreds of rock samples in his rambles about the Sierra Nevada, Rockies, Cascade, and Coast Range mountains during the late 1900s. After Evans returned to the East Coast, one of his specimens turned out to be a chunk of pallasite, a rare type of meteorite known as stony-iron. Although he did note that the irregular-shaped mass weighing an estimated 11 tons was found 40 miles from Port Orford, its precise location was not in his notes. Since the discovery of the meteorite fragment and Dr. Evan's sparse notes, the Port Orford Meteorite Society has led hundreds of attempts to find the meteorite, but its location remains a mystery.

The Beeswax Shipwreck of Neahkahnie Mountain

Neahkahnie Mountain, a 1,600-foot cape rising just north of Nehalem Bay, is the site of two of the most intriguing legends in Oregon history. When the first Europeans settled in the Nehalem country, they were amazed by a plenitude of wax on the beach. Tons of it! Some of the chunks weighed 200 pounds, others were candle-size. Skeptics claimed that the substance was natural paraffin produced by coal or petroleum. Then cakes of wax were found stamped with the letters HIS, the sacred monogram of the Catholic Church. The local Natives told a story of a beeswax ship wrecked by a storm. The survivors had been accepted into the tribe; some behaved so obnoxiously that they were killed, and others were adopted and produced fair-haired progeny.

Spanish shipping records give credence to the tale. One of their beeswax ships bound from Mexico to Manila in 1772 disappeared. So did the caravel San Jose, en route from La Paz to San Diego in 1769. It seems likely that one of their vessels, bound for distant Spanish missions, ended up illuminating the cedar huts of the Clatsop Nation.

GETTING HERE, GETTING AROUND

Bordered by the Coast Range mountains to the east and besieged by the Pacific Ocean to the west, the Oregon Coast requires some effort to get to and some effort to travel once you're here. Of course, the remoteness of the Coast is mostly a boon. The natural landscape is varied and dramatic and relatively unspoiled. The human landscape has also benefited from being remote. It hasn't completely succumbed to the modern project of making every town look exactly alike.

Traveling the Coast may bring some surprises. Parts of the road fall into the sea, sometimes closing it. Curvy two-lane highways make high speeds dangerous. Bends in the road may reveal views so amazing that they demand you pull over to look at them. The lesson here: Don't be in a big hurry.

BY CAR

Roads

U.S. Highway 101

US 101 runs the entire 400-mile length of the Oregon Coast, from California in the south to the Columbia River and Washington state in the north. The central artery of the Coast, it provides the main north-south route for tourists and residents alike, so it is heavily traveled. Sometimes the volume of traffic will astonish even the seasoned native. US 101 follows the shore, usually within sight of the ocean. Driving along US 101 you will see spectacular beaches, lush forests and lonely meadows, mysterious dunes and flourishing farms, and bustling tourist towns and fishing villages. Most exhilarating are Pacific vistas as the road clings to the rocky side of a bluff with the ocean crashing into the shore hundreds of feet below.

US 101 is susceptible to landslides and therefore road closures, making life difficult for both natives and tourists, who may have to travel miles and miles out of their way. This is one high-maintenance road. However, because of this susceptibility, it is also maintained very well by the hosts of engineers who are constantly evaluating its condition. You would be wise to call the Oregon Department of Transportation's road condition report at (800) 977-6368 or visit www.tripcheck .com, before going anywhere along US 101 and also for mountain pass information.

This highway has plenty of roadside services, but sometimes it's a long way between them, so keep an eye on the gas gauge. You should also be aware that US 101 is called "Highway 101" by most locals, though for the sake of consistency with road maps we have retained the technical name here. The highway also often changes names when it reaches a town, as in Brookings, where it is called "Chetco Avenue," or Gold Beach, where it is called "Ellensburg." But US 101 is still clearly marked, even if the street signs say something unfamiliar.

U.S. Highway 30

Following the Columbia River, this busy highway is the most direct route from Portland to Astoria. It is also the most direct route from Washington state. If you are coming from, say, Seattle, take I–5 south to Longview, Washington; from there, cross the Columbia River into Oregon over the Lewis & Clark Bridge, which will deposit you onto Oregon soil and US 30 at the little town of Rainier. Follow the road west toward Astoria.

Coast Range Roads

Most east–west roads to the Oregon Coast cross the Coast Range mountains, some following rivers for nearly their entire length. Some roads have significant changes in elevation and others have only modest elevation changes. Whether or not there are major changes in elevation, all the roads demand alert driving, since you will find dips, curves, deer, and little towns, and since you will be sharing the roads with trucks. US 26 is the way of choice for weekending Portlanders, who share the road with farm and logging trucks. The road stretches from Portland to a convenient location on US 101 between Cannon Beach and Seaside. In the winter, chains or other traction devices may be required. Highway 6 follows the Wilson River from west of Portland to Tillamook. A road of gentle curves, it can be a slow, if pleasant alternative to busy US 26, though the eastern end of it is more developed every minute. Highway 22 leads from Hebo to Salem; it crosses Highway 18, which leads from McMinnville to Otis, just north of Lincoln City. Locals say to beware of casino traffic on Highway 18. US 20 accompanies the Yaquina River from Corvallis to Newport, a good and very pretty road, though it can be pokey in places. Another pretty highway, Highway 34, follows the Alsea River from Corvallis to Waldport. Eugene residents take busy Highway 126 through timber towns to Florence and the sand dunes. Highway 38 is a pleasant road leading from Drain to Reedsport along the Umpqua River. It's the most direct east–west route to the South Coast. Highway 42 leads from the Umpqua Valley near Roseburg to Coos Bay through the aptly named town of Remote. You may see other east–west roads marked on your map that appear to lead to the Coast. Don't count on their being paved.

i The Oregon Department of Transportation (ODOT) has two excellent resources to alert you to state road conditions. Call (800) 977-6368 to check the latest road information or visit www.trip check.com. You will be able to see for yourself through cameras keeping watch at Port Orford and Yaquina Bay.

U.S. Highway 199

This road, nicknamed the "Redwood Highway," lies between Grants Pass and Crescent City, California. South Coast residents traveling home from Ashland and Medford use it, detouring into California for nearly 60 miles. They also sometimes use US 199 to connect them to I–5 in Grants Pass when they want to go to Portland and beyond, on the theory that driving the length of Oregon on I–5 will be faster than driving the length of Oregon on US 101. The road winds from Grants Pass to Crescent City with gentle curves and wide lanes, through the lonely mountain country where the Siskiyous meet the Coast Range. While most of the route is easily traveled, the western end of the road is very slow as it accompanies the Smith River and twists through the beautiful redwood groves of Jedediah Smith State Park, before it spills abruptly into coastal California farmland. A 20-minute drive north puts you in Brookings. Note that when you reach the California border, not far past the town of O'Brien, there will be a State of California agricultural inspection, so eat up all the homegrown produce before then.

Renting a Car

It is not easy to rent a car on the Oregon Coast. Hertz has an outlet in Astoria at 1492 Duane St., (503) 325-7700. Enterprise also has rentals in Astoria at 644 W. Marine Dr., (503) 325-6500. If you're coming from far away and you want to drive while you're here, your best bet might be to fly into Portland International Airport and rent a car there.

BY BUS

GREYHOUND LINES
(800) 231-2222
www.greyhound.com
The Greyhound bus travels along US 101. Coastal Greyhound bus service is arranged by independent agents rather than official Greyhound ones, but many of the agents can give you tickets, a place for regularly scheduled stops, access to transfer routes, and package express delivery.

Sometimes the agents are within restaurants, travel agencies, convenience stores, or other businesses. Other stops along the route might be signs posted on the highway, with no ticketing or other services; for these you need to make arrangements with Greyhound.

NORTHERN LIGHTS
7316 SE 162nd, Portland
(877) 355-9195
www.northernlightstowncar.com
Provides personal transportation service to the north coast, including Cannon Beach, Seaside, Astoria and Warrenton.

Municipal Buses

Public transportation on the Oregon Coast is not particularly plentiful, but some cities have bus service. Sunset Empire Transportation District (800-776-6406, www.ridethebus.org) offers bus service in Astoria, Warrenton, and Hammond. They also have routes from Seaside to Cannon Beach. The Astoria Transit station is located at 900 Marine Dr. in Astoria. Call or visit the Web site for more information about routes and fees.

The Tillamook Transportation District has a route from Tillamook to Manzanita and Cannon Beach. They also have routes from Tillamook to Pacific City to Oceanside and Netarts. Call or visit their Web site for specific information on schedules and fares (800-815-8283, www.tillamookbus.com).

The Lincoln County Transportation District provides bus service for Lincoln City, Depoe Bay, Siletz, Toledo, Newport, Waldport, and Yachats. Call or visit their Web site for specific information on schedules and fares (541-265-4900, www.co.lincoln.or.us/transit/schedule.html).

Curry Public Transit offers bus transportation for the southern Oregon communities of Brookings and Gold Beach. They also offer Coastal Express buses that travel from Smith River, California, north on US 101 to Bandon, Coos Bay, and North Bend. Call or visit their Web site for specific information on schedules and fares (800-921-2871, www.currypublictransit.org).

Shuttle Service
CARAVAN AIRPORT TRANSPORTATION
(541) 994-9645
www.caravanairporttransportation.com
You can get to the Central Coast from Portland International Airport (PDX) by taking the Caravan Airport shuttle. It leaves Monday through Friday from the Portland International at 2 p.m. You'll find the shuttle at the airport outside the baggage claim area by the information booth; call to make a reservation or for more information.

BY AIRPLANE

North Coast
PORTLAND INTERNATIONAL AIRPORT
7000 Northeast Airport Way, Portland
(503) 944-7000, (877) 547-8411
www.portofportland.com
The largest, most convenient airport to the northern Oregon Coast is Portland International Airport, PDX. You can rent a car there, and take US 26 or US 30 to the North Coast. You can also take Caravan Airport Transportation to Lincoln City, or hire a charter service to fly you anywhere on the coast. Many airlines fly into PDX. Call your travel agent.

Central Coast
NEWPORT MUNICIPAL AIRPORT
169 SW Coast Hwy., Newport
(541) 867-7422
The Port of Newport is very proud of its instrument landing system, which is designed to help pilots manage their planes even when visibility conditions are poor.

South Coast
SOUTHWEST OREGON REGIONAL AIRPORT
1100 Airport Way, North Bend
(541) 756-8531
www.flyoth.com
Commercial air service connecting to Portland is offered by United Express. They can be reached at (800) 864-8331, www.united.com.

HOTELS AND MOTELS

T his chapter lists hotels and motels on the entire Oregon Coast organized by region—North, Central, and South—and then by city from north to south. These accommodations range from simple to extravagant. You'll find anything from a deluxe suite with an ocean view to a simple bungalow that is perfect for families. We've included price codes that will give you an idea of what you can expect to pay for two people for one night during the summer season. Winter season rates are usually discounted along the Oregon Coast. Hotels and motels accept all or most major credit cards unless otherwise noted. Some counties tax hotel rooms.

Price Code

$ . . . . $60 and less
$$ . . . . $61 to $100
$$$ . . . . $101 to $150
$$$$ . . . . more than $150

NORTH COAST

The greatest concentrations of hotels and other accommodations in the North Coast are in the Seaside and Cannon Beach areas, and there are many to choose from. We figure you won't need any help spotting the national and regional chains, especially the ones that sprawl over half the beach. Occasionally we have included the familiar names if they are especially good in that area, but we've concentrated on accommodations that offer something different. Perhaps it's a guest cottage a little way up a river or a lodge renowned for its service and luxury. Maybe it's a large resort perfect for family vacations or old-fashioned beach cottages where you can practice living simply. But all the listings here offer something special.

Astoria

CANNERY PIER HOTEL   **$$$$**
10 Basin St.
(503) 325-4996
www.cannerypierhotel.com
You will enjoy the luxury of this waterfront hotel

located in the heart of downtown Astoria. The rooms at this hotel have private balconies overlooking the Columbia River, fireplaces, hardwood floors, and high-speed Internet. As part of your stay, you will also receive a complimentary breakfast, complimentary wine and lox from 5 p.m. to 6 p.m. daily, and the use of a chauffeured 1939 Buick. This hotel also offers a full day spa, gift boutique, hot tub, exercise room, library, laundry facilities, and complimentary day use bicycles. Your furry friend can also bask in the luxury of this hotel with pet-friendly rooms. For an additional pet fee, your dog will receive a dog bed, treats, bottled water, complimentary leashes, and waste bags. Also note that this hotel is smoke free.

CREST MOTEL   **$$**
5366 Leif Erikson Dr.
(800) 421–3141
http://astoriacrestmotel.com
The Crest Motel sits on two-and-a-half manicured acres above the city; its views of the Columbia River are magnificent, and its location, away from downtown, makes it a relatively quiet place to stay. It's also pleasant, with patio chairs outside in the back overlooking the river and a covered Jacuzzi among its many amenities. Other amenities include a continental breakfast, coin laundry facilities, phones, and cable television. One building is dedicated to those who don't smoke. It's okay to bring the dog.

HOTEL ELLIOTT $$$$

357 12th St.
(877) 378-1924
http://hotelelliott.com

Built in 1924, the historic Hotel Elliott features 32 unique rooms that are all non-smoking and have all been updated with modern amenities. The rooms feature heated stone floors in each bathroom, some rooms have romantic marble fireplaces, free cable Internet, free TV and DVD players, terry robes, cedar closets, high end beds with goose down pillows, custom cabinetry, and wheelchair accessibility. This classic hotel also offers two, pet-friendly rooms. This hotel has a spectacular roof top terrace that has magnificent views of the Columbia River and Astoria's historic downtown district.

ROSEBRIAR HOTEL $$-$$$$

636 14th St.
(800) 487-0224
www.rosebriar.net

This unique building with 12 rooms with private baths used to house a convent; it's a historic landmark estate sitting on the hill above downtown Astoria with excellent views of the city and the Columbia River. The common rooms are lovely, with lots of intact moulding and a nice fireplace, with newspapers and coffee just waiting to be consumed by guests. The hotel also boasts an elaborate Captain's Suite with a fireplace, soaking tub, wet bar, kitchenette, and panoramic views of the Columbia River. Another recommended room is the Lewis and Clark Room that boasts wonderful views of the Columbia River, a queen bed, a sofa bed, and a romantic, gas fireplace. It also has a private collection of books that provide excellent reading about the Lewis and Clark expedition. A restaurant serves dinner to guests, and banquets and catering can be arranged. Complimentary continental breakfasts are served.

Gearhart

GEARHART BY THE SEA $$-$$$$

1157 North Marion Ave.
(800) 547-0115
www.gearhartresort.com

This large resort in Gearhart surprisingly does not hog the landscape. It's a four-building condominium complex. The central building is Gearhart House; just north of that is Pacific View. Just west, a little closer to the ocean, are Pacific Palisades and Pacific Terraces. And, in spite of the profusion of buildings, all the units have some kind of ocean view. Because the units are individually owned, they are all furnished differently and some of them are lush; moreover, the size and layout of the units are different. All units have a fully outfitted kitchen, fireplace (wood delivered daily), dining room, living room, and bathroom off each bedroom. (You can rent one- or two-bedroom units.) What's more, there are two indoor pools (the one for those staying at Gearhart House has a Jacuzzi). A golf course is on-site. Banquet and conference facilities are available, and it is recommended that you check out the McMenamins Sand Trap Bar & Grill that is located in the Kelly House across the street from the resort. As is common on the North Coast, a deposit is required, and rates are based on a two-night stay. While it seems pricey, because they are condos the rent can be distributed among more people. Pets are allowed in some units. A pet fee is charged.

GEARHART OCEAN INN $$-$$$$

67 North Cottage Ave.
(503) 738-7373, (800) 352-8034
www.gearhartoceaninn.com

The Gearhart Ocean Inn is a wonderful place to stay and offers studios and suites that have small kitchens and have coffeemakers, microwaves, and refrigerators that are stocked with coffee, tea, hot chocolate, and microwave popcorn. The studios and suites offer additional amenities including a TV with DVD player, iron and ironing board, hair dryers, fluffy terry robes, and a variety of books and magazines. Close to the shopping malls and tourist fun of Seaside and the golf course and beach fun of Gearhart, the Gearhart Ocean Inn is a quaint cottage-style motel restored to its old-fashioned charm. Decorated in Cape Cod style, these studios and suites offer comfortable furnishings and close access to the beach. Pets are allowed for $15 each per night. There is a maximum of two pets per unit per night. Children under age 18 stay for free.

Seaside

EDGEWATER INN $$-$$$$
341 South Prom
(503) 738-4142, (866) 783-3784
www.edgewaterinnontheprom.com

The Edgewater allows you to step out the front door, walk down the path, and find yourself in the middle of the Prom, the beloved walkway that fronts the beach at Seaside. A brief walk to the north will put you in the middle of the tourist district; one straight ahead will put you on the beach. But the Edgewater itself manages to convey a get-away-from-it-all feel. Maybe because it's a small hotel of 15 rooms that dare you to relax. All the rooms come with a Jacuzzi tub, a fireplace, a full kitchen, television and VCR/DVD player, sleeping room for four, and great views. There are also a few cottages; these have the same furnishings.

INN AT THE SHORE $$-$$$$
2275 South Prom
(800) 713-9914
www.innattheshore.com

The Inn at the Shore is, we admit, a rather large hotel on the beach. But unlike most of the hotels in Seaside, it is at the quieter south end of the beach near Tillamook Head, away from the arcades and candy stores. You can still stroll up the Prom to get your saltwater taffy and ride the bumper cars, but at the end of the day, you can stroll back and watch a beautiful sunset from a peaceful bit of sand. Eighteen suites provide all

the usual amenities and then some. In many of the suites, you'll find gas fireplaces, kitchenettes, wet bars, and balconies; in all of them, you'll find televisions with DVD and VHS players. The inn also offers free wireless Internet service and complimentary bike rentals. The Inn at the Shore is wheelchair accessible and has pet-friendly rooms. No smoking, please.

Cannon Beach

ARGONAUTA INN/THE WAVES
MOTEL $$$-$$$$
188 West 2nd St.
(503) 436-2205, (800) 822-2468
www.thewavesmotel.com/the_argonauta_inn.htm

Just five units, the Argonauta Inn is an oasis amid a downtown Cannon Beach that can get pretty feverish on a summer afternoon. Each of these lovely, well-furnished units comes with fireplace and kitchen. The units, which are separate buildings, range in size. The largest, Beach House, is good for the family reunion—it can sleep 10, and a large stone fireplace provides incentive to get people off the beach for dinner. The usual modern amenities apply—phones, televisions—and a spa pool is also available. Pets are not allowed.

CANNON BEACH HOTEL $$-$$$
1116 South Hemlock St.
(800) 238-4107
www.cannonbeachhotel.com

A small, European-style hotel, the Cannon Beach has a long history of providing comfort to the weary. It was built as a loggers' boarding house, but it has been fully remodeled and has graduated from its humble origins to become a delightful and cozy hotel and bistro. There are just nine rooms, one of which is a suite; they are custom-furnished; each has a private bath. Some rooms also have fireplaces and spa tubs. (All the rooms have television DVD/VCR.) Breakfast is delivered to your door each morning, and room service, which is relatively rare on the Oregon Coast, is available from the restaurant. The lobby is worth mentioning too—it's a welcoming room with a fireplace, a nice place to curl up with a cup of tea to read the paper. Please don't smoke here, or bring your children, and leave your pets at home.

MCBEE COTTAGES $$$–$$$$
888 South Hemlock St.
(800) 238-4107
www.mcbeecottages.com
Nothing could be as inviting as the 10 smoke-free Cape Cod style cottages of the McBee Motel. The cottages have inviting, cozy furnishings and most have fireplaces and kitchens. The cottages are located only a block from the beach and are pet friendly.

SCHOONER'S COVE INN $$$$
188 North Larch St.
(800) 843-0128
www.schoonerscove.com
The Schooner's Cove is one of a number of Cannon Beach hotels that manage to be at once upscale and down home. Here, you can relax on the front lawn of the cedar-shake hotel while you use the barbecue and watch the beachcombers, or if you don't feel like cooking, watch them from the spa, which faces the ocean. The 30 rooms each have deck, fireplace, and view, DVD players, free wireless Internet, and HBO. The suites have kitchens, too. You can also reserve a time to soak in the oceanfront spa and watch the surf. There is good coffee, laundry facilities for everyone, but no smoking or pets.

THE SEA SPRITE $$$$
280 Nebesna St.
(866) 828-1050
www.seasprite.com
The Sea Sprite is actually just south of Cannon Beach, and it's hard to find anything other than the word "cute" to describe it. It has just six units, but each of them looks out to the ocean and has a deck and porch from which you can admire the view or grill your dinner. You'll also find cable TV and DVD, CD player, telephone, free wireless

Internet access, and microwave to satisfy any urges to use electricity. If you'd rather curl up in front of the fire, though, you can do that too. If these rooms are full, you should check out The Sea Sprite at The Estuary located at 372 N Spruce St. in Cannon Beach. This location is a block from the beach and has five suites that sleep four to six people. The suites feature full kitchens, gas fireplaces, large soaking tubs, and balconies with spectacular ocean views. If you get extra grubby, don't worry: The Sea Sprite has washers and dryers. Please leave the smokes and pets at home.

THE STEPHANIE INN $$$$
2740 South Pacific
(503) 436-2221, (800) 633-3466
www.stephanie-inn.com
Luscious and quiet, the smoke-free Stephanie is a truly sophisticated New England-style country inn. There are 50 rooms, each with a fireplace and air-conditioning to make sure you're comfortable. And rooms come with Jacuzzis and cozy terry robes. A breakfast buffet and newspapers are available each day; a masseuse is on-site. Rooms come equipped with DVD players, cable television, cordless phones, and free, high-speed Internet access. In short, you are pampered in every way. Perhaps the most remarkable feature of the Stephanie is its sense of privacy. It doesn't leap out at you when you're walking on the beach ("They don't wreck the beach with floodlights," said one neighbor), and when you're back inside, the inn feels unhurried and quiet. A complimentary buffet breakfast in the dining room is also included with your stay. Children 12 and over are welcome. Please leave your pets at home.

Tolovana Park
TOLOVANA INN $$$–$$$$
3400 South Hemlock St.
(800) 333-8890
www.tolovanainn.com
Okay, so the Tolovana Inn is a big hotel on the beach (about 3 miles south of Cannon Beach), but it's an institution that still provides luxury and service, the kind that makes life easy on you. Several

nearby restaurants will deliver. If you don't want to amble down to Cannon Beach yourself, you can take the free city shuttle, which stops right at the inn. You'll also have privileges at the Cannon Beach Athletic Club. The rooms are very nice, in that big-hotel way. Besides televisions, DVD players, gas fireplaces, and kitchens, the Tolovana Inn also has an on-site masseuse, free morning coffee and newspapers, high-speed, wireless connectivity, and conference facilities, including a room with a 48-inch television screen so you can show home videos to all the relatives at the family reunion. They might flee to the indoor pool or the game room, however, and who could blame them? For once, the dog can come.

Nehalem

NEHALEM RIVER INN LODGE, RESTAURANT & WINE CELLAR $$$–$$$$
34910 Hwy. 53
(503) 368-7708
www.nehalemriverinn.com

The Nehalem River Inn is an attractive lodge that is a mile and a half east of US 101. The lodge is on the Nehalem River; it's small and lush and rustic, with pleasant views of the Nehalem River. (Some views are close-ups: You can soak in a hot tub on the river.) The lodge consists of three rooms, a cottage, and a spacious suite. The three rooms have private bathrooms and big windows. And there is satellite television. The small cottage has a kitchenette, a fridge, a microwave, and a coffeepot. The suite has a cozy living room and kitchenette. For entertainment, you'll find a fireplace and a two-person spa, as well as a television with DVD/VCR. But you're really going to want to hang out on the lawn or in the excellent restaurant where they serve locally produced cuisine and their own wines.

Wheeler

MAGGIE'S GUESTROOMS $$–$$$
47 Gregory St.
(503) 368-6881

Not all great stays on the Oregon Coast are right on the ocean. Maggie's Guestrooms is a wholly different experience from the usual standardized hotel routine. For one thing, it is a tiny establishment of just three rooms, and each has a theme. The room with the queen bed is the Travel Room; the room with a full-size bed is the Art Room; and the room with two twin beds is the Music Room. The small, beautiful ambience fits in with the mission at Maggie's: to help those seeking a calmer life, especially women. Owner Peg Miller gave up the frantic pace of her own life when she moved from Chicago to Oregon. She bought a building in the charming village of Wheeler in 1999 and hung out her shingle in January 2000, where she now provides respite for other refugees from frenzy. Her rooms are on the second floor of a two-story 1930s building (it was the original post office); they all have private baths. You'll receive a yummy continental breakfast and you can walk across the street to the renowned Treasure Cafe. If you have too much at breakfast, work it off in the pool and health club run by the North County Recreation District. Maggie's also sponsors writers' retreats and workshops and local arts events. If you stay over the weekend, you'll catch the Friday night salon, which enables guests to meet one another and to find out what else is happening in and around Wheeler. These little personal touches make Maggie's Guestrooms more relaxing—and encouraging—than a grand ocean resort. A two-night minimum stay is required for most summer weekends and holidays. Well-behaved pets may stay with approval from the owner of the inn.

Pacific City

INN AT CAPE KIWANDA $$$–$$$$
33105 Cape Kiwanda Dr.
(888) 965-7001
www.innatcapekiwanda.com

A 35-room inn in the unhurried community of Pacific City, the Inn at Cape Kiwanda is a great place for a family vacation—all rooms have a gas fireplace and ocean views—or a business retreat—all the rooms have dataports and you can make use of a large ocean-view meeting room. You can use it, that is, if you can tear your employees away from the day spa, book and gift stores, and galleries. If you can't, walk across the street to the Pelican Pub & Brewery and take the rest of the day off. Some rooms have Jacuzzis from which you can peacefully view the ocean. The inn is nonsmoking and pets are allowed in selected rooms for a fee. A two-night minimum stay is required on weekends in July and August and all legal holidays.

Neskowin

PACIFIC SANDS RESORT $$–$$$
48250 Breakers Blvd.
(503) 392-3101
www.oregoncoast.com/pacificsands

While the Pacific Sands looks unprepossessing, its location on a quiet stretch of beach in the little community of Neskowin is reason enough to stay there. Pacific Sands is a condo-style resort close to golf courses, the casino at Lincoln City (it's just shy of being on the Central Coast), hiking, and, of course, the beautiful beach right there out the front door. The resort has 12 one- and two-bedroom units, many of which face the ocean, and all units have fireplace, living room, kitchen, and patio or deck from which you can enjoy the view. All of this comes at very reasonable prices: Even in the summer months, you can find units for less than $100. Pacific Sands asks for a deposit of the first night's rent and a seven day's notice to get it back. All rooms are nonsmoking and pets are not allowed. From the third week in June to the third week in September, there is a one-week stay minimum requirement. A two-night minimum stay is required at all other times.

CENTRAL COAST

There are so many hotels on the Central Coast that anyone could become bewildered driving along US 101. What we do is turn off US 101. Many of the hotels listed below are off the beaten path. Hotels on this area of the Coast tend to be clustered in Lincoln City and Newport.

Lincoln City

THE O'DYSIUS $$$$
120 Northwest Inlet Court
(800) 869-8069
www.odysius.com

Lincoln City presents mile after mile of beach motels. Fortunately, the O'dysius is here to break up the monotony. This swank 30-room hotel on a rare peaceful stretch of beach by the D River is devoted to making your stay at Lincoln City as luxurious as possible. The interior of the building is lovely, with lacquered wainscoting, a slate entry hall, and a stone fireplace in the library. The furniture is custom-made, and the beds smothered in down comforters and pillows; you'll find whirlpool tubs and ocean views in all the rooms. Rooms also feature telephones and dataports. The hotel has many other nice little touches: wine in the evening, slippers at your bedside, shuttle service to the casino in Lincoln City, sheltered parking, and indoor corridors to keep you dry during winter storms. Some rooms are accessible by wheelchair. While this is an expensive hotel, the O'dysius offers senior discounts, seasonal rates, and corporate packages, so ask about them. Small, well-behaved pets are welcome, and so are children if they're older than 12. It's so nice here you won't want to leave. The hotel is completely nonsmoking.

Gleneden Beach

WESTIN SALISHAN $$$$
7760 US 101 North
(800) 452-2300
www.salishan.com

Salishan, as it's known to locals, is one of the oldest resorts on the Coast and one of the most beloved. A thousand acres, 205 units, a championship golf course, several kinds of pools, activities for the children, wine tasting for the adults, shopping, tennis, and the beach—these are only a few of the reasons that people return often. Fireplaces and balconies come with all the rooms, which are decorated according to Northwest principles of place (lots of stone and wood). Rooms are spacious. Cable TV and movies are available, of course. In other words, this is an outstanding destination resort that should not be missed, especially if you're a golfer. (See the Golf and Shopping chapters for more information.)

Otter Rock

INN AT OTTER CREST $$$-$$$$
301 Otter Crest Loop
(541) 765-2111, (800) 452-2101
www.innatottercrest.com

A large resort just to the north of Newport, the Inn at Otter Crest offers tennis, basketball, an oceanside pool, and many other activities for the person who is trying to find something to do beside tide pools. The Inn at Otter Crest sprawls over 35 acres of forest, beach, and meadow. Its grounds are lovely; its rooms are too. Rooms feature large windows and decks; many rooms have a fireplace and kitchen, cable TV, and high-speed wireless Internet access. Pets are not allowed, and this facility is smoke-free.

Newport

THE SYLVIA BEACH HOTEL $$$-$$$$
267 Northwest Cliff
(888) 795-8422
www.sylviabeachhotel.com

In a world where every hotel seems to have the same decorator, the Sylvia Beach Hotel provides a valuable public service by its relief from monotony. This 20-room hotel set 45 feet above Nye Beach opened in 1988 and is dedicated to book lovers everywhere: It's named after the prescient and heroic Sylvia Beach, owner of the Parisian bookstore Shakespeare & Company, publisher of *Ulysses*, and book supplier to Ernest Hemingway. And books are the focus here: Not only is each room dedicated to a favorite author, but there are no in-room televisions, radios, or telephones to distract you from reading them.

A fabulous reading room has amazing views of the Yaquina Head Lighthouse and the ocean if you can be bothered to look up from the books, puzzles, board games, or drinks that are offered. Rooms are charmingly appointed according to literary reputation and style. In the Hemingway Room, for instance, hunting trophies hang over the bed to guard you while you sleep; in the Edgar Allan Poe Room, it's a mechanized pendulum that keeps you company. You'll find three classes of room: "novels," "best sellers," and "classics." "Classics" are the most expensive—oceanfront suites with fireplaces and decks; "best sellers" are oceanview rooms that fall in the middle price range; and "novels" cost the least. They are without ocean views, though they do have patios.

Whatever your literary diet, the room comes with breakfast, served family style in the Tables of Content restaurant. Dinners are served too, if you make reservations (dinners are available to people who are staying elsewhere). They can be lively and long, since sharing tables with strangers seems to bring out everyone's most outrageous stories. The loyalty and admiration inspired by this unusual hotel is evident when you read through the journal-guest books in each room. Whether it's the quiet rooms, the stimulating dinner conversation, the immersion in literature, or the proximity of the beautiful beach, many people find their thinking improves upon staying here. Pets and smoking are not allowed at this Coast retreat.

THE VIKING'S COTTAGES AND CONDOS $$-$$$$
729 Northwest Coast St.
(541) 265-2477, (800) 480-2477
www.vikingsoregoncoast.com

The Viking's Cottages and Condos offer two different Nye Beach experiences. The Cottages are decorated in the shabby chic beach house style you remember from childhood, with wood paneling and white trim, lace curtains, and painted wood furniture. They are unstuffy and old-fashioned, built in 1925, though terribly clean, of course; they are also modern enough to make the television watchers in the family happy. Only two of the cottages have telephones, and the bathrooms have only showers, no tubs. But there are decks, stairs to the beach, fully equipped kitchens, and great views. The 36 condos, on the other hand, are contemporary; they are privately owned and rented out to you. The oceanfront condos have, in addition to patios or balconies, a spa and pool, cable TV, fully equipped kitchens, and some fireplaces. If you need a telephone, though, make sure you ask for one ahead of time. Not surprisingly, the condos run a little more, but there are still bargains to be had. Pets are welcome in the Family Beach cottage.

Waldport

CAPE COD COTTAGES $$-$$$
4150 Southwest Pacific Coast Hwy. (US 101)
(541) 563-2106
http://capecodcottagesonline.com
The Cape Cod Cottages, built in 1938, are the perfect retreat for those who like to comb the beach without having to fight the crowds for sand dollars. Situated on a beautiful 6 miles of beach between Yachats and Waldport, the one- and two-bedroom cottages of this sweet and economical establishment are clean, comfortable, and low key. They come outfitted with decks, kitchens, fireplaces, telephones, and cable TV; there are also nonsmoking and wheelchair-accessible rooms. There's also a four-bedroom beach house if you want to bring some friends with you. It sleeps a total of eight. Pets and smoking are not permitted in the cottages.

EDGEWATER COTTAGES $$
3978 Southwest Pacific Coast Hwy. (US 101)
(541) 563-2240
www.edgewatercottages.com
Each of the seven units of these charming cottages right next to the beach has a fireplace, a deck, and a view; it's hard to say which is the most attractive feature. The stretch of beach on which the cottages rest is one of the most beautiful beaches anywhere, so plan to stay awhile—and you can do it because each cottage also has an equipment-stocked kitchen. They're Fido-friendly here, as long as the dog is good and you pay the pet fee, and the place is also a favorite of families with children, in spite of, or maybe because of,

the fact that there are no phones (except in the Westwind cottage). Just calm down and enjoy the beach instead. The Edgewater Cottages are wildly popular; call early for reservations and ask about the minimum stay requirements. Credit cards are not accepted.

Yachats

ADOBE RESORT $$-$$$
1551 US 101
(541) 547-3141, (800) 522-3623
www.adoberesort.com
The Adobe is a resort right in the middle of Yachats, which means that a fine basalt beach is right there before you and you're still close to restaurants and shopping. The older section, with great views and fireplaces, allows pets for a $10 fee. The newer sections won't allow pets, but they do offer some in-room Jacuzzis, patios or porches, wet bars, and even kitchenettes to make up for it. Nonsmoking and wheelchair-accessible rooms are both available (there's an elevator too). The rooms here all come with phone, hair dryer, cable TV, coffeemaker, and refrigerator; the resort complex offers a Jacuzzi and sauna, as well as an exercise room, for everyone to use. A full-service restaurant serves breakfast, lunch, and dinner, as well as a Sunday champagne brunch. (There's a lounge with stunning views, too, for the grown-ups.) Ask about packages—a number of extended-stay deals, some of which include various combinations of meals, can net you a bargain.

THE FIRESIDE MOTEL $$-$$$
1881 US 101 North
(800) 336-3573
www.firesidemotel.com
This is an unpretentious motel that offers great value. Two buildings hold 43 rooms; the rooms of the West Building face the ocean and all have remarkable views. These rooms also have balconies, and some rooms here have gas fireplaces. In the North Building, there are still some rooms with views, but from some you can't see the water. There is, however, a largish suite in

this building; it has both a kitchen and a view. Wherever your room is, it will have cable TV/DVD player, a coffeemaker, a direct-dial phone, and a refrigerator. There are wheelchair-accessible rooms, and some rooms in each building are dedicated to smokers and pets.

OCEAN HAVEN $$–$$$
94770 US 101
(541) 547-3583
www.oceanhaven.com

The ambience of the Ocean Haven is very Oregon. This eight-unit motel is stunningly set just south of Yachats near beach trails and tide pools. The owners want you to experience the beach as it is meant to be, so no pets are allowed since they discourage the native eagles, elk, otters, and their compatriots. It's not sumptuous; instead, it's comfortable and beachy, attracting artists and writers who like its dramatic location and quiet atmosphere (no television, no telephones in the rooms, however, there is free WiFi). No smoking, either; a one night's 50 percent deposit is required.

THE OREGON HOUSE $$–$$$$
94288 US 101 South
(541) 547-3329
www.oregonhouse.com

The Oregon House is an interesting hotel a little south of Yachats. Reservations are recommended here, and they have a strict deposit policy (one night or 50 percent) and a rather complicated refund policy. Once you're here, you may have to stay at least two nights, and sometimes three if it's a holiday. Pets and smoking are unwelcome, and children may stay only in some units. But once you get past all that, the Oregon House is a splendid place to stay. A stream winds its way through the property and its wooded trails, and there are little bridges to cross it. A trail leads to the beach—it is illuminated at night. There are five buildings and ten units, all of which are distinctive, have been carefully remodeled, and have interesting histories behind them. Most

rooms include fireplaces and kitchens, two rooms have Jacuzzis, and most have ocean views.

OVERLEAF LODGE $$$–$$$$
2055 US 101 North
(800) 338-0507
www.overleaflodge.com

A modern resort, the Overleaf Lodge's motto, "Natural Beauty, Civilized Pleasures," couldn't be more apt. First of all, the Overleaf is just north of Yachats, so you can take advantage of the many recreational activities in the area, from beachcombing to hiking. Every room faces the ocean and many rooms have balconies from which to enjoy the views. The civilized pleasures include an exercise room, robes, fireplaces in some rooms, and an on-site day spa where you can enjoy massages, facials and other body restoring treatments. You'll also find television and DVD player, hair dryer, microwave, refrigerator, and coffeemaker in all the rooms. Rates are, as usual, based on double occupancy; extra folk are $8 apiece. Keep the cigarettes and furry friends at home. The Overleaf provides some wheelchair-accessible rooms.

SHAMROCK LODGETTES RESORT
AND SPA $$–$$$
105 US 101 South
(541) 547-3312, (800) 845-5028
www.shamrocklodgettes.com

The Shamrock's log cabins exude summer-camp charm, and taking a stroll down the big lawn that leads to the beach will revive buried feelings of pleasure at the thought that you don't have to go home because you're going to sleep right there. Only this time, you'll skip the s'mores and enjoy a massage or relax in the spa. The cabins all have stone fireplaces and kitchenettes. There are also motel rooms; these too have fireplaces, and some are suites with Jacuzzis. All rooms, no matter where they are, have phone, cable TV, daily paper delivery, and amazing views. Pets are welcome in the cabins only (for an additional fee). All units are nonsmoking.

YACHATS INN   **$$–$$$**
331 South Coast Hwy. 101 (US 101)
(888) 270-3456 (541) 547-3456
www.yachatsinn.com

A cute older motel with a newer addition and a Japanese teahouse for meetings, the Yachats Inn has managed to preserve its quaint hometown air while still bringing modern convenience to its rooms. And the view from most rooms is timeless—crashing surf and painfully beautiful beaches. There are two buildings. The original building, built in 1948, has both suites and singles. All rooms have electric heat and if yours is a room with a fireplace or wood stove, your wood will be restocked. Some rooms have sun porches. If you're bored, you can watch cable TV. The newer section is built in contemporary Northwest beach-house style, with shingled siding and white trim. The suites sleep up to four persons and are outfitted with full kitchen and a dining room. There are also gas fireplaces, bathtubs, telephones, two televisions and VCRs, and decks. The Teahouse is a handsome building with a vaulted ceiling, a wood stove, a kitchen, and a large (2,000-square-foot), glass-enclosed deck for a meeting or other event; it can be rented by the day or by the hour. Pets can stay in the older section for $10 per pet per night; children under three stay for free; and extra people in a room stay for $5 per night per person.

ZIGGURAT   **$$$**
95330 US 101 South
(541) 547-3925

The Ziggurat is an unusual lodging near Yachats. Covered in weathered cedar shake, it was built in the tall beach grass according to the principles of pre-Egyptian pyramids (ziggurat is the Sumerian word for pyramid); hence there are no square rooms here and each room is remarkably private. The first floor has two suites, the Southeast Suite and the West Suite.

The Ziggurat values privacy—within the suites bedrooms can be closed off; and decks, patios, alcoves, and rooms all have spaces to curl up in and ponder your manuscript without

fear of being interrupted. They ask that your children be at least 14 if they're coming with you. The Southeast Suite has a queen-size bed in an enclosed alcove, some ocean view, and its own sauna, and there's a twin bed for the 14-year-old. The West Suite has a glass-block shower (round) and an impressive 27-foot wall of glass that you can stare out of from your hand-carved bed. When you weary of all the privacy, or if you can tear yourself out of bed, a library on the first floor, with books and games, as well as a mini kitchen for making and storing snacks, will provide some entertainment. And then, too, there are two decks enclosed in glass to keep you out of the freezing breezes. You can stay at the Ziggurat in two modes: It can provide you with bed-and-breakfast service, but you can also inquire about extended stays. These will allow you laundry and some kitchen privileges (but you'll have to make your own bed and breakfast) and give you as much privacy as you need to finish your treatise. In any case, you'll have to stay at least two nights and give five days' notice if you want a refund of your deposit. Note well: Don't bring pets or smoking implements; and don't bring the plastic either. They don't take credit cards—just cash, personal checks, and traveler's checks.

Florence

THE LANDMARK INN   **$$**
1551 4th St.
(541) 997-9030, (800) 822–7811
http://presys.com/~landmarkinn

The Landmark Inn is a charming, small hotel conveniently set within walking distance of the Florence Events Center and the notably shoppable Old Town district. Not only will you find lovely views of the mountains, sand dunes, and Siuslaw River, but you will enjoy them from nicely decorated rooms, 12 in all, some suites with sitting rooms and kitchens, and spas. Guests may use a traditional Finnish cedar sauna that sits in a tiny pine grove away from the main building. The Landmark Inn was built in 1998 on top of a knoll above Old Town. Beware the steeply graded driveway, especially going down. The pavement bears the scars of hasty motorists who scraped the bottoms of their vehicles. And you can smoke outdoors only.

RIVER HOUSE MOTEL $$–$$$
1202 Bay St.
(888) 824-2750
www.riverhousemotel.com

The River House is not luxurious, but it is clean, quiet, and really friendly (they have cookies and coffee in the lobby for those who wander in), and sometimes that's what you need the most. The River House is tucked under the bridge spanning the Siuslaw River in Florence; it's just to the west of Old Town. There are phones, TVs, high-speed Internet, microwaves, refrigerators, free in-room coffee and tea and a continental breakfast is served daily. Children under age 12 stay for free. Pets must stay home, however. They also have an alluring spa.

Reedsport

BEST WESTERN SALBASGEON INN $$
1400 US 101
(541) 271-4831
www.bestwesternoregon.com

This may be the spot to rest your head after a long day of exploring the dunes. The Salbasgeon has 56 spic-and-span rooms, some of which have coffeemaker, refrigerator, microwave, fireplace, and whirlpool, and all of which have free movies on cable and high-speed Internet. You'll also be able to help yourself to a continental breakfast and swim in the indoor pool. Pets are allowed in some rooms for a little extra, and some rooms are wheelchair accessible.

SOUTH COAST

The South Coast features proportionally more destination resort hotels than other areas of the Coast. Places like Gold Beach are remote enough that once you get there, you want to stay awhile. Hotels are primarily clustered in Bandon, Gold Beach, and Brookings.

Coos Bay

EDGEWATER INN ON THE PACIFIC COAST $$
275 East Johnson Ave.
(541) 267-0423, (800) 233-0423
www.edgewater-inns.com

Usefully set just east of US 101, the Edgewater boasts that it's the only waterfront motel in Coos Bay; it even has its own fishing dock. Many of the rooms in this hotel have spa tubs, kitchenettes, and balconies overlooking the bay. They'll provide you with a continental breakfast and VCR; you can also take advantage of their exercise room or the indoor pool to rejuvenate your road-weary bones. They also have a business center with wireless Internet access. Because it's just off the highway, the Edgewater is a little quieter than some of the motels right on the US 101 strip, but you can still walk to the Coos Bay waterfront or poke around downtown.

Bandon

BANDON DUNES $$$$
57744 Round Lake Dr.
(541) 347-4380, (888) 345-6008
www.bandondunesgolf.com

The top-notch Bandon Dunes Golf Course is hailed as one of the most impressive golf courses in the United States. Once you're there, you might not want to leave; fortunately there are accommodations for you. The elegant Lodge at Bandon Dunes not only provides a wonderful full-service restaurant, a lounge, and a golf shop, but it also has 19 single rooms with private baths and queen-size beds and two suites with master bedrooms and card rooms (or sitting rooms, if you prefer). The suites will cost you $1,300 to $1,800 per night for one person plus a little more for additional guests, and the single rooms run from $200 to $250 for one person, per night. If you're exhausted from all that golf, you can soak in a hot tub, or if you want to keep the edge over your partner, you can work out in the exercise room. You can also stay in one of the Lily Pond Rooms, which run about $360 per night.

If you stay at the lodge, your greens fees will be reduced, and if you go during the winter, you can take advantage of the off-season rates. Shuttle service is available between Bandon Dunes and the North Bend Airport. See the Golf chapter for more information.

BEST WESTERN INN AT FACE ROCK $$$
3225 Beach Loop Rd.
(541) 347-9441
(800) 638-3092 (reservations)
www.facerock.net

Magnificent views of the ocean, Face Rock, and the Coquille River Lighthouse make this 74-room resort a great place to bring the family for a stay at Bandon. In addition to the beach access—which even includes its own beach house—the Inn at Face Rock is right next to a pleasant 9-hole golf course (see the Golf chapter for more information). Many of the suites have fireplaces, king- and queen-size beds, kitchenettes, and private patios. You'll find coffeemakers, microwaves, and refrigerators in other rooms. There is also a banquet room, a heated outdoor spa, and an indoor pool for the use of guests. Some good bargains may be had: There are discounts for groups and packages, and best of all, during the winter season, prices for many of the rooms drop.

COQUILLE POINT VACATION RENTALS $$$$
1260 Beach Loop Rd.
835 & 845 Beach Loop Rd.
(541) 347-2700, (800) 457-9141
www.tablerockmotel.com

Brought to you by the people at the Table Rock Motel (see later listing), these comfortable lodgings are a restful and economical alternative to motel living. Three three-bedroom suites accommodate up to six people, and up to four people can stay in the two-bedroom suite. Beds are queen-size; all bedrooms have private bathrooms; and all suites provide fully equipped kitchens, laundry areas, and cable TV, VCRs, and high-speed Internet. Rent the places by the week: Not only will you save money but you'll need at least that long to explore the wildlife reserve, play on the beach, golf, windsurf, and see the whales. Keep the pets at home and the cigs in the car.

SUNSET OCEANFRONT ACCOMMODATIONS $$$
1865 Beach Loop Rd.
(541) 347-2453, (800) 842-2407
www.sunsetmotel.com

Straddling Beach Loop Road and making the most of its breathtaking location, the Sunset provides a full array of services, including a restaurant and lounge. Some rooms have kitchens and fireplaces; some are right on the ocean; some rooms are designated for pets. You can sleep in standard or queen-size beds, and you can choose from among economy rooms or full suites. Cable TV and laundry facilities are available. And there are wheelchair-accessible rooms. If you stay in the units across the road, you can find some excellent bargains. It goes without saying that it's easy to get to the beach—just walk down the stairs. The Sunset offers beach house rentals in addition to its motel services.

TABLE ROCK MOTEL $$–$$$
840 Beach Loop Rd.
(541) 347-2700, (800) 457-9141
www.tablerockmotel.com

What this little motel lacks in luxury, it makes up for in its dramatic setting. Next to a wildlife sanctuary and overlooking Table Rock, Face Rock, and the other formations off the Bandon shore, the Table Rock Motel offers some rooms with kitchenettes, coffeemakers, radios, and refrigerators. All units have cable TV and DVD players; though you probably will be too busy exploring to turn it on. High-speed Internet access is available in rooms and a lobby computer is available for your use. Pets are allowed for a fee of $10 per pet per day.

WINDERMERE ON THE BEACH MOTEL $$–$$$
3250 Beach Loop Rd.
(541) 347-3710
www.windermerebythesea.com

This appealing motel is right across from a golf course, right on the beach, and just right for families. Beautiful ocean vistas are visible from all the rooms. All units have cable TV, HBO, and wireless Internet. You'll find a variety of bed sizes from doubles to kings. A number of the rooms have kitchens and sleeping lofts, making them ideal for longer visits. Its moderate prices ($98 for a queen-size bed and kitchen unit) can make the Windermere a good value for the vacationing family, but leave the family dog at home—they don't take pets.

Port Orford

CASTAWAY-BY-THE-SEA $$–$$$
545 West 5th St.
(541) 332-4502
www.castawaybythesea.com
Port Orford is the westernmost point in the lower 48 states, and this friendly motel might be the westernmost building. The Castaway overlooks historic Port Orford, and the ocean beyond from every room, and offers both suites and rooms with sun porches and decks from which you can enjoy the view. Amenities include beach access, easy walking distance to town, cable TV, WiFi, and nonsmoking rooms. Well-behaved pets can stay for only $10 per pet per night. The off-season rates are remarkably low.

Gold Beach

GOLD BEACH RESORT $$$
29232 South Ellensburg Ave. (US 101)
(541) 247-7066, (800) 541-0947
www.gbresort.com
The Gold Beach resort is a nice motel in a location from which you can take equal advantage of the river recreation on the Rogue River or the ocean recreation of the Pacific. It's also a good place to hold a reunion, wedding, or business meeting because the resort has convention facilities for up to 250 people. The Gold Beach Resort offers 39 rooms, all of which face the water. Each room also has a small refrigerator, a coffeemaker, a television with VCR, WiFi, and—just in case you actually

are in a wedding or at a business meeting—a hair dryer, iron, and ironing board. Some rooms are accessible by wheelchair. Staying in one of five condominiums is another way to enjoy the resort: Each condo comes equipped with full kitchen and fireplace, and some have washers and dryers. These units will accommodate from four to seven people. No pets are permitted, but you are welcome to munch from the continental breakfast buffet, swim in the indoor pool or spa, and stare at the beach from your balcony.

IRELAND'S RUSTIC LODGES $$$
29346 Ellensburg Ave. (US 101)
(541) 247-7718
www.irelandsrusticlodges.com
Rustic indeed, these little cottages just ooze down-home charm. Each cottage has an open fireplace stocked with wood (but don't try to cook over it). There are 40 rooms in all, some of them ordinary hotel rooms; try for a cabin. The grounds have a pretty garden and, of course, the beach right there in front of you. The owners really like deposits; otherwise they might give away your cabin. Pets and extra people cost more and no smoking here, either. If you're worried that your taste for rusticity will evaporate after dark, rest assured that you can still watch cable TV, and there is high-speed, wireless Internet connectivity.

JOT'S RESORT ON THE ROGUE RIVER $$$
94630 Wedderburn Loop
(541) 247-6676, (800) 367-5687
www.jotsresort.com
Jot's Resort benefits from its location right under the Rogue River Bridge and has installed its own marina and tackle shop from which you can charter boats and hire fishing guides. It's a rather large resort by Coast standards, with 140 rooms of varying sizes and degrees of luxury. Jot's features a heated indoor pool, a spa and sauna, and an exercise room for you to relax in. Children under 10 stay free; pets are welcome for a $10 fee. You'll also be able to eat at the restaurant if you had a bad day fishing. Best of all, the ocean is still right there around the corner.

TU TU' TUN LODGE $$$$
96550 North Bank Rogue
(800) 864-6357
www.tututun.com

Named after the Tuntuni Indians who used to live here, the small and beautiful Tu Tu' Tun Lodge is 7 miles east of the ocean on the Rogue River. This wonderful place is both intimate and refined. Sixteen rooms in a two-story building make up the bulk of the rooms; these have king- or queen-size beds, private patios or balconies, and some of them have fireplaces and outdoor soaking tubs. There are also two suites in the lodge and two houses. The Garden House, overlooking the apple orchard, is a three-bedroom cottage that can sleep up to six; it has an attractive stone fireplace and a full kitchen. The River House, a contemporary building that features a large cedar-vaulted living room, has two bedrooms, two bathrooms, a full kitchen, and an outdoor Jacuzzi. (It's available only from July to October.) If you stay in a suite, you'll have a kitchen in addition to an expansive living room and a view of the river. One suite has two queen-size beds; the other has, in addition, a twin sleeper in the living room. All rooms have telephones, satellite television, and refrigerators to store your catch.

The center of activity is the main lodge—that's where you'll find a cozy bar, a library, and a large stone fireplace that demands you linger in front of it. The dining room, which serves elegant, delicious, family-style meals is also housed in the main lodge. The dining room is closed in the off-season, though you'll be served a continental breakfast; otherwise, during the high season, meals are prix fixe and include breakfast, hors d'oeuvre, and dinner. (If you want to eat here and you're not staying at the lodge, you may do so by reservation only.) To work off all the calories from dinner, the lodge has on its grounds a lap pool, river paths, and hiking trails. You can also play a round of horseshoes, practice your putting on a four-hole golf course, or live out your Minnesota Fats fantasies at the antique pool table. Or explore the Rogue's white water and wild scenery by taking one of the boats that stop at the dock. But the biggest draw is the fishing: Many people use the Tu Tu' Tun as a kind of luxurious fishing camp. The lodge will provide you with the latest news on salmon and steelhead runs and other important information. The Tu Tu' Tun bases its rates on double occupancy. They require a deposit of one night's lodging, and if you change your mind about staying here, although we can't see how that would happen, you must tell them two weeks before the date of your reservation in order to get it back. And you can only smoke outside on the terrace. Leave the pooch at home.

Brookings

BEST WESTERN BEACHFRONT INN $$
16008 Boat Basin Rd.
(541) 469-7779
(800) 468-4081 (reservations)
www.bestwesternoregon.com

Every one of the 102 rooms at the Beachfront Inn has a small, private balcony overlooking the ocean, which may be within 50 feet of you. The Beachfront has the closest rooms to the ocean of any other motel on the Oregon Coast. Other attractive things about its location include walking distance to the marina and the new shopping district at the Port of Brookings and the fact that it's across the street from the only restaurant in town with views of the water. But the location is not the Beachfront's only charm: These immaculate rooms and suites are comfortable and loaded with amenities. In addition to phones, refrigerators, microwaves, satellite television with HBO, and high-speed Internet access. The Beachfront features rooms with Jacuzzis that look out upon the ocean. There are also several one-bedroom suites with kitchens and sitting rooms. Smoking is permitted in one building and pets are allowed on a limited basis. If you want to have a meeting, a room that can hold up to 50 people is available. There's a sunny outdoor pool if you get tired of the beach. A number of rooms are accessible to those in wheelchairs, and there are four rooms with roll-in showers.

CHETCO RIVER INN   **$$$–$$$$**
21202 High Prairie Rd.
(541) 251-0087
www.chetcoriverinn.com

This small retreat 18 miles up the Chetco River allows you to really get away from it all—you're even off the power grid (the inn is run with solar power and propane gas)! But don't let that worry you: It's as comfortable and modern as anything. The Chetco River Inn is a fishing lodge, and they'll hook you up with guides for drift boat or ocean fishing, but it is also urbanely furnished with marble floors, leather furniture, and oriental rugs; down comforters keep you cozy at night. The five rooms range from about $135 to $155 each night for two people, and that includes a big country breakfast. You can also arrange to have lunches and dinners made. You also have the option to stay in the cottage which sleeps four and has a kitchen, fireplace, and large indoor Jacuzzi. Children are welcome if they're 12 or over (they'll be staying in their own room), but Rover has to stay home. The Chetco River Inn asks that you send a deposit of one night's lodging, which can be refunded up to seven days before your scheduled stay. Your deposit and reservations may all be handled conveniently on the Internet (or by phone). They accept checks here. Smoking outside only, please.

BED-AND-BREAKFAST INNS

In this chapter you'll find bed-and-breakfast inns that range from turn-of-the-century houses filled with beautiful antiques to contemporary inns. The possibilities are endless—you can stay in a chateau in a private suite or you can stay in a stateroom aboard a paddleboat. You'll have the luxury of enjoying the privacy of your own room as well as the opportunity to visit with other guests and exchange stories with the innkeepers. The innkeepers we interviewed were happy to share their stories with us as well as their love of what they do. Their common goal is to make you feel at home and give you a chance to relax and enjoy the scenic beauty of the magnificent coast.

When you stay in a bed-and-breakfast, you'll always receive a home-cooked breakfast made from fresh local ingredients, which usually includes a main entree such as fresh crab omelets, applesauce pancakes, or fluffy French toast, accompanied by homemade breads and jam, fresh fruit, and gourmet coffee, juice, or tea. Some innkeepers serve you breakfast in your room and some in the dining area at a specified time in the morning. It's always a good idea to find out when and where breakfast is served so you don't miss out!

We've organized the bed-and-breakfasts by region—North, Central, and South—and then by city from north to south. In each of the listings you'll find the name and address, price code, phone, Web site, restrictions, a detailed description of the bed-and-breakfast itself—including what's for breakfast—and other things to see and do in the area. If a bed-and-breakfast doesn't accept major credit cards, we've indicated that. Keep in mind that most bed-and-breakfasts do not allow smoking or pets and many allow children only with prior approval.

Whichever bed-and-breakfast you stay at, we know you will enjoy good company, breathtaking views of the scenic Coast, and a hearty homemade breakfast that will make you want to come back again and again.

Price Code

Our price code chart reflects the average cost of overnight accommodations for two people during peak season that generally runs from May through October (not including local lodging tax). Here's the breakdown:

$	$65 and less
$$	$66 to $95
$$$	$96 to $150
$$$$	more than $150

NORTH COAST

Astoria

ASTORIA INN $$
3391 Irving Ave.
(503) 325-8153, (800) 718-8153
www.astoriainnbb.com
The Astoria Inn is a friendly Victorian farmhouse that is surrounded by a pretty yard in a quiet residential area and has four guest rooms with private baths. The Cape Lookout Room is located on the second floor and is furnished with 1860s

antiques, a queen-size bed, a private bath with shower, and magnificent views of the Columbia River; the Cape Mears Room is located on the second floor and has a queen-size bed, private bath with shower, and nice forest views; the Cape Virginia Room is located on the second floor, is decorated with Victorian furnishings, and has a queen-size bed, private bath with shower, and a pretty forest view; the Fort Stevens Room is located on the first floor, is decorated with Victorian furnishings, and has a queen-size bed and private bath with shower.

Additional amenities you'll find at this inn are a television and movie player in the communal front room, a cozy sitting room furnished with antiques and collectibles, and a veranda where you can watch the ships pass by on the Columbia River. You'll also be served a complimentary breakfast that includes fresh fruit, breakfast meats, egg entree, and coffee, tea, and juice.

Astoria is full of shops, museums, and galleries that you can explore, and Fort Stevens and Fort Clatsop are within a half-hour's drive of this inn. Restrictions: Smoking is permitted on the outside veranda only. No pets. No children.

BENJAMIN YOUNG INN BED AND BREAKFAST $$–$$$
3652 Duane St.
(503) 325-6172, (800) 201-1286
www.benjaminyounginn.com
The Benjamin Young Inn Bed and Breakfast was built in 1888 and is located in a quiet residential district in Astoria. This bed-and-breakfast is an outstanding example of Queen Anne architecture and is elegant yet unpretentious. The interior of the house has high ceilings with ornate mouldings, stained glass windows, and comfortable furnishings in five guest rooms, each with style and personality.

The Fireplace Suite, located on the ground floor, can accommodate up to seven people, has a large jetted tub, a king-size bed, and a second bedroom. The Honeymoon Suite is decorated in a bridal theme and has a fancy canopy bed decorated with delicate lace. The room is also

decorated with other wedding memorabilia and has the wedding certificate of the original owners of the house dating back to 1873 on the wall. This suite is perfect for a romantic getaway. Its cupola overlooks the Columbia River and the antique furnishings take you back in time. The Lady Ann Room is a large, elegant suite located on the second floor that is furnished with a queen-size bed, loveseat, and two large comfortable chairs and has outstanding views of the Columbia River and this estate's gardens. This suite also boasts a private bath with European tub and shower. The Dorothy Room is also located on the second floor and is a sun-filled room offering partial views of the Columbia River. This room is furnished with a queen-size bed, a twin-size bed, sofa, rocking chair, and a private bath. The Rose Room is a cozy room on the second floor that features outstanding views of the Columbia River, a queen-size bed, and a private bath and shower.

Additional amenities you'll enjoy at this romantic getaway include Columbia River views, river and ocean access, wood-burning fireplace, a piano, a historic carriage house, off-street parking, bicycle storage for cyclists, homemade cookies, and a comfortable front porch. A complimentary breakfast is served in the dining room overlooking the river between 8 and 10 a.m. Breakfast is an "event" at this inn, and the table is graced with china, silver, and crystal. Breakfast entrees include quiche with bacon, omelets, crepes, turkey, sun-dried tomato sausages, freshly baked muffins and breads, cranberry scones, a variety of fresh fruits, orange juice, and freshly brewed coffee.

With such close proximity to downtown Astoria, there are dozens of activities and exploring options for you. You can visit the Flavel House, Astoria Column, and the Maritime Museum or travel west and visit Fort Stevens State Park or Fort Clatsop. Restrictions: No smoking. No pets.

CLEMENTINE'S BED AND BREAKFAST $–$$$
847 Exchange St.
(800) 521-6801
www.clementines-bb.com
Clementine's Bed and Breakfast is an 1888 Victorian

house that was fully restored in 1994. This elegant bed-and-breakfast features five guest rooms decorated Victorian-style with queen-size beds and private baths and showers, luxurious English bath accessories, comfy robes, fresh flowers, and wireless Internet service. One room is wheelchair accessible. In addition, two large suites suitable for families with children are available. These suites have a TV, fireplace, and full kitchen. Additional amenities include beautiful flower gardens with more than 2,000 spring bulbs and an herb garden and a living room where you can enjoy beverages and snacks in the evening, browse the reading library, play games, or listen to music.

You'll enjoy a gourmet breakfast in the dining room, or, if you prefer, it can be served in your room. The inn also offers cooking classes, massage and spa appointments and laundry service.

Astoria is full of things to see and do. Clementine's has kayaks available for your use and hiking and biking are also popular activities around Astoria. You can explore the museums and shops in Astoria, rent a fishing charter, or go play on nearby beaches. If you have children or pets, you can stay in the Moose Temple Lodge that is next door to Clementine's. The lodge contains two, spacious suites that share a common area that contains a small kitchen, fireplace and dining table. It also features the Riverview Loft that has a full kitchen, private bath with shower, a gas fireplace, and laundry facilities and can accommodate up to six people. Restrictions: No smoking.

FRANKLIN STREET STATION
BED AND BREAKFAST $$–$$$
1140 Franklin St.
(503) 325-4314, (800) 448-1098
www.astoriaoregonbb.com
Sharon Middleton and Becky Greenway are the mother-and-daughter team who are your hosts at the Franklin Street Station Bed and Breakfast. Shipbuilder Ferdinand Fisher built this grand Victorian house in the early 1900s. The inn is filled with old-world craftsmanship and antique furnishings that make you take a step back in

time. A grandfather clock and an old-fashioned settee are some of the lovely antiques you'll find on the main floor.

The house has six guest rooms that are decorated with pretty pastel floral wallpaper. Each room has its own special mix of the following amenities: TV/VCR, antique queen bed, private mini balcony, wet bar, claw-foot tub, and magnificent Columbia River views. A home-baked breakfast is served to you in your room at 8 or 9 a.m. or in the dining area at 7:30, 8:30, or 9:30 a.m. Crepes, Belgian waffles, quiche, and fresh Oregon fruit are just a few of the delicious entrees you'll be served at breakfast.

If you are looking for things to see and do in the area, the inn is within walking distance of downtown Astoria that is filled with fun shops, museums, and restaurants. You are also a short drive away from Fort Stevens State Park and Fort Clatsop. Restrictions: No smoking. No pets.

i If you want to have a get-together with your family or friends, some bed-and-breakfasts and inns will rent their whole facility to you and your group for a discounted price.

GRANDVIEW BED AND
BREAKFAST $$–$$$$
1574 Grand Ave.
(800) 488-3250
www.pacifier.com/~grndview
The Grandview Bed and Breakfast is a turn-of-the-century Victorian house that features inset balconies, bay windows, a tower, and open staircase. This grand home is located on the Historic Homes Walking Tour and is close to museums and shops. When you visit this bed-and-breakfast, you'll have your choice of 10 guest rooms, some with private bath and some two-bedroom suites. Rooms are stocked with books and games. For breakfast you'll enjoy fresh fruit, homemade muffins, lox and bagels, coffee, tea, and juice. Restrictions: No smoking. No pets. No alcohol.

Seaside

SUMMER HOUSE BED AND
BREAKFAST$$–$$$
1221 North Franklin
(503) 738-5740, (800) 745-2378

Jack and Lesle Palmeri are the owners and inn-keepers at the 4,000-square-foot Summer House, which was built in 1910 and is nestled in a residential neighborhood located near The Prom (Promenade)—a mile-and-a-half-long walkway that parallels the wide, sandy beach in Seaside. Lesle describes their house as "a special home adorned with treasures from a lifetime of travels. The house is a typical beach house style and the rooms are decorated in bright and cheery pastels. We have seven guest rooms, each with its own private bath, and a small television. The first guest room is called The Taj. It has a queen-size bed and decorations that my father brought home from India. The second guest room has a queen-size bed and contains my grandmother's furniture and her collection of porcelain dolls. Next is the Whispering Seas Room. This room has a queen-size bed and is decorated with seashells and driftwood and other items you would find on the beach. Upstairs at the end of the hallway is the Sunrise Room. This formal, pampering room has a king-size bed and a cozy fireplace and has a large bathroom with a small refrigerator. This room has high cathedral ceilings and a nice view of the Coast Range. The Garden Room has a king-size four-poster bed, a small sitting area, and a romantic fireplace. It is decorated with an abundance of flowers and looks out over a small garden of its own. The Jungle Room is a favorite of small children and the Aztec Room can sleep a family of four."

Another element that will make your stay at this bed-and-breakfast a romantic one is to request a gift basket for your partner. Gift baskets can include flowers, cheese and crackers, cookies and fruit, and a nice bottle of wine or sparkling cider. Or, they can include balloons or bubble bath. The Palmeris can make you a gift basket that fits into your budget by request. All they ask is that you give them a budget and a basic idea of what you want, and they will do the rest. Additional amenities you'll find are books, games, and musical instruments.

A full complimentary breakfast is served as part of your stay, which includes your choice of fresh fruits, homemade bread, a main dish, coffee, tea, and juice. Sightseeing, shopping, beachcombing, and sandcastle building are fun activities that are just a short walk from the Summer House. Restrictions: No smoking. No pets. No children under age three.

i One of the most popular outings on the North Coast is a weekend trip to the Seaside Factory Outlet Center, US 101 and 12th Ave. in Seaside. After browsing the shops for brand name discounts, folks hit the beach, have dinner at their favorite restaurant, take in a show or live music at a local pub, and stay at one of the inns or motels.

Arch Cape

ARCH CAPE INN$$$–$$$$
31970 East Ocean Lane
(800) 436-2848
www.archcapeinn.com

Arch Cape Inn is a magnificent European-style chateau that has gorgeous ocean views and is filled with beautiful antiques and original works of art. The interior of the inn is reminiscent of a French country home with its rich, terra-cotta tile floor, rough plaster walls, and natural cedar windows. The inn has 10 large rooms and suites, which all have a gas fireplace, telephone, cable TV, VCR, WiFi, refrigerator, and private bath with tile shower. Dogs are allowed in designated pet rooms for an additional fee.

The premier suite of this bed-and-breakfast is the Provence, which is filled with antique pine furniture and has a sitting room leading to a private patio, a queen-size bed, and an inviting Jacuzzi tub. Fluffy robes are provided for guests and a video and reading library is also available. Your stay includes a multicourse breakfast and an early evening social hour.

While you are visiting this plush bed-and-breakfast, you can keep yourself busy during the day by sightseeing in Cannon Beach or visiting one of the many state parks in this area, which include Ecola, Arcadia Beach, and Hug Point, all of which are located to the north, and Oswald West State Park, located south off US 101. Restrictions: No smoking. No pets. Children 12 and older are welcome.

Manzanita

THE ARBORS BED AND BREAKFAST $$$
78 Idaho Ave.
(503) 368-7566, (888) 664-9587

The Arbors is a 1922 two-story cottage that is surrounded by pretty gardens and has two guest rooms with private baths. Additional amenities at this bed-and-breakfast include delicious homemade cookies and a selection of hot drinks. Breakfast is served family style and includes a fruit plate with a hot breakfast entree and freshly baked scones, biscuits, and muffins served with jam and your choice of coffee, juice, or tea. If you are looking for things to do, you are within walking distance of a long, flat, sandy beach, you can hike up to the top of Neakahnie Mountain, or you can check out the surfers at Short Sands Beach located in Oswald West State Park just south of Manzanita. Nehalem Bay State Park located north of Manzanita has uncrowded hiking and biking trails that are also sure to please. Restrictions: No smoking. No pets. Children over age eight are welcome.

Oceanside

SEA ROSE–A BED AND BREAKFAST $$$
1685 Maxwell Mountain Rd.
(503) 842-6126
www.searosebandb.com

Judy Gregoire and Puddin the cat are your hosts

at the Sea Rose, a three-story, 1938 Cape Cod-style house that has easy beach access and a spectacular ocean view. This cozy bed-and-breakfast features the Antoinette Room and the Nicole Room. The Antoinette Room is furnished with a comfy queen-size bed, antique table and chairs, cozy rockers, a private deck with an ocean view, and a private bath with a claw-foot tub. The Nicole Room is decorated with white wicker furniture, an oak writing desk, and a queen-size bed and has a private bath with a claw-foot tub.

Additional treats and comforts you'll find in the common area are shelves filled with interesting book titles, a piano, refrigerator and freezer, and your choice of coffee, tea, popcorn, and yummy Tillamook ice cream. Breakfast is served in the dining room or on the deck. A typical breakfast includes a fresh citrus bowl made up of grapefruit, oranges, and kiwis; shrimp quiche; broiled tomatoes; and heart-shaped baking powder biscuits served with homemade blackberry jam. Other choices include homemade muffins, apple pancakes served with sage and rosemary sausage, cinnamon bread, and hot rolls. While you are in this area, you can visit Cape Meares and the Cape Meares lighthouse, Cape Lookout, and Cape Kiwanda. Restrictions: No smoking. No pets. Children over 14 are welcome.

Pacific City

EAGLE'S VIEW BED AND
BREAKFAST $$$–$$$$
37975 Brooten Rd.
(503) 965-7600, (888) 846-3292
www.eaglesviewbb.com

This country-style bed-and-breakfast is located on a hillside with views of the Nestucca Bay and Nestucca River and is surrounded by four acres of coastal landscape filled with cultivated gardens mixed in with a natural landscape. Trails lead you through the grounds and give you a chance to take in some of the outstanding views of the river and bay.

The inn is light and bright and decorated with country pine furnishings. The architecture includes high ceilings and natural woodwork.

Vacation Rentals

Renting a house at the beach is a fine way to enjoy the Oregon Coast, and many rental companies are available to help you find one. They'll set you up in anything from a rustic cabin to a luxurious house or condominium. Most companies listed below handle a range of properties within their communities and in surrounding areas. They will also let you know about local regulations for renters. Be aware that you may pay for cleaning fees and taxes if you rent a house.

Cannon Beach Vacation Rental Homes
Cannon Beach, (877) 386-3402,
www.cbpm.com

Castle Rock Vacation Rentals
Arch Cape, (503) 436-3600,
www.castlerockvr.com

Sunset Vacation Rentals
Manzanita, (800) 883-7784, www.ssvr.com

Manzanita Rental Company
Manzanita, (800) 579-9801,
www.manzanitarentals.com

Edgewater Vacation Rentals
Netarts, (503) 842-1300, (888) 425-1050,
www.oregoncoastvacrentals.com

Kiwanda Coastal Properties Vacation Rental
Pacific City, (888) 684-3732,
www.kiwandacoastalproperties.com

Sea View Vacation Rentals
Pacific City, (503) 965-7888, (888) 701-1023,
www.seaview4u.com

All Seasons Vacation Rentals
Lincoln City, (800) 362-5229,
www.allseasonsvacation.com

Pacific Retreats Vacation Home Rentals
Lincoln City, (800) 473-4833,
www.pacificretreats.com

Beachcombers Haven Vacation Rentals
Gleneden Beach, (541) 764-2252,
(800) 428-5533, www.beachcombershaven.com

Fairhaven Vacation Rentals
Newport, (541) 574-0951, (888) 523-4179,
www.fairhavenvacationrentals.com

Ocean Odyssey Vacation Rentals
Yachats and Waldport, (541) 547-3637,
(800) 800-1915, www.ocean-odyssey.com

Moonlight Bay Vacation Rentals
Charleston, (541) 888-5166, (800) 962-2815

Exclusive Property Management
Bandon, (541) 347-3790, (800) 527-5445,
www.visitbandon.com

Arcadia on the Coast
Gold Beach, (888) 227-1963,
www.southcoastvacationrentals.com

Five guest rooms are available and they all have a private bath, satellite TV and VCR, DVD and CD player. In addition, three rooms have Jacuzzi tubs and all rooms are wheelchair accessible. The rooms are decorated with handmade quilts and dolls and feature antique wardrobes and armoires. The inn features a Great Room where guests can relax by a warm pellet stove and sip hot chocolate and eat homemade cookies. Expansive decks also surround the bed-and-breakfast and you can take a relaxing soak in the outdoor five-person hot tub.

Your homemade breakfast includes a hot beverage, fruit, granola, fresh muffins, and a main entree is smoked salmon with cream cheese or green onions and scrambled eggs served with freshly baked croissants. If you feel like exploring, you can visit Cape Kiwanda Beach, Cape Meares State Park and Lighthouse, and Cape Lookout State Park. Both of these state parks are located on the Three Capes Scenic Highway. Restrictions: No, smoking, pets or children under age 18.

CENTRAL COAST

Depoe Bay

CHANNEL HOUSE BED AND BREAKFAST $$$–$$$$

35 Ellingson St.
(541) 765-2140, (800) 447-2140
www.channelhouse.com

The Channel House is a contemporary bed-and-breakfast perched above the rocky shore of beautiful Depoe Bay. This bed-and-breakfast features 15 rooms and suites. The oceanfront suites have magnificent views of Depoe Bay and offer a separate sleeping and sitting area, a queen-size bed, a wet bar, coffeemaker, gas fireplace, private bath, and a private deck with an outdoor whirlpool tub. Oceanfront rooms are equipped with a queen-size bed, private bath, and private deck with whirlpool tub. In addition, all rooms contain plush robes, a television with HBO, and a refrigerator. The Channel House also features wireless Internet access. A hearty continental breakfast is served in the oceanside serving room and includes freshly baked breads and pastries, an assortment of fresh fruits, yogurt, cereal, coffee, tea, and a variety of juices.

Be sure to explore the charming shops in Depoe Bay, and if you are looking for more adventure, try a deep-sea fishing or whale-watching trip from one of the local outfitters in Depoe Bay. Restrictions: No smoking. No pets. No children.

Newport

GREEN GABLES BED AND BREAKFAST & BOOKSTORE $$–$$$

156 Southwest Coast St.
(800) 515-9065, (541) 574-0986
www.greengablesbb.com

Nestled in the friendly community of Nye Beach, the Green Gables Bed and Breakfast is a charming Victorian-style home adjacent to a 4-mile stretch of wide sandy beach. Green Gables was built in 1981 and an extra wing was added in 1996. It has two guest rooms. The Turret Suite is a bright, open room bathed with light that streams in from the bay and turret windows surrounding the queen-size bed. A French door leads to a balcony where you can gaze at the Pacific Ocean. An adjoining room provides a writing desk where you can sit and write letters to friends and comfortable chairs where you can lounge and enjoy a good novel. This suite also features a large, relaxing, two-person whirlpool tub.

The Gables Room, located on the top floor of the house, is filled with charming nooks and crannies, an antique secretary's desk, cozy chairs, and a queen-size bed. In addition, a relaxing two-person whirlpool tub is available in the large, private bathroom located down a flight of stairs. Each room also comes equipped with the following amenities: cable TV; VCR/DVD player; refrigerator; microwave; soft, fluffy robes; hot pot with teas and hot chocolate; and a radio. The common area of the house has a warm and cozy wood stove, piano, and video library. If you love to read, then you'll also want to visit the bookstore located in the bottom level of the house that specializes in women's mysteries and quality children's books. When you stay at Green Gables, breakfast is offered in the coffeehouse and bakery, which features delicious pastries, gourmet coffee, and other breakfast specialties.

There are endless opportunities for fun nearby. This bed-and-breakfast is only 1 block from the ocean and beach and a short walk to shopping and restaurants. Other activities that may interest you include hiking, fishing, whale watching, kayaking, canoeing, or visiting the Oregon Coast Aquarium or the Newport Performing Arts Center. Restrictions: No smoking. Children 16 and older are welcome. Pets are not allowed.

i **A nifty way to take in the historic charm of the Nye Beach area in Newport is to dress in period costumes and take in some of the nightlife in that beach zone that is full of nostalgia and historical buildings. Attend the Newport Performing Arts Center and then retire to the Sylvia Beach Hotel for a lovely dinner and stay in a period room named after and designed around a famous author.**

OCEAN HOUSE BED AND BREAKFAST $$$–$$$$
4920 NW Woody Way
(866) 495-3888
www.oceanhouse.com

Spectacular ocean views can be experienced at the Ocean House Bed and Breakfast. This bed-and-breakfast is located on a high bluff above Agate Beach and has many romantic rooms to choose from that have fireplaces, private spas, and ocean views. If you are looking for more room, you should stay in The Cottage that features a rock fireplace, kitchenette, and a soothing whirlpool tub. Free Wi-Fi is available and a TV/DVD player is available by request to watch movies. Restrictions: No smoking, pets, or children under age 12.

South Beach

NEWPORT BELLE BED AND BREAKFAST $$$
Newport South Beach Marina
2126 S.E. OSU Dr.
(541) 867-6290, (800) 348-1922
www.newportbelle.com

If you want to stay in a different type of bed-and-breakfast you'll have to reserve a stateroom at the Newport Belle—a replica of a stern-wheeler riverboat that is docked in Newport's Newport Marina. This 97-foot boat includes 3,100 square feet of living space on three different decks. This unique bed-and-breakfast features turn-of-the-century charm with modern conveniences. Aboard this boat you can have your pick of five large staterooms. All rooms have a private bath and shower. From every room you'll have a wonderful view of the hustle and bustle of the Newport Marina and of the Yaquina Bay Bridge. You can enjoy stunning sunsets from the open afterdeck or curl up by the cozy wood stove in the main saloon where you can read, play games, watch satellite TV, or visit with other guests. For breakfast you have the choice of granola, yogurt, cottage cheese, fresh fruit, assorted pastries, muffins, or croissants, and a homemade hot entree.

There are many attractions in the near vicinity of the Newport Belle including the Oregon Coast Aquarium, the Hatfield Marine Science Center, the historic Newport bayfront, Yaquina Outstanding Natural Area, Yaquina Bay State Park, and the Newport Performing Arts Center. Soft-soled shoes are requested and appropriate for both the boat and the dock. Restrictions: No smoking. No pets or children.

Yachats

BURD'S NEST INN BED AND BREAKFAST $$–$$$
664 Yachats River Rd.
(541) 547-3683

The Burd's Nest Inn can be easily recognized by its bright, multicolored tile roof. The roof is an eye-catcher due to its 26,000 pounds of tiles that are proudly displayed in 10 different colors! This bed-and-breakfast features over 5,000 square feet of space and is nestled on a tree-covered hillside above the Pacific Ocean and the Yachats River estuary. The house is decorated in a country Spanish motif and is furnished with willow stick furniture mixed with an eclectic assortment of antique toys, stuffed animals, handcrafted items, birds, and birdhouses.

This inn features three colorful guest rooms. The Robin's Nest is furnished with a king-size bed, has French doors opening to a balcony with a panoramic view of the Pacific Ocean and the mountains, and a private bath with a yellow Mexican tile shower. The Swallow's Nest is decorated in a 1930s motif and has the same amenities as the Robin's Nest except it has a claw-foot tub and a ring shower. The Eagle's Nest is decorated in a patriotic theme and includes all of the amenities of the other rooms except it has a decorative brass tub. Soft, fluffy robes, hair dryers, and curling irons are provided. Breakfast is served between 9 and 9:30 a.m. and hot drinks are available before that time for early risers. Breakfast usually begins with homemade oat bran muffins and a delicious fruit smoothie. The next course includes anything from veggie quiche with salsa to French toast stuffed with cream cheese. To top it off, you can have your choice of coffee, juice, or tea.

From the bed-and-breakfast you can walk to the beach or town. While in town you can check out the quaint shops, eat a gourmet meal, or visit the Little Log Church by the Sea museum. Other attractions in the area include Cape Perpetua, Devil's Churn, Strawberry Hill, Heceta Head Lighthouse, and Sea Lion Caves. Restrictions: No smoking. No pets. No children.

HECETA HEAD LIGHTHOUSE
BED AND BREAKFAST $$$–$$$$
92072 US 101 South
(866) 547-3696
www.hecetalighthouse.com

The Heceta Head Lighthouse Bed and Breakfast is a Queen Ann-style house surrounded by a white picket fence that was built in the late 1800s and is situated next to Heceta Head Lighthouse—thought to be one of the most scenic spots on the Oregon Coast. This fully restored inn has five guest rooms decorated with period furnishings. The Mariner's Room has a mesmerizing ocean view, a queen-size bed, antique furnishings, and a private bath. The Lightkeeper's Room has an exclusive view of Heceta Head Lighthouse and the ocean and is furnished with a queen-size bed. This room has a shared bath. Victoria's Room is decorated with a four-poster queen-size bed, a trundle bed, and a private bath. The romantic Queen Anne room has a four-poster bed and a Victorian Chaise lounge. The Cape Cove Room is filled with antique furniture and has views of the historic Cape Creek Bridge. A full seven-course gourmet breakfast is served. While you are visiting you can explore the lighthouse and beach, the Sea Lion Caves, and Cape Perpetua. Restrictions: No smoking or pets.

THE KITTIWAKE BED AND BREAKFAST $$$$
95368 US 101
(541) 547-4470

The Kittiwake is a contemporary bed-and-breakfast built on two and a half acres that have been carefully cultivated to build suitable habitat for the endangered silverspot butterfly. Some areas have been left natural to encourage elk and deer to graze on the property. The house sits atop a 20-foot bluff overlooking the Pacific and is only 100 feet from the ocean. The interior colors and furniture of this quiet getaway are earth tones accentuated with bright colors that make it feel warm, snug, and inviting. The Kittiwake has three ocean-facing guest rooms that are outfitted with queen-size beds, private baths, and entrances to a deck. Room 1 is the largest and is decorated with rattan furniture and Caribbean pastel colors and is a favorite of longer-staying guests due to its large size. Room 2 is furnished with a cherry sleigh bed, writing desk, and whirlpool bath for two. Room 3 faces north and west and has window seats with a panoramic ocean view. This room is furnished with a queen-size bow bed and chest and table that are made of rock maple. This room also features a two-person whirlpool tub that has an ocean view to the northwest.

Other amenities you'll find at this bed-and-breakfast include a guest lounge with overstuffed furniture and window seats, magazines, and a small collection of eclectic hardback titles; a coffee bar with mugs and stemware; a guests' refrigerator; rain gear; and colorful kites. A full breakfast is served in your room on individual trays at 8:30 a.m. A typical homemade breakfast includes grapefruit or fresh mixed fruit; muffins or bagels; smoked ham, smoked turkey, sturgeon, bacon, or sausage and apples; a German breakfast entree; a beverage of choice; and a scrumptious dessert. You may opt to eat your breakfast indoors or on the lower deck, where each room has a designated seating area. If you are an early riser, fresh hot coffee, tea, and cocoa are always available.

Wildlife watching is a popular activity at this bed-and-breakfast. Early risers may see elk and deer grazing on the property and eagles soaring on the air currents above the beach, as well as a variety of shorebirds. In addition, whales and seals are seen throughout the year, and if you love to look at tide pools, head to the beach where you can see a rich variety of tide pool creatures. Other activities that you'll enjoy in this area include dune buggy rides in the Oregon Dunes National Recreational Area south of Florence; horseback riding on the beach (C & M stables is 12 miles south of the Kittiwake); and Sea Lion Caves located 8 miles south of the Kittiwake. The Kittiwake is also within proximity of dozens of state parks and designated natural areas including Heceta Head Lighthouse, Devil's Elbow State Park, Carl G. Washburn State Park, and Cape Perpetua.

Restrictions: No smoking. No pets. No children. The owners request that you do not burn candles or incense in your room and also ask that you do not wear waffle-soled shoes or hiking boots in the house.

Florence

EDWIN K BED AND BREAKFAST $$$$
1155 Bay St.
(800) 833-9465
www.edwink.com

You'll enjoy your stay at this two-story 1914 Craftsman-style bed-and-breakfast. It has been fully restored to its original grandeur and is filled with period antiques. You'll have your choice of six large rooms with a private bath, or you can stay in a 1,000-square-foot bedroom suite that has cooking facilities and can accommodate up to six people. A phone and wireless Internet are available at a central location for your use. For breakfast you'll enjoy your choice of freshly baked breads, muffins, or delicious apricot and white chocolate scones, egg or cheese soufflé, a fresh fruit plate, ham and sausage, Marionberry compote, coffee, tea, and orange juice. Activities abound in the Florence area. You can explore Old Town Florence, walk the beach, hit a few rounds of golf, or try your hand at fishing and crabbing. Restrictions: No smoking. No pets. Children over age 12 are welcome.

THE JOHNSON HOUSE BED AND BREAKFAST $$$
216 Maple St.
(541) 997-8000

This beautiful Victorian bed-and-breakfast was built in 1892 and contains period furnishings throughout. Impressive gardens surround the house featuring a variety of fragrant herbs and perennials. Six guest rooms are available and three of these rooms have private baths. Personal touches you'll find at this bed-and-breakfast include comfy robes, a fully stocked reading library, current periodicals and newspapers, a pretty sitting room, and extravagant bedding and linens. When you wake up in the morning, you can look forward to a breakfast that includes a main entree of soufflés, omelets, or frittatas made with fresh herbs from the garden and fresh crab in season or Swedish waffles and maple syrup. Accompanying your entree are freshly baked muffins, croissants, and scones; fresh fruit; ground gourmet coffee; and orange juice. Restrictions: No smoking. No pets. Children 12 and older are welcome.

SOUTH COAST

Coos Bay

THE OLD TOWER HOUSE BED AND BREAKFAST $$–$$$
476 Newmark Ave.
(541) 888-6058
www.oldtowerhouse.com

The Old Tower House Bed and Breakfast was built in 1872 and is located in the historic Empire District of Coos Bay. This charming old-world house has a large main parlor with a bright sunroom where many guests like to relax and read. The main house has three rooms, the King's Room, the Blue Room, and the Rose Room, designed to fit a variety of tastes. The King's Room features a large king-size brass bed covered with a decorative antique quilt, an Oriental rug, a wicker rocker, and pedestal sink. The Blue Room is filled with antique furnishings, two comfortable twin beds, a delightful Persian rug, a blue-tiled washstand from Scotland, and a pedestal sink, and you can enjoy outstanding views of the bay through a gothic-style window. The Rose Room features a 150-year-old Barley Twist double bed, vintage linens, a handmade fishnet canopy, rose floral wallpaper, vintage antiques, and a pedestal sink.

If you want more privacy, you may want to consider staying in The Carriage House suite. This loft suite comes equipped with a large sitting room, complete kitchen, hand-painted queen-size bed, TV and VCR, and an old-fashioned claw-foot tub. If this doesn't quite suit your taste, you may want to stay in the Ivy Cottage, which is a reflection of a quaint English garden cottage and is decorated with ivy wallpaper and a floral bath. This cottage comes equipped with a sitting room with TV, microwave, coffee-maker, refrigerator, a comfortable bedroom, and a claw-foot tub. All of the rooms also have free Wi-Fi.

Before you head out for the day, you'll enjoy a full complimentary breakfast that is served in the sunroom on damask table linens. If you are looking for things to see and do in the area, you can spend the day fishing, crabbing, or digging for clams; or you may also just want to relax in the garden and gazebo located on the Old Tower House grounds. Restrictions: No pets. No smoking. Children 10 years and older are welcome.

THIS OLDE HOUSE $$$–$$$$
202 Alder Ave.
(541) 267-5224
http://thisoldehousebb.com

Sally White is your host at This Olde House, an elegant home built in 1893 that is decorated with beautiful inlaid wood floors, crystal chandeliers, and antique furnishings. The inn has four guest rooms that are furnished with king- and queen-size beds, televisions, private baths, and fluffy robes. With your stay, you'll also receive complimentary wine. Breakfast is served with homemade blackberry syrup. While you are in this area, be sure to visit Sunset Beach and Shore Acres State Parks and the Coos Art Museum. Restrictions: No smoking. No pets. No small children.

Bandon

BAILEY'S CEDAR HOUSE BED AND
BREAKFAST $–$$
Box 58739, Seven Devils Rd.
(541) 347-3356

This friendly bed-and-breakfast was built in 1993 in a quiet, country, wooded setting and has two guest rooms. The first room is a cozy suite with a private entrance, sitting room, kitchen, private bath, television, and queen bed. The second guest room has a private entrance, queen bed,

television, and private bath. A soothing hot tub is available outside. A full breakfast is served, which includes omelets made with local seafood, scones, homemade jams, fresh fruit, juice, and coffee. This bed-and-breakfast is only a short 10- to 15-minute drive from Bandon's Old Town, which is filled with shops, galleries, restaurants, and a busy marina. If you love to play golf, be sure to check out the world-class Bandon Dunes golf course. Restrictions: No smoking or pets.

LIGHTHOUSE BED AND BREAKFAST $$$$
50 Jetty Rd. SW
(541) 347-9316
www.lighthouselodging.com

This contemporary bed-and-breakfast is located on the beach directly across from the historic Bandon Lighthouse. The house has five guest rooms and panoramic views of the ocean and Coquille River estuary. The Gray Whale Room is at the top of the inn and has a dramatic view of the Coquille River and the lighthouse. This grand room features a California king-size bed, private bath with shower, TV, wood-burning stove, and a whirlpool tub for two. The Greenhouse Room is the most romantic room at the bed-and-breakfast, furnished with a king-size bed, private bath and shower, fireplace, whirlpool tub for two, TV, and a river view. The Deck Room has a private deck with a river view, a queen-size bed, and a private bath and shower. Karen's Room has an ocean and lighthouse view, queen-size bed, and a private bathroom across the hall. The Sunset Room includes a nice view of the Bandon Lighthouse and features a cozy queen-size bed and private bath with a shower.

In the evening you can relax and sip on complimentary wine in the Great Room and watch TV or listen to the stereo and visit with other guests. In the morning you are served a hearty breakfast of muffins, fresh fruit, egg dishes, French toast, ham or bacon, juice, coffee, or tea. The Bandon area is filled with fun activities. You can stroll through the antiques shops and art galleries located in downtown Bandon; visit the Bandon Cheese Factory; try out clamming, fishing, or crabbing; or go whale, seal, and bird-watching.

Restrictions: No smoking. No pets. Children 12 and older are welcome. Please let owners know you will be bringing your children.

Langlois

FLORAS LAKE HOUSE BY THE SEA $$$$
92870 Boice Cope Rd.
(541) 348-2573
www.floraslake.com
Floras Lake House by the Sea is a contemporary bed-and-breakfast built in 1991. It features four guest rooms that all have views of Floras Lake and the ocean, vaulted wood ceilings, private baths, and deck entrances. In addition, two rooms have cozy fireplaces. There are no TVs in the rooms or Great Room. However, they do offer wireless Internet and there are phone jacks in the rooms for laptop users who want to access the Internet via dial-up modems. A buffet-style breakfast is served in the living/dining room area between 8:30 and 10 a.m. Breakfast includes English muffins, bagels, fresh fruit, yogurt, homemade granola, and a hot breakfast entree. Hot entrees can include fluffy French toast, buttermilk pancakes, quiche, or homemade sticky buns.

There are dozens of activities you can participate in close by. You can walk on the beach that is just a few minutes from the bed-and-breakfast or take a windsurfing lesson from Floras Lake Windsurfing School (run by the owners of the bed-and-breakfast, Liz and Will Brady). You can also explore nearby Cape Blanco and the Cape Blanco Lighthouse or try out your golf swing at Bandon Dunes golf course. Restrictions: No smoking or pets.

Gold Beach

ENDICOTT GARDENS BED AND BREAKFAST $$
95768 Jerry's Flat Rd.
(541) 247-6513, (866) 212-1220
www.endicottgardens.com
Endicott Gardens Bed and Breakfast is a contemporary bed-and-breakfast that is surrounded by a variety of fruit trees, beautiful flowers, shrubs, and exotic plants. This home features four guest rooms. Each room has a private bath, and two rooms have private decks with views of the surrounding mountains and forest. If you wish to stay for a longer period of time, two fully furnished studio apartments are also available. Breakfast includes fresh fruits from the garden, freshly baked breads, a main entree, and coffee, juice, or tea. There are a variety of activities in the Gold Beach area—jet boat tours up the Rogue River, fishing, golfing, horseback riding, beachcombing, and hiking. Restrictions: No smoking. No pets. Children are welcome with prior arrangement.

INN AT NESIKA BEACH $$$
33026 Nesika Rd.
(541) 247-6434
The Inn at Nesika Beach is a stylish, Victorian-style inn located on a bluff overlooking the Pacific Ocean. The inn features four rooms with soft feather beds, cozy comforters, fluffy robes, and private baths with whirlpool tubs. In addition, three of these rooms have fireplaces and two rooms have private decks with wonderful ocean views. The Fireside Room is a communal area that is a great place to read, play music, sit by the fire, storm watch, and visit with other guests. Your complimentary breakfast is served in the dining room facing the ocean and features fresh homemade breads, seasonal fruits, and a variety of breakfast entrees such as apple French toast, soufflés, fluffy pancakes, and breakfast meats. Your meal is also accompanied by your choice of fresh, hot coffee, tea, or cocoa. World-class trout, salmon, and steelhead fishing can be found on the nearby Rogue River and you can brush up on your golf game at Cedar Bend Golf Course, located north of the inn. Credit cards are not accepted at the inn. Restrictions: No smoking. No pets. Children 13 and older are welcome.

Brookings

BROOKINGS SOUTH COAST INN $$$–$$$$
516 Redwood St.
(800) 525-9273
www.southcoastinn.com
Built in 1917, this 4,000-square-foot Craftsman-style inn features four guest rooms with private

bath, television, VCR/DVD player, and video library. Two rooms have an ocean view. One room also has a private kitchenette and garden. The inn also boasts a large reading parlor with an original stone fireplace and a vintage grand piano. Breakfast includes hot coffee and an entree such as Norwegian waffles with homemade jam. Brookings is full of outdoor activities that will fill your days with fun. Hiking, boating, camping, fishing, mountain biking, golfing, and shopping are some of the offerings here. Restrictions: No smoking or pets. Children age 12 and older are welcome.

LOWDEN'S BEACHFRONT BED AND BREAKFAST $$
14626 Wollam Rd.
(541) 469-7045, (800) 453-4768
www.beachfrontbb.com

Gary and Barbara Lowden are the innkeepers at this contemporary bed-and-breakfast located on the ocean where the Winchuck River empties into the Pacific. This bed-and-breakfast offers two guest suites that include a queen-size bed; private shower and bath; a living room furnished with a sofa, dining chairs, and a gourmet cart with dishes; fireplace; and a microwave, refrigerator, coffeemaker, toaster, cable TV, and VCR/DVD player. A complimentary fruit basket is provided and the refrigerator is stocked with juice, half-and-half, and distilled water. You'll also have your choice of all the coffee, tea, popcorn, and hot chocolate you want. A continental breakfast is served to you in the evening so you can enjoy it in the morning when it is convenient for you. Children are welcome. There are many activities in the Brookings area. The Winchuck River is a good place to kayak and raft, and the waves at the mouth of the river provide some fun boogie boarding and surfing. Wildlife watching is also a fun outdoor activity here—you'll be able to see seabirds, seals, otters, and whales. Restrictions: No smoking or pets.

PACIFIC VIEW BED AND BREAKFAST $$$
18814 Montbretia Lane
(800) 453-4768, (541) 469-6837

Ursula and Mac Mackey are your hosts at their bed-and-breakfast, which is located in a quiet country setting overlooking the ocean. They have a suite available with a private entrance, private bath, and a sunroom overlooking the ocean. You'll also enjoy a wonderful ocean view from your room. In the morning, you'll be served a home-cooked breakfast that includes fresh fruit, freshly baked breads, and a main entree such as Quiche Lorraine and chicken and apple sausages. Fresh juice and coffee are also served. Ursula and Mac are local experts on things to see and do in the Brookings area. You can take a hike on the Oregon Coast Trail, which is within walking distance, take a jet boat ride on the Rogue River, visit a grove of redwood trees, or play on the beach. Restrictions: No smoking. No pets. No children.

SEA DREAMER INN BED AND BREAKFAST $$
15167 McVay Lane
(541) 469-6629

Built in 1912, the Sea Dreamer Inn Bed and Breakfast is a country Victorian-style home located on spacious grounds and has an outstanding view of southern Oregon's famous lily fields and the Pacific Ocean. When you visit this bed-and-breakfast, you will truly feel at home in one of its four guest rooms. The Beachcomber Room has an ocean view, library filled with books, comfortable double bed, and private bath. The Siren Song Room comes equipped with a double bed and shared bath. The Port St. George Room boasts a library, queen-size bed, semiprivate bath, and ocean view. The Quarterdeck Room is simply furnished with a double bed, treetop view, and semiprivate bath. The complimentary breakfast is usually served between 7:30 and 10 a.m. The menu is always changing and ranges from empañadas and quiche to egg and vegetarian dishes. Credit cards are not accepted. Restrictions: Smoking outside on the porch only. Will consider well-behaved pets and children.

CAMPING

Welcome to camping on the Oregon Coast! From north to south you will find picturesque state, federal, and private campgrounds that are set in a variety of coastal ecosystems from coastal forest and sandy beach to freshwater lakes and coastal dunes. In this section we've listed all the state park campgrounds and selected USDA Forest Service campgrounds from north to south.

NORTH COAST

Horse enthusiasts may want to check out Nehalem Bay State Park campground located in Nehalem on the North Coast. This state park has campsites with corrals and plenty of trail options where you can take your equine friend. Many state park campgrounds also have hiker and biker camps for backpackers traveling the Oregon Coast Trail or cyclists who are riding the Oregon Coast Bike Route.

Many state park campgrounds take reservations, and we highly recommend that you call ahead to make reservations during the peak camping season from May 1 through September 30. You'll find that many state park campgrounds have yurts, which are circular tentlike structures that are 16 feet in diameter with a wooden floor and come equipped with a lockable door, electric heater, skylight, and three beds that sleep five people. These yurts make you feel as if you're still roughing it, but they have a few amenities that make your camping experience more comfortable. Yurts are very popular places to stay on the Oregon Coast so always be sure to call ahead to reserve one of these unique camping lodges. Most state park campgrounds do not allow pets in the yurts, except South Beach State Park.

i Remember that some campgrounds are not open during the winter months, generally from November through February.

Hammond

FORT STEVENS STATE PARK
Information: (800) 551-6949
Reservations: (800) 452-5687
www.reserveamerica.com
www.oregonstateparks.org/park_179.php
Fort Stevens State Park offers fun for everyone. To get there, travel about 4 miles south of Astoria (or 9 miles north of Seaside) on US 101; turn west and follow signs for 4.5 miles to the park and campground. As Oregon's third largest state park, Fort Stevens covers 3,763 acres of beach, sand dunes, shallow lakes, and coastal forest and is situated at the mouth of the Columbia River. Paved hiking and biking trails crisscross the park through a thick coastal forest of western hemlock, red cedar, big-leaf maple, and red alder trees. Hiking enthusiasts should also note that the Oregon Coast Trail can be accessed from the park. Fishing for brown bullhead, rainbow trout, steelhead, and yellow perch is popular at 50-acre Coffenbury Lake, situated in the park. The wreck of the *Peter Iredale* is another popular attraction. This four-masted British freighter ran aground on Clatsop Spit in a rough storm in 1906. Other activities that will tantalize you at this park are beachcombing, windsurfing, swimming, or learning about the park's history at the Fort Stevens Military Museum. The park is open year-round. Leashed pets are allowed. Please note: Reservations Northwest charges a $6 fee when you make a reservation using the number given here.

Cannon Beach

SADDLE MOUNTAIN STATE NATURAL AREA AND CAMPGROUND

(800) 551-6949

www.oregonstateparks.org/park_197.php

Saddle Mountain State Park campground is located in a thickly wooded forest made primarily of red alder trees. To get there from Cannon Beach, travel about 10 miles east on US 26 and follow signs to the park. This state park is a unique botanical area filled with bright and cheery wildflowers such as the white triangular flowers of western trillium; pink-flowered western columbine; the purple, bell-shaped flowers of the coast penstemon; vibrant orange tiger lilies; blue iris; red Indian paintbrush; white meadow chickweed; phlox; and larkspur. To see the park up close and personal, hike to the top of 3,283-foot Saddle Mountain from the campground on a 5.2-mile out-and-back trail. This steep and scenic trail takes you on a scenic tour of a unique coastal mountain landscape. Once you reach the summit, you'll have spectacular views of Nehalem Bay and the Pacific Ocean to the west, the Columbia River to the north, and the snow-capped Cascade peaks of Mt. Jefferson and Mt. Hood to the east. This state park is very popular and the campground can fill up fast. The campground is open from March 1 through the end of October. Leashed pets are allowed.

Nehalem

NEHALEM BAY STATE PARK

Information: (800) 551-6949

Reservations: (800) 452-5687

www.oregonstateparks.org/park_201.php

Nehalem Bay State Park campground is located on a sandy spit separating the Pacific Ocean and Nehalem Bay. To get there from Cannon Beach, travel 13.5 miles south on US 101 to Laneda Avenue, turn right, and follow signs to the park. Six miles of beachfront lure those wanting to play on the beach. Horse enthusiasts will enjoy a first-rate 7.5-mile equestrian trail, and cyclists can hop on their two-wheel steeds to cruise on a fun 1.75-mile bike trail. Walking along the bay beachfront, you can experience prime bird and seal watching. Boating, fishing, crabbing, and clamming in the bay are also popular activities at this scenic spot on Nehalem Bay. Visit Wheeler Marina at 278 Marine Dr. in Wheeler, (503) 368-5780, to rent a boat and crabbing equipment and to get advice on the fishing, crabbing, and clamming hot spots in Nehalem Bay. If you want to go on a guided trail or beach horseback ride, call Northwest Equine Outfitters (503) 801-7433, www.horserental.occybercafe.com/horserental/horse.shtml. They offer guided horseback rides from Memorial Day through Labor Day. The park is open year-round. Leashed pets are allowed. Please note: Reservations Northwest charges a $6 fee when you make a reservation using the number above.

Tillamook

CAPE LOOKOUT STATE PARK

13000 Whiskey Creek Rd. West

Information: (800) 551-6949

Reservations: (800) 452-5687

www.oregonstateparks.org/park_186.php

This popular coastal campground is located just inland from a long, skinny sand spit that stretches for 5 miles and separates Netarts Bay from the Pacific Ocean. To get there from US 101 in Tillamook, travel about 12 miles southwest on the Three Capes Scenic Highway. The sites are located within a pretty coastal forest and are spaced closely together. If you hike from the campground north to the tip of the sand spit, you'll have the opportunity to view shorebirds and harbor seals. If you want to try your luck clamming, the muddy bay side of the sand spit is prime habitat for butter, cockle, gaper, and littleneck clams. Netarts Bay is also an excellent place to try your luck at crabbing and fishing. If you want to rent a boat and crabbing or fishing gear, stop by Bayshore RV Park and Marina, (503) 842-7774, in Netarts. You can also take a hike to the tip of Cape Lookout by driving 2.7 miles south from the campground on the Three Capes

Scenic Highway to a signed parking area on the right (west) side of the road. The 5-mile out-and-back trail will take you through a thick grove of Sitka spruce trees to the tip of the cape, where you'll have a good opportunity to view migrating gray whales during their semiannual migration that takes place during December and January and March and April. The trailhead is located in the southwest corner of the parking lot. Be sure to take the trail that goes to the left. The park is open year-round. Leashed pets are allowed. Please note: Reservations Northwest charges a $6 fee when you make a reservation using the number above.

i You can buy an annual day use permit for $25 that will give you access to all Oregon state parks for free. To get an annual permit, call (800) 551-6949, Monday through Friday, 8 a.m. to 5 p.m. Note that if you are camping at a state park, the day use fee is included in your camping fee, so you do not have to purchase an additional day use permit for the day you are camping.

CENTRAL COAST

Welcome to camping on the Central Coast! You'll find picturesque state, federal, and private campgrounds that are set in a variety of coastal ecosystems from coastal forest and sandy beach to freshwater lakes and coastal dunes. In this section we've listed all the state park campgrounds and selected USDA Forest Service campgrounds from north to south on the Central Coast.

Lincoln City
DEVILS LAKE STATE PARK
1452 Northeast 6th St.
Information: (800) 994-2002
Reservations: (800) 452-5687
www.oregonstateparks.org/park_216.php

Devils Lake State Park campground sites are nestled among pretty shore pines just off the west shore of Devils Lake in Lincoln City. Activities abound in this area—take your pick of swimming, fishing, canoeing, or kayaking. A boat ramp and day use area can be accessed from Northeast 1st St. off US 101 in Lincoln City. You can also try exploring Lincoln City's beaches, galleries, or factory outlet stores located at 1510 East Devils Lake Rd. If you want to try your luck with cards, dice, or slots, be sure to check out the **Chinook Winds Casino** located at 1777 Northwest 44th St. in Lincoln City. The park is open year-round. Leashed pets are allowed. Please note: Reservations Northwest charges a $6 fee when you make a reservation using the number above.

Newport
BEVERLY BEACH STATE PARK
198 Northeast 123rd St.
Information: (541) 265-9278
Reservations: (800) 452-5687
www.oregonstateparks.org/park_227.php

Campsites at this popular campground are tucked into a thick forest adjacent to pebbly Spencer Creek. To get there from Newport, travel 7 miles north on US 101. Grassy picnic areas and a unique yurt village are some of the attractions at this state park campground. There is also a visitor information center, where you can learn more about the area and purchase books and souvenirs. If you want to check out the beach, a short walk from the campground proceeds under the highway and takes you to an endless expanse of sandy beach where you'll have views of Yaquina Head to the south and the headlands of Otter Rock to the north. Surfing is popular

i If you prefer peace and solitude and want to avoid crowds, try camping on the Central and South Coasts. The North Coast is close to some of Oregon's largest population centers (Portland and Salem) and tends to attract more people than the less crowded Central and South Coasts.

at the north end of the beach and kite flying, sandcastle building, and beachcombing are also fun activities here. For more information about attractions around the Newport area, see the Attractions chapter. The park is open year-round. Leashed pets are allowed. Please note: Reservations Northwest charges a $6 fee when you make a reservation using the number above.

South Beach

SOUTH BEACH STATE PARK
5580 South Coast Hwy.
Information: (800) 551-6949
Reservations: (800) 452-5687
www.oregonstateparks.org/park_209.php
South Beach State Park campground is adjacent to a wide expanse of beach, and the Oregon Coast Trail traipses right through the heart of this park. To get there from Newport, travel 2 miles south on US 101. If you like to hike, you can head north or south on the Oregon Coast Trail. You can also try your hand at beachcombing, kite flying, or sandcastle building. Sea kayak tours are also offered at this park. For more information, call (541) 867-6590. If you make your stay at South Beach State Park your home base for a few days, you can take a deep-sea fishing charter out of Yaquina Bay in Newport (see the Fishing, Clamming, and Crabbing sections of the Sports and Activities chapter for information on outfitters), visit the Oregon Coast Aquarium (see the Attractions chapter for more information), or visit the Yaquina Head Outstanding Natural Area where you can see large flocks of seabirds, explore tide pools, and visit the historic Yaquina Head Lighthouse. The park is open year-round. Leashed pets are allowed. Please note: Reservations Northwest charges a $6 fee when you make a reservation using the number above.

ℹ️ Hiking and wildlife watching are present at almost all the campgrounds listed in this chapter. To be prepared for these activities, always have handy a daypack, binoculars, water bottles, and plenty of snacks.

Waldport

BEACHSIDE STATE PARK
Information: (800) 551-6949
Reservations: (800) 452-5687
www.oregonstateparks.org/park_122.php
This wonderful campground located right next to the beach allows beach lovers plenty of room to roam on miles of sandy beach. To get there from Waldport, travel 4 miles south on US 101. Winter storm watching, beach-combing, kite-flying, sandcastle-building, and whale watching are popular activities at this state park campground. There are also excellent fishing, crabbing, and clamming opportunities in Alsea Bay to the north at Waldport. The park is open March 15 through October 31. Leashed pets are allowed. Please note: Reservations Northwest charges a $6 fee when you make a reservation using the number above.

Florence

ALDER DUNE
Information: (541) 750-7000
Reservations: (877) 444-6777
www.fs.fed.us/r6/siuslaw/recreation/tripplanning/newpflor/camp/alderdune.shtml
This pretty campground is located between three-acre Alder Lake and two-acre Dune Lake among pine and alder trees. Swimming, fishing, and hiking are favorite activities at this campground. To get there from Florence, travel 4.5 miles north on US 101. You can hike on a trail around Alder Lake or take a trail that heads to Sutton Campground through a coastal sand dune ecosystem. The facilities are open Memorial Day through Labor Day. Leashed pets are allowed.

CAPE PERPETUA
Information: (541) 750-7000
www.fs.fed.us/r6/siuslaw/recreation/tripplanning/newpflor/camp/capeperpetua.shtml
This campground is set in a coastal forest along the shores of Cape Creek. More than 23 miles of trails can be found throughout the Cape Perpetua Scenic Area, which lead you through

old-growth forest and to rocky tide pools filled with sea anemones, purple urchins, and bright sea stars. You'll also have the opportunity to see some historic structures built by the Civilian Conservation Corp. in the 1930s. Visit the Cape Perpetua Visitor Center to obtain a map of trails in the area. During the summer months, interpretive programs are offered on Friday and Saturday. The park is open May 10 through September 30. Leashed pets are allowed.

CARL G. WASHBURNE MEMORIAL STATE PARK

Information: (541) 547-3416
(800) 551-6949
Reservations: (800) 452-5687
www.oregonstateparks.org/park_123.php

The campsites in this campground are surrounded by a green expanse of coastal forest, and elk are often seen grazing in grassy areas in the campground. To get there from Florence, travel 14 miles north on US 101. Hiking trails lead to a sandy beach where you have opportunities to watch for whales, build sand castles, fly kites, or look for agates. A 3-mile trail heads south from the campground to Heceta Head Lighthouse. The park is open year-round. Leashed pets are allowed. Please note: Reservations Northwest charges a $6 fee when you make a reservation using the number above.

JESSIE M. HONEYMAN MEMORIAL STATE PARK

84505 US 101
Information: (541) 997-3641
Reservations: (800) 452-5687
www.oregonstateparks.org/park_134.php

Jessie M. Honeyman Memorial State Park campground is the second-largest overnight campground in Oregon and is filled with a wealth of activities. It is located 3 miles south of Florence on US 101. Cleawox and Woahink Lakes are adjacent to the campground and offer great opportunities for swimming, fishing, and boating. Several interconnected trails lead through a diverse coastal ecosystem of spruce, fir, hemlock, salal, and thimbleberry. Beautiful stands of wild rhododendrons line the lakes and dunes in this popular state park and begin blooming in early spring. This state park also has a hiking trail where you can explore the large sand dunes that are part of the Oregon Dunes National Recreation Area. The park is open year-round. Leashed pets are allowed.

SUTTON CREEK

Information: (541) 750-7000
Reservations: (877) 444-6777
www.fs.fed.us/r6/siuslaw/recreation/
tripplanning/newpflor/camp/sutton.shtml

This attractive campground offers large secluded sites surrounded by cedar, spruce, and alder trees as well as wild rhododendrons. To get there, drive 4 miles north of Florence on US 101. Turn left on Campground-Vista Road and proceed 1 mile to the campground. From the campground you can explore more than 6 miles of trails in the Sutton Creek Recreation Area that give you a close-up view of a diverse coastal ecosystem made up of sand dunes, coastal forest, Sutton Lake, Sutton Creek, and sandy beach. You can take a trail to the beach—but in order to reach the beachfront you'll have to wade across Sutton Creek. This beachfront area is prime nesting habitat for the Western Snowy Plover and signs ask that you do not take your dog to the beachfront so as not to disturb the nesting activity of these birds. You can even take a short walk through a bog located in the campground where you can view the interesting insect-eating plant, the cobra lily. Fishing and boating are also popular at Sutton Lake. Drive to Holman Vista parking area, which has a wheelchair-accessible walkway, to take in views of the rolling sand dunes, scenic beach, and rambling Sutton Creek. The facilities at Sutton Creek are open year-round. Leashed pets are permitted.

TENMILE CREEK

Information: (541) 750-7000
www.fs.fed.us/r6/siuslaw

This small campground is a best-kept secret that is located adjacent to Tenmile Creek. While you are in this area be sure to head approximately 3 miles north on US 101 from the junction with Forest Service Road 56 and Visit Cape Perpetua Scenic Area. Stop by the Cape Perpetua Visitor's Center to pick up a trail map and use it as a reference to hike on one of many trails that wind through coastal forest and tide pools. The facilities are open year-round. Leashed pets are permitted.

Reedsport

CARTER LAKE
Oregon Dunes National Recreation Area
855 US 101
Information: (541) 750-7000
Reservations: (877) 444-6777
www.fs.fed.us/r6/siuslaw/recreation/
tripplanning/florcoos/camp/carterlake.shtml
This campground rests in a coastal sand dune ecosystem adjacent to 28-acre Carter Lake and sites are surrounded by lush coastal vegetation. You may want to try reeling in some rainbow trout in the lake or take a refreshing swim. You can also take a wheelchair-accessible 0.75-mile trail from the campground to Taylor Dunes. Keep in mind there is no off-road vehicle use allowed in this area. The facilities at Carter Lake are open April 30 through September 28. Leashed pets are allowed. It is located 11 miles south of Florence on US 101.

WILLIAM M. TUGMAN STATE PARK
Information: (541) 759-3604
Reservations: (800) 452-5687
www.oregonstateparks.org/park_98.php
William M. Tugman State Park is an undiscovered campground that is located 8 miles south of Reedsport, next to the shore of Eel Lake, a prime freshwater fishing lake that supports healthy populations of black crappie, cutthroat trout, rainbow trout, and largemouth bass. Other activities on this lake include swimming, canoeing, sailing, and boating. If you want to explore a more secluded section of the lake, you can head out on a hiking trail that takes you around the south end of the lake. The park is open year-round. Leashed pets are allowed. Please note: Reservations Northwest charges a $6 fee when you make a reservation using the number above.

SOUTH COAST

Coos Bay

SUNSET BAY STATE PARK
10965 Cape Arago Hwy.
Information: (541) 888-4902
Reservations: (800) 452-5687
www.oregonstateparks.org/park_100.php
Rocky sandstone cliffs, rugged sea stacks, and a well-protected sandy beach await those who visit Sunset Bay State Park, located 12 miles southwest of Coos Bay. Numerous day use areas throughout this park encourage family activities and a system of well-connected trails takes you to high vistas that have spectacular views of the rugged coastline and Sunset Bay. Be sure to hike on the Oregon Coast Trail 2 miles south to **Shore Acres State Park,** which has a sheltered observation station and a botanical garden. Note that pets are not allowed in Shore Acres State Park. You can access this trail at the day use picnicking area inside **Sunset Bay State Park.** Look for the wooden Oregon Coast Trail marker located just to the right of the restrooms that indicates the start of the trail. If you continue south on this Oregon Coast Trail from Shore Acres State Park, you'll reach Cape Arago State Park in another 2.5 miles. Other activities in this area include swimming and boating. You can also try your luck at fishing or crabbing from the small fishing village of Charleston. The park is open year-round. Leashed pets are allowed. Please note: Reservations Northwest charges a $6 fee when you make a reservation using the number above.

UMPQUA LIGHTHOUSE STATE PARK
10965 Cape Arago Hwy.
Information: (541) 271-4631
Reservations: (800) 452-5687
www.oregonstateparks.org/park_121.php
The Umpqua State Park campground is located 6 miles south of Reedsport, not far from the mouth of the Umpqua River and has many activities that will make you want to stay and explore this beautiful area. The state park is only a mile from

Salmon Harbor and excellent fishing opportunities in Winchester Bay to the north. This campground features two cozy one-room cabins that have covered porches where you can relax and enjoy the view of Lake Marie. Trails in the state park take you on a tour of towering sand dunes that are part of the Umpqua Dunes Scenic Area. You can also explore a 1-mile hiking trail that circles Lake Marie. Another unique attraction in this area is the 65-foot Umpqua River Lighthouse and museum. Tours of the lighthouse are given from May 1 to September 30; call (541) 271-4631 for more information on tour schedules. The park is open year-round. Leashed pets are allowed. Please note: Reservations Northwest charges a $6 fee when you make a reservation using the number above.

Bandon

BULLARDS BEACH STATE PARK
Information: (541) 347-2209
Reservations: (800) 452-5687
www.oregonstateparks.org/park_71.php
The Bullards Beach campground rests in a grove of shore pines 2 miles north of Bandon and features a 1.5-mile paved trail to the beach that wanders through a coastal forest and changes to a dune environment before it reaches the beach. From this path you'll have views of the salmon-rich Coquille River, and if you are a wildlife lover, you should be sure to stop by the Bandon Marsh National Wildlife Refuge located just south of the park. You should also be sure to check out the Coquille River Lighthouse located on the north jetty in the park and reachable via a 3-mile-long hiking path or along a paved road that ends at the lighthouse. Equestrian lovers will enjoy a 7-mile equestrian trail and miles of beach riding. If you love to fish, the Coquille River is within easy access The park is open year-round. Leashed pets are allowed. Please note: Reservations Northwest charges a $6 fee when you make a reservation using the number above.

Port Orford

CAPE BLANCO STATE PARK
Information: (541) 332-6774
Reservations: (800) 452-5687
www.oregonstateparks.org/park_62.php
Large campsites protected from the coastal wind by sheltering trees and a thick understory of salal, salmonberry, and thimbleberry are what you will find at this state park campground, located 9 miles north of Port Orford off US 101. The Oregon Coast Trail can be accessed from the south end of the campground. This park has a lot of natural beauty including high chalky bluffs, black sand beach, and offshore sea stacks that are home to herds of sea lions and are also prime nesting sites for seabirds. From this campground, you have access to the Elk and Sixes Rivers, which offer good fishing opportunities and more than 7 miles of equestrian trails are present in the state park. In addition, you can also explore the Cape Blanco Lighthouse, which is the oldest

Hot Potatoes

A tasty side dish you can prepare when you are camping is red potatoes with onions and green bell pepper. For easy fixing and cleanup, wash and dice four to five red potatoes, one bell pepper, and one yellow onion into a mixing bowl.

Place the mixture in foil, sprinkle with salt and pepper, and add a few pats of butter on top. Wrap the foil tightly and place on a barbecue grill for 45 to 55 minutes. When the potatoes are done, peel back the foil, and enjoy a tasty side dish with the rest of your evening meal. You can serve the potatoes right out of their foil wrapping to save time and cleanup.

lighthouse in Oregon, or the Hughes House Museum also located in the state park. The park is open year-round. Leashed pets are allowed. Please note: Reservations Northwest charges a $6 fee when you make a reservation using the number above.

HUMBUG MOUNTAIN STATE PARK
Information: (541) 332-6774
(800) 551-6949
Reservations: (800) 452-5687
www.oregonstateparks.org/park_56.php
This scenic state park is set in a forested setting 6 miles south of Port Orford and is adjacent to 1,756-foot Humbug Mountain. A moderate 5.5-mile loop trail will take you to the summit of Humbug Mountain. Windsurfing and scuba diving are popular activities in this area. A walkway leads from the campground under the highway to a 4-mile stretch of sandy beach where you can go beachcombing. The park is open year-round. Leashed pets are allowed. Please note: Reservations Northwest charges a $6 fee when you make a reservation using the number above.

Brookings
ALFRED A. LOEB STATE PARK
1655 US 101
Information: (541) 469-2021
(800) 551-6949
Reservations: (800) 452-5687
www.oregonstateparks.org/park_72.php
This park is located 7.5 miles east of Brookings, adjacent to the salmon-rich Chetco River and offers two self-guided tours through a myrtlewood forest and a small grove of magnificent redwood trees. This campground is located at

i Always be prepared for all types of weather on the Oregon Coast, no matter what the season. Always bring a rain jacket and insulating layers of clothing, sturdy hiking shoes, mosquito repellent, sunscreen, sunglasses, and a wide-brimmed hat.

the gateway to the Siskiyou National Forest and the Kalmiopsis Wilderness. Fishing opportunities abound in Chetco River and ocean fishing is available out of Brookings Harbor. The park is open year-round. Leashed pets are allowed. Please note: Reservations Northwest charges a $6 fee when you make a reservation using the number above.

HARRIS BEACH STATE PARK
1655 US 101
Information: (541) 469-2021
(800) 551-6949
Reservations: (800) 452-5687
www.oregonstateparks.org/park_79.php
The campground in this state park, which is 2 miles north of Brookings, is located in a wooded area bordered with bright azaleas. Wildlife watching and beachcombing are favorite activities here. You can look for seabirds nesting on Bird Island and also watch for whales offshore during their semiannual migration. Walk along the sandy beach and admire the rocky coastline and look for sea lions and harbor seals on the offshore rocks. The park is open year-round. Leashed pets are allowed. Please note: Reservations Northwest charges a $6 fee when you make a reservation using the number above.

RESTAURANTS

This chapter introduces you to many of the delicious eateries on the Oregon Coast. You'll find everything from high-end seafood restaurants to small, friendly cafes and coffeehouses that beckon you to stay for a while. Some restaurants are tucked away in historic districts and others provide you with an ocean view. We've organized the restaurants by region—North, Central, and South—and then by city from north to south. Restaurants are wheelchair accessible and accept credit cards unless noted otherwise. The price codes are listed below and will give you a hint of what your meal will cost.

Price Code

The price code below reflects the cost of a single meal excluding tips and drinks. As with other Oregon purchases, there is no sales tax.

$	$10 and less
$$	$11 to $20
$$$	$21 to $30
$$$$	more than $30

NORTH COAST

Up on the hearty North Coast of Oregon, it is inevitable that a day jaunt on the beach or along one of the headland trails will cook up a big appetite. Here in one of the villages strung between the capes and stretches of wild sand and offshore rocks can be found a good selection of restaurants for all tastes and pocketbooks. They range from the homey and low-key Columbian Cafe in Astoria to the legendary down-home Otis Cafe in Otis to the Grateful Bread bakery in Pacific City with its terrific pastry and fun play on words in reference to the rock band. Not only will you find some of the best-prepared seafood anywhere, you will encounter the relaxed, cheerful attitude that characterizes folks along this wind-battered, sea-pounded coastline.

Astoria

COLUMBIAN CAFE $
1114 Marine Dr.
(503) 325-2233
www.columbianvoodoo.com/cafe.html
This little shoebox grill is one of the most famous eateries on the Coast. So, squeeze in and watch the cooks only a wild elbow away serve up some great vegetarian and seafood meals. Try the crepes! Or call upon the "Chef's Mercy," a daily concoction of the freshest seafood. The Columbian Cafe is open for breakfast, lunch, and dinner. No smoking is allowed. Monday through Friday 8 a.m. to 2 p.m. and Saturday and Sunday 10 a.m. to 2 p.m. They are open for dinner Wednesday through Saturday from 5 p.m. to 8 p.m.

GUNDERSON'S CANNERY CAFE $$
1 6th St.
(503) 325-8642
www.riverparksuite.com/rest.html
Sitting on pilings over the bay with a great view of the Columbia River, the Cannery is a restaurant in what was once a busy processing plant for huge salmon. Now you can enjoy fresh versions of the same, other choices of seafood, and Dungeness crab cakes. Specialties include the halibut burger, crab and shrimp cakes, and lime prawns. A full bar is available, and the restaurant

is nonsmoking. The Cannery is open during the winter months Tuesday through Saturday 11 a.m. to 8 p.m. and Sunday 9 a.m. to 6 p.m. During the summer months (June through September) the restaurant is open Monday through Saturday 11 a.m. to 8:30 p.m. and Sunday 9 a.m. to 8:30 p.m.

THE WET DOG CAFE $$
114 Eleventh St.
(503) 325-6975
This local brew house has a variety of local brews on tap and serves up delicious burgers, sandwiches, pizza, and seafood in a warm, warehouse style atmosphere on the banks of the Columbia River. Monday through Friday, 9 a.m. to 2 p.m. Saturday and Sunday. Dinner hours start at 5 p.m. to closing (time determined by the number of people at the restaurant) Wednesday through Saturday. Credit cards are not accepted.

i Curious about seafood? Want to repeat that outrageously tasty meal you just had at one of the North Coast's better eateries? How about taking a seafood cooking class at the Duncan Law Seafood Consumer Center, 2021 Marine Dr., #200, Astoria, (503) 338-6523, www.seafoodschool.org. Classes run $50-$75 for a three-hour session. You will learn how to cook paellas, blackened and grilled fish, and delicious Dungeness crab dishes and many more.

Gearhart
PACIFIC WAY BAKERY AND CAFE $$
601 Pacific Way
(503) 738-0245
This hip little scene combines lots of windows with views of downtown Gearhart, a charming hardwood floor, and a laid-back staff cheerfully dispatching cinnamon rolls, scones, and muffins from its bakery and "yuppy food," including freshly homemade sandwiches for lunch and a full selection of entrees for dinner from its cafe side. On the menu are crab cakes, cashew razor

clams, macadamia roasted halibut, and vegetarian ravioli. There is an extensive list of sparkling wines, bottled beer, and nonalcoholic beer to accompany the meals. Hours are Thursday through Monday 11 a.m. to 3:30 p.m. for lunch and 5 to 9 p.m. for dinner.

Seaside
DOOGER'S $$
505 Broadway
(503) 738-3773
1371 South Hemlock St.Cannon Beach
(503) 436-2225
www.cannon-beach.net/doogers
With its two locations serving steaks and fresh local seafood, Dooger's is a smoke-free, cozy eatery with service so friendly it feels as if you are visiting friends or relatives for a special occasion meal. The Cannon Beach location focuses on families and seniors. It's open for breakfast, lunch, and dinner, and if you don't mind waiting in line for a while, you'll enjoy steamer clams, scallops, and halibut. Dooger's has a full bar at the Cannon Beach site and a regionally based wine list at both restaurants.

MCKEOWN'S RESTAURANT & BAR $$-$$$
714 Broadway
(503) 738-5232
http://mckeownsrestaurant.com
This local restaurant is just blocks from the beach and serves delicious breakfasts and is well known for their Sunday bunch. This restaurant serves popular seafood dishes including cedar plank salmon, crab cakes, Willapa Bay oysters, and salmon stuffed with crab. They also serve steaks, chicken, and pasta dishes and have a very good happy hour menu. Open daily 8 a.m. to 9 p.m.

Cannon Beach
BILL'S TAVERN $-$$
188 N. Hemlock St.
(503) 436-2202
Enjoy a unique beer and hearty food in a brewpub atmosphere. Order a beer sampler to taste some unique microbrews.

THE BISTRO $$
263 North Hemlock St.
(503) 436-2661

As its name suggests, this is an intimate little bistro complete with a full bar, that serves a pleasant mix of French, Italian, and Continental cuisine with seafood stew and sautéed oysters as the favorites among its return customers. It's open for dinner from 4 to 10 p.m. during the season.

CANNON BEACH BAKERY $
240 North Hemlock
(503) 436-0399
http://cannonbeachbakery.com

This bakery is famous for their hearty Haystack Bread. You can also enjoy scrumptious Danish pastries, soups, and sandwiches. Open Wednesday through Monday 6:30 a.m. to 5 p.m.

CRANKY SUE'S $–$$
308 Fir St.
(503) 436-0301

This fun spot serves up unique sandwiches such as an eggplant parmesan sandwich, Willapa Bay Oyster sandwich, and other delicious dishes including coconut shrimp, salmon pockets and crab and shrimp salad. They also serve delicious hamburgers (including the vegetarian kind), chicken wraps and comfort foods such as chicken dumpling soup.

LAZY SUSAN CAFE $
126 North Hemlock St.
(503) 436-2816

Breakfast is the best bet at this popular, sunny spot with its gingerbread waffles and specialty omelets. Lunches and dinners include tuna hazelnut, seafood salad, quiche, and salads served with wine or beer. Hours vary, but they're generally open from 8 a.m. to 8 p.m. during summer except on Tuesday, and in winter, 8 a.m. to 2:30 p.m. Monday through Thursday and Sunday; 8 a.m. to 8 p.m. on Friday and Saturday. Credit cards are not accepted but checks are.

PIZZA 'A FETTA $
231 Hemlock St.
(503) 436-0333
www.pizza-a-fetta.com

Tucked between art galleries and gift shops in this tourist-lively town, Pizza 'a Fetta serves pizza by the pie or slice, pasta, soup, and salad all made from scratch. "We specialize in taste," says the cook. Microbrewed beers or Italian wines are served by the bottle or the glass. Hours are 11 a.m. to 9 p.m. seven days a week in summer, and it closes Wednesday and Thursday in winter.

i Want a fresh cup of espresso to take with you as you walk along the beach? If so visit Bella Espresso, 231 North Hemlock St., (503) 436-2595.

Manzanita

MANZANITA NEWS AND ESPRESSO $
500 Laneda Ave.
(503) 368-7450

This local coffeehouse serves up delicious coffee and bagels and has a large selection of magazines and newspapers you can browse while you sip your cup of Joe.

TERRA COTTA CAFE $$–$$$
725 Manzanita Ave.
(503) 368-3700
www.terracottacafe.net/menuside1.htm

This cozy dinner cafe offers a unique menu including steamed halibut with spinach, mushrooms, onions, parmesan, lemon and fresh herbs, grilled swordfish steak, shrimp and filet mignon and also serves a variety of seafood pastas and salads. This dinner house has seasonal hours and it is recommended that you call ahead to make a reservation.

Oceanside

ROSEANNA'S OCEANSIDE CAFE $$
1490 Pacific Ave.
(503) 842-7351
www.roseannascafe.com
In a converted old country store with a great view of the Pacific, Roseanna's is both charming and upscale. Specialties include Tillamook Bay oysters, salmon, halibut, tiger prawns, cod, red snapper, and "the best chowder around." Roseanna's has a limited bar, along with wine and beer, and is open for lunch and dinner. The old building is somewhat wheelchair accessible, and the owner says many in wheelchairs eat there regularly. Hours are weekends 11 a.m. to 9 p.m. and weekdays 11 a.m. to 8 p.m.

Pacific City

GRATEFUL BREAD BAKERY $
34805 Brooten Rd.
(503) 965-7337
www.pacificcity.org/GratefulBread/home.html
Perhaps one of the best eateries on the Oregon Coast, this always-packed spot is a haven for hungry travelers as well as a hangout for locals. With its terrific bakery supplying specialty breads, scones, brownies, and cookies, the cafe side serves up pizza, lasagna, seafood, and vegetarian options. Breakfast temptations include French toast with blackberry and apple compotes and gingerbread pancakes. There is no alcohol served. Hours are Thursday through Monday 8 a.m. to 4 p.m., closed on Tuesday and Wednesday.

PELICAN PUB & BREWERY $$-$$$
33180 Cape Kiwanda Dr.
(503) 965-7007
www.pelicanbrewery.com
To taste an Oregon-made award-winning microbrew and have a fantastic ocean view, you should visit the Pelican Pub & Brewery. This brewery features beers and fresh fish and seafood. You can also feast on a hearty breakfast of crab cakes Benedict, biscuits and gravy, or steak and eggs. Vegan potatoes and vegetarian scramble will also entice the vegetarian crowd. Examples of featured beers include India Pelican Ale, Doryman's Dark Ale, Kiwanda Cream Ale, MacPelican's Scottish Style Ale, and Tsunami Stout. The brewery is open Sunday through Thursday from 8 a.m. to 10 p.m. and Saturday and Sunday 8 a.m. to 11 p.m.

RIVERHOUSE RESTAURANT $$-$$$
34450 Brooten Rd.
(541) 965-6722
www.riverhousefoods.com/index.php
Situated on the scenic Nestucca River, this small cafe is a sanctuary from the hubbub along US 101 3 miles westward. The menu is casual gourmet with sandwiches, seafood, buckets of steamer clams, and tasty apple pie. Don't miss the Riverhouse blue dressing on your salad. There is a full bar, and Visa and MasterCard are accepted for the price of the meal only. Hours are 11 a.m. to 9 p.m. daily.

Otis Junction

OTIS CAFE $
1259 Salmon River Hwy.
2 miles east of US 101 on Hwy. 18 at
Otis Junction
(541) 994-2813
Here is a gem of an old-time country restaurant. Many folks detour in its direction just for the legendary food. The prices are cheap, the grub is terrific, and the portions are big. Try the king-size burgers with legendary fries or hash browns. One of their signature items is buttery black bread that's also sold to go. This down-home spot also offers beer and wine and is open for breakfast and lunch every day and for dinner Friday through Sunday. If you're visiting on a weekend, you'll probably have to wait for a table.

CENTRAL COAST

From Lincoln City to Florence there are lots of ports of call for the hungry visitor. The most famous is Mo's with its internationally renowned, not-to-be-missed clam chowder; the most upscale is the Whale's Tale; and the eatery that gets lots of raves is Tidal Raves. Probably Newport and Florence have the most higher-end restaurants along this portion of the Oregon Coast. Both have animated Old Towns that are usually packed with out-of-towners who are served well by local restaurateurs. The top of the try-list along this strip is definitely Dungeness crab—tasty in a crab roll or mixed in pasta, or—the ultimate coastal meal—crab with a crisp salad and a loaf of French bread.

Lincoln City

BAY HOUSE $$$

5911 Southwest US 101
(541) 996-3222
www.bayhouserestaurant.com

Here is one of the sparkling gems of the Oregon Coast. With its classic ambience of finished wood and brass, the Bay House offers innovative entrees with an emphasis on seafood. One scrumptious example is salmon with hazelnut crust, another is pan-fried oysters in an Asian lemongrass broth. Or try the Dungeness crab legs with angel hair pasta. They have a large and impressive wine list, as well as a full bar. Open at 11:30 a.m. Tuesday through Saturday and open at 5:30 p.m. for dinner on Sunday and Monday. Reservations are recommended.

BLACKFISH CAFE $$–$$$

2733 US 101
(541) 996-1007
www.blackfishcafe.com

Fresh local fish and seafood dishes will satisfy your hunger after a day of shopping or beachcombing. Crispy corn meal oysters, steamed Manila clams, grilled Ling Cod, Rockfish and Chips, and Cavatapi Pasta with Alder Smoked Chinook Salmon, are some of the favorites here. Open Wednesday through Monday at 11:30 a.m. for lunch and at 5 p.m. for dinner.

DORY COVE $–$$

5819 Logan Rd.
(541) 994-5180
www.dorycove.com

Nestled next to Road's End Wayside, a small state park with easy access to the beach, Dory Cove is a great place to stop when you are tired and hungry from traipsing about the coastline. A large variety of meals are offered for lunch and dinner, including clam chowder, shrimp salad, all sorts of burgers, and a very popular tenderloin steak. Wine and beer are served.

Gleneden Beach

THE DINING ROOM AT WESTIN
SALISHAN RESORT $$$

7760 US 101 North
(800) 452-2300
www.salishan.com

With a spectacular view of Siletz Bay, this gourmet restaurant at the noted resort complex offers loin of lamb, duckling, venison, New York strip steak, North Coast cioppino, and grilled salmon, halibut, or scallops. Along with this upscale cuisine is a large variety of wines and cocktails. Open only for dinner, hours are 6 to 9 p.m. in winter (starting in October) and 6 to 10 p.m. in summer, which usually starts in April. It is closed Monday and Tuesday. There is no dress code, just dress comfortably.

Depoe Bay

GRACIE'S SEA HAG RESTAURANT
AND LOUNGE $$

58 US 101
(541) 765-2734

This spot claims that its "seafood is so fresh the ocean hasn't missed it yet." Examples of this bounty from the Pacific are baby shrimp, scallops, oysters, smoked tuna, and salmon stuffed with crab and shrimp. On Friday night there's an all-you-can-eat seafood buffet. Hours vary but they are usually open from 9 a.m. to 10 p.m.

TIDAL RAVES $

279 Northwest US 101
(541) 765-2995

A popular dining spot for folks ambling over from the Willamette Valley, Tidal Raves has one of the best views in Depoe Bay. It also has great grub including its famous Pasta Rave with crab, shrimp, and lingcod cuddling with the noodles. Another good choice is the Thai prawns. Hours are 11 a.m. to 9 p.m. daily.

Newport

BIG GUY'S DINER $
1801 North Coast Hwy.
(546) 265-5114
One of the many '50s-style restaurants that combine nostalgia and tasty fare, Big Guy's Diner offers a farm-style breakfast featuring an 8-oz. chicken breast, biscuits, and gravy; huge hamburgers; and a variety of classic dinner items all under $10. Hours are 6 a.m. to 9 p.m. daily.

BRIDGES RESTAURANT AND LOUNGE $$
1000 Southeast Bay Blvd.
(541) 265-8521
www.embarcadero-resort.com/index.html
As the eatery portion of the Embarcadero resort, hotel, and marina with a host of sailing options and a great view of Yaquina Bay, the restaurant offers a sumptuous Sunday brunch with champagne and fresh seafood and lunch and dinners specializing in steaks and seafood. Breakfast is served on Saturday and Sunday. Call or visit their Web site for the most current hours.

CANYON WAY BOOKSTORE AND
RESTAURANT $$
1216 Southwest Canyon Way
(541) 265-8319
This lovely oasis away from the hubbub of hectic Newport has delights for the mind and body. After browsing an impressive bookstore and gift shop, settle into a tasty lunch or early dinner with selections ranging from low-priced sandwiches to fresh pasta dishes. Be sure to check out the local art adorning many of its walls. Hours are 11 a.m. to 3 p.m. and 5:30 to 9 p.m. Tuesday to Saturday.

MO'S $
622 Southwest Bay Blvd.
(541) 265-2979
Easily the most famous restaurant on the Oregon Coast, Mo's is synonymous with hearty, affordable chow—particularly clam chowder and oyster stew. Other favorites are an all-you-can-eat seafood buffet and an excellent prime rib special. If this cozy spot is packed with customers, walk across the street to Mo's Annex, (541) 265-7512, for the same menu.

PANACHE $$–$$$
614 West Olive
(541) 265-2929
www.panachenewport.com
This restaurant prides itself on serving fresh, locally caught seafood, hormone free beef, lamb and pork, and organic vegetables and offers a variety of vegetarian dishes. The location is a carefully restored 1919 house that has a cozy, tiled gas fireplace and antique tables and chairs. Local artwork is also displayed and is available for purchase.

ROGUE ALES PUBLIC HOUSE $
748 Southwest Bay Blvd.
(541) 265-3188
www.rogue.com
Tucked in Old Town Newport, this big rollicking pub is the international headquarters for sampling some great microbrews made at the Rogue Ales Brewery, also located in Newport. Tasty additions to the brew samples are delicious burgers, soups, seafood, and salads and a large appetizer menu. You'll also find the usual sandwich suspects, including roast beef, turkey, and ham. Hours are 11 a.m. to 1 a.m. Monday through Thursday and 11 a.m. to 2 a.m. Saturday and Sunday.

i A quick treat that will echo a long way back into the history of the Oregon Coast is a stop at the Siletz Tribal Smokehouse. Here you can sample smoked salmon and tuna and then take home a few cans of these delicious delicacies prepared in ancient Native American fashion. The smokehouse is at 272 US 101 in Depoe Bay, (541) 765-3349, www.oregonsmokedfoods.com.

Waldport

LEROY'S BLUE WHALE   **$**
on US 101 across from the Visitor
Information Center
(541) 547-3397
The Waldport franchise of this family-style restaurant offers a sumptuous menu of traditional American food with an emphasis on seafood, including prawns and calamari (squid). Hours are 7 a.m. to 8 p.m. daily in winter, and 7 a.m. to 9 p.m. in summer. Also, try the Blue Whale in Yachats.

Yachats

ADOBE RESORT   **$$**
1555 US 101
(541) 547-3141
www.adoberesort.com
In this glass-encased dining room reaching out above Smelt Sands Beach, breakfast features Eggs Adobe, poached eggs with bay shrimp and artichoke bottoms topped with hollandaise sauce; brunch with French toast; and dinners including salmon ricotta and shrimp fettuccine. Hours are breakfast and lunch, 8 a.m. to 2:30 p.m. Monday through Saturday and 9 a.m. to 1 p.m. for Sunday brunch. Dinner hours are 5 to 9 p.m. Sunday through Thursday and 5:30 to 9:30 p.m. Friday and Saturday.

LA SERRE   **$$**
160 West Second St.
(541) 547-3420
The name means "greenhouse," and the atmosphere is cheerful and comfy with overhead skylights and a tall, beamed ceiling. Inside, you can order gourmet as well as healthy fare including charbroiled steaks, crab cakes, cioppino, or famous Umpqua oysters. Dinner starts at 5 p.m. Wednesday through Monday. Reservations are recommended.

YACHATS CRAB AND CHOWDER HOUSE   **$**
131 US 101
(541) 547-4132
In every coastal village from Cape Cod to Venice, California, there are those fish and chips joints that vend quick, cheap, and tasty baskets of marine grub. The Yachats Crab and Chowder House is a solid example. Here you can grab some crab and garlic bread or rock cod and halibut fish and chips. Hours for lunch and dinner are 11:30 a.m. to 8:30 p.m. Tuesday through Thursday, 11:30 a.m. to 9 p.m. on Friday and Saturday, and 11:30 a.m. to 8 p.m. on Sunday.

YACHATS LEROY'S BLUE WHALE   **$**
580 US 101
(541) 547-3397
The Yachats franchise of this family-style restaurant offers a sumptuous menu of traditional American food with an emphasis on seafood, including prawns and calamari (squid). Hours are 7 a.m. to 8 p.m. daily in winter, and 7 a.m. to 9 p.m. in summer. Also try the Blue Whale in Waldport.

YANKEE CLIPPER   **$**
125 Ocean Dr.
(541) 547-4004
This small sandwich parlor with a view of the Yachats Estuary offers clever soup and sandwich combos, homemade desserts, and tasty coffee. Hours are 11 a.m. to 3 p.m. daily. Credit cards are not accepted.

Florence

THE BLUE HEN   **$**
1675 US 101
(541) 997-3907
Although there are lots of chicken dishes at this small cafe operating out of a home, it is also famous for its chowder—complete with 14 ingredients—and huge biscuits. Wine and beer are served.

**THE BRIDGEWATER SEAFOOD
RESTAURANT AND OYSTER BAR**   **$$**
1297 Bay St., Old Town Florence
(541) 997-9405
This is the most upscale eatery in Old Town, where fresh fish is often cooked with a Cajun flavor. Some claim that it is the winner in the clam chowder contest with Mo's. But only your palate

can win that contest! Another hit here is the All-You-Can-Eat seafood dinner buffet for $10 or slightly more. Hours are 11:30 a.m. to 9 p.m. during the week and 9 a.m. to 9 p.m. on weekends.

CLAWSON'S WINDWARD INN $$
3757 US 101
(541) 997-8243

This highly acclaimed gourmet restaurant has a sophisticated ambience in which you can sample an innovative menu including fresh mussels broiled with hazelnuts and chicken and veal sausage, lobster, and steak. Hours for breakfast, lunch, and dinner are 7 a.m. to 10 p.m. in the summer and 7 a.m. to 9 p.m. in winter. There is a full bar.

i **A great spot to pick up your own seafood for an on-site snack, for a picnic, or for your own kitchen is the International C-Food Market, 1498 Bay St., Florence, along the dock of the Siuslaw River. Fishing boats arrive with their catches of crabs, oysters, clams, and whitefish. Call (541) 997-9646.**

MO'S $
1436 Bay St., Old Town Florence
(541) 997-2185

There are six Mo's Restaurants along the Oregon Coast at Cannon Beach, Lincoln City, two at Otter Crest, Newport, and here at Florence. Located along the Siuslaw River dock, this particular outlet of the notable chowder palace chain is a big rambling place. With its reasonable prices, a large variety of seafood dishes, bustling service, and an atmosphere of fun at the beach, Mo's is probably the most attractive restaurant in Old Town. Hours are 11 a.m. to 8 p.m. Sunday through Thursday and 11 a.m. to 9 p.m. Friday and Saturday.

TRAVELER'S COVE $$
1362 Bay St.
(541) 997-8194

Crab is a big part of the menu here at this combination gift shop and restaurant. There are crab enchiladas, crab quiche, and Caesar salad loaded with Oregon's legendary Dungeness crab. If this creeping cuisine makes you crabby, try other sandwiches and salads that are also tasty. Take your lunch out to the dining deck with a river view.

Lakeside

LAKESHORE LODGE $$
290 South 8th St.
(800) 759-3951
www.lakeshorelodgeor.com

Dining on the lakefront of the many-fingered Ten-Mile Lake in a big-windowed room enhances the choice of a family-style chicken dinner, prime rib, fresh local seafood, steaks, homemade pizza, and fresh pastas. Hours are 8 a.m. to 9 p.m. daily, with earlier openings on the weekends for fisherfolk.

SOUTH COAST

Down on Oregon's South Coast are dozens of great restaurants, particularly in Bandon, a revitalized destination resort town that suffered a devastating fire in the 1930s. Back in the mid-to-late 1970s, Bandon government officials and local boosters worked hard to get funding to rebuild much of Old Town. Now, in this historic and charming strip along with the scenic Beach Loop Drive that winds along the bluff overlooking some of the loveliest beach and offshore rocks in the Pacific Northwest, lots of new eateries help to amplify Bandon's reputation as a hot spot to visit. But don't ignore the fine eateries in Coos Bay and Charleston to the north and Wedderburn and Brookings to the south. There are lots of great choices for repast as you pass by these salty towns.

i **A quick and tasty alternative to a formal restaurant is Cone 9 Cookware and Espresso Bar in the Pony Village Mall, 1611 Virginia Ave., North Bend, (541) 756-4535. You can nab a heap of pasta, a sandwich, a salad, bowl of soup, or a combination. Then, after fast service, you can take your tray out to the mall plaza to people-watch as you munch.**

North Bend

ALDER SMOKEHOUSE $
1055 Virginia Ave.
(541) 756-9599
This specialty spot offers lip-smacking smoked and barbecue meals for dining in or taking out. Their most popular item is a tri-tip sandwich with sides of pasta salad, potato salad, or cole slaw. A popular side dish is their smokehouse chili beans. Hours are Tuesday through Thursday 11 a.m. to 3 p.m. and Friday and Saturday 11 a.m. to 7 p.m.

THE PLANK HOUSE IN THE MILL CASINO $$
East side US 101
(800) 953-4800
www.themillcasino.com/dining/
plankhouse.cfm
On the bay side of the Coquille tribe's humming casino, beyond the video poker and gaming tables, is the Plank House restaurant open twenty-four hours a day. The best bet here is the all-you-can-eat lunch or dinner buffet. It also serves seafood as well as traditional sandwiches. If you dine between 4 p.m. and 6 p.m. you can take advantage of their early bird dinner specials which include prime rib, the local catch of the day, fettuccine and shrimp alfredo, traditional fish and chips, and two cheese ravioli.

Coos Bay

BENNETTI'S ITALIAN RESTAURANT $$–$$$
260 South Broadway
(541) 267-6066
You'll find unique and delicious dishes and a friendly and warm atmosphere at this family owned Italian restaurant. Specialties include veggie calazone, gnocchi, and Steak Sugo which is a cubed New York Steak and sautéed with green and red peppers, roasted onions, mushrooms and wine. This is added to their homemade meat sauce and served over pasta.

BLUE HERON BISTRO $$
110 West Commercial
(541) 267-3933
www.blueheronbistro.com
Probably the most European-flavored and -furnished eatery in Coos County, the Blue Heron Bistro offers healthy and affordable eatables from waffles and genuinely good coffee to nitrate-free German sausage to prime rib. Hours are 11 a.m. to 9 p.m. Monday through Saturday.

GOURMET COASTAL COFFEES $$
273 Curtis Ave.
(541) 267-5004
Located a few blocks off the main drag in Coos Bay, this very popular coffee shop and sandwich parlor has a wide variety of coffee drinks, pastries, and their big hit, the Zestie Veggie Sandwich. This is known as a place where you can stop by and read all the Sunday paper, meet with friends for a lively discussion, or amble back to a charming little patio for a quiet sip of java among the greenery. Live music is a casual affair with drum circle on Thursday night. Hours are 6 a.m. to 6 p.m. Credit cards are not accepted.

KUM-YON'S $
835 South Broadway
(541) 269-2662
Although there are a number of Asian restaurants in Coos Bay and North Bend, most are nondescript and not worth a traveler's effort. Except for Kum-Yon's, a pleasant little spot featuring South Korean cuisine. They also serve sushi, sashimi, chow mein, and yakitori in sizable portions. They offer beer and wine. Hours are 11 a.m. to 9 p.m. Tuesday through Friday and 11 a.m. to 9:30 p.m. on Friday and Saturday.

SUMIN'S $
298 South Broadway #B
(541) 267-0119
The first sign that this is a hot spot for fans of sushi and other Asian cuisine is a packed house of smiling customers. But be patient and wait for seats. Your reward is some of the finest sushi on the Oregon Coast. The service is swift and cordial and the food is fresh and innovative. Open seven days a week.

Coos Bay folks in the know head for the Scenery in the morning for a brisk cup of java and their choice of a freshly baked scone. They also have soup and sandwiches later in the day for lunch. The Scenery is at 190 Central Ave., Coos Bay, (541) 267-5600.

Charleston
PORTSIDE $$
63383 Kingfisher Rd.
(541) 888-5544
www.portsidebythebay.com
Lots of folks from "The Bay Area" come over the bridge at the Charleston Boat Basin to dine at the Portside. Here in this darkly lit room, you can get a window seat and watch the fishing boats come and go as you sample dishes of fresh seafood including Cajun blackened catch of the day, shrimp Louie, lobster bisque, seafood gumbo, and traditional fish and chips. On Friday the chef prepares a generous seafood buffet. The restaurant is open for lunch and dinner.

Bandon
BANDON BILL'S STEAK & SEAFOOD $$
3225 Beach Loop Dr.
(541) 347-7302
Located at the Inn at Face Rock out on the scenic Beach Loop Drive overlooking a gorgeous strip of beach and offshore rocks, Bandon Bill's offers a terrific view and opulent cuisine. Examples are mesquite chicken quesadilla, shrimp and crab stuffed scallops, and Kahlua honey-smoked game hen. The chef is also very proud of his special clam chowder! Hours are 4 p.m. to 9 p.m. Sunday through Thursday and 3 p.m. to 10 p.m. Friday and Saturday.

BANDON DUNES GALLERY
RESTAURANT AND PUB $$–$$$
2450 North Lakeview, Round Lake Rd.
(541) 347-4380
www.bandondunesgolf.com

Whether you are trying out this world-class golf course along the bluff north of Bandon, designed in the spirit of Scotland's ancient links tradition; enjoying its spa; staying at one of the suites at the lodge or at their Lily Pond Cottages; or just stopping by for a meal, their restaurant has lots to offer the hungry duffer or visitor. Breakfast features the Bandon Dunes Scramble—smoked lox salmon scrambled with eggs, capers, red onions, and the famous Bandon cheddar cheese. Lunch ranges from crispy oysters to Grandma Thayer's meatloaf sandwich, and dinners offer aged prime New York steak, pan-seared Pacific snapper, steamed Oregon little-neck clams, and fried calamari. Dinner reservations are recommended. Hours are 6 a.m. to 10 p.m. daily.

BEACH JUNCTION MARKET & DELI $
(541) 347-6978
At the corner of US 101 and the southern end of Beach Loop Road, this market and deli is handy for picnic fixings, a quick snack, or stocking up for camping. They have homemade biscuits and gravy, specialty sandwiches, cold beverages, and gourmet coffees.

HARP'S RESTAURANT AND THE
HIDEAWAY LOUNGE $$
480 1st St. Southwest
(541) 347-9057
Harp's is a culinary incarnation with its fresh, creative dishes that will fulfill almost anyone's palate. With fresh pasta made every day, a unique seasoning to go with its grilled oysters, and a hot

For organic nibbles, there are two options in the Coos Bay/Bandon area. The Coos Head Food Store, 1960 Sherman Ave., North Bend, (541) 756-7264, has more than 300 bulk food items, freshly squeezed carrot and wheat grass juice, as well as organic produce. The other store is Mother's Natural Grocery, 975 2nd St., Bandon, (541) 347-4086, with vegetarian treats as its specialty.

New York strip steak basted with Tabasco sauce, this comfy little spot is one of the best options for fine dining in Bandon. Open Tuesday through Saturday from 5 to 9 p.m. daily. There is a full service bar.

LORD BENNETT'S $$
1695 Beach Loop Rd.
(541) 347-3663
http://lordbennett.com
Named after the dour Irish lord who established the town of Bandon, this fine eatery poised on the bluff along Beach Loop Road with a stunning view of the Pacific Ocean offers a wide range of entrees. Lunch items include shrimp omelet, broiled red snapper, and a crab sandwich with avocado and melted jack cheese; dinner specialties are stuffed sole, blackened red snapper, lobster, and a combination seafood plate. They are open for Sunday brunch and lunch from 10 a.m. to 2:30 p.m. and for dinner daily from 5 to 9 p.m.

WHEELHOUSE RESTAURANT & CROW'S NEST LOUNGE $
125 Chicago Ave., Old Town Mall
(541) 347-9331
With its nautical theme and close view of the local working fishing fleet moored across the street, the Wheelhouse is a lively and tasty spot to dine while visiting this friendly, cheerful tourist stop. Try fresh native seafood, local lamb, or the homemade clam chowder and have delicious vegetarian dishes. Another hit is the fish fried in a beer batter. Hours are daily from 11:00 a.m. to 9 p.m. depending on the crowd.

Gold Beach

ROD 'N' REEL $
94321 River Rd.
(541) 247-6465

A neat little cafe close to the jet boat docks where you begin your adventure zooming up the Rogue River, Rod 'n' Reel serves breakfast, lunch, and dinner—all tasty and all low cost. Try the grilled shrimp or crab sandwiches. Hours are 6 a.m. to 2 p.m.

Brookings

O'HOLLERANS RESTAURANT $$
1210 Chetco Ave.
(541) 469-9907
As one of Brookings oldest restaurants, you won't find fancy furnishings but you will find good steaks, seafood, and other hearty American fare.

RUBIO'S MEXICAN RESTAURANT $
1136 Chetco Ave.
(541) 469-4919
Rubio's is a good bet if you are craving Mexican or Tex-Mex cuisine. The salsa is a big hit, and the house specialty is seafood doused with jalapeño sauce, butter, garlic, and wine. Also, try their chiles rellenos. Hours for lunch are 11 a.m. to 5 p.m. and dinner is served concurrently from 11 a.m. to 8 p.m. on weekdays and 11 a.m. to 9 p.m. on the weekends.

WILD RIVER PIZZA $
16279 US 101
(541) 469-7454
www.wildriverbrewing.com/wrp-br.html
This big and bustling pizza parlor is a great spot to feed the family that's starved after a hearty time at the beach. Along with the usual choices for pizza, you may also want to try hearty fried chicken, deli sandwiches, homemade desserts, and handcrafted microbrews. Hours are 11 a.m. to 10 p.m. daily.

NIGHTLIFE

After a fun day at the beach or touring a historic shopping district, you may be ready to check out the lively nightlife on the Oregon Coast. This chapter provides you with a variety of entertainment choices including clubs with dancing and live music, playhouses featuring local theatrical productions, and casinos with cards and slots. The entertainment possibilities are listed north to south by region and then by city.

NORTH COAST

Oregon's tame but pleasing beach world is a far distance from the bright lights of Atlantic City or Las Vegas, but there are a few choices of nightlife that will entertain visitors as well as introduce them to the local cultural flavor. In Astoria, the oldest village in Oregon, you can catch the antics of the Astor Street Opry Company or join the gang at Cafe Uniontown, the hot spot for live music here. Farther south, there are some great shows at the Coaster Theater in Cannon Beach for folks who have stopped by this artsy town to view the painting and crafts.

Astoria

ASTOR STREET OPRY COMPANY
129 West Bond St.
(503) 325-6104
www.shanghaiedinastoria.com
A local theater troupe presents *Shanghaied in Astoria*. This play, with chase scenes, bar fights, and lots of Scandinavian jokes, is based on Astoria's dubious distinction as a notorious shanghai port during the late 1800s. Call the number listed to purchase tickets and to find out the current days and times.

> **i** To zero in on your tastes in evening entertainment, this Web site will give you plenty of choices: www.coastarts.org. It lists concerts, plays, and other fun events.

CAFE UNIONTOWN
218 West Marine Dr.
(503) 325-8708
This hot spot under the Astoria Bridge is the town's jazz scene with both jazz and blues. Also fun are the piano sing-alongs in the bar. Call for the current entertainment schedule. There is usually a cover charge.

THE WET DOG CAFE
144 11th St.
(503) 325-6975
This haven for both old hipsters and Gen-X types has local and regional groups playing blues to alternative rock on Friday and Saturday. This fun spot has pool tables and plenty of pasta dishes, pizza and other seafood dishes. Shark Rock Red, Frenchie's Scottish Ale, Rye PA, Pacific Pale ale, and a Peacock Spit Golden.

Seaside

GIRTLE'S RESTAURANT & LOUNGE
311 Broadway
(503) 738-8417
www.girtles.com
On Friday and Saturday nights you can enjoy listening to fun dance music from the Smoke and Mirrors band. During the week you can try karaoke.

Cannon Beach

BILL'S TAVERN
188 North Hemlock St.
(503) 436-2202
This legendary lounge has emerged as the center of Cannon Beach nightlife. A hand-carved sign with a wooden crow perched on top is a relic from the original tavern founded 65 years ago. Now it is home to local blues and rock groups who take the stage once or twice a month.

COASTER THEATRE
108 North Hemlock St.
(503) 436-1242
www.coastertheatre.com
This lively theater company runs its plays on Friday and Saturday with tickets ranging from $14 to $20. Recent productions include *Sherlock's Secret Life, Grace and Glorie, Hello Dolly* and *Dames at Sea.*

Manzanita

GALES BAR & GRILL
165 Laneda Ave.
(503) 368-4253
On Friday and Saturday night, this cozy little nook offers live rock music by local and Portland bands with dinners of steaks, pasta, and seafood—particularly their popular Captain's Platter of mixed seafood. The live music continues after dinner from 9 p.m. to 1 a.m.

Pacific City

TIDEWATERS
34455 Brooten Rd.
(503) 965-6960
Musicians of all flavors are brought in from Portland and other urban zones to perform at the Tidewaters with no cover charge. Along with a 50-seat restaurant, there is a lounge with a festive maritime motif and a wide view of the bay at Pacific City. There is also a wild karaoke party on Friday night.

CENTRAL COAST

From Lincoln City down to Florence, the Oregon Coast hums both day and night with scenic wonder and lively entertainment. In just about every town there is a performing arts center, if only a modest renovation of a grange hall. It's a great way to meet the locals and you may be surprised by the quality of entertainment particularly in the realm of community theater.

Lincoln City

CHINOOK WINDS CASINO
1777 Northwest 44th St.
Casino information: (888) 244-6665
Entertainment and bus reservations:
(888) 624-6228
www.chinookwindscasino.com
One of the most successful Native American gaming ventures in Oregon, Chinook Winds Casino offers a variety of games including blackjack, poker, bingo, slots, keno, and a large stage and entertainment theater. Newer entertainments include craps, roulette, Pai Gow poker, Let-it-Ride, Caribbean Stud, Aruba Stud, Progressive Blackjack, and Big 6 Wheel. It all adds up to gambling fun of all flavors. Other amenities include a restaurant and lounge: The Rogue River Lounge, with live entertainment several nights each week and a sumptuous dance floor. Hours are 9 a.m. to 12:30 a.m. Sunday through Thursday and 9 a.m. to 1:30 a.m. Friday and Saturday. There is child care available, a video arcade for kids, and a gift shop.

Newport

BAY HAVEN TAVERN
608 Southwest Bay Blvd.
(541) 265-7271
Established in 1908, this ancient fisherman's saloon has served all sorts of folks, including Jack London and John Steinbeck. Perhaps its greatest claim to fame was as a location in the screen version of Ken Kesey's *Sometimes a Great Notion.* Nowadays and nights, its identity is as "Home of the Blues."

THE NEWPORT PERFORMING ARTS CENTER
777 West Olive
(541) 265-2787
www.coastarts.org

In 1986, they burned down the historic Bluebird Cottages at Nye Beach to make room for the Newport Performing Arts Center. With its 400-seat Alice Silverman Theater and auxiliary Studio Theatre, the center is the largest performing arts venue on the Oregon Coast. While traveling through Newport, it is always a good idea to check its schedule for music, theater, or lectures. One of the popular events is a monthly Nye Beach Writers Series that runs spring through fall with two designated writers reading each month, followed by an "open mike."

PORT DOCK ONE
325 Southwest Bay Blvd.
(541) 265-2911

A large restaurant and lounge reminiscent of the three-story, stick-porched hostels of the Caribbean, the Port Dock One is on Newport's bayfront next to the Underseas Gardens. Stop by in the evening for live and usually danceable music.

Yachats
YACHATS COMMONS
101 2nd St.
(541) 547-4142

Sponsored by the Friends of Yachats Commons, this cozy little venue for jazz, acoustic, and classical music offers visitors a treat for a modest charge.

Florence
FLORENCE EVENTS CENTER
715 Quince St.
(541) 997-1994
www.eventcenter.org

Here at the Events Center you can find a wide variety of evening entertainment including brass orchestra concerts, storybook theater by the Last Resort Players, rhododendron shows, and art exhibits. While in town, call for current events on tap.

THE LOTUS
1150 Bay St.
(541) 997-7168

Nestled under the bridge crossing the Siuslaw River, The Lotus is a calmer night scene than the Fisherman's Wharf but just as fun for its live music of local bands covering '50s rock 'n' roll and blues.

SOUTH COAST

North Bend

LITTLE THEATRE ON THE BAY
2100 Sherman Ave. (US 101 & Washington)
(541) 756-4336
www.ltob.net

Maybe it's the legendary grey skies or the communal energy of a coastal village, but it seems that live theater is a booming force in North Bend, Coos Bay, Bandon, and Coquille. A good example is Little Theatre on the Bay. This ambitious outfit has been mounting full-scale musicals as well as serious drama for decades. Examples of their shows include *Paint Your Wagon* and *Of Mice and Men*.

THE MILL CASINO
3201 Tremond Ave.
(541) 756-8800, (800) 953-4800
www.themillcasino.com

Here in the sprawl of a renovated plywood mill along US 101 is a lively yet perfectly safe gambling parlor operated by the Coquille tribe. You can stop by every night and play slots, bingo, blackjack, and poker. There is also live entertainment six nights a week with rock, country and western, and oldies to dance to while the house bags up your winnings. There is free RV parking.

NORTH BEND LANES BOWLING CENTER
1225 Virginia Ave.
(541) 756-0571

This modern bowling center is a complete operation with pool tables and a giant screen TV and is a luncheon spot with salads, sandwiches, and homemade soup.

ROGER'S ZOO
2047 Sherman Ave.
(541) 756-2550
This smoke-free pub has great pizza and often has live music. The sounds are usually rock or jazz. This is a haunt of locals who want a quiet good time.

Coos Bay

BLUE MOON RESTAURANT AND LOUNGE
871 South Broadway
(541) 269-9004
This old saloon is a bit rough around the edges but is the real McCoy as a country tavern in downtown Coos Bay. Live country music fills the saloon on Friday and Saturday nights with no cover charge. It also offers free pool on Monday 5 p.m. to close.

GOONEY'S SPORTS BAR & GRILL
3290 Ocean Blvd.
(541) 266-8815
This full-service bar has good grub, 10 satellite-access TVs, pool tables, darts, a jukebox, video golf, and Oregon lottery games. There is live music every other weekend at 9 p.m., no cover charge. The sounds include highly danceable Cajun swamp rock and a local band that calls itself the Beat Dragons.

GENEVIEVE'S RESTAURANT
1088 Newmark Ave.
(541) 888-4353
Another great resource that's accessible without your laptop is *Hipfish* (www.hipfishmonthly .com), an arts and culture monthly that covers the nightlife events from Astoria down to Lincoln City. You can snap up this free, very comprehensive, and well-produced tabloid at most stores and shops. Located en route to the Coast from downtown Coos Bay, Genevieve's has family-style dining as well as live music and DJs spinning CDs on Friday and Saturday.

OLD CITY HALL GRAND BALLROOM
375 Central Ave.
(541) 266-0526
The old seat of power only a block away from the new city hall has been remodeled into a dance hall, where you can spend an evening taking dance lessons. Bands play rock 'n' roll and Big Band sounds. There is a cover charge for events.

ON BROADWAY THEATER
845 S. Broadway #107
(541) 269-2501
www.geocities.com/obthespian
As well as presenting adult drama, this lively group also mounts shows with teenage thespians involved in Alternative Youth Activities. There is also a Children's Theatre for younger children. Call or visit their Web site to purchase tickets and to view current productions. The theater has three different venue locations: Genevieve's, 1088 Newmark Ave.; Coos Bay Children's Theater at the Pony Village Mall, 1611 Virginia Ave.; and North Bend Egyptian Theatre, 229 S. Broadway, Coos Bay.

WANDA'S
740 Koos Bay Blvd.
(541) 267-6293
Wanda's is another reliable venue for the best of local bands playing blues and rock on Friday and Saturday night usually with no cover.

Coquille
SAWDUST THEATRE
114 North Adams St.
(541) 396-4563
www.sawdusttheatre.com
This hilarious and highly entertaining theater group is worth a side jaunt east from US 101 to Coquille.

Bandon
LLOYD'S
119 2nd St.
(541) 347-4211
Fondly known as "Lloyd's of Bandon," this venerable pub has been the scene of lots of live music

brought in from Portland and other larger scenes. The bands play every other Friday and Saturday from 9 p.m. to 2 a.m. The restaurant side menu is available in the lounge side. Best bet is classic cheeseburger and fries.

LORD BENNETT'S RESTAURANT AND LOUNGE
1695 Beach Loop Rd.
(541) 347-3663

You can enjoy live entertainment in the lounge of this popular steak and seafood restaurant. Additional perks are fantastic views of the rugged, rocky beach.

SPRAGUE THEATER
1202 11th St.
(541) 347-7426

You can enjoy a variety of plays put on by the amateur Bandon Theater Group. Recent performances have included Gian Carlo Menotti's Christmas Story *Amahl and the Night Visitors*.

Pistol River

PISTOL RIVER FRIENDSHIP HALL
P.O. Box 6086, Pistol River 97444
(541) 247-288
www.pistolriver.com

In the old country tradition of grange halls and barn dances, the Pistol River Friendship Hall stages lots of great acoustic entertainment. Located along a small river flowing to the ocean halfway between Gold Beach and Brookings. Call or visit the Web site for current show schedules and ticket prices. Pistol River is located 10 miles south of Gold Beach off US 101.

Brookings

REDWOOD THEATER
621 Chetco Ave.
(541) 469-4632
www.redwoodtheater.com

Probably the most southern nightlife venue on the Oregon Coast, the Redwood Theater, an old movie house actually constructed with redwood, shows films and presents live music concerts. The Friends of Music schedule five concerts of classical chamber music on Sunday afternoons in spring and fall.

SHOPPING

The Oregon Coast offers a variety of shopping experiences. You'll find everything from outlet malls to small upscale shops in quaint historic districts. Many shops are locally owned and feature one-of-a-kind arts and crafts, toys, clothing, jewelry, candy, and everything in between. The shops in this chapter are listed from north to south.

NORTH COAST

The shopping ambience varies considerably on the North Coast of Oregon. You'll find outlet centers and main streets, crowded tourist strips and destination stops, and everything in between. Each of the towns on the Oregon Coast has a distinctive retail character. Cannon Beach, for instance, has many fine, upscale shops and galleries; Seaside's colorful shopping district serves customer demand for candy, beach toys, and souvenirs; Astoria's old-fashioned main street-style downtown area demands hours of browsing and exploring. In fact, many of the towns on the Coast have lively main streets to investigate, areas that retain their qualities of independence and eclecticism. While Cannon Beach is a tourist mecca, it also doesn't allow franchises, so family-owned businesses are common and the town is attractively idiosyncratic. The main street area of Tillamook (actually called Main Avenue) is worth exploring for the opposite reason: because apparently tourists hardly ever do. It has a distinctively local flavor, with Sears, hardware stores, building supplies, secondhand stores, groovy record shops, and farmers' co-ops all mixed up together. These districts are full of surprises, adding adventure to the other pleasures of buying local.

Astoria

Maybe it's because downtown Astoria looks like the movie set of a small mid-century town, or maybe it's because this shopping district is for everyone, locals and tourists alike, but whatever the secret ingredient to the retail charm of this area, it works. Chocolate fiends will linger in **Columbia Chocolates,** 1332 Commercial St., where they sell candy made right there in town. **Let It Rain,** 1124 Commercial St., sells everything to keep you dry in coastal storms. **Finn Ware,** 1116 Commercial St., is the source for all things Scandinavian, from sauna supplies to crystal. **Custom Threads,** 1282 Commercial St., will keep you in splendid yarns and needles and hooks during all your knitting and crochet projects. Notable bookstores in the area include **Lucy's Books,** 348 12th St., and **Godfather's Books,** 1108 Commercial St., and right nearby, the **Backroom Bookstore** at 1052 Commercial St. *The Daily Astorian,* the local newspaper, also maintains a bookstore that specializes in local history; you can find them at 949 Exchange St.

COLUMBIA RIVER MARITIME MUSEUM
1792 Marine Dr.
(503) 325-2323
www.crmm.org
Museum gift shops are often excellent resources for unusual birthday, anniversary, and wedding gifts, and the shop at this well-planned museum is no exception. Comprehensive books and monographs on Indian art, Oregon history, maritime history, fishing, shipwrecks, lighthouses, and other water-related items are for sale, and so are elegant sand glasses and ships' lanterns. Their teaching resources are outstanding; in addition to all the books, there are maps, charts, graphs, and videos. If none of those sound like the right gift, try the jewelry.

LUCY'S BOOKS
348 12th St.
(503) 325-4210

Lucy's is a bookstore with a strong local focus, and Astoria is a town with a lot of writers. Lucy's has not only an excellent selection of books about the Pacific Northwest but carries the local writers too; you can find things here that you cannot find anywhere else, like anthologies of poems collected from the Fisher Poets Gathering, which takes place in February. Lucy's also has a good section on women's writing and a decent travel section. It's closed Sunday.

Seaside

CLEANLINE SURF SHOP
719 First Ave., Seaside
(503) 738-7888
171 Sunset Blvd., Cannon Beach
(503) 436-9726
www.cleanlinesurf.com

Both branches of this store sell surfboards, skateboards, and snowboards. But that's not all: You can also repair your board or rent one for the day—they feature complete surf rental packages. Or if you'd feel safer in a kayak, they can help you get set up with that too. In addition to gear, Cleanline also sells wet suits and simple shoes; you'll keep warm with the Ugg sheepskin boots and the Patagonia jackets. Or you'll cool down with Billabong shorts.

SEASIDE ANTIQUE MALL
39 South Holladay
(503) 717-9312

There are about a dozen stores in Seaside that sell antiques; the Seaside Antique Mall is the largest, and browsing here is a splendid way to spend a rainy Oregon day. In addition to the usual china, glass, and linens, you can also score some great finds in the advertising, Indian artifact, and art pottery departments. You can find a lot more than that, too: 88 antiques and collectibles dealers have pooled their resources at this mall. Open Sunday to Friday 10 a.m. to 5 p.m.; Saturday 10 a.m. to 8 p.m.

SEASIDE CAROUSEL MALL
300 Broadway
(503) 738-6728
www.seasidecarouselmall.com

Broadway is Seaside's waterfront shopping district, and there you will find many candy, souvenir, and wacky T-shirt shops. In the middle of it all is the appropriately named Seaside Carousel Mall, which houses a beautiful carousel in addition to the shops. After the little ones go for a ride on a big ginger cat or a unicorn, take them to Under the Big Top Toys for more indulgence. Then perhaps something for you is in order from Signature Imports, which sells furniture and decorating items in addition to beautiful leather bags, handknit sweaters, and batik sarongs. Mary Anna's $12.99 Store carries nothing that costs more than $12.99 and much of it is surprisingly chic; By the Sea has a nice selection of nautical-themed gifts and shells; and Seaside Mostly Hats carries, well, mostly hats, but it's awfully convenient when you've forgotten yours. North Coast Leathers carries motorcycle leathers, jackets, coats, wallets, belts, hats, and handbags. Or, try some delicious taffy candy at Rascals. Open 10 a.m. to 9 p.m. Monday through Saturday and 10 a.m. to 6 p.m. on Sunday.

SEASIDE FACTORY OUTLET CENTER
111 North Roosevelt
(503) 717-1603
www.seasideoutlets.com

One of the favorite activities of visitors to the North Coast is spending the day at the shopping mall, and in this case big savings are in store. You'll see some familiar outlet names at this 25-store complex—Kitchen Collection, OshKosh B'Gosh, Bass Shoes, and Dress Barn all have spaces here. Our favorites include the Black & Decker store for small appliances, Nike for sportswear and shoes, and Eddie Bauer for outdoor apparel and gear. Open January and February 10 a.m. to 7 p.m. Monday through Saturday and 10 a.m. to 5 p.m. on Sunday. During the rest of the year, they are open 10 a.m. to 8 p.m. Monday through Saturday and 10 a.m. to 7 p.m. on Sunday.

Cannon Beach

BRUCE'S CANDY KITCHEN
256 North Hemlock St.
(503) 436-2641
www.brucescandy.com

This plank-floored, false-fronted building sells handmade chocolate and saltwater taffy and it's a Cannon Beach institution. It's a full-service candy store; you can get swirly rainbow lollipops and gummi bears. You can watch them make the candy right there, and watching it being made imparts an even more delicious flavor. They don't pull every flavor in their saltwater taffy line; that means that the butterscotch, root beer, butter, and cinnamon varieties are stickier and harder (and usually the first ones eaten, as long as no dental work is in jeopardy). Bruce's also makes a line of sugar-free candy; it's quite good.

CANNON BEACH BOOK COMPANY
132 Hemlock #2
(503) 436-1301, (800) 312-5045
www.cannonbeachbooks.com

A fine bookstore, the Cannon Beach Book Company is a great supporter of writers and literary events in the area, so stop by to see what's happening and what local writers have published lately. While you're there, check out the contemporary fiction and literary nonfiction—and anything else, for this is a shop that believes in browsing. You'll also find a good mystery section and books for children.

CENTER DIAMOND
1065 South Hemlock St.
(503) 436-0833, (888) 305-0854
www.centerdiamond.com

This shop is helping to feed the mania for quilting, and after a visit, it's easy to see why. It's a must-stop for North Coast quilters. The Center Diamond really is a center—not only do they sell beautiful fabrics, patterns, and notions for quilting, but they also feature classes and workshops. You might try a "Slumber party," which is an extended retreatlike workshop on doll making, quilting, or related topics. Open every day 10 a.m. to 5 p.m.

ECOLA SQUARE
123 South Hemlock St.

Ecola Square has some of the most interesting shops in Cannon Beach. Its attractively faded, white-trimmed exterior just begs to be visited. Some highlights of this village mall are Ecola Square Books, which specializes in books for children as well as books about the region. and the Wild Bird Shop, which features everything you need to learn about birds. Ecola Square is very Cannon Beach, and a great place to spend a rainy day when you can't have the real thing.

i If you need a place to park and public restrooms, you can park at the intersection of 2nd and Spruce Streets in downtown Cannon Beach. This parking area is also directly across the street from the Cannon Beach Information Center.

EL MUNDO FOR MEN
231 North Hemlock St.
(503) 436-1002, (888) 662-4927
www.elmundoformen.com

El Mundo for men was doing Casual Friday long before anyone else; in 1975 the owner, George Vetter, was convincing college students that they should skip the necktie and mellow out. Now he carries a lot of attractive natural-fiber clothing for men; he also has quite a selection of joke T-shirts. When the beach look won't do, El Mundo's can also spiff you up in a dinner jacket by Ralph Lauren or Christian Dior; they have all sizes, including those for children.

GEPPETTO'S TOY SHOPPE
299 North Hemlock St.
(503) 436-2467

This shop is a longtime favorite of vacationers to Cannon Beach, and those families know that Geppetto's is a must-stop before a long car trip home. It specializes in entertaining and educational toys, and the folks who work there are imaginative about travel and rainy-day activities. Also noteworthy is the good selection of arts-

and-crafts kits appropriate for different ages and all the sand toys a child could ever want.

JUPITER'S RARE AND USED BOOKS
244 North Spruce St.
(503) 436-0549

Used bookstores are awfully fun, and Jupiter's is no exception. You can find that copy of Plato you were looking for or pick up last month's Stephen King novel, all for really great prices. And like many of the bookstores on the Coast, they feature local writers, especially hard-to-find editions of them. You'll also find some first editions.

i Large, full-service grocery and drug stores such as Safeway, Fred Meyer, or Wal-Mart tend to be concentrated in or near population hubs. If you're staying in an out-of-the-way place, keep this in mind so you don't have to drive 45 miles in the middle of the night to find toothpaste or aspirin.

M. SELLIN
215 North Hemlock St.
(503) 436-1572

This clothing shop for women features natural-fiber garb that is as stylish as it is comfortable. In addition to the wonderful dresses, skirts, trousers, and shirts, M. Sellin carries a good selection of fashionable shoes and jewelry. Recently, they have started featuring yummy-smelling skin care products too. M. Sellin is an institution here in Cannon Beach, and so is its sister store on Hawthorne in Portland.

PUPPY LOVE BY THE SEA DOG BOUTIQUE
271 North Hemlock St. #1
(503) 436-9800
www.puppylovebythesea.com

This friendly pup boutique lets you shop with your dog and features a wide assortment of canine apparel, doggie backpacks, float coats, collars, leashes, and gourmet dog treats.

Manzanita
MANZANITA NEWS AND ESPRESSO
500 Laneda Ave.
(503) 368-7450

Manzanita News is a dangerous and distracting heaven for magazine fanatics, who probably should stop reading them and get outdoors. But no one could break the habit with the 435 titles here to tempt them. Not only does the shop carry *Martha Stewart Living* and *Atlantic Monthly*, but it also carries the *Sun and Film Quarterly*. And there are lots of maps and newspapers and very inviting spaces to sit and read. Add to this the Portland Roasting Company coffee and the cookies, muffins, and scones by Temptations, a local baking company, and you might forget to go back out to the beach (we'd tell you how good the gingerbread scones were, only then there might not be any left for us).

MOTHER NATURE'S NATURAL FOODS
298 Laneda Ave. #1
(503) 368-5316

Mother Nature's has a cafe that serves delicious, seasonal organic food made right there, a fresh produce case, and organic wine. Mother Nature's is also a full-service natural foods store that sells vitamins, health supplements, beauty aids, cards, and gifts in addition to the groceries. The produce is excellent; they try to buy as much as they can from local producers. The cafe is great—one of few alternatives for a healthful lunch in Manzanita.

Tillamook
LATIMER CENTER GIFT SHOP
2105 Wilson River Loop Rd.
(503) 842-8622
www.latimerquiltandtextile.com

The Gift Shop at the Latimer Center helps to pay for the extraordinary conservation and study of the textile arts that the Latimer Center has undertaken. You can purchase patterns for Latimer-designed quilts, baskets, wall hangings, bags, and handmade papers. If you're a textile artist your-self, you can purchase Northwest plant fibers; if you'd like to become a textile artist, you can take classes. And this doesn't even count the works by local textile artists that you can purchase and take home with you.

Pacific City

MIGRATIONS ESPRESSO AND BOOKS
33105 Cape Kiwanda Dr., Suite 1
(503) 965-4661

So much more than a shop, this space is actually a coffee shop that features organic coffees and teas and delicious bakery things in addition to being a book and nature store. The bookstore has a wide assortment of books and magazines for vacationing travelers and serious readers, while the nature store carries everything you'll need when you put the book down and venture out on your own. Field guides, binoculars, knives, some rain gear, and day packs are among the fea-tured items; for backyard adventurers there are birdbaths and feeders. Sip some coffee while you look over your purchases and enjoy the lovely ocean view from this interesting store.

CENTRAL COAST

Like the North Coast, the Central Coast has enough variety in its shopping to keep it lively. Those who love shopping malls will like the Lincoln City Factory Stores and the Marketplace at Salishan. Those who adore exploring old-fashioned main street shopping will enjoy the Nye Beach area in Newport with its funky shops in Victorian buildings and the Old Town district of Florence. And all along US 101 you'll find little shops that will have you making U-turns.

Lincoln City

BOOK END BOOKS
4095 A Logan Rd.
(541) 994-9393

The perfect place to spend a rainy afternoon in Lincoln City, Book End offers free coffee to its customers, encourages browsing, and carries a wide selection of magazines and new books. It's also a good source for a miscellany of cards and CDs. Book End is a pleasant space; you may get so absorbed stocking up on beach reading that you'll forget to go to the beach to read it once the sun comes out.

THE FACTORY STORES AT LINCOLN CITY
1500 Southeast East Devils Lake Rd.
(541) 996-5000
www.tangeroutlet.com/lincolncity

Built to resemble a village, the Factory Stores at Lincoln City, which are at the intersection of Devils Lake Road and US 101, have lawns and benches and courtyards. It's pleasant and rare to encounter grass at an outlet mall; that alone makes this one worth a visit. Cooks will love visit-ing the Kitchen Collection and Le Gourmet Chef. You'll find a lot of great clothing deals at Eddie Bauer, Dress Barn, Coldwater Creek, Pendleton Woolen Mills, Gap Kids, and Gap Outlet. Other compelling reasons to shop here: outlets for Columbia Sportswear, Nike and Reebok.

JUDITH ANNE ANTIQUES
412 Southeast US 101
(541) 994-9912

Judith Anne Antiques is the place to go if you find your mouth watering at the idea of good dishes—without any food on them. She carries a great selection of china, art pottery, and jewelry. Some delicious-looking Victorian necklaces are available and from time to time she'll get her hands on a cameo. Here you'll also find American art pottery from Fiesta, Weller, Franciscan, Bauer, Roseville, and even Rookwood, as well as Bel-leek porcelain, older Royal Doulton, and other imports. And she has a number of interesting oyster plates. A good stop for collectors.

i Oregon has no sales tax, making shopping even more fun than usual.

Gleneden Beach

THE MARKETPLACE AT SALISHAN
7760 US 101 North
(541) 764-2371
(888) SALISHAN (725-4742)
(541) 764-3282
www.salishan.com

Shopping the Marketplace at Salishan brings many advantages—not only are there fabulous stores, but if you're staying at the Westin Salishan, you don't even need to leave the premises to see them. Start off at the Coast Roast Coffee Company for a cup of Joe and a pastry, then (after you've finished) begin your wandering. Le Domaine carries beautiful linens, accessories, and furniture for the beach house, while Hot Pots will outfit the kitchen. After you've dressed your house, dress yourself at The Sweater Shoppe specializing in hand-knit sweaters, hats, and jackets. The Wooden Duck carries toys, puzzles, and games for the little ones, and Scribbles offers a fine selection of writing paper so you can tell your friends at home what they're missing. Pick out a special Oregon wine at Wine and Romance.

Newport

There are two appealing areas for shopping in Newport, the waterfront and Nye Beach. The waterfront has a selection of shops mostly geared toward tourists (everybody else down there is too hard at work to go shopping) but still worth visiting. If you're there, you can check out **Cat House** (which advertises "an unexpected variety of gifts from around the world for cats and their slaves"), 410 Southwest Bay Blvd. and **Northwest Kitchens**, 420 Southwest Bay Blvd., which stocks Oregon wines and gourmet food in addition to an ample supply of kitchen gadgets.

Turn off US 101 and drive toward the ocean anywhere from 6th to 2nd Streets in Newport, and you will run right into **Nye Beach,** the historic district that was the summering spot for well-to-do residents of the Willamette Valley and the home of a sanatorium run by Herbert Hoover's stepfather. People still summer here,

and you might say they come here for their mental health. Now in these blocks you will find the impressive **Newport Performing Arts Center** (777 West Olive St.) and the **Yaquina Art Center** (839 Northwest Beach Dr.), lovely hotels and inns, and some great shopping. The stores here are really delectable. The gift shop at the **The Sylvia Beach Hotel,** 267 Northwest Cliff, is worth checking out: It carries books, gifts, and cards. **Toujours Boutique,** 704 Northwest Beach Dr., has beach-stylish clothing in natural fibers. **Tsunami Ceramics,** 310 Northwest Coast St., has bisqueware ready for you to paint, as well as a potter's wheel and clay to play with—the perfect activity for a blustery coastal day. And then there is **Tea and Tomes,** 716 Northwest Beach Dr., which will appease your appetite for British imports and serve you tea as well. On the outskirts, at 156 Southwest Coast St., you'll find **Green Gables,** which is both a bed-and-breakfast inn and a coffee and bookstore featuring books for children, books on the Northwest, mass-market fiction, mysteries, science fiction, and Westerns.

CANYON WAY BOOKSTORE
1216 Southwest Canyon Way
(541) 265-8319

This independent bookstore has been feeding opinions, brains, and souls since the early 1970s and keeping the flame of thoughtful bookselling alive for coastal residents. In addition to the more than 30,000 titles in stock, Canyon Way Bookstore also carries interesting cards and calendars and an eclectic collection of CDs. They don't just feed your soul here, though; there is also a little restaurant for the rest of you. Don't miss this Newport institution.

CHEAP FRILLS
116 Southwest Coast Hwy. (US 101)
(541) 265-9588

You'll find really great vintage clothing at this shop, and these days really great vintage clothing is hard to come by. Some standouts are the collections of delicate, frothy lingerie and becoming Victorian hats. Also look for Victorian and Art Nouveau jewelry; it is worth the trip to search through these collections. Men may find suits, leather jackets, and funky ties.

COTTAGE GARDENWARE AT NYE BEACH
732 Northwest Beach Dr.
(541) 574-7706
Paradise for Martha Stewart fans: That sums up the atmosphere and product lines of this delightful shop. Look for fine tools, hats, and gloves; a variety of seeds; and wonderful garden themed gifts. But you don't have to actually have a garden to enjoy this shop; it also features a gorgeous selection of furniture and decorating items, beautifully displayed. Choose wisely and you can feel like you're in a garden without doing any of the work.

Yachats
LUNA SEA FISH HOUSE
153 Northwest Hwy. 101
(541) 547-4794, (888) 547-4794
www.lunaseafishhouse.com
The Luna is a tough old fishing boat built in 1925 and restored to picturesque working condition. The folks who own it process their own fish rather than selling it to a processor; that way the product is as fresh as possible. They marinate and smoke their catch right away, and the result is incredibly delicious smoked salmon, smoked tuna, and all kinds of cheeses and spreads. You can't get much fresher than this.

PLANET YACHATS
281 US 101 South
(541) 547-4410
www.planetyachats.net
Yachats really is sometimes like another planet, and for those times, check out Planet Yachats. This lapidary sells amazing crystals, minerals, and fossils for when you're feeling in tune with terrestrial forces. It also features beautiful jewelry made of polished stones. Planet Yachats is an inspired choice for unusual gifts for life's big ceremonies.

Old Town Florence
The Old Town district of Florence is a wonderful place to hang out. Attractions and public facilities, art galleries and antiques shops, food and drink, hotels, clothing stores, gift stores, bookshops, and specialty stores all combine to form an atmosphere that is charming and festive. It's much more than a shopping district; like all good market squares, it provides a center for village social life (even though it's not actually a square). It's a fun place to hang out, read the paper at a sidewalk or riverside cafe, and get caught up on the local news. Old Town is fun for visitors too. Wander leisurely through and watch the glassblowers make raindrops at the **Raindrop Factory,** 1278 Bay St., or watch a new movie at the vintage **Harbor Theater,** 1377 Bay St. Pick up a kite at **Catch the Wind,** 1250 Bay St. Finish up your day with a sternwheeler cruise on the Siuslaw at **Mo's,** 1436 Bay St.; have an ice cream at **BJ's,** 1441 Bay St.; and go home.

DIVINE DECADENCE
1297 Bay St.
(541) 997-7200
A scrumptious shop in Old Town Florence, Divine Decadence will incite drooling in the most dignified jewelry lover. Divine Decadence carries both costume jewelry and the real stuff, both modern and vintage confections. This is definitely a browsing store; also look here for vintage clothes, for gifts, and for other kinds of unclassifiable "eclectica." This shop is an excellent source for gifts for those you love, especially you.

GRAPE LEAF
1368 Bay St.
(541) 997-1646
This shop showcases regional wines but it also features an excellent selection of international wines. And it sells the accessories to go along with the wine: openers, good glassware, wine guides, and everything else you need to sample and compare. Grape Leaf sells high-end food and gifts as well—and you can try before you

buy at the charming riverside wine tasting room and deli.

LOVEJOY'S IMPORTS
195 Nopal
(541) 902-0502

Maybe it's all the rain, maybe it's the seaside, but something about the Oregon Coast reminds people of England. For those times when you'd rather be in Bristol, check out Lovejoy's Imports. There you'll find delicious English teas, gifts, and imported foods, as well as other edible delights from other parts of the world.

SOUTH COAST

The shopping areas on the South Coast are stretched out with miles of road separating them, though you'll sometimes find an interesting store in between centers of population. The major shopping areas are in Coos Bay/North Bend, Bandon, and Brookings. Coos Bay has a pedestrian-friendly, old-fashioned downtown area with charming street lamps. Near the Coos Art Museum, just up from the waterfront, this district sports a tidy, bustling Rite-Aid, cafes and pubs, and some shops worth seeing (see below). Bandon's Old Town district, just off US 101, is especially charming and popular; in addition to the many shops, with souvenirs and luxury items as well as books, gifts, and clothes, are funky diners and bars and a nice boardwalk along the harbor where you can get fresh seafood. Brookings has two main shopping areas, one along US 101 and one at the Port of Brookings (technically known as "Harbor"). To get there, take Harbor Drive west off US 101. Some excellent shops lie along the main strip of US 101 but they can be hard to spot, for it's an area that suffers from minimal sprawl. Still, there's a little core of buildings in the middle of town that provide a coherent shopping experience.

Coos Bay

HARVEST BOOK SHOPPE AND THE COFFEE CORNER
307 Central Ave.
(541) 267-5824

A friendly and wide-ranging bookstore in downtown Coos Bay and run by knowledgeable people, the Harvest Book Shoppe has everything from Robert Ludlum to Plato, Stephen King to Shakespeare. Especially notable are the works on Northwest and local history, culture, and natural history. The Harvest is a steady supporter of downtown Coos Bay and does all it can to increase knowledge about this richly historical area and the whole community. Stop there before or after a visit to the Coos Art Museum up the street.

THE OREGON CONNECTION
1125 First St.
(541) 267-7804
www.oregonconnection.com

This store features all kinds of gifts you can purchase made out of beautiful Oregon myrtlewood. This shop also features specialty foods that feature Oregon huckleberries and Marionberries. You'll find jams, preserves, salsa, syrups, and other delicious gourmet foods.

THREADS THAT BIND
120 Central Ave.
(541) 267-0749

This vigorous store provides all that the quilter needs to be in heaven. Lovely fabrics, helpful books, thread, and notions are all here so you can stock up for the winter. They carry a special collection of lighthouse quilt patterns based on lighthouses on the coasts of Oregon, Washington, and California. Threads That Bind is well connected, too, so they can set you up with sewing circles and lessons. They provide a machine quilting service, too, making life simple for you.

Bandon

BIG WHEEL GENERAL STORE
130 Baltimore St.
(541) 347-3719
www.bandonbythesea.com/bigwheel.htm
Few stores are like this one, which supplies the weary tourist with delicious fudge and the locals with pet food. The Big Wheel General Store is in an old building with a wide-planked floor that creaks delightfully as you walk around to look at the free driftwood museum or decide whether you should buy a wooden lighthouse, marbles, or shells. In addition to many tourist items, the Big Wheel also sells some old stuff—farm implements, glass, and other oddities—and some practical things like dog flea spray. There is a very decent selection of guidebooks and field guides.

THE COBBLER'S BENCH
110 2nd St.
(541) 347-9012
www.bandonbythesea.com/cobblar.htm
Wolf Daniel Braun has been a leathersmith since 1977, and he branched out and opened the Cobbler's Bench in 1985. He will resole your Justins or custom design a wallet. But he'll also provide you with ready-made leather products from a variety of respected suppliers, a number of them from Oregon. The Cobbler's Bench has a notably good selection of belts, briefcases, and bags. They carry Birkenstocks and other name brands and an attractive selection of men's and women's clothing and Native American jewelry. This is an excellent store for personal gifts for women and men.

CRANBERRY SWEETS
280 Southeast First St.
(541) 347-9475
The sweets here are made with cranberries and other local products. (There are plush toys and gifts, too, to round out the picture.) Every kind of cranberry candy you could imagine is here, along with other fruit candies and chocolates, and they're all handmade and delicious. The most renowned, and deservedly so, are the chewy jelly candies called Cranberry Nut. Try the cheddar cheese fudge.

FORGET ME KNOTS QUILTING & NEEDLEWORK
125 Baltimore Ave.
(541) 347-9021
Our spies tell us that quilting is very big in the South Coast area, perhaps, the theory goes, because winters can be long and lonely and quilting brings people together. When they do get together, chances are it's at this homey shop to pick up supplies. Patterns, notions, fabric paint, and even precut squares are all available here.

HARBOR LIGHTS BOOKS
175 Second St.
(541) 347-2371
www.bandonbythesea.com/harbor_b.htm
A delightfully musty little bookshop that specializes in used books and book searches, Harbor Lights carries a broad selection of usefully organized materials. You can find things here that are hard to find in cities, where the bookstores are gleaned more thoroughly. Harbor Lights seems to prompt interesting conversations between strangers; it must be the wide selection of books in a small space.

OREGON COAST JAMS
48053 US 101
(888) 795-1719
www.oregonjam.com
Oregon Coast Jams makes every kind of jam imaginable—hot pepper, pumpkin, pomegranate, even jelly made out of beer. They specialize in local fruit jams, though—cranberry, wild huckleberry, wild blackberry, and Marionberry are perennial favorites. They also make exceptional honeys (try the Lemon Blossom). They never use corn syrup or coloring. They're open every day except Christmas and they close early on Thanksgiving.

WINTER RIVER BOOKS
170 2nd St.
(541) 347-4111

This bookstore is bright and light, just the thing for a gray day. Leisurely browsing is required. Winter River carries best sellers and a number of sale books and remainders, and the selection is quite broad, from gardening to mysteries to classics. There's a good children's section and, like many bookstores on the Coast, a competent section of books about the Oregon Coast. Winter River also carries a nice selection of cards, crystals, music, and pottery, and they occasionally have author events.

Port Orford
TIMEWORN TREASURES
345 North Oregon St.
(541) 332-2046

This little gem is in an old house on US 101 just down the hill from the Castaway. The treasures are not too time-worn—they look good—but you'll find some Victorian furniture pieces; pretty, embroidered old linens; china dishes; memorabilia; and things like the glasses that gas stations gave away when you filled your tank

Gold Beach
GOLD BEACH BOOKS, BISCUIT COFFEEHOUSE AND ART GALLERY
29707 Ellensburg Ave.
(541) 247-2495
www.oregoncoastbooks.com

This fun store features over 50,000 books and also serves fresh coffee, smoothies, homemade bakery items and features art work for local artists.

Brookings
BANANA BELT TRADING COMPANY
654 Chetco Ave. (US 101)
(541) 469-6087, (877) 276-3141

The Banana Belt Trading Company is the place to go for the person who has everything, because you'll find something here that he definitely doesn't have. Oregon products—especially, but not exclusively, gourmet food items—are featured in this interesting and eclectic shop on Brookings's main strip. It carries an unusual assortment of souvenirs and gifts. There are some good aromatherapy products, fun T-shirts, leather goods, and the only risqué card collection in town.

BEACHFRONT GIFTS
16011 Boat Basin Rd.
(541) 469-8025

The mania for fudge on the South Coast is matched only by the mania for saltwater taffy on the North Coast. But after eating the fudge at Beachfront Gifts, you can see how a mania would develop. Beachfront Gifts sells T-shirts and other souvenirs, but the focus is on Oregon crafts and other products. This is an excellent gift shop; it has everything from plastic pails and shovels for your kids to fine baubles for you, and everything is attractively displayed.

BOOK DOCK
16364 Lower Harbor Rd.
(541) 469-6070, (800) 230-3591

The Book Dock is in the Port of Brookings Harbor and it takes advantage of its pleasant location by offering fireside chats, book discussions, and author events in addition to its new and used books. The fireside chats are favorite events: Local experts are asked to present talks on topics of interest (like lighthouses or whales), tea is served, and the place is jammed with interested listeners. The Book Dock sells music and gifts in addition to their books; books on Oregon history and natural history are especially well represented but there are also lots of mysteries and other vacation reading.

FLORA PACIFICA
15447 Ocean View Dr.
(800) 877-9741
www.florapacifica.com

Flora Pacifica is the place for flowers: fresh, dried,

preserved, or wreathed. They supply cut flowers and bouquets, as well as plants for landscaping or potting, from their own 11-acre farm. They also grow and sell herbs; books, crystals, and floral arts and crafts are for sale as well. The wreaths, swags, garlands, potpourri, and other dried flowers are extraordinary, as are the flower arrangements—these are the reasons that brides and businesses alike flock to Flora Pacifica. The shop also maintains an experimental viewing garden and offers classes on flower arranging, herb growing, wreath making, and more.

WORDS AND PICTURES
407 Oak St.
(541) 469-7067
Words and Pictures is both an art gallery and a bookstore. The bookstore part, which also sells alluring gifts and CDs, features a good range of new books, "from best sellers to special treasures," in the words of owner Pat Stewart. Some highlights of her collection are pleasantly crowded shelves of cooking and gardening books, as well as an excellent children's book section. You can also find audio books—occasionally good bargains are to be found among them. After stocking up on best sellers and blank books, wander into the next room and look at the art.

OREGON LIGHTHOUSES

Oregon's lighthouses are a direct link to our maritime past, and there are nine lighthouses along the coastline that were built close to estuaries or major headlands between 1870 and 1896 as dictated by the former U.S. Lighthouse Board. The U.S. Corps of Engineers built the lighthouses and maintenance of the lighthouses was given to the Coast Guard. In the 1960s, the Coast Guard installed automated beacons in the lighthouses and ownership of many of the lighthouses was handed over to state and federal agencies. This prompted a movement to protect and preserve these beautiful historic structures. All the lighthouses on the Oregon Coast are on the National Register of Historic Places and many are open for tours.

TILLAMOOK ROCK LIGHTHOUSE
Cannon Beach

Nicknamed "Terrible Tilly," the Tillamook Rock Lighthouse stands 62 feet high and rests on a large chunk of basalt rock that is more than a mile offshore from Tillamook Head. This lighthouse was built in 1881 and acted as a lifesaving beacon for ships headed for the Columbia River. The lighthouse is privately owned and does not allow public access. You can view this lighthouse from Indian Beach at Ecola State Park located 3 miles north of Cannon Beach. There is a $3 day use fee at this state park and you need to purchase a day use permit at the entrance station.

CAPE MEARES LIGHTHOUSE
Tillamook
(800) 551-6949
www.capemeareslighthouse.org

The 38-foot-tall Cape Meares Lighthouse was built in 1890 and is the shortest lighthouse tower on the Oregon Coast. The lighthouse is open daily May through September and on the weekends in October, March, and April. A gift shop is located in the lighthouse and is open from 11 a.m. to 4 p.m. daily from May through September. This lighthouse is on a scenic headland in Cape Meares State Park, 10 miles west of Tillamook on the Three Capes Scenic Highway.

YAQUINA HEAD LIGHTHOUSE
Newport
(541) 574-3100

The Yaquina Head Lighthouse stands 93 feet tall and was commissioned in 1873. This lighthouse is the tallest on the Oregon Coast and was built to aid the navigation of ships entering Yaquina Bay. This lighthouse is located in the Yaquina Head Outstanding Natural Area 4 miles northwest of Newport off US 101. Drive north 3 miles on US 101 and turn left onto Lighthouse Drive. Drive 1 mile on Lighthouse Drive to the Yaquina Head Lighthouse parking area. Note there is a $5 entrance fee to enter this area, which has trails to tide pools, a rocky beach, and spectacular viewpoints. It is recommended that you begin your tour by stopping by the Interpretive Center that is located 0.7 mile from US 101 on Lighthouse Drive. The Interpretive Center has exhibits, video presentations, and hands-on displays about the geology and cultural and natural history of Yaquina Head. The Interpretive Center is open in the summer months from 10 a.m. to 6 p.m. and in the winter months from 10 a.m. to 4 p.m.

YAQUINA BAY LIGHTHOUSE AND MUSEUM
Newport
(541) 574-3100
www.yaquinalights.org

Commissioned for service from 1871 to 1874, the 40-foot-tall Yaquina Bay Lighthouse is one of the rare lighthouses on the Pacific Coast that was built with a Cape Cod style light keeper's house as part of its tower. Located in scenic Yaquina Bay State Park, this lighthouse—filled with period furniture and with great views from every window—is one of the most visited on the Oregon Coast. In addition, the bottom portion of the lighthouse houses a gift shop that has books on coastal lighthouses, wildlife, and much more. Visiting hours are from 11 a.m. to 5 p.m. daily from Memorial Day through Labor Day and from noon to 4 p.m. the rest of the year (weather permitting). Admission is free although donations are encouraged. The lighthouse is located in Yaquina Bay State Park at the north end of the Yaquina Bay Bridge off US 101 in Newport.

HECETA HEAD LIGHTHOUSE
Florence
(866) 547-3696
www.hecetaheadlighthouse.com
The 56-foot Heceta Head Lighthouse was commissioned in 1894 and rests on a rocky headland 205 feet above the ocean. Adjacent to the lighthouse is the Heceta House, the original light keeper's house, which was built in 1893 and now is operated as a bed-and-breakfast. The lighthouse can be accessed from the Heceta Head Lighthouse State Viewpoint parking area located 12 miles north of Florence on US 101 on the west side of the highway. There is a $3 day use fee at this site. You can purchase a permit from the automated pay station in the parking area. You can tour the lighthouse daily March through October from 11 a.m. to 5 p.m.

UMPQUA RIVER LIGHTHOUSE
Reedsport
(541) 271-4631
The 65-foot Umpqua River Lighthouse is located at the entrance to Winchester Bay and is adjacent to Umpqua Lighthouse State Park. This lighthouse was illuminated in 1894 and replaced an earlier lighthouse that was built on the north spit of the Umpqua River in 1857. You can get to the lighthouse by driving 6 miles south of Reedsport on US 101 to the Umpqua Lighthouse State Park entrance. Tours are available May 1 through September 30. Call for the updated days and times.

CAPE ARAGO LIGHTHOUSE
Coos Bay
(541) 756-0100
The 44-foot Cape Arago Lighthouse was commissioned in 1934 and is located 12 miles southwest of Coos Bay adjacent to Gregory Point. This lighthouse is the most recent lighthouse in service on the Coast and it replaced lighthouses that were built in 1866 and 1908. This lighthouse is not open to the public but it can be seen from trails at Sunset Bay State Park. To get to Sunset Bay State Park from US 101 in Coos Bay, follow the signs to Charleston Harbor and Ocean Beaches and drive on the Cape Arago Highway 12 miles southwest to the park.

COQUILLE RIVER LIGHTHOUSE
Bandon
(541) 347-2209
The Coquille River Lighthouse is located on the

For more information . . .

Contact these organizations for more information about coastal lighthouses:

Oregon Chapter of the U.S. Lighthouse Society
P.O. Box 600, Lakeside 97449
(541) 759-3920

Yaquina Lights, Inc.
P.O. Box 410, Newport 97365
(541) 574-3100

Friends of Cape Meares
P.O. Box 282, Oceanside 97134
(503) 842-5270

north bank of the Coquille River in Bullards Beach State Park. The lighthouse was illuminated in 1896 to help steer mariners across the hazardous bar. Interestingly, this lighthouse is powered by solar energy. The lighthouse is open year-round during daylight hours and you can tour the tower watch room by request. To get to the lighthouse, drive 2 miles north of Bandon on US 101 to the entrance to Bullards Beach State Park.

CAPE BLANCO LIGHTHOUSE
Port Orford
(541) 756-0100

The 59-foot tower of the Cape Blanco Lighthouse is located on Cape Blanco, the westernmost point in Oregon. The lighthouse is in Cape Blanco State Park. To reach Cape Blanco State Park drive 46 miles south of Coos Bay or 4 miles north of Port Orford on US 101 to the junction with Cape Blanco Road. Turn west and drive 5 miles on Cape Blanco Road to the state park entrance. For more information about Cape Blanco State Park, see The Great Outdoors chapter.

ATTRACTIONS

If you're a history buff, like to find unique and out-of-the-way places, and enjoy a variety of things to see and do, then this chapter is for you! In this chapter we've listed a wide range of attractions including museums and historic monuments, lighthouses, casinos, cheese factories, micro-breweries, wineries, interpretive areas, and a few other odds and ends. We've organized these attractions by region of the Coast—North, Central, and South—and then by city from north to south.

While we've done our best to make sure times and admission prices are up to date, we recommend that you call ahead to verify times and prices for the attractions listed. Also, many of the attractions in this chapter have seasonal hours and have longer, more extended hours usually from May 1 through September 30.

If you still want to find out more things to see and do on the amazing Coast, be sure to check out fun ideas in our other chapters on Kidstuff, Annual Events and Festivals, The Great Outdoors, and Day Trips.

NORTH COAST

Astoria

ASTORIA COLUMN
1 Coxcomb Dr.
(503) 325-2963
Built in 1926, the 125-foot Astoria Column rises prominently from its high vantage point from the top of Coxcomb Hill and offers outstanding views of the mouth of the Columbia River where it meets the Pacific Ocean, Mount Saint Helens, Youngs Bay, downtown Astoria, and the Astoria Bridge, which links Oregon and Washington. To reach the top of the column, you'll climb up a narrow 166-step spiral staircase to a viewing platform. The outside of the column features painted murals of the settlement and exploration of this area. The Astoria Column is open from 9 a.m. to dusk seven days a week.

COLUMBIA RIVER MARITIME MUSEUM
1792 Marine Dr.
(503) 325-2323
www.crmm.org
The Columbia River Maritime Museum is a 37,000-square-foot facility that celebrates the seafaring history of the Astoria area. The museum has seven galleries that include displays about the history of the salmon-packing industry, specifics on different types of boat design, and artifacts from the *Peter Iredale* shipwreck that occurred near the mouth of the Columbia in 1906. The museum is located at the edge of the scenic Columbia River and also has a dock where you can tour the lightship *Columbia*—a historic floating lighthouse. This museum also has some modern maritime artifacts from the *New Carissa*, a wood-chip freighter that ran aground off of Coos Bay in February of 1999. The museum is open 9:30 a.m. to 5 p.m. daily. The admission fee is $10 for adults; $8 for seniors 65 and up; $5 for children ages six to 17; and children under six are free. The museum is closed Thanksgiving and Christmas.

FLAVEL HOUSE
441 8th St.
(503) 325-2203
If you want to take a step back in time to view the wealthy lifestyle of shipping tycoon George Flavel, be sure to visit the Flavel House. This

Queen Ann Victorian-style mansion was finished in 1885 and from its three-story octagon tower you'll have outstanding views of downtown Astoria and the Columbia River. When you tour the inside of this magnificent house, you'll find winding staircases, Persian rugs, 14-foot ceilings, and exquisite fireplaces. You'll also find clothing displays, artwork, and other household items from this opulent era. The Flavel House is open daily from 10 a.m. to 5 p.m. from May through September and from 11 a.m. to 4 p.m. October through April. The admission price is $5 for adults, $4 for seniors and AAA members, $2 for children ages six to 17, and free for children six and under. This admission fee also includes entrance to the Heritage Center Museum and the Upper-town Fire Fighters Museum.

FORT CLATSOP NATIONAL MEMORIAL
92343 Fort Clatsop Rd.
(503) 861-2471
www.nps.gov
The Fort Clatsop National Memorial is administered by the National Park Service and is a memorial to the camp set up by Lewis and Clark, who spent the winter of 1805–06 in this area. The members of the expedition befriended the Clatsop Indians and decided to name their encampment after this resident Native American tribe. The national memorial is a reconstruction of the expedition's camp based on sketches made by Lewis and Clark. One of the main attractions at this memorial is the reenactment of the day-to-day activities of Lewis and Clark's party. Park rangers wearing 19th-century garb demonstrate how members of the expedition tanned hides; made candles, moccasins and clothing, jerky, canoes, and lead bullets; loaded muskets; used flint and steel to make fires; and much more. The memorial also has a visitor center adjacent to the fort with interesting displays that recount the events of the expedition, artifacts from the Clatsop Indians, and video and slide presentations. Well-maintained trails and picnic areas are also present at the memorial, making this a fun place to spend the day. Fort Clatsop is open every day year-round

except Christmas Day. The visitor center is open 9 a.m. to 5 p.m. from mid-September through mid-June and from 9 a.m. to 6 p.m. from mid-June through mid-September. Admission prices are $3 for those 16 and older or $5 per car.

HERITAGE CENTER MUSEUM
1618 Exchange St.
(503) 325-2203
The Heritage Museum is made up of two stories of exhibits that explore the history and the cultural diversity of the Astoria area. Several galleries in the museum contain weapons, tools, photos, and other mementos depicting Astoria's colorful past. An entire room explores the rich history of the Clatsop tribe. The museum is open daily in the summer from 10 a.m. to 5 p.m. and 11 a.m. to 4 p.m. in the Winter. The admission price is $4 for adults, $3 for seniors and AAA members, $2 for children ages six to 17, and free for children six and under. This admission fee includes entrance to the Flavel House and the Uppertown Fire Fighters Museum (see the write-ups in this chapter).

UPPERTOWN FIREFIGHTERS MUSEUM
2986 Marine Dr.
(503) 325-2203
This museum houses a fine collection of vintage fire fighting equipment including horse-drawn and motorized vehicles that were in service from 1877 to 1921 as well as an interesting collection of fire extinguishers and photos from some of Astoria's most devastating fires. The museum is open 10 a.m. to 2 p.m. Wednesday through Friday and 10 a.m. to 3 p.m. on Saturday. Admission is $4 for adults, $3 for seniors and AAA members, $2 for children ages six to 17, and free for children six and under. This admission fee also includes entrance to the Flavel House and the Heritage Center Museum.

Seaside

THE PROMENADE PROM STREET
(503) 738-6391
Seaside is famous for its concrete boardwalk, known as "The Promenade," which parallels the

Pacific Ocean along an endless sandy beach. When you walk on the promenade, you'll see miles of flat, sandy beach, bikers, skaters, and other visitors enjoying the view. This spot is a classic tourist trap, but this adds to its charm. Benches and restrooms are present along this 1.5-mile boardwalk. You can get to the Promenade by turning west onto Avenue A from US 101 in downtown Seaside and following it west until you reach Prom Street. Expect crowds during the height of the summer months and be patient, because finding a parking spot can prove to be challenging.

SEASIDE HISTORICAL MUSEUM
570 Necanicum Dr.
(503) 738-7065
www.seasidemuseum.org

The Seaside Historical Museum has many informative displays that document the history of the Seaside area beginning with Native American artifacts and moving on to displays from the 19th century. An antique print shop display demonstrates how newspapers were printed at the turn of the 19th century, and a display of century-old fire fighting equipment shows how firefighters equipped themselves. Next to the museum is a beach cottage display called "The Butterfield Cottage." This cottage is a wonderful restoration of one of the original beach cottages in Seaside at the beginning of the 19th century and gives you a feel for what it was like to live in a beach town in a simpler time. The museum is open 10 a.m. to 4 p.m. Monday through Saturday and noon to 3 p.m. on Sunday mid-March through October 31. From November 1 through mid-March, the museum is open noon to 3 p.m. daily. The admission charge is $3 for adults, $2 for seniors age 62 and older, $1 for students, and children under the age of six are admitted free.

Cannon Beach

HAYSTACK ROCK
(503) 436-2623

Located 0.5 mile south of downtown Cannon Beach, 235-foot Haystack Rock can be accessed by parking in downtown Cannon Beach and walking west on Harris Street to the beach and then walking 0.5 mile south. Haystack Rock is part of the Oregon Islands Wildlife Refuge and is an important nesting site for pigeon guillemots, tufted puffins, pelagic cormorants, and western gulls. At the base of this monolith are rocky tide pools that are fun to explore. You may see bright green sea anemones, orange starfish, purple crabs, chitons, and limpets.

Tillamook

BLUE HERON CHEESE COMPANY
2001 Blue Heron Dr.
(503) 842-8281, (800) 275-0639
www.blueheronoregon.com

You can taste fine wines and cheese at the Blue Heron Cheese Company. Specialty cheeses such as Brie and Camembert are popular, and this company also sells specialty fruit products, mustard, honey, and jams. The Blue Heron Cheese Company is open from 9 a.m. to 6 p.m. October through February and from 8 a.m. to 8 p.m. March through September.

LATIMER QUILT AND TEXTILE CENTER
2105 Wilson River Loop Rd.
(503) 842-8622
www.latimerquiltandtextile.com

A fine collection of pioneer quilts can be seen at the Latimer Quilt and Textile Center. The center is housed in the historic Maple Leaf School and features a research library. Demonstrations on quilting, rug making, basketry, spinning, and weaving are also given at the center. The center is open 10 a.m. to 5 p.m. Tuesday through Saturday and noon to 4 p.m. Sunday (March 1 through October 31). Admission is $3 for adults, children under age six are admitted free. For groups of ten or more, admission is $2 each.

TILLAMOOK AIR MUSEUM
6030 Hangar Rd.
(503) 842-1130
www.tillamookair.com

The Tillamook Air Museum features more than

two dozen vintage aircraft that are housed in a World War II blimp hangar. Some examples of planes you'll see at this interesting museum are the B-25 Mitchell Bomber, A-26 Invader, Mk-8 Spitfire, FM-2 Wildcat, Mig-17, P-47, and T-6 Texan. The museum also features a 1940s-style cafe, gift shop, theater, and exhibits that display World War II artifacts. To get to the museum, drive 2 miles south of Tillamook on US 101 to a blinking yellow light. Turn left onto Long Prairie Road and follow the signs to the museum. The museum is open from 9 a.m. to 5 p.m. daily. The museum is closed Thanksgiving and Christmas Day. Admission is $7.50 for adults and seniors, and $4 for children ages six to 17. Children five and under are free.

TILLAMOOK CHEESE FACTORY
4175 US 101 North
(503) 815-1300
www.tillamookcheese.com

Tillamook Cheese factory makes some of the finest cheddar cheese in the world. Tillamook County has a mild climate and plenty of moisture to support large herds of Holstein, Guernsey, and Jersey cows that produce fresh, sweet milk. When you visit the Tillamook Cheese Factory, you can get a first-hand glimpse at how the cheese is actually made. A glass viewing area lets you watch the master cheese makers at work. In addition, you can learn about the history of cheese making in Tillamook County. This facility also makes high-quality butter, ice cream, and cheese spreads. If you want to taste-test some ice cream, visit the ice-cream counter, or if you want to purchase their products and take some souvenirs home, check out the gift shop. The Tillamook Cheese Factory is located 2 miles north of Tillamook on US 101 on the east side of the highway. It is open 8 a.m. to 6 p.m. October through May and 8 a.m. to 8 p.m. June through September. Admission is free.

TILLAMOOK PIONEER MUSEUM
2106 2nd St.
(503) 842-4553
www.tcpm.org

The Tillamook Pioneer Museum is located in the old courthouse and features an interesting mix of exhibits that are worth checking out. The museum has displays that give the history of the Tillamook tribe; a rock and mineral collection; a pioneer home and workshop; replicas of early automobiles; a natural science display of shorebirds and waterfowl; beeswax candles from a 17th-century shipwreck; and carved stones that are thought to be related to a buried treasure at the base of Neahkahnie Mountain. Travel and history books about the Tillamook area are available in the museum's bookstore. The museum is open 10 a.m. to 4 p.m. Tuesday through Saturday. Admission is $3 for adults, $2.50 for seniors 62 and older, 50 cents for children ages 12 to 17, and kids under 12 are free.

Pacific City
CAPE KIWANDA

Cape Kiwanda is a golden sandstone headland sculpted by the frothy ocean waves of the Pacific and is located at Pacific City. Pacific City is 25 miles south of Tillamook and 20 miles north of Lincoln City off US 101 on the Three Capes Scenic Loop. Pacific City is most well known for its fleet of dory boats. Dory boats are flat-bottomed fishing boats that are launched off the flat, sandy beach at the base of Cape Kiwanda. Locals still launch these boats into the calm morning surf to fish for halibut, lingcod, and other commercial fish species that are plentiful around offshore Haystack Rock. If you want to experience fishing from a dory boat, call Haystack Fishing, owned by Joe & Wendy Hay, (866) 965-7555; www .haystackfishing.com. This state-licensed outfitter offers chartered trips where you can catch halibut, sturgeon, salmon, and lingcod. If you just want to look and not catch, this outfitter also offers chartered whale-watching trips. Many visitors come to Cape Kiwanda beach to watch the dory boats ride the ocean waves back into shore and come to a sliding stop on the sand. Mixed in with the dory fleet, you will also see surfers and ocean kayakers playing in the waves. Walk along Kiwanda Beach at the base of Cape Kiwanda and investigate the rocky tide pools that are home to anemones, sea stars, mussels, and hermit crabs. You may also find sand dollars, mussel shells, and other beach treasures by walking along the flat, sandy beach south from Cape Kiwanda. If you like hiking up steep sand dunes, you can hike to the top of Cape Kiwanda from Cape Kiwanda beach. The soft, sandy, strenuous trek to the top of Cape Kiwanda is well worth the effort. You will have spectacular views of Haystack Rock, Nestucca Bay to the south, and Cape Lookout to the north. Kids can spend hours climbing, jumping, and running down the face of this expansive sand dune. A public parking area and restrooms are available at Cape Kiwanda beach. If you want to try a local microbrew, check out the Pelican Pub & Brewery located adjacent to the public parking area.

CENTRAL COAST

Lincoln City

ALDER HOUSE II
611 South Immonen Rd.
(541) 994-6485
www.alderhouse.com
Alder House II is a glassblowing studio that welcomes visitors to view the ancient art of turning molten glass into vases, bowls, paperweights, and so on. The studio is open from 10 a.m. to 5 p.m. March 15 through the end of November. The studio is located 4 miles south of Lincoln City off US 101 on Immonen Road. If you are coming from the south, drive 0.5 mile past the entrance to Salishan Lodge on US 101 and turn right on Immonen Road. If you are coming from the north through Lincoln City on US 101, you'll cross the Siletz River Bridge and you'll see Immonen Road approximately 0.5 mile from the end of the bridge. Turn left and the studio entrance is approximately 0.75 mile from US 101.

CHINOOK WINDS CASINO
1777 Northwest 44th St.
(888) CHI-NOOK (244-6665)
www.chinookwindscasino.com

Chinook Winds Casino is owned and operated by the Confederated Tribes of the Siletz Indians of Oregon and is packed full of fun activities. The inside decor of the casino is filled with wood beams that reflect its rustic outdoor theme, a pond with a cascading waterfall, and great views of the Pacific Ocean. The casino is 20,000 square feet in size and contains convention facilities, guest rooms, and gaming areas for blackjack, Caribbean stud poker, craps, roulette, keno, bingo, and slot machines. Complimentary Starbucks coffee and soft drinks are also available to visitors. The casino also has a gift shop, day-care center, and video arcade, as well as three restaurants. If you are staying at a local Lincoln City motel or RV Park, Chinook Winds offers a complimentary shuttle service to and from the facility you are staying at. You can request shuttle service between 9 a.m. and 1 a.m. by calling (541) 921-1652. This casino also attracts well-known entertainers such as Kenny Loggins, the Beach Boys, and Julio Iglesias.

NORTH LINCOLN COUNTY MUSEUM
4907 Southwest US 101
(541) 996-6614
www.northlincolncountyhistoricalmuseum .org
The North Lincoln County Museum has exhibits and artifacts that depict the lives of the first homesteaders that came to the Lincoln City area. Exhibits of an early day classroom, bedroom, and kitchen with period pieces and handmade furniture can be seen. Native American artifacts and logging implements are also present in this museum. Admission is $2 per person over age 12. Children 12 and under are $1. Families are admitted for $5. The museum is open noon to 5 p.m. Wednesday through Sunday from May 15 to October 15. During the winter months, October 16 through May 14, the museum is open noon to 5 p.m. Wednesday through Saturday. The museum is closed December 15 through January 31 and major holidays.

Grand Ronde

SPIRIT MOUNTAIN CASINO

27100 Southwest Salmon River Hwy.

(800) 760-7977

www.spirit-mountain.com

Spirit Mountain Casino is owned by the Confederated Tribes of the Grand Ronde Community of Oregon. This facility on Highway 18 is more than 90,000 square feet and houses a casino (smoking and nonsmoking) with 1,100 slot machines, craps tables, roulette tables, blackjack tables, Let It Ride poker tables, Pai Gow poker tables, and a Big 6 Wheel. In addition to the fun gaming activities, the casino has the 100-room Spirit Mountain Lodge, a SuperPlay Kids Club that provides supervision for children from the ages 18 months to 12 years, four restaurants, and first-class entertainment. Spirit Casino is open twenty-four hours a day, seven days a week, all year round.

Otter Rock

FLYING DUTCHMAN WINERY

915 1st St.

(541) 765-2553

www.dutchmanwinery.com

This winery produces fine Pinot Noir, Chardonnay, and Pinot Gris wines. The winery is located in a spectacular setting overlooking the ocean and has picnic facilities. The winery also features a one-of-a-kind gift shop where you can find unique wine-related gifts, nautical items, and original art pieces by featured Oregon artists. The winery is open from 11 a.m. to 6 p.m. June through October and from 11 a.m. to 5 p.m. the rest of year. They offer free samples of all their fine wines.

i If you are traveling with your pet, remember not to leave him locked in the car in hot weather—it only takes a few minutes before he can die of heat exhaustion. Also, always carry a leash with you and plastic bags. Many attractions on the Oregon Coast require that your dog be leashed and that you pick up and dispose of your pet's waste.

Newport

HATFIELD MARINE SCIENCE CENTER

2030 Southeast Marine Science Dr.

(541) 867-0100

http://hmsc.orst.edu/visitor

The Hatfield Marine Science Center offers a variety of displays that give you a closer look at the plants and animals that live on the Oregon Coast. You'll find tide pools filled with colorful starfish, sea anemones, sea urchins, and mollusks, and one of the main attractions is a display with a large octopus that often captivates kids. A whale skeleton gives you an idea of how large these mammals really are and informative marine science films also further educate you about Northwest marine life. Be sure to visit the bookstore to find educational books on marine science, Oregon history, and wildlife, as well as games and puzzles, gifts, posters, videos, and DVDs. You can also hike on the 1-mile paved Estuary Trail that begins on the left side of the chain-link fence on the south side of the parking lot. The center is open Thursday through Monday from 10 a.m. to 5 p.m. May through September and during whale watch weeks. Call ahead to verify dates and times. Closed Thanksgiving and Christmas. Admission is by donation.

LINCOLN COUNTY HISTORICAL SOCIETY MUSEUMS

545 Southwest 9th St.

(541) 265-7509

Be sure to stop and explore two museums run by the Lincoln County Historical Society. The Log Cabin museum contains maritime displays, a logging display, and exhibits that contain Siletz Indian artifacts such as beaded robes, headdresses, baskets, and tools. Adjacent to the museum is the Burrows House, which was originally a boarding house and now displays a collection of household items and furniture from the early part of the 20th century. You should also browse through the bookstore, which features many local history titles. The museum is open from 10 a.m. to 5 p.m. Tuesday through Sunday (June to September).

They are open 11 a.m. to 4 p.m. Tuesday through Sunday the rest of the year. Admission is free although donations are encouraged.

OREGON COAST AQUARIUM
2820 Southeast Ferry Slip Rd.
(541) 867-3474
www.aquarium.org
The Oregon Coast Aquarium is a special place that everyone should visit. This aquarium contains several indoor and outdoor displays about Northwest plant and animal marine life. One of the most popular displays is the jellyfish tank—dozens of beautiful jellyfish swim freely in a circular tank in the middle of a large room filled with huge aquarium displays. Another favorite is the touch tank where you can touch tidal pool creatures such as sea anemones, starfish, and other mollusks. The outside displays are just as interesting. You can view California sea otters, harbor seals, and sea lions and walk through an outdoor aviary where you can watch tufted puffins, pigeon guillemots, common murres, and other seabirds swimming and feeding in a natural environment. The Passages of the Deep exhibit lets you view three underwater habitats. As you walk through a clear acrylic tunnel, you'll have a close-up view of a southern Oregon reef; Halibut Flats, which introduces you to bottom-dwelling fish; and the Open Sea, which features large sharks, salmon, and bat rays. A crowd favorite is the sea otter display that holds 65,000 gallons of seawater and offers five viewing points where you can watch the otters feeding, swimming, or playing. Trails outside the aquarium lead through gardens of native plants with interpretive signs. The aquarium also has a bookstore and cafe. The aquarium is open from 10 a.m. to 5 p.m. daily from mid-September through the end of May and 9 a.m. to 6 p.m. June through mid-September. Admission is $14.95 for ages 13 to 64, seniors 65 and older are $12.95, children ages three to 12 are $9.45, and children age two and under are free.

Waldport
ALSEA BAY BRIDGE HISTORICAL INTERPRETIVE CENTER
(541) 563-2002
Stop at this interpretive center to learn about the history of travel routes on the Oregon Coast beginning with Indian trails and leading to road routes. Photos of different coastal bridges are on display and there is also a model of the Alsea Bay Bridge. Located at the southern end of the Alsea Bay Bridge off US 101, the center is open from 9 a.m. to 4 p.m. daily from Memorial Day through Labor Day and from 9 a.m. to 4 p.m. Wednesday through Sunday during the rest of the year. Admission is free.

Yachats
CAPE PERPETUA INTERPRETIVE CENTER
(541) 547-3289
www.newportnet.com/capeperpetua
The Cape Perpetua Interpretive Center is located 3 miles south of Yachats off US 101 on the east side of the highway. This center provides you with a wealth of information about coastal ecology, coastal tides and weather, whale migration, and exhibits about the Alsea tribe. You can also pick up a trail brochure that describes all the trails in the Cape Perpetua area. The center has a bookstore that has a good collection of titles on local history. The center is open from 9 a.m. to 6 p.m. daily from May to September and from 10 a.m. to 4 p.m. on Saturday and Sunday from October through April.

SEA LION CAVES
91560 US 101
(541) 547-3111
www.sealioncaves.com
When you visit Sea Lion Caves, you'll descend 208 feet in an elevator to an observation point about 50 feet above a large sea grotto where sea lions gather in large groups and reverberate their raucous barks in a large natural amphitheater. The lions are present in this rocky cave in the fall and winter months and during the rest of the

Chambers of Commerce/Visitor Centers

Be sure to stop by one of the following chamber of commerce offices or visitor centers for the area you are visiting. The helpful staff at these centers can provide you with information on things to see and do and with brochures and coupons for attractions and meals.

Astoria/Warrenton Chamber of Commerce
111 West Marine Dr., Astoria,
(800) 875-6807,
www.oldoregon.com

Bandon Chamber of Commerce
300 Southeast Second St., Bandon,
(541) 347-9616, www.bandon.com

Bay Area Chamber of Commerce
145 Central Ave., Coos Bay,
(800) 824-8486,
www.oregonsadventurecoast.com

Brookings-Harbor Chamber of Commerce
16330 Lower Harbor Rd., Brookings,
(800) 535-9469, www.brookingsor.com

Cannon Beach Chamber of Commerce
207 North Spruce, Cannon Beach,
(503) 436-2623, www.cannonbeach.org

Charleston Information Center
P.O. Box 5735, Charleston 97420,
Boat Basin and Cape Arago Highway,
(800) 824-8486

Coquille Chamber of Commerce
119 North Birch, Coquille, (541) 396-3414,
www.coquillechamber.com

Depoe Bay Chamber of Commerce
70 Northeast US 101, Depoe Bay,
(541) 765-2889,
www.depoebaychamber.org

Florence Area Chamber of Commerce
270 US 101, Florence, (541) 997-3128,
www.florencechamber.com

Garibaldi Chamber of Commerce
235 Garibaldi Ave., Garibaldi,
(503) 322-0301, www.garibaldioregon.com

Gold Beach Chamber of Commerce/ Visitors Center
29279 Ellensburg Ave., #3, Gold Beach,
(800) 525-2334,
www.goldbeachchamber.com

Lincoln City Visitors & Convention Bureau
801 Southwest US 101, Lincoln City,
(800) 452-2151, www.oregoncoast.org

Myrtle Point Chamber of Commerce
424 5th St., Myrtle Point,
(541) 572-2626

year they occupy the offshore rocks. Note that you access the elevator through the gift shop. This Oregon Coast attraction is sometimes called an overrated tourist trap, but is worth a stop if you are curious. Admission prices are $8 for those age 16 and up, $4.50 for children between ages 6 and 15, and children age five and under are free. Visiting hours are 9 a.m. to 6 p.m. July and August and 9 a.m. to 3:30 p.m. the rest of the year. Sea Lion Caves is located 10 miles north of Florence on US 101.

Florence

SIUSLAW PIONEER MUSEUM
85294 US 101 South
(541) 997-7884

Located in a historic church, the Siuslaw Pioneer Museum contains a good collection of artifacts from the Siuslaw tribe. In addition, there are exhibits depicting the early life of those who settled in this area including a kitchen exhibit from the beginning of the 20th century. The museum is open noon to 4 p.m. Tuesday through Sunday. Admission $3. Children and museum members are admitted for free.

Nehalem Bay Area Chamber of Commerce/Visitors Center
425 Nehalen Blvd., Nehalem,
(877) 368-5100,
www.nehalembaychamber.com

Nestucca Valley Chamber of Commerce
P.O. Box 75, Cloverdale 97112,
(503) 392-3445

Newport Chamber of Commerce
555 Southwest Coast Hwy., Newport,
(800) 262-7844,
www.newportchamber.org

Oregon Coast Visitors Association
137 Northeast 1st St., Newport
(888) 628-2101,
www.visittheoregoncoast.com

Pacific City Chamber of Commerce
P.O. Box 331, Pacific City 97135,
(503) 965-6161, www.pacificcity.net

Port Orford Chamber of Commerce
520 Jefferson & US 101, Port Orford,
(541) 332-8055,
www.portorfordoregon.com

Reedsport/Winchester Bay Chamber of Commerce
Junction of US 101 and Oregon Highway 38,
Reedsport, (800) 247-2155,
www.reedsportcc.org

Rockaway Beach Chamber of Commerce
103 South 1st St., Rockaway Beach,
(503) 355-8108, www.rockawaybeach.net

Seaside Visitors Bureau
7 North Roosevelt, Seaside,
(888) 306-2326, www.seasideor.com

Tillamook Chamber of Commerce
3705 US 101 North, Tillamook,
(503) 842-7525, www.tillamookchamber.org

Toledo Chamber of Commerce
311 Northeast 1st St., Toledo,
(541) 336-3183

Waldport Chamber of Commerce & Visitors Center
620 Northwest Spring St., Waldport,
(541) 563-2133

Yachats Area Chamber of Commerce & Visitors Center
241 US 101, Yachats,
(800) 929-0477, www.yachats.org

Reedsport

DEAN CREEK ELK VIEWING AREA
(541) 888-5515

Learn more about the magnificent Roosevelt elk by stopping at this interpretive area to read the interesting facts about these beautiful animals—best of all you get to see a herd of 100 elk that feed in the adjacent meadow. Other wildlife residents you may see in this area include black-tailed deer, osprey, blue herons, and Canada geese. The best viewing times are early morning and evening. The interpretive area is located 3 miles east of Reedsport on Highway 38.

OREGON DUNES VISITOR CENTER
855 Hwy. Ave.
(541) 271-3611

The Oregon Dunes Visitor Center is a must-stop to find out about all the activities available in the Oregon Dunes National Recreational Area. The center has a film that gives you an interesting look into dune formation and numerous brochures that describe plant and animal life, hiking opportunities, and information on off-road vehicle use and recommended places to camp. Many interpretive programs are offered during the summer months. The center is open from

8 a.m. to 4:30 p.m. Monday through Friday and from 10 a.m. to 4 p.m. Saturday and Sunday from May 28 through Labor Day. During the rest of the year, the center is open 8 a.m. to 4:30 p.m. Monday through Friday.

SOUTH SLOUGH ESTUARY INTERPRETIVE CENTER
61907 Seven Devils Rd.
(541) 888-5558
This interpretive center offers a first-hand glance at an estuary ecosystem. The center is located adjacent to a large estuary that is filled with a variety of shorebirds and other wildlife. Several interpretive trails lead you through the rich maze of life that is present here. The center is open Monday through Saturday from 8:30 a.m. to 4:30 p.m. from Memorial Day weekend through Labor Day weekend and from 8:30 a.m. to 4:30 p.m. Monday through Friday the rest of the year.

UMPQUA DISCOVERY CENTER MUSEUM
409 Riverfront Way
(541) 271-4816
Visit this museum to learn about the culture of the Umpqua Indians and early explorers and the natural history of the Umpqua River Valley. The center is open from 9 a.m. to 5 p.m. daily from June 1 through September 30 and from 10 a.m. to 4 p.m. the rest of the year. Call for current admission prices.

SOUTH COAST

North Bend

COOS COUNTY HISTORICAL MUSEUM
1220 Sherman Ave.
(541) 756-6320
www.cooshistory.org
This museum contains a diverse collection of artifacts and exhibits that tell the history of the Coos tribe as well as those who originally settled here. You'll find intricately beaded aprons, ceremonial robes, baskets, and shells, as well as finely chiseled arrowheads. You will also find pioneer implements and artifacts from the area's prominent shipping past. The museum is open 10 a.m. to 4 p.m. Tuesday through Saturday. Closed on holidays. Admission is $2 for adults and $1 for children ages 7 to 11.

Coos Bay

OREGON CONNECTION HOUSE OF MYRTLEWOOD
1125 South 1st St.
(541) 267-7804, (800) 255-5318
www.oregonconnection.com
If you want to see how myrtlewood souvenirs and other products are produced, stop by the House of Myrtlewood, take a free factory tour, and view a 12-minute video that shows the production of bowls, clocks, and other myrtlewood souvenirs. A gift shop sells the items made in the factory as well as other Oregon-made products. Business hours are 9 a.m. to 5 p.m. Monday through Saturday and 11 a.m. to 4 p.m. on Sunday.

Bandon

THE WOOL COMPANY
990 2nd St.
(541) 347-2912
www.woolcompany.com
You'll be impressed by the inventory of wool products in this unique spinning, knitting, and weaving shop. You'll find natural fiber yarns, books, equipment, dyes, fibers, buttons, and patterns. The shop also offers classes and individual lessons. The Wool Company is open from 9 a.m. to 5 p.m. Monday through Saturday.

Port Orford

HUGHES HOUSE
91814 Cape Blanco Rd.
(541) 332-6774
www.hugheshouse.org
Built in 1898 by Patrick Hughes, the 11-room, two-story Victorian-style house was built out of old-growth Port Orford cedar at a cost of $3,800.

This Victorian mansion is open for tours from 10 a.m. to 3:30 p.m. Tuesday through Sunday during the summer and is filled with delightful antique furniture and old photos depicting the life of the former 1,000-acre dairy ranch that the house sits on. The Hughes House also features a gift shop that carries cranberry glass and teapots, in addition to other unique items.

Gold Beach

CURRY COUNTY MUSEUM
920 South Ellensburg Ave.
(541) 247-6113
www.curryhistory.com
Here you'll find out about the gold fever that struck this area during the late 1880s. You'll also learn about what the interior of a gold miner's cabin looked like and other interesting gold rush trivia. In addition, you'll learn about the history of the Native Americans and other settlers who came to this area. The museum is open 10 a.m. to 4 p.m. Tuesday through Saturday. Admission is $2 for adults and 50 cents for children under age 16.

Brookings

CHETCO VALLEY HISTORICAL SOCIETY
15461 Museum Rd.
(541) 469-2753
To see an ancient cypress tree with a trunk diameter of 27 feet, be sure to stop by the Chetco Valley Historical Society Museum. The 100-foot-tall tree is adjacent to the museum and is thought to be one of the oldest cypress trees in the world. This museum is located inside the old stagecoach station and trading post and has displays of 20th-century Japanese swords and a dugout canoe in addition to late 19th-century furniture, tools, and arrowheads. The museum is open 1 to 5 p.m. Friday through Sunday. Admission is free but donations are encouraged.

THE ARTS

The natural beauty of the Oregon Coast inspires writers, artists, and musicians to express themselves in a variety of ways. Use this chapter as your stepping stone into the Oregon Coast art and culture scene, where you'll find dozens of activities that will satisfy your artistic cravings.

In this section you'll find a listing of art museums that feature traditional and contemporary artwork, and writing events and retreats where you'll find out about workshops you can attend. Also you'll find eclectic events such as the Fisher Poets Gathering, which features the lyrics of salty seafarers and gives you a chance to recite your own verse, and an overview of selected stages where you can attend theater and music performances plus the rich offering of music festivals and events that are present throughout the year. You'll also find a comprehensive listing of art galleries that showcase the talents of Northwest artists in a variety of mediums. The galleries listed are a mix of working studios, traditional art galleries, and galleries that are often combined with a bookstore, gift shop, or other retail enterprise. Many of these galleries hold art shows during the summer months but may have shorter hours during the winter months. Keep your eyes and ears open, for every place you visit on the scenic Oregon Coast you'll find that the arts are alive and are celebrated year-round.

ART MUSEUMS

COOS ART MUSEUM
235 Anderson, Coos Bay
(541) 267-3901
www.coosart.org
The Coos Art Museum is housed in an art deco-style building and has a permanent collection of nearly 400 pieces of artwork. The interior of the museum is decorated in a modernistic style and has three galleries. The Maggie Karl Gallery is downstairs and the Oregon Gallery and Mabel Hansen Gallery are upstairs. These galleries display paintings, prints, and photographs by Northwest artists and all of the art pieces are available for purchase. The gallery also has the Prefontaine Memorial Gallery, which displays photos, trophies, and awards of Olympic runner Steve Prefontaine of Coos Bay. The museum has an additional permanent collection of paintings, prints, and sculptures with the highlight of this collection being 110 original graphics from well-known artists such as Robert Rauschenberg, Alexander Calder,

Red Groms, Larry Rivers, James Rosenquist, and Warrington Colescott. Many pieces of the permanent collection can be viewed online at the museum's Web site. The museum is open 10 a.m. to 4 p.m. Tuesday through Friday and from 1 to 4 p.m. on Saturday. Closed all major holidays.

NEWPORT VISUAL ARTS CENTER
777 Northwest Beach Dr., Newport
(541) 265-6540
www.coastarts.org/vac
The Newport Visual Arts Center showcases the art of many Northwest artists in the 1,000-square-foot Runyan Gallery and the 300-square-foot Upstairs Gallery. Examples of artwork you'll see at this impressive cultural center include paintings of "The Oregon Territory" by Jim Shull, photography from local photographers, and selected pieces from local glass artists. The William Runyan Gallery hosts 12 shows per year featuring new artists from the Northwest. Admission to the center is free. The Runyan Gallery is open from 11 a.m. to 6 p.m. Tuesday through Sunday, and the Upstairs

Gallery is open from noon to 4 p.m. Tuesday through Saturday.

ART GALLERIES

North Coast

ART CENTER GALLERY CLATSOP COMMUNITY COLLEGE
1653 Jerome, Astoria
(503) 338-2473
www.clatsopcc.edu
The Art Center Gallery at Clatsop Community College features a collection of sculpture, photography, painting, drawing, printmaking, and mixed media artwork by local and regional artists.

PACIFIC RIM GALLERY
One 12th St., Astoria
(503) 325-5450
Stop by the Pacific Rim Gallery to find a unique blend of fine arts and crafts combined with a small espresso bar and deli. The gallery holds art shows every eight weeks featuring different mediums, such as bronze sculpture.

RIVERSEA GALLERY
1160 Commercial St., Astoria
(503) 325-1270
This local gallery features contemporary works by Northwest and national artists in a variety of mediums including prints, paintings, pastels, photos, glass, clay, wood, fiber, sculpture, and an extensive selection of jewelry.

VALLEY BRONZE OF OREGON FINE ART GALLERY
1198 Commercial St., Astoria
(800) 559-2118
www.valleybronze.com
This 3,400-square-foot gallery is host to a premier fine art foundry where they work with metals including bronze, silver, stainless, aluminum, and steel. They feature sculptures, paintings, and prints by nationally and internationally known artists. Artists include George Carlson, Barbara Chen, David Crawford, Chester Fields, Dorothy Fowler, Elle George, Michael Gorbon, Nano Lopez, Maimon, Walter Matia, Royo, and Mike Smith.

EXPOSURE ART GALLERY
609 Broadway St., Seaside
(503) 738-8030
www.shopseaside.com/ea
The Exposure Art Gallery features original works by local and regional artists. In this gallery you'll find a wonderful collection of art glass, intricate basketry, candles and scents, beautiful bronze and clay sculptures, jewelry, and dazzling pottery.

NECANICUM GALLERY & PICTURE FRAMING
1928 South Holladay Dr., Seaside
(503) 738-3168
The Necanicum gallery features wonderful watercolor prints by Rie Munoz and Nancy Loukkula.

SHEARWATER GALLERY
111 Broadway St. #11, Seaside
(503) 738-0328
The Shearwater Gallery features the artwork of Earl Hamilton, Joachim McMillan, Nho Nguyen, Mimi Fox, and Lisa Albinger. They also offer functional art for sale such as tableware and pottery, artistic lamps, end tables, coffee tables, and other home furnishings. They also feature handmade jewelry and whimsical bird feeders.

BRONZE COAST GALLERY
224 North Hemlock St. Suite #2,
Cannon Beach
(503) 436-1055
www.cannon-beach.net
Representing Northwest artists, this gallery features limited edition bronzes, paintings, giclées, photographs, and life-size heroic monuments.

CANNON BEACH ARTS ASSOCIATION GALLERY
1064 South Hemlock St., Cannon Beach
(503) 436-0744
www.cannonbeacharts.org
The Cannon Beach Gallery was founded in 1986

and represents local professional and non-professional artists. The Cannon Beach Arts Association sponsors the gallery and features solo artist exhibits and also hosts juried shows throughout the year. The gallery promotes excellence in visual art through education and exhibition. It sponsors an internship program for Seaside High School students and also sponsors students from Clatsop Community College. Visit the Web site or call to find out the current exhibitors.

DRAGONFIRE INTERACTIVE STUDIO AND GALLERY

123 South Hemlock St., Cannon Beach
(503) 436-1533
www.dragonfirestudio.com

This gallery features acrylic art by Miska, mixed media by George Abboud, watercolor landscapes by Paula Carlson, acrylic on canvas by Joann Chartier, and stunning wave and sea life photographer Clark Little. The gallery promotes local artists and also offers classes for beginners and professionals.

HAYSTACK GALLERY

183 North Hemlock St., Cannon Beach
(503) 436-2547
www.haystackgallery.com

The Haystack Gallery features a collection of watercolors, bronze, and metal sculptures, hand-blown glass, lithographs, giclées, raku pottery, and hand-tinted etchings.

HOUSE OF THE POTTER

183 North Hemlock St., Cannon Beach
(503) 436-2504
www.houseofthepotter.com

The House of the Potter in the Cannon Beach Mall features hand-thrown stoneware by Jay Steward and also sells a wide variety of nondenominational Christian books, gift cards, and inspirational gifts.

ICEFIRE GLASSWORKS

116 East Gower St., Cannon Beach
(503) 436-2359

Icefire Glassworks is a working studio where you'll be able to see James Kingwell and Suzanne Kindland making free-blown glass vases, bowls, weights, and sculptures through a glass observation window.

THE JEFFREY HULL GALLERY

172 North Hemlock, Sandpiper Sq.,
Cannon Beach
(503) 436-2600, (888) 436-2606
www.hullgallery.com

This spacious second-floor gallery at Sandpiper Square showcases original watercolors, limited edition lithographs, mini-cards, and boxed cards by featured artist Jeffrey Hull. Jeffrey Hull is a member of the American Society of Marine Artists and is one of Oregon's premier seascape watercolorists. The gallery participates in the Story Weather Art Festival events held the first weekend in November by hosting an open house to unveil their newest prints.

NORTHWEST BY NORTHWEST GALLERY

232 North Spruce St., Cannon Beach
(503) 436-0741

This Cannon Beach gallery houses a variety of arts and crafts that focus on glass media.

OREGON GALLERY

223 North Hemlock St., Cannon Beach
(503) 436-0817

This gallery houses a good collection of scenic Northwest photography, wall decor, and a large selection of gifts made in Oregon. If you want to bring home a special gift that was made in Oregon, be sure to stop by this gallery.

THE PURPLE PELICAN

140 North Hemlock, Cannon Beach
(503) 436-1390, (877) 436-1390
www.rarediscovery.com

The Purple Pelican features metal garden art by Tom Torrens that includes bells, bird feeders, and gongs. The Purple Pelican also has a fine collection of baskets, ceramics, glass, pottery, sculpture, and woodcarvings by international artists.

STEIDEL'S ART
116 South Hemlock St., Cannon Beach
(503) 436-1757
The gallery features watercolors and pastels by William M. Steidel and specialized matting and framing by Sam Steidel.

WHITE BIRD GALLERY
251 North Hemlock St., Cannon Beach
(503) 436-2681
www.whitebirdgallery.com
Evelyn Georges established the White Bird Gallery in 1970 and has represented the finest local, regional, national, and international artists for more than 35 years. When you visit this gallery, you'll be able to view oil, watercolor, and acrylic paintings, and clay, glass, and wood sculptures. Artwork is featured during art shows given throughout the year. The gallery is open daily from 11 a.m. to 5 p.m. during the summer and 11 a.m. to 5 p.m. Thursday through Monday during the winter. All major credit cards are accepted.

WILD BIRD SHOP—NATURE ARTS AND SOUNDS
123 South Hemlock St., Cannon Beach
(503) 436-9806, (800) 281-9806
www.wildbirdshop.com
If you are a nature lover, you should be sure to visit Wild Bird Shop in Ecola Square. This shop features birding supplies, decorative fountains, nature-oriented art, crafts and gifts, music, and wildlife arts and crafts by local Oregon artists.

OSBORNE STUDIO & GALLERY
641 Manzanita Ave., Manzanita
(503) 368-7518
www.osbornestudio.com
This gallery exhibits the paintings of Donald Osborne. Visit his Web site to view the current painting available.

SHEPHERD GALLERY
12905 US 101, Nehalem
(503) 368-6247
The Shepherd Gallery showcases beautiful goldsmith work, paintings, and fine crafts.

CARVERS & DESIGNERS
19485 US 101, Rockaway Beach
(503) 355-8508
Unique woodcarvings, photography, furniture, and paintings are exhibited at the Carvers & Designers gallery.

PACIFIC MOON GALLERY
111 South Miller St., Rockaway Beach
(503) 355-2212
Photography, oils, watercolors, pottery, and stained glass are some of the art mediums you'll find at the Pacific Moon Gallery.

ARTSPACE GALLERY & CAFE
9120 5th St. (US 101 and 5th St.), Bay City
(541) 377-2782
This gallery showcases contemporary Northwest art including colorful multimedia paintings, marble sculptures, and interesting wood carvings. In addition, this gallery has a cafe that serves fresh seafood and other daily specials.

PACIFIC CITY GALLERY
35350 Brooten Rd., Pacific City
(503) 965-7181
www.pc-gallery.com
This gallery features the artwork of over 100 Northwest artists. You can find glass, pottery, wall art, jewelry, and beautiful handmade gifts at this large gallery. Open 10 a.m. to 5 p.m. daily. Closed Tuesday and Wednesday from January through March.

SOARING CRANE GALLERY
33105 Cape Kiwanda Dr., Pacific City
(503) 965-7848
Featured artwork at this gallery includes art quilts, wood, paper, antler carvings, recycled glass dishware, a fine jewelry collection, and panoramic photography.

Central Coast
ALDER HOUSE II
611 South Immonen Rd., Lincoln City
(541) 996-2483
www.alderhouse.com

The Alder House II is a glassblowing studio that welcomes visitors to view the ancient art of turning molten glass into vases, bowls, paperweights, and so on. Open 10 a.m. to 5 p.m. March 15 through the end of November.

AMERICAN SHADOWS
825 Northwest US 101, Lincoln City
(541) 996-6887, (800) 215-3781
This gallery was established in Arizona in 1990 and then moved to the Oregon Coast in 1993 where its Southwest art collection was expanded to include the artwork of the Northwest Coastal Native Americans. This gallery proudly exhibits woodcarvings by the following Native American artists: Ken Hatch (Siletz tribe), Micah Vogel (Makah tribe), and Odin Lonning (Tlingit tribe). The gallery also features the watercolors of April White and Linda Nelson. Other artists featured include Barry Herem, J. D. Challenger, and Howard Terpning. Some of the mediums you'll find at the gallery include original paintings, hand-pulled and offset lithographs, bronze and alabaster sculptures, kachina carvings, American Indian artifacts, Northwest Coastal carvings, masks, Brentwood boxes, and Western and wildlife art. This gallery also has one of the largest selections of traditional and contemporary jewelry on the Oregon Coast.

EARTHWORKS
620 Northeast US 101, Lincoln City
(541) 557-4148
The Earthworks gallery features blown and fused glass and functional and decorative ceramics. In addition, you'll find handmade baskets, fine wood pieces, and paintings.

FRAME CELLAR & GALLERY
2150 Northwest Mast Place, Lincoln City
(541) 994-8556
The Frame Cellar & Gallery houses a collection of oil paintings, sculptures, and watercolors.

FREED GALLERY
6119 Southwest US 101, Lincoln City
(541) 994-5600
www.freedgallery.com
The Freed Gallery exhibits furniture, pottery, jewelry, glass, sculpture, clay, wood, and photography. The gallery features the contemporary paintings by Beth Ames Swartz, unique clay pieces by Brian Mackin, and glass art by Andrea Mullans Weir. Open daily 10 a.m. to 5 p.m.

i You can find out about performances and upcoming exhibits by reading the local newspaper in the community you are visiting. See the Media chapter for more information about local newspapers. Another good source for finding out about art and musical events is the local chamber of commerce or visitor center.

RYAN GALLERY
4270 US 101 North, Lincoln City
(541) 994-5391
The Ryan Gallery displays a diverse collection of oils, acrylics, watercolors, pastel and mixed media paintings, ceramics, glass, sculpture, and jewelry.

LAWRENCE GALLERY AT SALISHAN
7755 US 101 North, Gleneden Beach
(541) 764-2318
www.lawrencegallery.net
Located not far from the beautiful Salishan Links golf course at the Marketplace at Salishan, the Gallery at Salishan exhibits contemporary fine arts and crafts from national and international artists.

MOSSY CREEK POTTERY
483 Immonen Rd., Gleneden Beach
(541) 996-2415
Mossy Creek Pottery features unique handmade earthenware, stoneware, and porcelain pottery.

NYE BEACH GALLERY
715 Northwest 3rd St., South Beach
(541) 265-3292

This gallery features the beautiful bronze, copper, and concrete sculpture of artist Lon Brusselback.

FORINASH GALLERY
856 Southwest Bay Blvd., Newport
(541) 265-8483
www.forinashgallery.com
This gallery specializes in photography by Chuck Forinash and prints of scenic coastal images featuring lighthouses and bridges.

INSCAPES GALLERY
818 Southwest Bay Blvd., Newport
(541) 265-6843, (800) 359-1419
www.inscapesgallery.com
Located on Newport's historic bayfront, the Inscapes Gallery features oil originals and other art pieces from more than 400 artists. At the gallery, you'll find original oil paintings, steel wall hangings, photography, jewelry, dichroic and fused glass, bronze sculptures, and furniture.

OCEANIC ARTS
444 Southwest Bay Blvd., Newport
(541) 265-5963
Stan Pickens established the Oceanic Arts gallery in 1974 to showcase art pieces with Northwest flair. This gallery features fine art prints and contemporary crafts in wood, glass, pottery, metal, and other mediums.

RICKERT GALLERY
640 Southwest Bay Blvd., Newport
(541) 265-5430, (800) 732-8831
www.rickertart.com
The Rickert Gallery features the seascapes of Sharon Rickert, landscapes by Lyn Lasneski, watercolors by Jan Kunz, and metal sculptures by John Cabalas. In addition, the gallery exhibits original bronzes, lithographs, pastels, and prints. Open daily from 9 a.m. to 5:30 p.m.

MICHAEL GIBBONS GALLERY
The Vicarage, 140 Northeast Alder St., Toledo
(541) 336-2797
www.michaelgibbons.net/toledo.htm
This gallery is housed in a historic home built in 1926. The gallery features the paintings in oil and reproductions of the Pacific Northwest and Southwest desert by Michael Gibbons.

BRIAN MCENENY WOODCARVING GALLERY
10727 US 101, Seal Rock
(541) 563-2452
www.woodcarvinggallery.com
You don't want to miss the unique wildlife carvings made out of black walnut, cedar, hibiscus, maple, myrtle wood, and redwood at this unique gallery.

EARTHWORKS GALLERY
2222 US 101 North, Yachats
(541) 547-4300
www.gocybervision.com/gocybervision/
earthwork/index.htm
Steve Dennis established the Earthworks Gallery in 1990. Steve has exhibited his functional and artistic ceramics nationally and many of his pieces are represented in public, corporate, and private collections. This gallery represents more than 150 artists working in clay, glass, wood, and metal, and it has one of the largest showings of glass pieces in Oregon. The gallery also features landscape paintings, watercolors, oils, and pastels.

TOUCHSTONE GALLERY
2118 US 101 North, Yachats
(541) 547-4121
Robin Mathews fulfilled a lifelong dream when she opened the Touchstone Gallery in 1998. Her gallery specializes in ceramics, glass, wearable art, sculpture, and paintings.

BLUE HERON GALLERY
1385 Bay St., Florence
(541) 997-7993
Established in 1990, the Blue Heron Gallery showcases a mix of different mediums from local and internationally acclaimed artists. You'll see woodcarvings, bronze sculpture, jewelry, glassworks, and metalwork pieces that are shown with award-winning presentation. In 1999 *Niche* magazine rated this gallery as one of the top 100 galleries in the United States, and if you stop by you'll see why.

FLORENCE EVENTS CENTER GALLERY
715 Quince St., Florence
(541) 997-1994, (888) 968-4086
www.eventcenter.org/gallery/gallery.html
The Florence Events Center Gallery features the artwork of local and regional artists throughout the year. Visit their Web site to view the current gallery schedule.

FRAMES OF FLORENCE–GALLERY 101
1361 1st St., Old Town Florence
(541) 997-2043
While you are browsing through the shops in Old Town Florence, be sure to stop by the Frames of Florence–Gallery 101. This gallery exhibits Charles Draper's color photos, Dan Looney's watercolors and mixed media, Stephanie Lochow's pottery, Tom Turk's scrimshaw, Don Jenson's gyotaku (fish rubbings), Lane Sharkey's limited edition prints of dried flowers, and a permanent display of Barclay Cook's black and white photographs of local scenes.

MINDPOWER GALLERY
417 Fir Ave., Reedsport
(541) 271-2485, (800) 644-2485
www.mindpowergallery.com
The Mindpower gallery features original artwork in 2-D and 3-D. The gallery also has a gift shop that carries music, books, and original handmade crafts and offers custom framing services.

MYRTLEWOOD GALLERY
1125 US 101, Reedsport
(541) 271-4222
www.myrtlewoodgallery.com
The Myrtlewood Gallery features gifts and art pieces made from wood as well as original paintings and sculptures.

South Coast

CRYSTAL DOLPHIN GALLERY
1901 Sherman Ave., North Bend
(541) 756-1989
You'll find many unique art items at the Crystal Dolphin Gallery. This gallery features contemporary jewelry, glass, paintings, and sculpture.

FROGBLOSSOM STUDIO & GALLERY
1554 Sherman Ave., North Bend
(541) 756-2844
Emily Ashworth established the Frogblossom Studio & Gallery and gift shop in 1998 to market her own artwork, which includes abstract, architectural, floral, and whimsical original framed and unframed acrylic paintings, cards, bookmarks, and frog collectibles. Emily is usually creating a new painting in her studio, and she asks that you call before you visit or knock on the door of her studio to view her artwork.

BAY MOSS STUDIO
180 Central, Coos Bay
(541) 269-0965
You'll find ceramics, glass, furniture, jewelry, paintings, woodturnings, and much more by local and regional artists at Bay Moss Studio.

BANDON GLASS ART STUDIO AND GALLERY
240 US 101, Bandon
(541) 347-4723
www.bandonglassart.com
Be sure to stop by this working glassblowing studio. Through an observation window you can watch master glassblowers create colorful glass vessels and paperweights. In this hot glass shop, you'll find the amazing work of Dutch Schulze, who creates vases that are characterized by the flow of complex multicolored strands and orbs against a background of vibrant color.

CLOCK TOWER GALLERY
198 2nd St. SE, Bandon
(541) 347-4721
Located in downtown Bandon, the Clock Tower Gallery exhibits artwork in a variety of mediums including prints, posters, watercolors, oils, drawings, stained glass, ceramics, and myrtlewood.

SECOND STREET GALLERY
210 2nd St., Old Town, Bandon
(541) 347-4133
www.bandon.com/gallery
This gallery proudly exhibits the artwork of more than 100 artists, including paintings in oil, acrylic, and watercolors; sculptures in stone, bronze, steel, wood, and clay; fine furniture; blown glass, fused glass; wearable art; contemporary jewelry; decorative ceramics; functional pottery; basketry; and weavings. Open 10 a.m. to 5:30 p.m. daily.

SPIRIT OF OREGON
112 2nd St., Bandon
(541) 347-4311
The Spirit of Oregon is an artists' cooperative that displays handmade pottery, sea kelp and sea grass baskets, paintings, jewelry, wearable art, sculptures, fiber, and African arts.

COOK GALLERY
705 Oregon St., Port Orford
(541) 332-0045
www.harborside.com/~randj/rcookgallery
.htm
This gallery focuses on the wood art and also exhibits contemporary and traditional paintings, sculpture, and fine crafts.

GRANTLAND MAYFIELD GALLERY
246 Sixth St. (US 101), Port Orford
(541) 332-6610
This gallery contains an eclectic mix of art pieces, including blown glass, silk ensembles, jewelry, paintings, and sculpture.

ART & SIGN
29282 Ellensburg Ave., Gold Beach
(541) 247-6528
Art & Sign is a working studio that showcases acrylics and watercolors by Magda Druzdzel.

GALLERY 101 AT THE BOOKWORM BOOKSTORE
29401 Ellensburg Ave., Gold Beach
(541) 247-9033
This gallery features oils, watercolors, multimedia, photography, ceramics, jewelry, photography, and woodworking by local and regional artists.

THE GRAY WHALES GALLERY
29830 Ellensburg Ave., Gold Beach
(541) 247-7514
The Gray Whales is a gallery and gift shop that is owned and operated by Ed and Maggi Frazier. The gallery features a variety of mediums from local artists including pottery; watercolor, oil, and acrylic mixed media paintings; bronze, stone, wood, and clay sculptures; stained glass; weavings; basketry; Native American drums and rattles; and gyotaku or fish rubbings.

J. ADER GALLERY
29272 Ellensburg Ave., Gold Beach
(541) 247-0148
Jean Ader's original oils of local scenes, wildlife, and birds are featured.

JUDY'S CORNER FRAME SHOP
15608 US 101, Unit One, Brookings
(541) 469-5839
This shop exhibits collage work, jewelry, pastels, watercolors, and stained glass.

MORY'S MINI GALLERY
810 Chetco Ave., Brookings
(541) 469-4856
Mory's Mini Gallery features a variety of art pieces by local coastal artists. The gallery exhibits acrylic, oil, and watercolor paintings, ink drawings, mixed media, sculpture, pottery, and prints.

PELICAN BAY ARTS ASSOCIATION
509 Pine St., Brookings
(541) 469-1807
The Pelican Bay Arts Association displays visual arts, porcelain, textile, and sculpture artwork by member artists. The Pelican Bay Arts Association is a nonprofit organization and is supported by an endowment fund, membership dues, gifts, and donations.

WORDS AND PICTURES

407 Oak St., Brookings
(541) 469-7067

This combined gallery and bookstore features the work of more than 50 local and regional artists in a wide variety of mediums. Paintings, sculptures, carvings, glass, photography, basketry, pottery, fiber art, and prints are some of the types of artwork you'll find on display in this warm and friendly gallery. In addition to browsing the gallery, you may also want to browse through the vast collection of book titles, greeting cards, and music titles.

WRITING EVENTS/RETREATS

FISHER POETS GATHERING

Astoria
(503) 325-6311
www.clatsopcc.edu/fisherpoets

The three-day Fisher Poets Gathering is a get together of salty seafarers who recite their lyrics at places like the Wet Dog Cafe in downtown Astoria. This working person's poetry revival entices anglers from up and down the West Coast from California to Alaska to recite stories about their experiences at sea. Jon Broderick, a one-time commercial fisherman turned high school teacher in Astoria, started this event in an effort to preserve the seafarer's verse, which is much like cowboy poetry. The gathering features 15 hours of readings and various workshops on history, photography, and poetry about life at sea. One of the favorite events at this gathering is the limerick contest, where contestants write passages under the clock. Call ahead for specific times and locations.

NEWPORT PERFORMING ARTS CENTER

777 West Olive St., Newport
(541) 265-9231
www.coastarts.org

The Nye Beach Writers series features readings from award-winning poets and writers throughout the year. Visit the Web site for a list of current events in this series.

OREGON WRITER'S COLONY

P.O. Box 15200, Portland 97293-5200
(503) 827-8072
www.oregonwriterscolony.org

The Oregon Writer's Colony was formed to support writers, establish a permanent writers' retreat on the Oregon Coast called the Colony House, and sponsor a variety of writing workshops throughout the year. The Colony House is a log house located in Rockaway Beach with great views of the Pacific Ocean and Lake Lytle. The house has four bedrooms, two full bathrooms, a well-equipped kitchen, and many windows with views. Members of the Oregon Writer's Colony can reserve a room with a shared bathroom and kitchen year-round.

SITKA CENTER FOR ART AND ECOLOGY

P.O. Box 65, Otis 97368
(541) 994-5485
www.sitkacenter.org

Tucked into the slopes of Cascade Head on the central Oregon Coast, Sitka Center for Art and Ecology is a unique educational facility and working artists' studio that celebrates the relationship between nature and art. This special facility is located in a beautiful natural setting adjacent to the Nature Conservancy preserve, in the midst of an 8,000-acre national scenic area and overlooking the Salmon River estuary, which inspires artists with its natural beauty. The Sitka Center is operated by the Neskowin Coast Foundation and offers a variety of workshops and special residency programs for artists, writers, and naturalists. The facilities at the center consist of studios where classes and workshops are held. The facility itself is surrounded by the Harold Hirsch Garden, which provides a natural setting for conducting outdoor workshops. Classes and workshops are offered throughout the year in books and journaling, drawing, ecology, fibers, photography, printmaking, sculpture, and other art media, and writing. The center also hosts various shows, readings, and music events. Visit the center's Web site for a current course catalog and a current list of events.

MUSIC

NEWPORT PERFORMING ARTS CENTER
777 West Olive St., Newport
(541) 265-9231
www.coastarts.org
The 23,000-square-foot Newport Performing Arts Center is the pride of Newport and was opened in 1988 to promote performing, literary, and visual arts, and as part of its offering features a variety of musical as well as theater, film, and literary events throughout the year. To see the current calendar of musical events, you can visit the center's Web site.

FLORENCE EVENTS CENTER
715 Quince St., Florence
(541) 997-1994
www.eventcenter.org
The 8,000-square-foot Florence Events Center is a modern, state-of-the-art facility that combines meeting and exhibit space with a 500-seat theater. The center is a community venue for theater, ballet, art shows, concerts, and a variety of other community events. Call for a schedule of current concerts or visit the Web site.

THEATER

North Coast

ASTOR STREET OPRY COMPANY
129 West Bond St.
(503) 325-6104
www.shanghaiedinastoria.com
A local theater troupe presents *Shanghaied in Astoria*. This play, with chase scenes, bar fights, and lots of Scandinavian jokes, is based on Astoria's dubious distinction as a notorious shanghai port during the late 1800s. Call the number listed to purchase tickets and to find out the current days and times.

i To view an events calendar that covers the arts and cultural scene for the entire Coast, visit the Oregon Coast Council for the Arts Web site at www.coastarts.org.

CEDAR BAY RESTAURANT
2605 12th St., Tillamook
(503) 815-8272
The Cedar Bay Restaurant often hosts fun dinner shows such as *The Odd Couple*. Shows usually begin at 7:30 p.m. and an average ticket price is $20 per person. Call ahead for a current show schedule.

COASTER THEATRE
108 North Hemlock St.
(503) 436-1242
www.coastertheatre.com
This lively theater company runs its plays on Friday and Saturday with tickets ranging from $14 to $20. Recent productions include Sherlock's Secret Life, Grace and Glorie, Hello Dolly and Dames at Sea.

TILLAMOOK BAY COMMUNITY COLLEGE
2510 1st St., Tillamook
(503) 815-8272
www.tillamookbay.cc
Tillamook Bay Community College often hosts plays throughout the year. Call ahead for a current show schedule and ticket prices.

Central Coast

FLORENCE EVENTS CENTER
715 Quince St., Florence
(541) 997-2051
www.eventcenter.org
The Florence Events Center hosts several plays throughout the year, including such classics as *The Wizard of Oz*, with an all-star cast from *The Last Resort Players Storybook Theatre*. Visit the events center Web site to find out about current show offerings or call for more information.

NEWPORT PERFORMING ARTS CENTER
777 West Olive St., Newport
(541) 265-ARTS (265-2787)
www.coastarts.org
The Newport Performing Arts Center features a variety of plays throughout the year. To see the current schedule of plays and ticket prices, visit the center's Web site.

THEATRE WEST
3536 Southwest US 101, Lincoln City
(541) 994-5663
www.theatrewest.com
Theater West entertains the local community by featuring different plays throughout the year such as *Habeas Corpus,* a comedy about mistaken identity and middle age. Shows are usually held Thursday, Friday, and Saturday nights at 8 p.m. Call for a current show schedule and ticket prices.

South Coast

BANDON PLAYHOUSE
P.O. Box 1047, Bandon 97411
(541) 347-7708
http://bandonplayhouse.net
The Bandon is a community theater that features a variety of plays throughout the year at different locations in Bandon. You can call or visit their Web site to view a upcoming productions.

ON BROADWAY THEATER
845 S. Broadway #107, Coos Bay
(541) 269-2501
www.geocities.com/obthespian
As well as presenting adult drama, this lively group also mounts shows with teenage thespians involved in Alternative Youth Activities. There is also a Children's Theatre for younger children. Call or visit their Web site to purchase tickets and to view current productions. The theater has three different venue locations.

SAWDUST THEATRE
114 North Adams St.
(541) 396-4563
www.sawdusttheatre.com
This hilarious and highly entertaining theater group is worth a side jaunt east from US 101 to Coquille.

MUSIC FESTIVALS AND EVENTS

CASCADE HEAD MUSIC FESTIVAL
Peter the Fisherman Lutheran Church, Campus Building
1226 Southwest 13th St., Lincoln City
(877) 994-5333
www.cascadeheadmusic.org
This festival features beautiful orchestral pieces from orchestras from all over the world. Different orchestras are featured and play on weekday and weekend evenings during the month of June. Delicious Oregon wines, cheeses, and handmade desserts are offered at each concert. Call ahead for specific locations, times, and ticket prices.

ERNEST BLOCH MUSIC FESTIVAL
Newport Performing Arts Center
777 West Olive St., Newport
(541) 265-2787, (888) 701-7123
www.baymusic.org
This annual music festival commemorates composer Ernest Bloch who lived and composed on the Oregon Coast from 1940 to 1959. During the festival you'll hear music composed by Bloch, Richard Strauss, Saint-Saëns, Poulenc, Chen Yi, and many others. The festival is held from the end of June through mid-July. Call or visit the Web site for specific dates, times, and ticket prices.

OREGON COAST MUSIC FESTIVAL
P.O. Box 663, Coos Bay 97420
(877) 894-9350
www.oregoncoastmusic.com
This music festival is one of the big events of the summer season on the Oregon Coast. This two-week event is held in mid-July and features chamber, choral, and symphony music as well as performances that feature the sounds of Big Band, bluegrass, blues, and jazz. Call for specific locations, times, and ticket prices.

OREGON DIXIELAND JUBILEE
P.O. Box 813, Seaside 97138-0813
(503) 738-6894
www.jazzseaside.com

The Oregon Dixieland Jubilee is a huge event where nine bands play Dixieland-style music at the Seaside Convention Center and other locations in Seaside. This event has included bands such as The Titan Hot Seven, New Pacific Jazz Band, Clint Baker's New Orleans Jazz Band, and Chicago Six with Yve Evans. This annual event takes place during the last part of February. Call ahead for specific locations, times, and ticket prices.

ART FESTIVALS AND EVENTS

ART FAIRE
Florence Events Center
715 Quince St., Florence
(541) 997-2051
www.eventcenter.org
The last weekend in August, the Florence Events Center sponsors an art show and sale from local and regional artists working with all media and high-quality crafts. You can support local artists by attending this fun event.

AZALEA FESTIVAL ART SHOW
Azalea Park, Brookings
(800) 535-9469
www.brookingsor.com
Held during the last weekend in May, this festival celebrates the brightly flowered azaleas that are at their peak bloom during May in Azalea Park. Held since 1939, this festival features a floral parade and queen coronation, arts and crafts, and food booths. The art show features pieces in watercolor, oil and acrylic, pastel, mixed media/collage, drawing, and graphics.

CRANBERRY FESTIVAL
Cranberry Festival Association
P.O. Box 348, Bandon 97411
(541) 347-9616
www.bandon.com
Be sure to attend the annual Cranberry Festival held the third weekend in September. At this historic Bandon festival, you can view a variety of arts, crafts, and photography and enjoy on-stage music and entertainment as well as a street fair and Grand Parade.

GLASTONBURY RENAISSANCE FAIRE
South Beach State Park, Newport
(541) 265-9231
www.oregonstateparks.org/park_209.php
Held the second weekend in May at South Beach State Park, the Glastonbury (pronounced Gloss-on-brie) Renaissance Faire includes over 30 booths that feature unique pieces made by regional artists. This art fair is sponsored by the Oregon Coast Arts Association and has a medieval theme where the myths, history, and legends of this time in history are celebrated. The Glastonbury Renaissance Faire is open from 10 a.m. to 6 p.m. Saturday and Sunday. Call for current admission prices.

YACHATS ORIGINAL ARTS AND CRAFTS FAIR
Yachats Commons
4th St. and US 101, Yachats
(800) 929-0477
www.yachats.org
Held the third weekend in March, the Yachats Original Arts and Crafts Fair features more than 75 exhibitors displaying items such as paintings, drawings and photos, glasswork, pottery, ceramics, woodworking, furniture, and lamps.

IN SUPPORT OF THE ARTS

OREGON ARTS COMMISSION
775 Summer St. Northeast Suite 200, Salem
(503) 986-0123
www.oregonartscommission.org
Established in 1967, the Oregon Arts Commission supports the arts to ensure their excellence in the state of Oregon. Nine commissioners in this organization determine policies, establish long-range plans, and review applications to grants programs to determine funding levels. The commission provides ongoing funding for the operations for almost 100 nonprofit arts organizations. This organization's Web site has links to dozens of arts organizations and also lists internship and grant opportunities for Oregon writers and artists. Many music venues on the Oregon Coast sell out quickly. Buy major concert tickets in advance so you are guaranteed a good seat as well as admission.

OREGON COAST COUNCIL FOR THE ARTS (OCCA)
P.O. Box 1315, Newport 97365
(888) 701-7123
www.coastarts.org
The Oregon Coast Council for the Arts is a non-profit organization that is part of a national network of local arts agencies that serves the entire coastal region. The organization assists arts and humanities organizations and individual artists by providing grants, cultural planning and programs, and management expertise for arts facilities. Their Web site includes a comprehensive events listing of cultural and art happenings for the entire Coast and also includes links to other arts organizations.

OREGON COAST EXTENDED ARTS NETWORK (OCEAN)
P.O. Box 1315, Newport 97365
(888) 701-7123
www.coastarts.org/ocean/home.html
The Oregon Coast Extended Arts Network is one of 10 regional art councils that serve under the Oregon Arts Commission. This organization is an eight-county arts advocacy organization that promotes the arts for Oregon's coastal communities. This organization provides grants and funding; marketing; cultural facilities planning; community and downtown renewal; art education, classes, residencies, and training; and promotes performances and exhibits.

KIDSTUFF

For kids, the more than 300-mile stretch of the Oregon Coast is one long playground with all sorts of fun stuff to do, from gazing up at huge concrete dinosaurs to peering down closely at the strange critters in a small puddle of a tide pool. There are lots of sand dunes to romp on, docks to try your skill at crabbing and fishing, and neat spots for hiking, biking, horseback riding, wading, and walking where pioneers, explorers, sailors, and Native Americans once trod. We've organized the activities by region and city from north to south. So bring along jeans or cutoffs for your own adventure, buckets and scoops for sandcastle building, toss in a couple of kites for flying on a breezy day, fishing gear for when the perch or flounders are biting, and, of course, rain gear for every day of the year. It's pretty hard for a kid to have a bad day on the Oregon Coast.

NORTH COAST

Astoria

ASTORIA'S RIVERFRONT
Starts at 1700 block of Marine Dr.
(503) 325-6311
Astoria's riverfront promenade has 2.8 miles of shoreline where you can walk along plank docks and watch freighters heading for the Columbia Bar or out to sea to Japan and China. There are also chances to watch fishing boats bringing in their catch. A nifty Sixth Street Pier viewing tower is a fun spot to observe the ships and boats as well as climb high enough to look down at the crowds.

COLUMBIA RIVER MARITIME MUSEUM
1792 Marine Dr.
(503) 325-2323
www.crmm.org
At this terrific museum, there's lots of interactive stuff, including a replica of a steamboat pilothouse in which kids can man the helm, operate a 5-foot-high wheel, and send commands to the engine room through a voice tube. The navigation bridge from the USS *Knapp*, a World War II destroyer, is also a great place to scramble about.

Near this intriguing museum with its professionally presented exhibits is the lightship *Columbia*, which once served as a floating lighthouse near the river of the same name. Kids can also climb about the *Columbia*. The museum is open 9:30 a.m. to 5 p.m. daily. The admission fee is $10 for adults; $8 for seniors 65 and up; $5 for children ages six to 17; and children under six are free. The museum is closed Thanksgiving and Christmas.

FORT CLATSOP
92343 Fort Clatsop Rd.
(503) 861-2471
www.nps.gov
Fort Clatsop is a precise replica of the fort where Meriwether Lewis, William Clark, and their Corps of Discovery wintered during the winter of 1805–06. Summers are great times to visit the fort to watch the rangers in costume enact "living history," make candles and moccasins, and demonstrate how to shoot a muzzle-loader. Of particular interest to kids is the Junior Ranger Program in which children can participate in pioneer activities to earn a certificate. At the Interpretive Center there's a 32-minute film and a 17-minute slide show. Located off US 101, 6 miles south of Astoria, the fort is open daily year-round except

Christmas Day. The visitor center is open 9 a.m. to 5 p.m. from mid-September through mid-June and from 9 a.m. to 6 p.m. from mid-June through mid-September. Admission prices are $3 for those 16 and older or $5 per car.

FORT STEVENS STATE PARK
(503) 861-1671
www.oregonstateparks.org/park_179.php
Named for a Union General killed in the Civil War, this fortification dates from that era. Located 10 miles west of Astoria off US 101, it was used to keep a lookout for Confederate warships. There was also concern that British ships-of-war would appear as a response to Britain's possible alliance with the Southern Confederacy. During World War II, Japanese submarines shelled the area, making it the only spot in the continental United States that received fire. Shortly after World War II, the battery was dismantled but there is still enough for kids to clamber about on. There are 6 miles of bike trails, guided tours, and summer reenactments of the Civil War. There is a $3 day use fee for this park.

A Drive into History

One of the most popular outings for kids on the Coast is a drive up to the top of Coxcomb Hill on the east side of Astoria to the Astoria Column. Take Marine Drive to 16th Street and follow the signs to this towering oddity—a 125-foot climb spiraling up inside the column to the viewing deck where you can see across the Columbia River to Mount St. Helens (on a clear day). Curved around the column are drawings of Lewis and Clark's Expedition and other events that made history in the Pacific Northwest.

UPPERTOWN FIREFIGHTERS MUSEUM
30th and Marine Dr.
(503) 325-2203
This 1890s fire station houses a horse-drawn fire engine built in 1878 and a 1912 fire truck that was America's first motorized fire engine. Also at the museum are other examples of fire fighting equipment. The museum is open 10 a.m. to 4 p.m. Monday through Saturday and noon to 3 p.m. on Sunday mid-March through October 31. From November 1 through mid-March, the museum is open noon to 3 p.m. daily. The admission charge is $3 for adults, $2 for seniors age 62 and older, $1 for students, and children under the age of six are admitted free. This admission includes entrance to the Flavel House and the Heritage Center Museum.

Seaside
THE SALTWORKS
Lewis and Clark Way
This monument, reproduced from descriptions in the journals of the Lewis and Clark expedition and located 8 blocks south of Broadway, between Beach Drive and the Promenade, commemorates the work of boiling seawater into salt. It took seven weeks to make four bushels of salt. Kids will learn about some of the difficulties the Lewis and Clark expedition faced out west.

SEASIDE AQUARIUM
200 North Promenade
(503) 738-6211
www.seasideaquarium.com
An old-time building that served as a swimming pool (natatorium) more than 60 years ago, this aquarium is home to seals that the kids can feed. There are also sea stars, wolf eels, a sand shark, and many other types of marine life. Open daily from 9 a.m. to 5 p.m. in summer; 9 a.m. to 5 p.m. Wednesday through Sunday from November through February.

TOWN CENTER CAROUSEL
300 Broadway
(503) 738-6728
Seaside's antique carousel was exchanged for a newer model in 1990. Located near the beach at the center of Seaside Town Center, the carousel is a real kid pleaser. This wild ride has a dozen horses, a flying pig, and a huge rabbit.

Garibaldi
OREGON SCENIC RAILROAD
(503) 842-7972
www.ocsr.net
Kids will have fun on the 1.5-hour round trip ride on the scenic railroad between Garibaldi and Rockaway beach. To find the railroad travel to Garibaldi and turn left on Third Street and follow the signs to Lumberman's Park. Due to the railroad's popularity, reservations are recommended. Call or visit the Web site for the current ticket prices and trip times.

Tillamook
BLUE HERON CHEESE COMPANY
2001 Blue Heron Dr.
(503) 842-8281, (800) 275-0639
www.blueheronoregon.com
A somewhat smaller establishment than the Tillamook Cheese Factory, this is just as fun—with lots of free samples of cheese, syrups, and jams. A delicatessen and gift shop are onsite, as well. Open from 9 a.m. to 5 p.m. October through February and 8 a.m. to 8 p.m. March through September.

i If the weather turns really rough while you are out and about along the Oregon Coast, and you're looking for ways to entertain disappointed kids, give the local library a call for a schedule of its children's events. Most libraries sponsor storytelling, crafts, sing-alongs, and puppet shows. They are always free of charge.

TILLAMOOK CHEESE FACTORY
4175 US 101 North
(503) 815-1300
www.tillamookcheese.com
Opened in 1949, the Tillamook Cheese Factory is renowned for its delicious cheese rendered from dairy farms in the county, where the land is too salty to grow crops. There are self-guided tours with lots of great old photos, free cheese, and an ice-cream bar. A restaurant and gift shop are available for tasty meals and nifty mementos. Open daily, 8 a.m. to 8 p.m. from June through September and 8 a.m. to 6 p.m. the rest of the year.

CENTRAL COAST

Newport
HATFIELD MARINE SCIENCE CENTER
2030 South Marine Science Dr.
(541) 867-0226
http://hmsc.oregonstate.edu/visitor/index.html
A splendid companion to the Oregon Coast Aquarium, this science center opened in 1996. Primarily designed as a place to research and study marine life, it is also a great place for kids to get the real feel for the ocean via hands-on activities, such as petting the octopus, playing with sea anemones, and handling starfish. Also in this intriguing spot are exhibits, demonstrations, and field trips. The center is open daily 10 a.m. to 5 p.m. from Memorial Day weekend through Labor Day. They are open daily from 10 a.m. to 4 p.m. Thursday through Monday the rest of the year. Visit their Web site for the current schedule. There is no admission fee but donations are encouraged.

OREGON COAST AQUARIUM
2820 Southeast Ferry Rd.
(541) 867-3474
www.aquarium.org
In the 40,000 square feet devoted to marine life, this famous aquarium off US 101 has a giant octopus, sea otters, and sea lions cavorting about in front of your wide eyes. There are also lots

of fluffing puffins and other seabirds in a huge outdoor aviary. As well as learning lots about the life of an ocean and its residents, you can watch the feeding of the animals and observe various special programs. Tickets are $14.95 for adults, $12.95 for seniors, $9.45 for children ages three to 12. The aquarium is open from 10 a.m. to 6 p.m. daily from Memorial Day weekend through Labor Day and 10 a.m. to 5 p.m. the rest of the year.

RIPLEY'S BELIEVE IT OR NOT!
250 Southwest Bay Blvd.
(541) 265-2206
www.marinersquare.com

Ripley's Believe It Or Not! is packed with strange items that will appeal to the kid in all of us. For example, children get a chance to pretend they are astronauts speeding through space. Be careful that younger ones aren't too spooked. Open daily, except for Christmas. Summer hours are 9 a.m. to 8 p.m.; the rest of the year, it's 10 a.m. to 5 p.m. Visit the Web site or call for admission fees.

THE WAX WORKS—A LIVING MUSEUM
250 Southwest Bay Blvd.
(541) 265-2206
www.marinersquare.com

Another roadside attraction that will certainly entertain kids is The Wax Works, where legendary and famous characters, some animated, seem to come alive. Open daily, except for Christmas, the summer hours are 9 a.m. to 8 p.m., the rest of the year, 10 a.m. to 5 p.m. Visit the Web site or call for admission fees.

YAQUINA HEAD LIGHTHOUSE, INTERPRETIVE CENTER, AND TIDAL BASIN
750 Lighthouse Dr.
(541) 574-3100
www.blm.gov/or/resources/recreation/
yaquina/index.php

Yaquina Head is home to more than 25,000 shorebirds that nest on nearby offshore islands during spring and summer and a wide variety of marine life including a fairly new population of whelkins, sea stars, anemones, sculpins, shore crabs, and other rockgrippers setting up shop in tidal basins scooped out of the quarry by the Bureau of Land Management.

Quarry Cove, at the base of Yaquina Head, a promontory of lava flow and basaltic cliffs, juts out a mile into the Pacific 3 miles north of Newport on Oregon's Central Coast and was once an abandoned rock quarry. Now, along with the lighthouse on the bluff above, it has been designated as an Outstanding Natural Area by the BLM. Specially built to be wheelchair accessible, the cove is a natural spot (well, not quite natural) to observe the growth of tide pools.

Up the hill, the Interpretive Center has kid-friendly, hands-on exhibits and lively videos that present the geological, biological, and social chronicles of the area. Tourists and townspeople from nearby Newport get a chance to learn about the first Americans who lived here 4,000 years ago and consider the lonely, vigilant lives of the lighthouse keepers who kept ships at sea safe from the rocky lips of the Oregon shore.

If visitors have any time or energy left after visiting the tide pools, lighthouse, and museum, there are trails crisscrossing the 100-acre site worth investigating. Salal Hill Trail is a short but steep 12-minute hike leading to terrific views and wildflowers in the spring. A walk up Communications Hill Trail takes a hiker into a woodsy flank of shore pine, Sitka spruce, and a lively neighborhood of chipmunks, chickadees, and wrens. The Coast Guard maintains navigation communications equipment on top of the hill. A third trail leads down from the lighthouse bluff to Cobble Beach. It's an easy, five-minute descent to a shore composed of tons of cobbles the size of baseballs. A while back, 14 million years or so, boiling hot lava rushed to the sea and exploded into shards that have slowly been ground smooth by the tides.

Yaquina Bay lighthouse was built in 1871 and the Yaquina Head lighthouse was constructed in 1873. After three years, the lighthouse down at the harbor was extinguished, leaving the other lighthouse, at 162-feet above sea level, a higher, brighter beacon reaching 19 miles out to sea. A glimpse of its 9-foot high, 6-foot wide, two-ton

Fresnel lens is a visual cue that this light is indeed powerful. The lens was first illuminated by burning 2½ gallons of lard oil each night. This was replaced by a kerosene/mineral oil combination that lighted up the lamp until 1911, when a kerosene mist similar to a Coleman stove was used. In 1933, an electrical element was installed. Eventually, the lighthouse was automated and is now staffed by BLM tour guides. The lighthouse is Newport's oldest building. In 1869, Congress set aside money for harbor improvements that included two lighthouses. One would be at the harbor entrance and the other was to be built on Yaquina Head, then known as Little Cape Foulweather.

Thousands of school kids have been bussed to Yaquina Head to spend mesmerizing moments staring down into these quietly undulant lagoons and later to wander about a cool museum with lots of buttons to push and stuff to play with and out to the tip of the cliff to this lighthouse that has a gigantic light bulb in a window at the top.

Also, there's a neat deck where you can watch for whales. Look for spouts and what they call breaching when those big guys roll around on the surface of the water. The ranger says that not only are there migrating whales going by but also a resident pod of gray whales that likes it here better than Alaska or Baja California. You can also scope out those fat and happy harbor seals lying around on Seal Island down below and, starting in March and going through summer, check out the birds on Colony Island and other offshore rocks just below the lighthouse on the northwest side of the bluff. There's a "starwheel" on the deck to help identify Brandt cormorants, tufted puffins, oystercatchers, pelicans, and other feathered characters.

Yaquina Head Outstanding Natural Area is not only a terrific spot for kids but also eminently worthy of a visit for adults, particularly those intrigued by natural history. Yaquina Head, open from dawn to dusk, is 4 miles northwest of Newport, off US 101 on Lighthouse Drive. The Interpretive Center is open daily; hours change during different seasons. The entrance fee is $7 for one to nine passengers.

How about a trip of a lifetime for young folks? Try a kayak paddle excursion along Nehalem Bay, a 6-mile estuary about 20 miles south of Cannon Beach. Not only do you get to take a great boating excursion with your kids, you also get to observe lots of birds and seals who live in this lovely spot. Call the Nehalem Bay Kayak Company at (503) 368-6055. They are at 395 US Hwy. 101, Wheeler.

Florence
DARLINGTONIA WAYSIDE
As you walk along wooden platforms through a patch of skunk cabbage in a steamy bog, you will encounter a collection of pitcher plants called Darlingtonia. These exotic cobra lilies are freakish carnivorous plants that lure insects by enchanting them with their sweet smell. The bugs crawl into the mouth of the Darlingtonia, can't crawl back up, and eventually fall to the base of the stem where they are digested. Most all adults and surely all kids will be fascinated with these little critters that are plants that eat animals! Located 5 miles north of Florence, on US 101 on the east side of the road, the wayside is for day use only. There are nearby picnic benches and tables if the visit makes you hungry.

DOLLY WARE'S DOLL MUSEUM
On US 101 at 36th Street
(541) 997-3391
If you have kids who like dolls, you may want to stop and visit this museum, which houses 2,500 dolls of all ages and descriptions. This collection of dolls from Germany, France, and Italy also includes a pre-Columbian doll. Collector's items such as Kewpie dolls and Shirley Temple dolls are also on display. The museum is open daily from 10 a.m. to 5 p.m. except Monday.

JESSIE M. HONEYMAN MEMORIAL STATE PARK
(800) 551-6949, (541) 997-3641
www.oregonstateparks.org/park_134.php
This charming old state park is one of the most

child-friendly spots on the Oregon Coast. Kids can swim, hike, beach comb, and build sandcastles or you can rent a boat or canoe for a family cruise. If you have a boat or canoe with you, you will find a boat launch available, or you can rent a canoe, rowboat, or paddle boat at the concession stand in the park. Located 3 miles south of Florence on US 101, the park is open year-round. For a campsite reservation, call (800) 452-5687.

SAND DUNES FRONTIER AND THEME PARK
85366 US 101
(541) 997-8087
www.sandland.com
Dune buggy rides operated by trained drivers will escort your family on an exciting outing to the world-famous dunes 4 miles south of Florence on US 101. Licensed drivers can also rent buggies for their own excursions. Open daily from March 1 to November 1.

SANDLAND ADVENTURES
85366 US 101
(541) 997-8087
www.sandland.com
This wild and wooly adventure gives kids a chance to scoot about the dunes in a dune buggy. You can hire a guide or rent a buggy for yourself to pilot. If no one wants to go dune buggying, there are also go-karts, miniature golf, and bumper boats. Open daily 9 a.m. to 7:30 p.m. from June 1 to Labor Day. Open 9 a.m. to 5 p.m. Tuesday through Saturday during the rest of the year. Closed January 1 and December 25.

SEA LION CAVES
(541) 547-3111
www.sealioncaves.com
This special location, 11 miles north of Florence, on US 101, is a natural wonder worth visiting. An elevator will take you 208 feet down to the world's largest sea cave—it's the size of a football field. Safe behind glass (and keeping the seals safe), you can still hear the uproar from the seals as you watch them loll and swim and cavort in large heaps. Up on top there is a gift shop and an observation deck to try and sight a whale spouting. Open 9 a.m. to 5 p.m., admission is $11 for adults, $10 for seniors, $7 children age seven to 12, and kids age two and under are admitted for free. Closed Christmas day.

SOUTH COAST

Coos Bay

BLOSSOM GULCH NATURE TRAIL
The trail can be found by turning left off US 101 onto Central just as you enter downtown Coos Bay. Follow Central to 10th Street, turn left and continue to the Blossom Gulch Elementary School at 10th and Anderson. Walk along the north side of the school past the playground to signs welcoming you to the trail.

Blossom Gulch sounds like the title of a western novel written for young adults. In real life, it's a boggy grove on the outskirts of Coos Bay laced with trails and dotted with signs explaining the nature of watershed enhancement.

Located behind Blossom Gulch Elementary School in a mixed thicket of fir, cedar, and alder, the Blossom Gulch Nature Trail starts with a boardwalk built over a swamp of cattails, skunk cabbage, and bunchgrass. A few steps along the trail, a covered deck offers information about Watershed Connections, a local wetland enhancement project. A collaboration between Oregon Department of Fish and Wildlife, South Slough Estuarine Reserve, and other local agencies, the project mobilized school children who spent many hours cleansing the gulch of invasive plants like English ivy.

Beyond the deck, the boardwalk passes by a slow brook rippled only by a Lilliputian cavalcade of a mother duck and five youngsters scurrying to catch up. Then the trail heads uphill switching back along a ridge trail of sun-dappled duff—a fecund mélange of twigs, needles, and decaying wood pulp strewn on hard-packed soil. Alongside the trail are thick carpets of tangy wood-sorrel, spiky clusters of bracken fern, and broad-leafed stalks bereft of their orange-sweet salmonberries. Above all this, slim Douglas firs billow and creak in the whisper of a southwesterly wind.

The walk ends at its entry point or continues on a spur along the south side of the school's playground. A modest, educational trek through a microcosm that serves as a gallery of broader environmental restoration, Blossom Gulch Nature Trail is also a natural for younger children who may not grasp watershed rehabilitation at work but will enjoy an up-close look at life in a swamp.

Charleston

SOUTH SLOUGH NATIONAL ESTUARINE RESERVE

61907 Seven Devils Rd.
(541) 888-5558
http://oregon.gov/DSL/SSNERR/index.shtml
A glossy bit of trickery takes place on a micro-scale at South Slough, a 4,700-acre estuary on the southern Oregon Coast off Cape Arago Highway just west of Charleston. On one of those remarkable coastal days when the sun chooses to power through the clouds, thousands of little sundew plants sparkle with what appear to be baubles of dew. Unfortunately for thirsty insects, the tasty drops are actually sticky digestive juice that renders bugs into snacks for carnivores with roots. Folks who have been to Darlingtonia Wayside will get a sense of déjà vu.

These critter-gobbling plants and lots more intriguing flora and fauna are on view at a place still close to its original wild and natural state that scientists have dubbed it "The Richest Place on Earth." One of the few estuaries in the world to have escaped development into a large port city, this arm of the Coos Bay estuarine system offers a rare chance to see a fresh watershed blending into a saltwater bay.

Here in this tranquil locale, visitors can trace the trickle of a small freshwater stream down a hillside of cedar and fir; through tunnels of alder to a valley floor carpeted with pickleweed, a succulent that holds freshwater in its fleshy leaves to dilute inundations of salt; through waving eelgrass meadows to a saltmarsh combed with saltgrass, a slender weed that excretes salt through its leaves. Beyond this adaptive vegetation lie the tideflats—ancient sediment replenished by the moving waters of ocean and stream where a vast community of shellfish, shrimp, and worms burp and wiggle out their quiet lives.

First stop is the interpretive center at the top of the hill. Inside are several exhibits about estuarine ecology and displays of plants and animals that live in or near South Slough. Staff members will happily answer questions about upcoming programs, direct you toward appropriate nature walks, and introduce you to live feathered or furry animals that are often hanging around the center. Slide shows and films are scheduled almost daily and a bookstore offers books, T-shirts, and other related gifts.

Next, it's time to choose a trail down the hill. There are three basic paths, each with a particular slant: A 1.5- to 3-mile-long Estuary Study Trail—this easy-down, puffer-up trek is the most notable of South Slough's hikes. It follows Hidden Creek as it tumbles 100 feet down from the uplands to the slough. The trail starts in the parking lot of the interpretive center (follow the sign marked TRAILHEAD). The trail then meanders through a series of habitats, crisscrossing the creek a number of times until it becomes a boardwalk across a wetland. One of the most dramatic stretches along the boardwalk is a stroll through a squat jungle of skunk cabbage with huge rubbery leaves that conjure up the dinosaur days. Shortly after this delightful journey through the Pleistocene, you'll come to an observation platform that offers a vista of fresh- and saltwater marshes. Beyond the platform, the trail emerges from the forest to spread out into a braid of paths. One leads to agricultural dikes built by farmers to keep salt water out of their fields. Another leads to Sloughside Pilings—once an elevated railroad for log trains chugging down from high ridges to dump logs into the slough for a boom-tow down to the mills at Empire, North Bend, and Coos Bay.

Ten Minute Loop is an easier 0.25-mile hike particularly suitable for young children. Starting at the interpretive center, this loop offers a glimpse of recovering forest habitat. Along the trail, local flora are labeled for easy identification, and a short way down this path you'll come to a viewpoint overlooking the slough and surrounding watershed.

Wasson Creek Trail is a moderate 0.75-mile trail that covers a variety of habitats in a short distance. The trail begins at a freshwater wetland, crosses the valley, and returns through an upland forest. Hawks, songbirds, beaver, elk, and deer are all common citizens of the Wasson Creek drainage. To get there, head south from the interpretative center on Seven Devils Road to another preserve sign. Take this left turn onto Hinch Road and travel for about a mile, then turn right at a small binocular sign. This is the trailhead for Wasson Creek Trail.

Hoofing is not the only way to tour South Slough. Many visitors canoe South Slough to get to habitats inaccessible by trail. Canoe launch areas are available in the preserve and at Charleston, but it's a good idea to call or stop by the interpretive center first for information about tides and winds. One great way to slide through the slough is with a trained interpretive guide paddling his own canoe. To participate in this 6-mile trip, bring along your own canoe, paddles, lifejackets, and sack lunch.

Although the preserve is open all year, the interpretive canoe trip and most organized events are held during the summer. Don't be shocked by the news that it gets seriously damp at the slough. But also, if you want to take your chances, it can also be blessed by a perfectly mild and sunny day deep in the middle of winter.

A trek that kids really like is "Mudflat Mysteries," a goopy hands-on examination of clams and other critters that live below the muddy surface. Another program for young students (age six to 12) is "Slough Safari," a hike that gives children a chance to learn about the science of this magical spot.

Lastly, "Big Cedar Guided Walks" offers an access trail for individuals with physical disabilities. These free walks lead groups on a 0.5-mile, easy journey to the observation platform near the edge of the marsh.

The slough is also an educational experience for biologists and ecologists, who use the area as a living laboratory. As one of the most active biological areas on the planet, it is a rare locale where scientists can observe and research the nature of the beasts and their habitat. The interpretive center is open 8:30 a.m. to 4:30 p.m. Monday through Saturday from Memorial Day weekend to Labor Day and from 8:30 a.m. to 4:30 p.m. Monday through Friday the rest of the year. For more information, write to South Slough National Estuarine Reserve, P.O. Box 5417, Charleston, OR 97420.

Bandon

WEST COAST GAME PARK SAFARI
(541) 347-3106
www.gameparksafari.com

Here in what is claimed to be the largest wild animal petting zoo in America, kids get a chance to pet little critters and observe the bigger wildlife. Included in the roaming tribe you can observe as you drive through are tigers, bears, cougars, lions, buffalo, elk, zebras, and camels. Free-roamers include goats, llamas, deer, and peacocks. Located 7 miles south of Bandon on US 101. Call or visit the Web site for hours and admission prices.

i Another terrific jaunt is pounding down a hard, sandy beach on a well-seasoned pony. Try the Bandon Beach Riding Stables, (541) 347-3423, 54629 Beach Loop Dr., 1/4 mile south of the Inn at Face Rock. They are open all year come rain or shine. While you're there, take a peek at Face Rock and see if your kids can see that famous brow, nose, and lips jutting out of the Pacific waters.

Port Orford

PREHISTORIC GARDENS
36848 US 101 South
(541) 332-4463
This melodramatic roadside attraction with its looming dinosaurs is a bit startling to those driving by. In operation since the mid-1950s, the garden presents these ancient reptiles in a rain forest setting. Built to the correct shape and size, the dinos are also accompanied with interpretive signage. It's a self-guided tour through the garden so it's easy to take your time to absorb the knowledge as well as the fun. Open all year, daily from 8 a.m. until dusk.

Brookings

ALFRED A. LOEB STATE PARK
(541) 469-2021
www.oregonstateparks.org/park_72.php
Located 6 miles north of the California-Oregon border is a stretch of mild climate on both sides of Brookings that the locals proudly call the Banana Belt. Alfred A. Loeb State Park has a good sampling of the famed myrtle tree (it's actually the largest grove in Oregon). There are some good swimming holes in the Chetco River and lots of picnic nooks.

ANNUAL EVENTS AND FESTIVALS

You'll be amazed at the variety of annual events and festivals that are held on the Oregon Coast. Many feature arts and crafts by local artisans, delicious seafood such as crab and salmon, and live entertainment. Other events are centered on favorite beach pastimes such as sandcastle building or kite flying. Or they focus on the natural beauty of the plants and animals present on the coastline. For example, twice a year you can participate in whale-watching week and look for spouting gray whales on their semiannual migration, or if you love flowers you should check out the Azalea Festival in Brookings or the Rhododendron Festival in Florence, both during the month of May. If you want to combine great seafood with fine Oregon wines, then you should be sure to attend the Newport Seafood and Wine Festival held in February in Newport. We've tried to include events that are big crowd pleasers as well as small-town gatherings, and we've also included events such as the Great Oregon Beach Cleanup where you can volunteer to help keep the Oregon Coast beautiful.

In this chapter we've listed annual events and festivals alphabetically in the months that they occur. We've noted the time of the month the event is taking place and we always recommend that you call ahead to verify specific places and times. Note that concerts and writing events are not included in this chapter, but, instead, are listed in the Arts chapter.

JANUARY

WINTER WHALE WATCH WEEK
Along the Oregon Coast
Oregon State Parks and Recreation
Whale Watching Center
119 SW US 101, Depoe Bay
(541) 765-3407
www.whalespoken.org

During Winter Whale Watch Week you can stop by more than 29 locations on the Oregon Coast from December 26 through January 2 and watch for gray whales migrating south. Trained volunteers can help you spot these magnificent creatures and can provide you with information about gray whale migration. Volunteers are present from 10 a.m. to 1 p.m. at designated sites that are identified by a WHALE WATCHING SPOKEN HERE sign. You can find out where the designated whale-watching locations are by visiting www .whalespoken.org. The Oregon Parks and Recreation District, the Oregon Coast Aquarium, and other private and governmental agencies sponsor this semiannual event.

YACHATS LIONS ANNUAL CRAB FEED
Yachats Lions Hall 4th and Pontiac, Yachats
(541) 547-3495

The last weekend in January you can enjoy an all-you-can-eat crab feast that includes French bread, coleslaw, baked beans, soda, and coffee for $25 per person.

ℹ️ You'll have better luck spotting gray whales on calm days with the sun at your back. Look for the signature "blows" the whales give when they are surfacing for air. Be sure to dress warmly and bring a pair of binoculars.

ℹ️ To find out about more events and festivals held on the Oregon Coast, call the Oregon Tourism Commission at (800) 547-7842 and request The Events Calendar–Oregon or visit their Web site at www.traveloregon.com.

FEBRUARY

CHARLESTON MERCHANTS' ANNUAL CRAB FEED
Charleston Elementary School
5200 Seven Devils Rd., Charleston
(541) 888-2311
www.charlestonmarina.com
Join the fun at the annual Charleston Merchants' Crab Feed held in mid-February. The local Charleston Merchants sponsor a dinner of a whole or half crab, fresh green beans, fluffy French bread, and a beverage. The dinner is held from 11 a.m. to 4 p.m. and proceeds from this event benefit the Charleston Visitors Association.

NEWPORT SEAFOOD & WINE FESTIVAL
Newport Marina Exhibit Hall, Newport
(541) 265-8801
www.seafoodandwine.com
This festival was established in 1976 and is one of the premier festivals on the Oregon Coast. Held the last weekend in February, this event features more than 100 exhibitors including the food booths that cook up sinfully delicious seafood specials. You'll also be able to taste-test a variety of wines from representatives from most of Oregon's wineries as well as well-known wineries from California and Washington. Arts and crafts booths filled with photography, original paintings, handcrafted jewelry, woodcarvings, wall hangings, and handcrafted pottery are part of the fun. The festival hours are Friday from 2 to 9 p.m., Saturday 10 a.m. to 6 p.m., and Sunday from 10 a.m. to 4 p.m. You must be over 21 years of age to attend and the admission price is $10 on Friday, $15 on Saturday, and $5 on Sunday.

MARCH

GREAT OREGON BEACH CLEANUP
Entire Coast
(503) 844-9571
www.solv.org
You can help keep the Oregon coastline beautiful by joining more than 5,000 volunteers to take part in the Oregon Beach Cleanup that takes place the last Saturday in March and the second Saturday in September to collect 20 to 30 tons of debris along the scenic coastline. Dozens of designated cleanup sites are available all along the Coast and you are asked to pick up trash between 10 a.m. and 1 p.m. Plastic bags are provided. Bring rubber gloves to protect your hands from sharp objects. Call ahead for specific locations.

OREGON DUNE MUSHERS MAIL RUN
P.O. Box 841, North Bend 97459
(541) 677-8393
www.oregondunemushers.com
Held the first weekend in March, this annual three-day event is a 70-mile endurance mush from North Bend to Florence through the Oregon Dunes National Recreation Area. Dryland dog teams (dogs pulling a cart on wheels) and their owners brave sand dunes, trails, hard-packed roads, and sandy beaches.

SPRING WHALE WATCH WEEK
Along the Oregon Coast
Oregon State Parks and Recreation
Whale Watching Center
119 SW US 101, Depoe Bay
(541) 765-3407
www.whalespoken.org
During Spring Whale Watch Week, you can stop at more than 28 locations on the Oregon Coast during the last week in March and watch for gray whales migrating north. Trained volunteers can help you spot these magnificent creatures and can provide you with information about gray whale migration. Volunteers are present from 10 a.m. to 1 p.m. at designated sites that are

identified by a WHALE WATCHING SPOKEN HERE sign. You can find out the 28 designated whale-watching locations that are part of this program by visiting www.whalespoken.org. The Oregon Parks and Recreation District, the Oregon Coast Aquarium, and other private and governmental agencies sponsor this semiannual event.

YACHATS ARTS & CRAFTS FAIR
Yachats Commons 4th Street and US 101, Yachats
(541) 547-3530
www.yachats.org
Held the third week in March, the annual Yachats Arts & Crafts Fair is filled with fun sights and sounds for everyone. Cruise through booths filled with handcrafted wares made from clay, leather, and fabric. If you get hungry, be sure to stop by the food booths filled with fresh seafood delicacies, yummy desserts, and other concoctions that will make you want to go back for seconds. The arts and crafts fair is open from 9 a.m. to 5 p.m. on Saturday and from 10 a.m. to 4 p.m. on Sunday.

APRIL

ASTORIA-WARRENTON CRAB & SEAFOOD FESTIVAL
Hammond Mooring Basin, Hammond
(503) 325-6311
www.oldoregon.com
Thousands of people attend the annual Astoria-Warrenton Crab & Seafood Festival held the last weekend in April. More than 150 craft, food, and wine vendors are present, with the main event being the traditional crab dinner. This festival features a variety of entertainment, a colorful carnival, a kids corner, and many more activities that will appeal to all members of the family. The festival is open Friday evening from 4 to 9 p.m., Saturday from 10 a.m. to 8 p.m., and Sunday from 11 a.m. to 4 p.m. Call for admission prices.

MAY

AZALEA FESTIVAL
Azalea Park, Brookings
(800) 535-9469
www.brookingsor.com
Held during the third weekend in May, this festival celebrates the brightly flowered azaleas that are at their peak bloom during May in Azalea Park. Held since 1939, this festival features a floral parade and queen coronation, arts and crafts, and food booths.

MUTT MASTERS DOG SHOW & OLYMPICS
1545 SE 50th, Lincoln City
(800) 452-2151
www.oregoncoast.org/mutts/index.php
In Mid-May you can take your canine friend to attend a fun-filled afternoon of dog events including a Frisbee contest, fetch contest, and high jump contest. You can also cruise through the human food booths and find plenty of pet information, goodies, and gifts. A suggested donation is $5 per person and you are encouraged to bring bags of dry food that will be donated to the Lincoln County Animal Shelter.

RHODODENDRON FESTIVAL
Florence
(800) 524-4864
www.florencechamber.com
The beautiful blooms of the rhododendron are celebrated at this annual event held during the third weekend in May. A variety of events such as an arts and crafts fair, floral parade and queen's coronation, flower show, and Rhodie Run are some of the fun events at this festival.

JUNE

BEACHCOMBER DAYS
Waldport
(541) 563-2133
www.waldport-chamber.com
Beachcomber Days is an annual celebration held during the third weekend in June for the commu-

nity of Waldport and sponsored by the Waldport Chamber of Commerce. The whole town comes alive with arts and crafts vendors selling unique items, food booths featuring seafood delicacies, and live entertainment. Kids will love the parade and carnival that are also held in conjunction with this annual event.

CANNON BEACH SANDCASTLE CONTEST
Cannon Beach
(503) 436-2973
www.cannonbeach.org
This annual event is held in Cannon Beach on the second Saturday in June and draws sandcastle builders and spectators from all over Oregon. The event is held from 9 a.m. to 2 p.m. and is limited to 150 participants organized into divisions by age, individual or team, and type of building implements used. Each individual or team is assigned a building plot and can use only natural materials such as rocks, seaweed, shells, and sticks to build their sandcastle.

CASCADE HEAD MUSIC FESTIVAL
Peter the Fisherman Lutheran Church,
Campus Building
1226 Southwest 13th St., Lincoln City
(541) 994-5333
www.cascadeheadmusic.org
This annual event is held in mid-June and features musicians from all over the world that play compositions by classic Viennese masters such as Beethoven and Schubert. Delicious Oregon wines, cheeses, and handmade desserts are offered at each concert. Call for specific dates and times.

CHAINSAW SCULPTURE CHAMPIONSHIPS
Rainbow Plaza, Reedsport
(541) 361-9080
www.odcsc.com
This annual event is held the second weekend in June and features professional chainsaw carvers who create one-of-a-kind wood sculptures in timed events. Wood sculptures are offered for sale after the contest. Call for specific dates and times.

TILLAMOOK COUNTY RODEO
P.O. Box 65, Tillamook 97141
(503) 842-5855
www.tillamookrodeo.com
This fun family event is held the last weekend in June and features the Dairy Parade, rodeo, dance, and Buckaroo Breakfast. Call for schedule and admission prices.

JULY

FOURTH OF JULY CELEBRATION
Rockaway Beach
(503) 355-8108
www.rockawaybeach.net
Join in the festivities at Rockaway Beach, which include a parade, auction, races, games, and treasure hunt. End the day by watching a grand display of colorful fireworks on the beach at dusk.

OCEAN FESTIVAL
Beach Boulevard, Winchester Bay
(541) 271-3495
www.reedsportcc.org
The Ocean Festival has a rich set of activities that will satisfy anyone. Arts and crafts booths, a children's carnival, a classic car show, a quilt show, a dance, and a seafood dinner are some of the highlights of this annual event that is held the fourth weekend in July.

PANCAKE BREAKFAST & PARADE
Downtown Manzanita
(877) 368-5100
Come join the rest of the Manzanita community for a homemade pancake breakfast and a small-town Fourth of July parade. The communities of Wheeler, Nehalem, and Manzanita participate in this fun annual event. Local seniors have their own float and kids dressed up in brightly colored costumes march proudly for their parents in this small-town parade. The pancake breakfast is held from 8:30 to 11 a.m. and the parade starts at 1:00 p.m. Be sure to stick around for the fireworks off the beach at Manzanita at dusk.

TOLEDO SUMMER FESTIVAL
Memorial Field, Toledo
(541) 336-9550
www.toledosummerfestival.com
This fun community event is held the last weekend in July and features a logging show, carnival, parade, dances, delicious food, and Toledo's famous fireworks display. Call for specific dates and times.

AUGUST

BLACKBERRY ARTS FESTIVAL
50 East Central, Coos Bay
(541) 269-0215
Juicy, sweet blackberries are the heart and soul of this arts and crafts festival that is held at the end of August in downtown Coos Bay. At this fun festival you can taste-test blackberry pie, blackberry cookies, blackberry scones, and blackberry jams and jellies—just for starters. You can also check out almost 100 booths that are filled with local arts and crafts. Many of these talented craftspeople will demonstrate how they make their wares and if you ever wanted a handmade German leather cap, you'll find it here.

SEPTEMBER

BANDON CRANBERRY FESTIVAL
Bandon
(541) 347-9616
www.bandoncranberryfest.com
This annual festival is held the first part of September in Bandon's Old Town and features arts and crafts, food vendors, live music, a parade and queen's coronation, and the Cranberry Bowl Football game.

CHOWDER BLUES AND BREWS FESTIVAL
Florence Events Center
715 Quince St., Florence
(541) 997-3128
www.florencechamber.com
This three-day festival is held at the end of September and features a chowder cook-off, micro-brew tasting and competition, food booths, and live music.

FALL KITE FESTIVAL
Lincoln City
(800) 452-2151
www.oregoncoast.org
You'll be amazed at all the colorful kites that come in all shapes and sizes and are flown at this annual kite festival that is held the third weekend in September. Kite flyers from all over the world participate in a variety of contests including team kite-flying, lighted kite night fly, and many more. Call ahead for specific times and location.

INDIAN STYLE SALMON BAKE
City Park, Depoe Bay
(541) 765-2889
www.depoebaychamber.org
If you love salmon and want to participate in a more than 40-year-old annual event, then you should plan on spending the third Saturday in September at this salmon fest. Hundreds of pounds of salmon are baked on the beach in a festive atmosphere filled with music, clowns, and other fun happenings.

OCTOBER

DOG SHOW AT THE BEACH
Surfsand Resort
148 West Gower, Cannon Beach
(800) 547-6100, (503) 436-2274
www.surfsand.com
This community event is held in mid-October and is sponsored by the Surfsand Resort. You and your dog can participate in 14 events, such as cutest dog, oldest dog, biggest dog, and smallest dog. Others include Frisbee catch, best bark, an obstacle course race, best tail wag, the 25-yard doggy dash, obedience trials, best trick, a "so ugly you're cute!" award, best costume, and a pet/owner look-alike contest. In addition to the events and awards ceremony is the auction/raffle and Parade of Champions at the day's end. Proceeds go to the Clatsop County Animal Shelter.

OREGON SHOREBIRD FESTIVAL
Charleston
(541) 867-4550
www.oregonsadventurecoast.com
Learn about Oregon's shorebirds at this annual festival sponsored by the Cape Arago Audubon Chapter. You can participate in boat birding trips, land field trips, and informative lectures. Call for specific dates and times.

NOVEMBER

HOLIDAY GIFT FAIR
Seaside Convention Center
415 1st Ave., Seaside
(800) 444-6740
www.seasidechamber.com
During this gift fair, held the last weekend in November, you can shop for handmade crafts and holiday decorations at more than 130 booths. Additional highlights of this event include holiday caroling, a visit from Santa, and a tree lighting ceremony at Quatat Park in Seaside.

STORMY WEATHER ARTS FESTIVAL
Cannon Beach
(503) 436-2623
www.cannonbeach.org
This festival celebrates drama, poetry, music, and artwork of Oregon artists at different locations in Cannon Beach. You can listen to hot country fiddles, classical piano music, or attend a variety of short plays. Another crowd pleaser is the Quick Draw Event where 14 artists have one hour to paint and frame their artwork in front of an audience. The art is then sold by auction. This festival is held the second weekend in November. Call ahead for event times, ticket prices, and locations.

DECEMBER

NEWPORT LIGHTED BOAT PARADE
Newport Harbor, Newport
(800) 262-3183
www.christmasboatparade.com
During the third week in December, the Christmas Boat Parade lights up Newport Harbor with an array of colorful holiday lights. Some boats are decorated with animated Christmas scenes and carolers. The boats travel 14 miles around Newport Harbor allowing viewers to enjoy the lights from restaurants, public beaches, and private homes. The parade takes place five consecutive nights and starts at 6:30 p.m. each night.

OREGON COAST AQUARIUM'S "SEA OF LIGHTS"
2820 Southeast Ferry Slip Rd., Newport
(541) 867-3474
www.aquarium.org
Twinkling lights, traditional caroling, and a gingerbread village are part of the holiday magic that takes place the first weekend in December from 6:30 to 9:30 p.m. at the Oregon Coast Aquarium. Kids can make holiday crafts and visit Santa and his elves and adults can enjoy hot chocolate and other holiday goodies while looking at the fascinating exhibits at the aquarium.

i **There are many celebrations and events happening in all coastal cities during the Fourth of July weekend and the Christmas holidays. To find out more about holiday events and celebrations, call the local chamber of commerce for the city you are visiting.**

THE GREAT OUTDOORS

The recreational opportunities along the Oregon Coast are as limitless as your imagination. In this chapter you'll find information on the coastal landscape, geology, climate, plants, and animals. In addition, you'll find detailed listings of state parks, recreation sites, and natural areas. The beach is the big attraction at many state parks. You can fly a kite along the shore, play Frisbee or beach volleyball, build sandcastles, play in the surf, or watch for wildlife. Almost all state parks have hiking trails that wander through scenic coastal forest, along wide, sandy beaches, or on scenic bluffs that overlook the ocean. You'll have the chance to watch for whales, explore tide pools, and learn about coastal plants and animals by reading interpretive signs. In addition to beach access, many state parks and recreation areas have picnic areas nestled in a coastal forest or perched above the beach offering scenic ocean views.

NATURAL WORLD

The natural world of the Oregon Coast is a kaleidoscope of sights, sounds, and smells. With a diverse landscape made up of mountains, beaches, rivers, dunes, bays, and estuaries, the Oregon Coast is filled with colorful plants and viewable wildlife waiting to be experienced. If you were to paint a canvas of the Oregon Coast, you would begin by painting the north-south running Coast Range of mountains that is covered by a patchwork of deep green cedar and fir forest. This young mountain range separates the Oregon coastline from the green Willamette Valley to the east. Roaming this lush, green range of mountains you would find majestic Roosevelt elk, swift black-tailed deer, and lumbering black bear. Flowing from the mountains you would paint the wide-running coastal rivers like the Nehalem, Wilson, Siuslaw, Rogue, and Chetco that are stocked by fish hatcheries with salmon, trout, and steelhead. Mixed in with these major waterways you would draw outlines of large, rounded coastal bays, lakes and estuaries that support a myriad of bird species such as blue herons, Canada geese, kingfishers, loons, and mallard ducks.

As you near the edge of the Pacific Ocean, you would paint high cliff walls, spectacular headlands, and rocky islands that are home to colonies of seabirds like common murres, pigeon guillemots, gulls, cormorants, and tufted puffins. Mixed between the high rocky cliffs you would paint long, flat strokes for sandy beaches and swift strokes for the high, sweeping sand dunes that change with wind and tide. Chasing the tides on the sandy beaches you would sketch black oystercatchers, sanderlings, snowy plovers, and western sandpipers. Flying just above the break, you draw a group of stately brown pelicans scouting for their next meal. Along the shoreline, you would also capture the intricate shadows of craggy tide pools that are home to creatures like sea-green anemones, bright orange starfish, prickly purple sea urchins, gregarious crabs, black oval mussels, and rough-shelled barnacles. And last, you would apply brushstrokes for the Pacific Ocean that pulses with the rise and fall of the tide with its undulating swells and pounding waves. This blue-green ocean is home to migrating gray whales, harbor seals, and barking Stellar's sea lions.

The sights and sounds of the Oregon Coast natural world are waiting to be discovered by you. With more than 300 miles of scenic coastline, there are dozens of opportunities to pull off US 101, the main coast arterial highway, into a scenic viewpoint or state park where you may have the opportunity to observe sea lions resting on offshore rocks, nesting seabirds catching fish and feeding young, a bald eagle soaring high above on the lofty air currents, the spout of a gray whale, or interesting tide pools that serve as a window to the undersea world.

In this chapter we will introduce you to the geologic events that shaped the coastal landscape, give you a taste of what the climate has in store for you, and tell you about some of the diverse plants and animals you may see while you are on your journey through this rugged and magnificent place. We'll also guide you through our wonderful state parks, which all have something unique to offer.

GEOLOGY

Molded and shaped by a series of geologic events, the Oregon Coast mountains are relatively young in relation to their Cascade mountain cousins located in the central part of the state. The Coast mountain range began as seafloor sediments and basalt seamounts. When the North American continent collided with these seamounts more than 45 million years ago, a shallow sea floor was created that filled with sediment over the next 20 million years. About 25 million years ago, the Coast Range was pushed upward from the sea and over the next 7 million years the Oregon Coast landscape evolved into what you see today.

Other volcanic episodes also shaped the basalt headlands along the coast. Over 15 million years ago, as many as 12 huge basalt lava flows, originating in eastern Oregon and Washington, traveled west to the Pacific Ocean through the ancient Columbia River channel and formed Tillamook Head, Cape Falcon, Cape Meares, Cape Lookout, Cape Kiwanda, Yaquina Head, Depoe Bay, Otter Rocks, and Seal Rocks.

CLIMATE

There is no disputing the fact that it is wet in Oregon. As a matter of fact, the coastline has the highest rainfall in the entire state. For example, Astoria and Newport receive an annual rainfall

of over 80 inches, and Brookings, nicknamed "the banana belt of the Oregon Coast" for its often warm and sunny weather, comes in with an average rainfall of about 10 inches less. You can expect average temperatures on the Coast in the low to mid-60s in the summer months with occasional warm sunny days that reach into the mid 70s. In the winter months, you can expect average temperatures to be in the 40s and 50s. Remember, the weather on the Coast can resemble the moods of a two-year-old—it can be sunny and bright; cloudy and foggy; rainy and windy; or a combination of any of the above. With this thought in mind, it is always best to be prepared for all types of weather. In the winter months, bring along a sturdy rain jacket and insulating layers such as polar fleece or a wool sweater as well as sturdy, waterproof shoes and insulating socks. In the summer months, be sure to wear sunscreen and sunglasses and a wide brimmed hat, and keep a rain jacket and other insulating layers on hand in case the weather decides to turn on you.

The climate on the Coast is influenced by a variety of natural forces, including sun, wind, and tides. Heavy winter rainstorms create green coastal forests, and salt-laden winds constantly reshape sand dunes, beaches, and coastal vegetation. The moody weather is all a part of the area's attraction. Walking through a forest filled with sea-green fog and mist captures the mystery of the woods. Walking along the rocky coast on a stormy day, you can watch huge, white, frothy breakers crash into offshore rocks creating a thundering roar. Or, you may happen to be walking on a long, flat, sandy beach on a bright, summer day with the salty wind whipping your hair, surfers catching fast waves, and kids flying brightly colored kites. These images are all possibilities along the scenic Oregon Coast.

i To learn more about weather on the Oregon Coast, visit the Oregon Climate Service home page on the World Wide Web at www.ocs.oregonstate.edu.

THE COASTAL LANDSCAPE

Forests

The Oregon Coast landscape is dynamic and always changing. The coastal mountains are laden with a patchwork forest made up of western hemlock, Sitka spruce, red cedar, and Douglas fir. In southern coastal forests there are small islands of orange-barked madrone trees, Port Orford cedar, coastal redwood trees, and myrtle trees. The myrtle tree is a member of the laurel family and is related to avocado, camphor, cinnamon, and sassafras. Scented candles and perfumes are made from the oil present in the myrtle's fragrant and spicy leaves. The leaves also serve as an excellent seasoning for soups and sauces. Furniture and souvenirs are made from the beautiful wood of this tree, and dotted along the Oregon Coast you'll find souvenir shops selling myriad products made from it. Large areas of coastal forest are a patchwork of different ages and types of trees due to logging. It is not uncommon to see large tracts of clearcuts that have been replanted with young seedlings. In areas that have been heavily cut, you'll find thick groves of big-leaf maple and red alder trees. You can recognize red alders by their grayish white bark and thick covering of green moss and lichens. The coastal Indian tribes made utensils and carvings from the wood of this tree and also steeped the bark in hot water to cure rheumatic fever.

To see a rare grove of myrtle and redwood trees, visit **Alfred A. Loeb State Park** located 7.5 miles east of Brookings off of North Bank Chetco River Road. Walk on the River View Nature Trail to view the myrtle trees and the Redwood Nature Trail to view the 600- to 800-year-old grove of redwood trees. An informative brochure that corresponds to numbered trail markers along each trail is available at the trailhead.

There are only a few pockets of old-growth trees on the Oregon Coast. One of the best places to walk through a grove of old-growth trees is **Oswald West State Park** located 9 miles west of Cannon Beach off US 101.

The coastal forests have a rich variety of understory plants. In the spring months you'll have the opportunity to view many wildflowers such as the delicate, white triangular flowers of western trillium; the pink-flowered western columbine; the purple, bell-shaped flowers of the coast penstemon; and the cloverlike leaves and delicate white flowers of wood sorrel. Woven into this forest recipe are the distinctly shaped leaves of sword fern, deer fern, and maidenhair fern that thrive in the cool, wet environment. Wildflowers that grow in sunny, open areas include vibrant orange tiger lilies, blue iris, red Indian paintbrush, white meadow chickweed, phlox, and larkspur. **Saddle Mountain State Park** is a rich botanical area featuring many different species of wildflowers. It is east of Cannon Beach off US 26.

Many coastal headlands are covered with a variety of grasses and unique wildflowers such as red fescue, wild rye, goldenrod, coastal paintbrush, wild iris, blue violet, lupine, and yarrow. **Cascade Head** is designated as a National Scenic Preserve and is haven to a rare meadowland ecosystem that protects the threatened Oregon silverspot butterfly. Cascade Head is one of six remaining areas where this butterfly is found. Its current range is along the coasts of northern California, Oregon, and Washington. The best time to see the butterfly is from August through September when it is in the adult stage. Adults lay eggs on the tall grasses in August and September and the caterpillar emerges in early spring. The caterpillar forms a cocoon in early summer and reaches the adult butterfly stage in midsummer. The butterfly is about 1 inch wide and has orange and brown markings on the top of the wings and silver spots under the wings. Cascade Head is located 4 miles north of Lincoln City on US 101.

Black-tailed deer inhabit the coastal forests and feed on bark, buds, leaves, and grasses. These graceful mammals are named for the distinctive dark brown tail with black trim, which has a white underside. Smaller than their mule deer cousins, black-tailed deer can be most frequently seen grazing in open clearings in the evening and early morning hours.

Black bears can also be found roaming the mountains and valleys of the Coast Range. Varying in color from rich, dark brown to light cinnamon, these bears range from 35 to 40 inches tall when on all fours and have a length of 4½ to 6 feet. Depending on area and level of nutrition, black bears weigh from 125 to 600 pounds, with males being about a third larger than females. Black bears have taste buds for virtually anything that is edible. About 75 percent of their diet is made up of roots, berries, flowers, grasses, sedges, herbs, and tubers. They also feed on decaying animal carcasses, fish, small marine animals, insects, and small mammals.

One of the most magnificent mammals you may see is the Roosevelt elk. Mature bull elk can weigh up to 1,000 pounds and are usually reddish-brown in color. Roosevelt elk are primarily grazers and tend to congregate in open meadows where grasses are plentiful. A dominant bull elk is usually in charge of a herd of about 20 cows. Every spring, the bulls grow a set of antlers that are used to ward off rival males during the fall breeding season. Once the breeding season is over, the antlers are shed. To see a herd of Roosevelt elk, visit Cascade Head or the **Jewell Meadows Wildlife Area** located 1.5 miles west of Jewell off Highway 202. The best viewing months are September through March. Another place to view Roosevelt elk and black-tailed deer is the **Dean Creek Elk Viewing Area** located on the south side of Highway 38 three miles east of Reedsport.

Estuaries

As you move down from the mountains, coastal rivers meander through lush coastal valleys and eventually flow into the transitional zone of estuaries. The Oregon coastline is rich with estuaries that are formed when tides cause seawater to flood the mouths of coastal rivers, mixing freshwater and seawater. The level of the water in estuaries rises and falls with the tide. Estuaries are very productive places due to the fairly calm rise and fall of the water that creates a safe haven for estuarine plants and animals to live. Estuaries have a flat, muddy bottom that is created from the accumulation of decaying plants, animal matter, and fine sediment that is brought down from the coastal mountains in the rivers. Shellfish such as butter clams, razor clams, and oysters thrive in this rich, muddy environment and, in turn, shorebirds find an ample supply of crustaceans, fish, snails, and worms. Estuaries are an excellent place to view different varieties of birds such as blue herons, belted kingfishers, loons, grebes, and a variety of geese and ducks. Plants that thrive in the nutrient-rich soil include arrow grass, giant vetch, salt rush, cattails, bull rushes, and bull thistle.

If you'd like to view birds and other wildlife in this rich coastal zone, visit **Bayocean Peninsula** at Tillamook Bay, **Netarts Bay** or **Siletz Bay Park** in Lincoln City, **Yaquina Bay** in Newport, the **South Slough National Estuarine Reserve** south of Charleston, and the **Bandon Marsh National Wildlife Refuge** located across the river from Bullards Beach State Park, located 2 miles north of Bandon on US 101.

Sand Dunes

Oregon's sand dunes form desertlike landscapes that intermingle with coastal forest and freshwater lakes creating different types of coastal ecosystems. The Oregon Dunes stretch from Heceta Head south to Cape Arago and are protected as part of the Oregon Dunes National Recreation Area, established in 1972. This recreation area protects more than 50 square miles of dunes between Florence and Coos Bay. These ever-changing dunes sit on top of a marine sandstone layer called the Coos Bay Dune Sheet. Wind, tides, and wave action have pushed sand as far inland as 2.5 miles over thousands of years to create some of the world's largest dunes. The wind sculpts and shapes the dunes by blowing at a constant rate of about 14 miles per hour from the northwest. Winter storm winds that blow in from the southwest can exceed 100 miles per hour and also have a great influence on dune formation. Ocean currents flowing north in the winter months and south in the summer months also act as a partner in sculpting the dunes by keeping sand deposited by coastal rivers at the shoreline. Large waves then push the sand onto shore and strong winds blow the sand inland.

Rocky Shore

The rocky shore has been shaped by its never-ending struggle with the sea. Winter storms and high tides form pounding waves that crash into rocky islands, arches, sea stacks, and cliffs. During this process, the ocean carves out its own masterpiece for all of us to enjoy. Atop the headlands and bluffs, you'll find the twisted and bent trunks of shore pines often referred to as *krumholz* that are sculpted by the relentless winds that whip in from the sea. Among these sturdy trees, hardy salal and ceanothus bushes make their stand in the·wet, windy environment. Open meadows of grasses and bright wildflowers also grace the slopes along the rocky coast and brave succulents gain a foothold on the steep cliff faces and rocky outcroppings.

Where the ocean meets the rocky shore, sea caves, tide pools, and cobblestone beaches are home to a variety of seashore animals and birds. The most common bird we all associate with the seashore is the vivacious gull. Five different species of gulls live along the coastline, the glaucous-winged gull being the largest and most common. You can identify this gull species by its white head and chest, gray wings, and yellow bill with a distinctive red spot. Sharing the rocky cliffs with the gulls are the penguin-like common murres, which can be identified by their dark brown feathers and white undersides, and pigeon guillemots, which are distinguished by their black bodies, white wing patches, and bright red beaks and feet. Tufted puffins also nest on rocky cliffs and offshore islands. The males have bright orange beaks, white eye patches, yellow feather tufts, and dark plumage. They feed on small minnowlike fish that they catch by diving underwater and swimming with their wings. Other birds that nest on the rocky ledges and offshore islands are pelagic and brandt's cormorants. These long-necked birds have dark,

iridescent plumage and can often be seen resting on rocks with their wings outstretched. This curious behavior is due to the fact that their feathers become saturated with water after they have been diving for fish. In order to regain flight, these birds have to dry out their waterlogged feathers in the sun. Bald eagles also soar on the air currents above the rocky shoreline searching for ill or injured fish. The bald eagle has beautiful dark brown plumage and distinctive white head, neck, and tail feathers. The rocky coast also supports large groups of Stellar's sea lions, which rest and breed on offshore islands. They feed on fish and squid, and males can weigh up to 2,200 and reach lengths of up to 11 feet. You can hear the barklike sounds of large herds of Stellar's sea lions up to a mile away.

Another common sight along the coastline is the spout of migrating gray whales during their semiannual migration. Gray whales can be seen migrating south to their breeding lagoons in Baja California during December and January and migrating north during March and April to feed in the rich Arctic seas. Mature gray whales are about 35 to 45 feet long, weigh 22 to 35 tons, and can live up to 60 years. These gentle giants feed on shrimplike amphipods by scraping up mud from the ocean bottom and then filtering unwanted material through their baleen (a horny substance in their jaws) leaving the tasty amphipods behind, which they then swallow.

If you are exploring the rocky shoreline in the tidal zone, you'll have a unique opportunity to view a wealth of plant and animal life. The black stain you see on some rock faces in the tidal zone is hardy black lichen that consists of algae and fungi that have developed a symbiotic partnership. Rough-shelled acorn barnacles also cluster closely on exposed rocks. When the tide is out, these small creatures seem lifeless, but when the tide comes back in and the shells become submerged, these tiny creatures thrust out a netlike appendage that catches microscopic plankton. Acorn barnacles share their rocky home with limpets and snails that are also especially adapted to

(Q) Close-up

Dune Walk

To walk among some amazing dunes in the Oregon Dunes National Recreation Area, check out these trails:

TAYLOR DUNES TRAIL

This 3.2-mile moderate out-and-back trail takes you through a beautiful coastal forest and dune environment. Start by hiking north from the parking area and crossing the Carter Campground entrance road. Follow the forest path as it parallels quiet Taylor Lake on the right. At 0.3 mile you'll arrive at a trail junction. Go left and continue 0.2 mile to a viewing platform surrounded by big Sitka spruce trees. After enjoying views of the dunes and far-off beach, head back to the trail junction and turn left. Follow the blue-banded posts for 0.5 mile to a beautiful beach (your turnaround point). Retrace the route back to the trailhead. To get there from Reedsport, travel 12 miles north (or 9 miles south of Florence) on US 101 to the Taylor Lake Trailhead.

DUNES OVERLOOK

This easy 2-mile hike takes you to a scenic viewpoint overlooking expansive dunes in the Oregon Dunes National Recreation Area. From the parking area walk out to a viewing platform and then take a paved sidewalk and long wooden ramp to the start of the sandy hiking trail. Use the guideposts to find your way across the dunes to a secluded beach (your turnaround point). To get there from Reedsport, travel 11 miles north (or 10 miles south of Florence) on US 101 to the Dunes Overlook Trailhead.

UMPQUA DUNES

This 1-mile interpretive loop takes you through a madrone and manzanita forest, wetlands, and magnificent coastal dunes. If you feel like a longer hiking adventure, continue through the dunes 2.5 miles to the beach. Look for posts with blue bands to guide your way. To get to this hike, travel 10.5 miles south of Reedsport on US 101 (or 12 miles north of North Bend) to the signed Umpqua Dunes Trailhead.

TAHKENITCH CREEK LOOP

This pleasant 1.5-mile loop route takes you through a coastal dune environment along picturesque Tahkenitch Creek in the Oregon Dunes National Recreation Area. To get there from the junction of Highway 38 and US 101 in Reedsport, travel 9.2 miles north (or 12 miles south of Florence) on US 101 to the Tahkenitch Creek Trailhead.

SUTTON CREEK RECREATION AREA

The 2,700-acre Sutton Creek Recreation Area has over 6 miles of trails to explore, giving you a close-up view of a diverse coastal ecosystem made of sand dunes, coastal forest, freshwater lakes, coastal stream, and sandy beach. The Sutton Creek Campground has a short walk through a bog where you can view the insect-eating plant, cobra lily. To get to the Sutton Creek Campground Trailhead, drive 4.2 miles north of Florence on US 101 to Sutton Beach Road and turn left (west) at the Sutton Recreation sign. For more information on these trails, contact the Oregon Dunes National Recreation Area, 855 Highway Ave., Reedsport, OR 97467; call (541) 271-3611; or visit www.fs.fed.us/r6/siuslaw/recreation/tripplanning/oregondunes.

live with the changing tide. In the tidal zone you'll also find greenish yellow rock weed and bright green sea lettuce, whose wrinkled fronds resemble a head of Romaine lettuce. In tide pools, black oval-shelled mussels cluster tightly together on the craggy rocks, sharing their underwater habitat with vibrant orange starfish, prickly purple sea urchins, and emerald-green sea anemones. Other plants that live here include the light yellowish brown sea cauliflower, green sea cabbage, and olive-brown crisp leather seaweed. Bustling about in these craggy pools are hermit crabs, purple shore crabs, and Oregon rock crabs.

The Oregon Islands National Wildlife Refuge protects all these species and many more. More than 56 islands are part of this system and stretch along the entire Oregon Coast. You can view birds and mammals from many designated viewpoints along our coastline. Some of the best viewing areas are **Ecola State Park,** located 3 miles north of Cannon Beach; **Cape Meares State Park,** located 9 miles west of Tillamook on the Three Capes Scenic Highway; **Oceanside State Park,** located 2 miles south of Cape Meares on the Three Capes Scenic Highway; **Cape Lookout State Park,** located 11 miles southwest of Tillamook on the Three Capes Scenic Highway; **Yaquina Head Outstanding Natural Area,** located 3 miles north of Newport on US 101; and **Devil's Elbow State Park** and **Oregon Islands National Wildlife Refuge,** located 12 miles north of Florence on US 101. To learn more about coastal species and to see them up close, we highly recommended that you visit the **Oregon Coast Aquarium,** which has interactive displays hands-on exhibits, and natural outdoor displays that house a variety of species that live on the coast. The Oregon Coast Aquarium is located just south of Newport's Yaquina Bay Bridge, off US 101. To find out more about the aquarium, see the Attractions chapter.

COASTAL PARKS

North Coast

FORT STEVENS STATE PARK
(Camping and Day Use)
www.oregonstateparks.org/park_179.php
Located about 1 mile south of Hammond, Fort Stevens State Park encompasses 3,763 acres and offers a coastal habitat with a wonderful mix of shallow lakes, wetlands, coastal forest, and sandy beach. Paved biking trails and hiking trails are present throughout the park. You can hike 2 miles around scenic Coffenbury Lake, and a 1-mile trail takes you from the campground to the wreck of the *Peter Iredale,* a four-masted British freighter that ran aground on Clatsop Spit in a rough storm in 1906. Watch for whales at a viewing tower located in parking lot C at the north end of the park.

You may also want to explore the abandoned gun batteries of the Fort Stevens Military Reservation, which guarded the mouth of the Columbia River from the Civil War until World War II. You can view military artifacts and interpretive displays at the Fort Stevens Military Museum, (503) 861-2000, which is located off of Ridge Road adjacent to the park and is open from 10 a.m. to 6 p.m. from June through September and 10 a.m. to 4 p.m. the rest of the year. The Oregon Coast Hiking Trail passes through the park and if you are backpacking on this trail, hiker/biker campsites are available at Fort Stevens. Other popular activities in the park are swimming, windsurfing, picnicking, and beachcombing. The day use fee is $3.

DEL REY BEACH STATE RECREATION SITE
(Day Use)
www.oregonstateparks.org/park_177.php
Del Rey Beach is located 2 miles north of Gearhart off US 101. You'll find a flat, sandy beach only a short walk from your car at the Del Rey Beach State Recreation Site. This beach is a great place to watch the surf, take a long walk, fly kites, play Frisbee, build sandcastles, or play in the surf on a hot summer day. There is access to the Oregon Coast Trail. There is no day use fee.

SADDLE MOUNTAIN STATE NATURAL AREA
(Camping and Day Use)
www.oregonstateparks.org/park_197.php

Saddle Mountain State Natural Area is located 17 miles northeast of Cannon Beach off US 26. The area encompasses 2,911 acres and is rich in botanical diversity. Saddle Mountain rises 3,283 feet above the park, and a 5.2-mile out-and-back strenuous hiking trail leads you to the summit of this lofty peak. If you plan on hiking to the summit, note that the upper section of the trail can be somewhat treacherous. Wooden walkways and handrails have been put in place to help you reach your goal, but some parts of the trail are precipitous. However, once you arrive at the top you'll have far-reaching views to the west of Nehalem Bay, Onion Peak, Tillamook Head, and the coastline from Seaside to Clatsop Spit. To the east, you'll be able to see the Cascade Mountains as well as the surrounding Coast Range. This natural area is home to more than 300 species of plants. Ten primitive campsites are present in this park and they tend to fill up fast. Restrooms, picnic facilities, and water are available. There is no day use fee.

ECOLA STATE PARK
(Day Use)
www.oregonstateparks.org/park_188.php

Ecola State Park is located off US 101 2.5 miles north of Cannon Beach on Tillamook Head. The park covers 1,304 acres and affords many breathtaking views from several different viewpoints. From the main parking area, a short, paved trail leads you to viewpoints looking south toward Cannon Beach and Haystack Rock. In addition, you can take a 2-mile stroll on the Clatsop Loop Trail. This interpretive trail winds through a Sitka spruce forest and follows the footsteps of Lewis and Clark. There are several picnic tables located in a grassy area adjacent to the parking area where you can soak in the view while enjoying your lunch. Also from the main parking area, you can hook up with the Oregon Coast Trail and hike 1.5 miles north through a pretty coastal forest to Indian Beach. Along the way, you'll pass three spectacular viewpoints. From Indian Beach, you'll have great views of the 62-foot-high Tillamook Rock Lighthouse that rests on a large chunk of basalt rock that is more than a mile offshore from Tillamook Head. This lighthouse was built in 1881 and acted as a lifesaving beacon for ships headed for the Columbia River.

Instead of parking in the main parking area, you can continue driving to the Indian Beach parking area. This scenic, rocky beach is popular with surfers and boogie boarders. If you need to rent surfing or boogie boarding gear, stop by **Cleanline Surf Shop,** 171 Sunset Blvd., Cannon Beach, (503) 436-9726; www.cleanlinesurf.com.

There is fishing at the park as well as a hike-in camp at Indian Creek. The day use fee is $3.

Coast Safety

When you are visiting Oregon's scenic beaches, keep the following in mind:

Avoid hiking to isolated rocks, tide pools, beaches, or headlands during the incoming tide. You can view tide tables online at hmsc.oregon-state.edu/weather/tides.html.

Be aware that water-saturated logs weigh several tons and could crush you should they roll on you.

Don't wade out too far in the surf.

Strong currents and waves can swiftly carry you offshore. In addition, ocean temperatures are very cold and can quickly sap your strength.

Watch for sneaker waves that can knock you off exposed rocks, headlands, and jetties.

Don't climb on steep cliffs or rocks.

Always assume that all cliff edges are unstable and stay away from them.

TOLOVANA BEACH STATE RECREATION SITE
(Day Use)
www.oregonstateparks.org/park_199.php
Tolovana Beach is located 1 mile south of Cannon Beach off US 101. It is a flat, sandy beach that offers access to Haystack Rock. This interesting rock formation is the basalt remnant of volcanic eruptions that occurred 17 million years ago. It is also part of the Oregon Islands Wildlife Refuge and is an important nesting site for puffins, pelagic cormorants, pigeon guillemots, and western gulls. At the base of Haystack Rock, you'll find tide pools filled with a variety of colorful creatures, such as sea anemones, starfish, mussels, and hermit crabs. The flat, sandy beach is a great place to take a bike ride. If you need to rent a bike go to **Mike's Bike Shop** at 248 North Spruce St. in Cannon Beach, (503) 436-1266.

Other activities include picnicking, fishing, and kiteflying. There is access to the Oregon Coast Trail. There is no use fee.

ARCADIA BEACH STATE RECREATION SITE
(Day Use)
www.oregonstateparks.org/park_187.php
Arcadia Beach is located 3 miles south of Cannon Beach off US 101. The long, flat, sandy stretch of beach offers picnicking, fishing, beachcombing, and kiteflying, as well as access to the Oregon Coast Trail. Arcadia beach is a great place to spend the afternoon after exploring the shops, galleries, and restaurants in nearby Cannon Beach. There is no day use fee.

HUG POINT STATE RECREATION SITE
(Day Use)
www.oregonstateparks.org/park_191.php
Hug Point is located 5 miles south of Cannon Beach off US 101. The beach at Hug Point State Recreation Site is a historic wagon route and settlers headed south on the beach at low tide to reach the town of Arch Cape. Settlers had to "hug" closely to the headland to get around the point at low tide. Hug Point is a pretty beachside cove that houses two sea caves that are fun to explore. Fall Creek runs through this area. A great hike is to head north on the Oregon Coast Trail

5.2 miles north to Third Street in Cannon Beach. If you plan on completing this hike, make sure it is at low tide so you can trek around several of the headlands. Other activities include picnicking, fishing, kiteflying, and sandcastle building. There is no day use fee.

OSWALD WEST STATE PARK
(Camping and Day Use)
www.oregonstateparks.org/park_195.php
Oswald West State Park, located 10 miles south of Cannon Beach on US 101, covers 2,474 acres and offers breathtaking scenery. Arch Cape, Neahkahnie Mountain, Cape Falcon, and Smuggler's Cove are all contained within this park. A 1-mile out-and-back hiking trail leads you to Short Sands Beach—a popular beach for surfers and boogie boarders. The Oregon Coast Trail passes through the park and if you go north you can hike a 5-mile out-and-back trail to Cape Falcon. If you hike south on the Oregon Coast Trail, you can take a strenuous trek to the top of Neahkahnie Mountain, which is about 3.6 miles from the parking lot. The views from the summit are some of the best on the coast. There is no day use fee.

NEHALEM BAY STATE PARK
(Camping and Day Use)
www.oregonstateparks.org/park_201.php
Nehalem Bay State Park covers 890 acres and is located adjacent to Nehalem Bay and the Pacific Ocean, about 3 miles south of Manzanita. The campground in this park has sites for camping with horses. On one side of the campground is scenic Nehalem Bay and on the other side are sand dunes that lead to a sandy beach that extends for 4 miles to the end of the Nehalem Bay Spit. If you want to crab in the bay, you can launch your boat at the boat ramp located in the park. You may also want to launch your kayak or canoe in the bay. You can ride your bike on the 1.7-mile bike path that winds through open dunes adjacent to the bay. While riding on this bike path, you may see deer, elk, and a variety of other wildlife. Horseback riders can enjoy the 7.5-mile equestrian trail that takes you to the end of Nehalem Bay Spit. Hikers who walk along the

bay beachfront can experience prime bird-and seal-watching. The Oregon Coast Trail passes through the park and there is a hiker/biker camp here. Try horseback riding by renting a horse from **Northwest Equine Outfitters,** (503) 801-RIDE (801-7433), which operates a horse concession Memorial Day through Labor Day. Find them at the day use area in the park. There is a $3 day use fee at the park.

MANHATTAN BEACH STATE RECREATION SITE
(Day Use)
www.oregonstateparks.org/park_193.php
Manhattan Beach is located 2 miles north of Rockaway Beach off US 101. This day use park offers several picnic tables nestled among beautiful shore pines. A short access trail leads to a pretty beach where you can go beachcombing, fly a kite, build a sandcastle, or play Frisbee. There is also fishing and access to the Oregon Coast Trail. There is no day use fee.

i Bring a thermos with you on your visit to the Oregon Coast. Stop by a local coffee shop to fill your thermos with hot, steaming coffee that you can enjoy as you explore the many beautiful beaches along Oregon's rugged coast.

CAPE MEARES STATE SCENIC VIEWPOINT
(Day Use)
www.oregonstateparks.org/park_181.php
Cape Meares is located 10 miles west of Tillamook on the Three Capes Scenic Loop. One of the park's main attractions is the Cape Meares Lighthouse that was built in 1890. You can tour the lighthouse daily May through September and on the weekends in October, March, and April. A gift shop is located in the lighthouse and is open from 11 a.m. to 4 p.m. daily from May through September. A wide, paved path leads from the parking area to the lighthouse and along the way you'll have the opportunity to stop at several different viewpoints where you'll be able to see

nesting seabirds that include common murres, tufted puffins, pigeon guillemots, cormorants, and gulls. In addition, 3 miles of hiking trails take you through an old-growth spruce forest where you can view a tree shaped like an octopus. There is no fee for day use.

OCEANSIDE BEACH STATE RECREATION SITE
(Day Use)
www.oregonstateparks.org/park_182.php
Oceanside Beach is located 11 miles west of Tillamook off US 101 in the small community of Oceanside. When you visit this area, you can walk on the beach and hunt for agates, fly a kite, try surfing or kayaking in the fun waves off the beach, or check out the wildlife. A half-mile offshore is Three Arch Rocks, home to 13 species of seabirds that nest on these sea stacks. The rocks are designated wilderness and all animals that live here are protected. While you're visiting the Oceanside area, be sure to stop at **Roseanna's Oceanside Cafe,** 1490 Pacific St., Oceanside, (503) 842-7351. This local restaurant has a mouth-watering seafood menu and a great view of Three Arch Rocks and the pounding surf. Other popular activities include hang gliding and fishing. There is no day use fee.

CAPE LOOKOUT STATE PARK
(Camping and Day Use)
www.oregonstateparks.org/park_186.php
Located 12 miles southwest of Tillamook, Cape Lookout State Park covers 2,014 acres that include Netarts Spit and the jutting headland of Cape Lookout that is covered with a fern-filled coastal forest. Hiker and biker campsites are available. The campground is located adjacent to the ocean and has a few sites with an ocean view. A variety of hiking trails in the park will satisfy all levels of hikers. A very scenic trail is the 5.4-mile out-and-back Cape Trail that takes you to the tip of Cape Lookout, which is a good spot to look for whales. This trailhead is located 2.7 miles south of the state park campground entrance on the Three Capes Scenic Loop. If you're looking for a shorter hike, two nature trails are also present in the park. The 0.25-mile self-guided nature trail begins adjacent

to the campground registration booth. The Jackson Loop Nature Trail begins off the park entrance road east of the RV dump station.

Other activities include picnicking, fishing, and kayaking. There is access to the Oregon Coast Trail. The day use fee is $3.

CAPE KIWANDA STATE NATURAL AREA
(Day Use)
www.oregonstateparks.org/park_180.php
Cape Kiwanda State Natural Area, about 15 miles north of Lincoln City, encompasses 185 acres and is composed of a pretty beach adjacent to Cape Kiwanda, which is made of a spectacular sand dune. This area is best known for its fleet of dory boats that are launched from the beach. Once they're in the surf, it takes a bit of skilled maneuvering to start their engines; then they're off, racing over the waves. Bottom fishing in this area is excellent next to offshore Haystack Rock. If you want to fish from a dory, you can rent a charter boat; call **The Haystack Fishing Club** at (877) 965-7555; www.haystackfishing.com. Kids love to climb up the sand dune and have races down the hill as well as explore the tide pools at the base of Cape Kiwanda. Surfers and kayakers also enjoy playing in the surf off Cape Kiwanda beach. You'll also find hiking, kiteflying, sandcastle building, and paragliding. Public restrooms and a parking area are adjacent to the beach. There is no day use fee.

ROBERT ("BOB") STRAUB STATE PARK
(Day Use)
www.oregonstateparks.org/park_183.php
At this flat, sandy beach in Pacific City, you can explore Nestucca Spit. Go to the end of the spit by turning left (south) and hiking about 3.2 miles. Good fishing opportunities exist at the tip of the spit. Clamming is also good along the shores of Nestucca Bay. There is no day use fee.

NESKOWIN BEACH STATE RECREATION SITE
(Day Use)
www.oregonstateparks.org/park_223.php
Neskowin Beach is located in the community of Neskowin on US 101, 33 miles south of Tillamook and 10 miles north of Lincoln City. Kids can enjoy wading in Neskowin Creek as it skirts the base of Proposal Rock. If you feel like taking a hike, you can head north up the beach that ends at the Nestucca River. While you are here be sure to check out the town of Neskowin. There is no day use fee.

Central Coast
ROADS END STATE RECREATION AREA
(Day Use)
www.oregonstateparks.org/park_225.php
Located about 3 miles south of Lincoln City, Roads End offers a popular spot for windsurfing, surfing, and boogie boarding. To rent surfing or boogie board gear, visit **Safari Town Surf Shop,** 3026 Northeast US 101 #3, Lincoln City, (541) 996–6335. A short trail takes you to the beach that is nestled in a sheltered cove. From here you'll have views of Cascade Head and at low tide you can explore the tide pools. If you go north along the beach for about 1.5 miles, you can hike around the tip of the headland to a secluded cove that can only be accessed during low tide. If you hike to the cove, be sure you return before the tide comes back in! There is no day use fee.

D RIVER STATE RECREATION SITE
(Day Use)
www.oregonstateparks.org/park_214.php
D River is located in Lincoln City just off US 101, adjacent to the D River (the shortest river in the world) that flows 120 feet from Devils Lake to the ocean. A fall kite festival is held here the last weekend in September. If you need a kite, visit **Catch the Wind Kite Shop,** 266 Southeast US 101, (541) 994-9500; www.catchthewind.com. Other popular activities include fishing and hiking. There is no day use fee.

DEVILS LAKE STATE PARK
(Camping and Day Use)
www.oregonstateparks.org/park_216.php
If you love water sports, you'll enjoy your stay at Devils Lake, which covers 678 acres and has an

average depth of 10 feet. Docks are adjacent to the campground, and boat launches in the park's day use areas are located west of the campground and across the lake in the park's East Devils Lake location. Picnicking, windsurfing, water skiing, knee boarding, jet boating, sailing, hiking, and fishing are also fun activities here. The lake is home to rainbow trout, bluegill, yellow perch, catfish, black crappie, and Chinese grass carp. Located in Lincoln City, this park is surrounded by wetlands and marshes that attract migratory geese and ducks. Bald eagles are known to nest here. There is no day use fee.

i If you are going to cook your crabs at home, store them in a cooler on crushed ice until you get home. Cook your crabs by boiling them for about 20 minutes in fresh water with a few teaspoons of salt and some lemon slices.

GLENEDEN BEACH STATE RECREATION SITE
(Day Use)
www.oregonstateparks.org/park_221.php
Gleneden Beach is located 7 miles south of Lincoln City off US 101. This recreation area has a nice picnic area set against a backdrop of shore pines. A paved path leads to a sandy beach where surfers and boogie boarders like to catch a few waves. You may get lucky and spot sea lions playing in the surf or try your hand at fishing. If you want to rent surfing or boogie boarding gear, stop by the **Safari Town Surf Shop,** 3026 Northeast US 101 #3, Lincoln City, (541) 996-6335. There is no day use fee.

FOGARTY CREEK STATE RECREATION AREA
(Day Use)
www.oregonstateparks.org/park_220.php
Fogarty Creek State Recreation Area is located 2 miles north of Depoe Bay off US 101. Bubbling Fogarty Creek meets the sea at this scenic state park. Picnic tables are scattered across a grassy lawn that is bordered by a forest canopy of west-

ern hemlock, Sitka spruce, and shore pine. Trails cross charming footbridges over the creek and lead to the sandy beach. On the beach you'll have plenty of opportunities to watch waves crashing into offshore rocks, watch seabirds, or enjoy other beach activities, such as fishing.

BOILER BAY STATE SCENIC VIEWPOINT
(Day Use)
www.oregonstateparks.org/park_213.php
Boiler Bay is located 1 mile north of Depoe Bay off US 101. The viewpoint rests atop scenic rocky bluffs and has picnic tables. From here you'll more than likely see gray whales spouting in the far distance (be sure to bring your binoculars!). You may also see sea birds such as oystercatchers, pelicans, grebes, loons, and jaegers. Another popular activity here is watching waves crash into the rocky cliffs during the winter months. There is no day use fee.

OTTER CREST STATE SCENIC VIEWPOINT
(Day Use)
www.oregonstateparks.org/park_224.php
Otter Crest is located 10 miles north of Newport off US 101. From this scenic viewpoint perched 500 feet above the ocean, you'll have spectacular views of Cape Foulweather and Devils Punchbowl, and you may also spot some gray whales. There is no day use fee.

DEVILS PUNCH BOWL STATE NATURAL AREA
(Day Use)
www.oregonstateparks.org/park_217.php
Located about 8 miles north of Newport, Devils Punchbowl is aptly named after its punch bowl-shaped rock formation that is thought to be the remnants of a sea cave. Waves come crashing into the rocky bowl creating a frothy white brew. This small park has picnic tables and a hiking trail that leads down to a rocky tide pool area. You have the option of heading down a set of stairs and walking south on scenic Beverly Beach. Surfers also brave the surf off the rocky shoreline. You'll have a good chance at spotting whales at this park. There is no day use fee.

BEVERLY BEACH STATE PARK
(Camping and Day Use)

www.oregonstateparks.org/park_227.php

Beverly Beach State Park, about 7 miles north of Newport, has a large campground and day use area with picnic tables in a grassy area surrounded by coastal forest. A trail leads under the highway to a broad sandy beach. Surfers should check out the north section of the beach that promises a good break. The Oregon Coast Trail passes right through the park and if you are backpacking, you'll be happy to know that in addition to biker and horse campsites, this park has hiker campsites and showers. If you feel like a short hike, take a leisurely 0.75-mile self-guided nature trail that parallels Spencer Creek. The trail can be accessed between campsites C3 and C5. If you have kids, you may want to take them to the playground that is adjacent to campsite E9. Other popular activities include fishing, whale watching, and wildlife viewing. There is no day use fee.

AGATE BEACH STATE RECREATION SITE
(Day Use)

www.oregonstateparks.org/park_212.php

Agate Beach is located 1 mile north of Newport off US 101. This day use area offers picnicking and beach access and is a good clam digging and surfing beach. If you want to go surfing or boogie boarding, get local advice and gear from **Ocean Pulse Surfboards,** 428 Southwest Coast Hwy., Newport, (541) 265-7745, www.oceanpulsesurf .com. There is no day use fee.

YAQUINA BAY STATE RECREATION SITE
(Day Use)

www.oregonstateparks.org/park_208.php

Yaquina Bay State Park in Newport covers 32 acres and its star attraction is the 40-foot-tall Yaquina Bay Lighthouse that was commissioned for service from 1871 to 1874. The lighthouse also has a gift shop that has books on coastal lighthouses, wildlife, and much more. Visiting hours are from 11 a.m. to 5 p.m. daily from Memorial Day through Labor Day and from noon to 4:30 p.m. the rest of the year (weather permitting).

The lighthouse stands on a scenic bluff that has views of the Yaquina River and the Pacific Ocean. The park also has several picnic tables that are set among shore pine and spruce trees. There is no day use fee.

Paved trails lead to sand dunes along the north jetty. If you go north, you can walk along the beach all the way to Yaquina Head. Keep your eye out for a variety of shorebirds including sandpipers and dunlins. From the park you can also head east to Newport's bayfront where you can watch the fishing fleet or try fishing off the docks. You are also in the close vicinity of the **Oregon Coast Aquarium** and the **Hatfield Marine Science Center** that are worth visiting.

Another area to visit is the **Yaquina Head Outstanding Natural Area** that is managed by the Bureau of Land Management (BLM), (541) 574-3100. At this scenic stop you'll learn about the natural history of this part of the Central Coast and you'll be able to view the 93-foot **Yaquina Head Lighthouse** that was commissioned in 1873. A visitor center and hiking trails take you on a journey to tide pools, rocky beach, and grassy headlands.

The Yaquina Head Outstanding Natural Area is located 4 miles northwest of Newport off of US 101. Drive north on US 101 for 3 miles and turn left onto Lighthouse Drive. You'll reach the interpretive center in 0.7 mile. Note there is a $7 entrance fee to visit this area.

SOUTH BEACH STATE PARK
(Camping and Day Use)

www.oregonstateparks.org/park_209.php

South Beach State Park, which offers a long stretch of sandy beach, encompasses 434 acres and is located at the southern end of Yaquina Bay, about 2 miles south of Newport on US 101. The park has a large campground with a playground. If you like to hike, be sure to check out the 1-mile Cooper Ridge Trail that can be accessed at the hiker/biker camp or at campsite C37. Cyclists may want to try the South Jetty Trail, which has a paved 10-foot-wide pedestrian/ bicycle path connecting the park's day use area to South Jetty Road. Other trails lead to the beach where you can participate in all kinds of fun beach activities including beachcombing, kite-flying, and sandcastle building. Windsurfers and surfers may like the waves off this beach. If you need to rent gear, visit **Ocean Pulse Surfboards,** located at 428 Southwest Coast Hwy., Newport, (541) 265-7745.

Fishing is popular off the south jetty. You may catch lingcod, sea bass, perch, and salmon. There is no day use fee at the park.

LOST CREEK STATE RECREATION SITE
(Day Use)
www.oregonstateparks.org/park_205.php
Lost Creek State Recreation site is located 7 miles south of Newport off US 101. You'll be able to have a picnic with an ocean view as well as views of Yaquina Head and Seal Rock. From the parking area a trail leads to a long expanse of sandy beach. The Oregon Coast Trail passes through this state park and can be hiked as a day hike or as a longer backpack trip. Other activities include kiteflying and surf fishing. There is no day use fee.

ONA BEACH STATE PARK
(Day Use)
www.oregonstateparks.org/park_206.php
Covering 237 acres, 8 miles south of Newport, Ona Beach State Park offers a wide sandy beach for swimming and other recreational opportunities on Beaver Creek, which empties into the ocean at Ona Beach. Ona is a Native American word that translates to "razor clam." At one point in time these tasty clams were abundant at this beach. A boat ramp is located on the east side of the highway and allows you access for launching a canoe or kayak on the creek. Picnic sites are located along the creek in a large grassy area. While you are paddling you may spot otters, blue herons, mallard ducks, and other wildlife. There is no day use fee at the park.

SEAL ROCK STATE RECREATION SITE
(Day Use)
www.oregonstateparks.org/park_207.php
The scenic recreation site is located atop a bluff

about 10 miles south of Newport, with fantastic views of offshore rocks where you can view sea lions and seabirds. Before you begin exploring this spot, you can have lunch in the picnic area that is surrounded by shore pines and thick stands of salal. After lunch hike down a short path to explore the beach and rocky tide pools. There is no day use fee.

DRIFTWOOD BEACH STATE RECREATION SITE
(Day Use)
www.oregonstateparks.org/park_203.php
Located 3 miles north of Waldport, Driftwood Beach has scenic picnic spots set among pretty shore pine trees. You have direct access to a flat sandy beach that is perfect for a variety of beach activities, such as fishing. There is no day use fee.

GOVERNOR PATTERSON MEMORIAL STATE RECREATION SITE
(Day Use)
www.oregonstateparks.org/park_117.php
This recreation site is located along a scenic stretch of sandy beach 1 mile south of Waldport. From the parking area you can walk north to Yaquina John Point located at the edge of Alsea Bay where you'll have a good chance of seeing seals lounging on the sandy shore. You'll also have a good chance of spotting brown pelicans flying overhead. Some windsurfers try their luck at the mouth of the bay if the wind conditions are right. You may also want to try surf fishing in this area. At the picnic area you can take a break and enjoy ocean views. If you are hiking the Oregon Coast Trail, you'll continue walking south on the beach through this recreation area toward Yachats. While you're here, be sure to visit the **Alsea Bay Bridge Historical Interpretive Center,** 620 Northwest Spring St., (541) 563-2002, located at the southern end of the Alsea Bay Bridge off US 101 in Waldport. At this interpretive center, you'll learn about the history of travel routes on the Oregon Coast beginning with Indian trails and leading to road routes. There is no day use fee.

i For more information about Oregon's coastal parks, contact Oregon State Parks and Recreation, 725 Summer St. Northeast, Suite C, Salem; (800) 551-6949; www.oregon.gov/OPRD/PARKS/index.shtml.

BEACHSIDE STATE PARK
(Camping and Day Use)
www.oregonstateparks.org/park_122.php
The park is located 4 miles south of Waldport on US 101 right next to a wide expanse of sandy beach and is one of the few campgrounds on the Oregon Coast that has campsites with an ocean view. A bubbling creek is the dividing line between the campground and the day use area. Beach activities are the highlight here. You can fly a kite, build a sandcastle, play Frisbee or volleyball, or go beachcombing. A wealth of other activities is close by. You can try clamming or crabbing in Alsea Bay 4 miles north of the park or try fishing in the Alsea River for steelhead and salmon. You should also be sure to stop by the **Cape Perpetua Visitor Center,** (541) 547-3289, located 7 miles south off US 101. At the interpretive center you'll learn about coastal ecology, coastal tides and weather, whale migration, and the Alsea tribe. You can also pick up a trail brochure and map that describes all the trails in the Cape Perpetua area. The center is open from 9 a.m. to 5:30 p.m. daily June through August and from September to May from 10 a.m. to 4 p.m. daily. There is a $5 day use fee.

SMELT SANDS STATE RECREATION AREA
(Day Use)
www.oregonstateparks.org/park_128.php
This recreation area in north Yachats is well known for its annual smelt run (small silvery fish related to salmon) and is also a good whale-watching spot. At this recreation area you can also hike on the historic 804 Trail. The 0.75-mile trail starts from the parking area, takes you past two spouting horns (areas where the ocean is pushed through cracks in the lava rock and sends sprays of water into the air), and then through a wind-blown coastal ecosystem. After 0.75 mile you'll reach the beach, but if you continue hiking you'll get to Vingie Creek in another 0.8 mile, Tillicum Beach picnic area in another 2.7 miles, or, if you really feel like walking, the Governor Patterson Memorial State Recreation Site in 6.3 miles. The Oregon Coast Trail is accessible from Smelt Sands. There is no day use fee.

YACHATS STATE RECREATION AREA
(Day Use)
www.oregonstateparks.org/park_133.php
This recreation area is located in the heart of Yachats, it has a nice picnic area and views of the Yachats River as it meets the ocean. You can explore tide pools, watch for whales, or try your luck at fishing from this scenic spot. There is no day use fee.

YACHATS OCEAN ROAD STATE NATURAL SITE
(Day Use)
www.oregonstateparks.org/park_132.php
This scenic natural area in Yachats has many viewpoints of Yachats Bay and the Pacific Ocean. Trails give you access to the beach and tide pools. You'll also have a good chance at spotting whales. There is no day use fee.

NEPTUNE STATE SCENIC VIEWPOINT
(Day Use)
www.oregonstateparks.org/park_126.php
Neptune State Scenic Viewpoint covers 302 acres and is located adjacent to the Cummins Creek Wilderness 3 miles south of Yachats. Cummins Creek meets the ocean here and hiking trails offer beach access from both sides of this stream. If you hike south on the beach, you can explore the rocky shore and tide pools. You'll also have good opportunities to see whales and other sea mammals here. Other activities include picnicking, fishing, and windsurfing. If you want to hike a strenuous 8.5-mile loop to the Cape Perpetua Visitor Center from Neptune, you can hook up with the Cummins Creek Trailhead that is located east of US 101 and follow the Cummins Creek Trail to

the Cooks Ridge Trail to the visitor center. From the visitor center, you can access the Oregon Coast Trail to return to your starting point. There is no day use fee.

STONEFIELD BEACH STATE RECREATION SITE
www.oregonstateparks.org/park_130.php
You can enjoy beach activities and watching for wildlife on this uncrowded beach 6 miles south of Yachats. There is no day use fee.

MURIEL O. PONSLER MEMORIAL STATE SCENIC VIEWPOINT
(Day Use)
www.oregonstateparks.org/park_125.php
This scenic viewpoint, located 16 miles north of Florence on US 101, has access to 5 miles of wide sandy beach that is a great stop for all kinds of beach activities including windsurfing and fishing. This is also a good spot to watch for whales. There is no day use fee.

CARL G. WASHBURNE MEMORIAL STATE PARK
(Camping and Day Use)
www.oregonstateparks.org/park_123.php
One of the highlights of this park, located 12.5 miles north of Florence, is a 6-mile out-and-back hike to Heceta Head Lighthouse from the campground. You'll begin this hike on the Valley Trail that is located before the pay station to the campground. The trail follows China Creek and then leads you to an open, grassy meadow where you may get to see some Roosevelt elk. The trail then takes you through a boggy area, and then you'll reach US 101. Cross the highway and continue your adventure by turning onto Hobbit Trail. You'll hike for a short way on this trail and then come to a trail junction. Turn left onto the Heceta Head Trail that will take you to the Heceta Head Lighthouse. Once you reach the lighthouse, you can watch for seabirds nesting in the high cliffs surrounding the lighthouse. If you aren't up for such a long hiking adventure, you can hike 0.5 mile to the beach and enjoy beach

activities, such as fishing. The Beach Trail can be accessed between campsites B40 and B42. There is no day use fee.

> **i** The Oregon Department of Fish and Wildlife has a wealth of information on fishing regulations, species identification, weekly fishing reports, and fish restoration programs available on their Web site at www.dfw.state.or.us.

HECETA HEAD LIGHTHOUSE STATE SCENIC VIEWPOINT
(Day Use)
www.oregonstateparks.org/park_124.php
The Heceta Head Lighthouse State Scenic Viewpoint is located 12 miles north of Florence and 14 miles south of Yachats off US 101. The 56-foot lighthouse was commissioned in 1894 and it rests on a rocky headland 205 feet above the ocean. Adjacent to the lighthouse is the Heceta House, the original light keeper's house that was built in 1893 and now is operated as a bed-and-breakfast. To reach the lighthouse you can take a gravel path from the parking lot and walk 0.5 mile through a thick coastal cedar and fir forest dotted with sword fern, wild iris, and salal. You'll also enjoy the view of the rocky shore and the Cape Creek Bridge from the picnic tables along the path. From the lighthouse you'll have great views of puffins, cormorants, and other seabirds nesting on the offshore cliffs. You can also hike to the beach and enjoy exploring tide pools and other beach activities. You can hike to Carl G. Washburne State Park from the lighthouse on the Heceta Head Trail. Tours of the lighthouse are given daily. Call ahead for tour times. There is a $3 day use fee at this park.

DARLINGTONIA STATE NATURAL SITE
(Day Use)
www.oregonstateparks.org/park_115.php
When you stop at this 18-acre state natural site, located 5 miles north of Florence, you'll be able

to take a short walk on a boardwalk through a bog to view the interesting insect-eating plant *Darlingtonia californica*. This hungry plant traps flies and other insects into its tubelike opening and then digests the insects to get much-needed nutrients. After you take your tour, you can eat your lunch at the picnic area in a shady forest setting. There is no day use fee.

> ℹ️ Watch for brown highway signs with a binocular symbol that indicate wildlife viewing areas.

JESSIE M. HONEYMAN MEMORIAL STATE PARK
(Camping and Day Use)
www.oregonstateparks.org/park_134.php
Jessie M. Honeyman has something to offer everyone. Located 3 miles south of Florence on US 101, this popular state park is next to scenic sand dunes and also provides camping and access to 82-acre Cleawox Lake and 350-acre Woahink Lake. These lakes offer all kinds of water activities, including swimming, boating, waterskiing, and fishing. Boat ramps and picnic sites are available on both lakes. Windsurfers may want to try these lakes. Canoeing and kayaking are other fun activities.

Or you can hike on one of the park's many hiking trails. A 0.5-mile trail takes you from the Cleawox Lake picnic areas to the shore of Lily Lake that is bordered by colorful rhododendrons. A second nature trail connects the Cleawox day use area with the group camp on Woahink Lake. To reach the beach you'll have to hike over 2 miles of dunes from the Cleawox area. There is a $3 day use fee at the park.

BOLON ISLAND TIDEWAYS STATE SCENIC CORRIDOR
(Day Use)
www.oregonstateparks.org/park_114.php
This scenic spot 5 miles north of Reedsport has a hiking trail that takes you on a tour of the island.

On this trail you'll have a good chance at spotting a variety of birds. You'll also have a scenic view of the Umpqua River. There is no day use fee.

UMPQUA LIGHTHOUSE STATE PARK
(Camping and Day Use)
www.oregonstateparks.org/park_121.php
This state park, 6 miles south of Reedsport, has a campground and day use area that is centered on scenic Lake Marie and hilly sand dunes. Lake Marie offers fishing and nonmotorized boating, making canoeing and kayaking a popular activity. Canoeists and kayakers enjoy exploring the mouth of the nearby Umpqua River where different species of birds can be observed. Swimmers like the small sandy beach that provides good access to the lake. If you want to look for whales, check out the whale-viewing platform located just north of the lake—this viewpoint has interpretive signs that fill you in on the migration and feeding patterns of gray whales. If you feel like a short hike, you can walk on one of three paths from the campground that take you to the 1.4-mile lakeshore loop. A short trail leads off the lakeshore loop to a viewpoint of the sand dunes. If you are feeling ambitious, you can hike over the dunes to the beach.

The other highlight of this area is the 65-foot Umpqua River Lighthouse. The lighthouse is within walking distance of the state park and you can tour the lighthouse May 1 through September 30. Call Douglas County Parks, (541) 271-4631, for the current tour schedule. There is no day use fee.

South Coast
WILLIAM M. TUGMAN STATE PARK
(Camping and Day Use)
www.oregonstateparks.org/park_98.php
This state park and campground is located 8 miles south of Reedsport on US 101, next to 350-acre Eel Lake, which supports healthy populations of black crappie, cutthroat trout, rainbow trout, largemouth bass, and brown bullhead. The lake has a boat ramp as well as a fishing dock set up for anglers with disabilities. Windsurfing, canoeing,

and kayaking are also popular here. If you like to picnic, you'll like this state park's large, grassy lawns with facilities set against a backdrop of shore pines and other coastal forest vegetation. If you're a hiker, you'll enjoy exploring a trail that leads around the south end of the lake where you might see ospreys, eagles, and black-tailed deer. Other activities include swimming and bicycling. There is no day use fee.

SUNSET BAY STATE PARK
(Camping and Day Use)
www.oregonstateparks.org/park_100.php

Sunset State Park is nestled in a scenic cove between sandstone cliffs 12 miles southwest of Coos Bay. The campground here is located on the east side of the highway, and Big Creek meanders through it, which may explain its popularity. Day use facilities along the bays have picnic tables set on a grassy expanse of lawn. Beach lovers have access to a sandy beach and there are also facilities to launch boats.

From the day use picnic area, you can hook up with the Oregon Coast Trail and hike south to Shore Acres State Park and Cape Arago State Park. You'll reach Shore Acres State Park in a little over 2 miles. Along the way, you'll have spectacular views of the 44-foot Cape Arago Lighthouse, which was commissioned in 1934. After approximately 4.5 miles you'll reach Cape Arago State Park. There is no day use fee at the park.

SHORE ACRES STATE PARK
(Day Use)
www.oregonstateparks.org/park_97.php

Shore Acres State Park, located on a high bluff above the Pacific Ocean about 13 miles southwest of Coos Bay, was once the private estate of lumberman and ship builder Louis B. Simpson. He built a summer home here that boasted three stories, a ballroom, and a heated indoor swimming pool. He also cultivated five acres of formal gardens.

You can tour the grounds that contain two spectacular rose gardens, a Japanese garden with a lily pond, and other formal flower gardens. During December, the gardens are festooned with colored lights and holiday decorations. Different flowers are planted at different times of year for a garden that blooms almost year-round. Peak blooming time for bulbs and daffodils is late February through March; the tulips open late March through April; rhododendrons and azaleas flower from April through mid-May; annuals and perennials are the attraction from May through September and roses from June through September; and dahlias bloom August through mid-October. The gift store and information center are situated at the entrance to the gardens. The Friends of Shore Acres State Park sponsor a variety of horticultural and cultural events here throughout the year.

In addition to the gardens, you'll find an observation building perched atop a rugged bluff. From this point you'll have spectacular views of the waves crashing into the sandstone cliffs and you'll also have the opportunity to spot whales from December through June. You'll have access to the Oregon Coast Trail and Simpson Beach, where you can participate in all kinds of beach activities. Note that dogs are not allowed at this park. The day use fee is $3.

CAPE ARAGO STATE PARK
www.oregonstateparks.org/park_94.php

Cape Arago State Park is located 14 miles southwest of Coos Bay on a rocky headland that rises 200 feet above the Pacific. Picnic tables are located on scenic viewpoints along the bluff offering good opportunities for whale watching and for spotting nesting seabirds in the spring months. Simpson Reef is located off this cape and is the home of seals and sea lions. You can access the beach at North, Middle, and South Coves. Note that North Cove is closed March 1 to June 30 while sea lions are birthing and raising their pups. South Cove has numerous tide pools that are fun to explore. A 4.5-mile section of the Oregon Coast Trail links this park to Shore Acres State Park and Sunset Bay State Park (located to the north). There is no day use fee.

ℹ️ Visit the Oregon State Parks and Recreation Web site at www.oregon .gov/OPRD/PARKS/index.shtml for a wealth of information about coastal state parks including maps, descriptions, camping information, reservation information, and much more.

SEVEN DEVILS STATE RECREATION SITE
(Day Use)
www.oregonstateparks.org/park_69.php
Located 10 miles north of Bandon, the Seven Devils recreation area has a picnic area adjacent to Merchants Beach where you can participate in all kinds of activities, such as fishing, beachcombing, kite-flying, and sandcastle-building. There is no day use fee.

BULLARDS BEACH STATE PARK
(Camping and Day Use)
www.oregonstateparks.org/park_71.php
Bullards Beach State Park, located 2 miles north of Bandon, has a campground with hiker/biker campsites as well as horse campsites and also a 7-mile equestrian trail. The park is sandwiched between the Coquille River and the Pacific. A 1.5-mile trail gives hikers and bikers access from the campground to the beach where you can participate in all kinds of beach activities. Another 3-mile trail takes you to the North Jetty that is home to the historic Coquille River Lighthouse, built in 1896. Memorial Day through Labor Day you'll find interpreters who will tell you about the lighthouse's history. You can fish in the Coquille River for steelhead, coho, and chinook salmon. Kayakers will also enjoy exploring the estuary at the mouth of the Coquille River, which has been designated as the Bandon Marsh National Wildlife Refuge. The park has a boat launch and access to the Oregon Coast Trail. There is no day use fee.

FACE ROCK STATE SCENIC VIEWPOINT
(Day Use)
www.oregonstateparks.org/park_66.php
This park is located 1 mile southwest of Bandon

off US 101. Here you'll have wonderful views of Face Rock and a series of pointed sea stacks. You'll also be able to take a trail to the beach where you can explore tide pools and participate in other beach activities, such as fishing. If you are looking for a longer hike, you can trek 3 miles north on the beach to downtown Bandon. There is no day use fee.

BANDON STATE NATURAL AREA
(Day Use)
www.oregonstateparks.org/park_64.php
This park has several access points off of US 101 from 1 to 5 miles south of Bandon. The first access point is a viewpoint overlooking Face Rock. The face on this rock is supposed to represent Ewauna, the daughter of Chief Siskiyou. You'll also be able to see a series of sea stacks that are part of the National Wildlife Refuge system. From here a trail leads down to the beach and to a picnic area with tables.

If you continue south on US 101, the next access point is the Devil's Kitchen area. Hiking trails lead to the beach and a picnic area next to a pretty creek. Continuing south on US 101, you'll come to two more access points, that feature beach access but do not have picnic or restroom facilities. There is no day use fee at these areas.

BOICE COPE COUNTY PARK
(Camping and Day Use)
Located 2 miles south of Langlois on US 101, Boice Cope County Park features a campground at Floras Lake with 22 paved spaces with water but no hookups. There are also 12 tent sites. Restrooms and showers are available. You cannot reserve these sites; they are first come first served. On summer weekends this park fills up fast, and you'll have the best luck finding a camping site during the middle of the week. Floras Lake is popular with windsurfers due to its warm temperature, sandy bottom, and strong 15 to 25 mph northwest winds. You can rent windsurfing gear and take lessons March through mid-October from **Floras Lake Windsurfing,** which is owned by the same people who run **Floras Lake**

House by the Sea Bed and Breakfast, 92870 Boice Cope Rd., Langlois, (541) 348-2573, www .floraslake.com. Windsurfing rentals and instruction are available April through September. Call ahead to make reservations for gear and lessons. Sea kayak rentals are also available. There is no day use fee at the park.

FLORAS LAKE STATE PARK
(Day Use)
Located about 7 miles north of Port Orford, Floras Lake State Park is wild and undeveloped. The 1,371-acre park encompasses 2.5 miles of ocean, including Blacklock Point, and also includes the west side of Floras Lake. Wild rhododendrons and salal thrive here along with wild blueberries and huckleberries. If you want to explore this area, you can start hiking on a dirt road that is located to the left of the gated entrance to the airport. You'll hike through hardy coastal forest. After 0.8 mile cross a creek and turn left at the trail junction. Follow the Oregon Coast Trail marker signs at the next three junctions and you'll arrive at Blacklock Point in a little over a mile. To reach the beach, which is filled with driftwood logs and huge boulders, stay to the left and navigate your way down—note this can be a bit tricky There are other trail options that take you to Floras Lake—but be forewarned that the trails are not maintained and the intersections are confusing. There is no day use fee at the park.

i To be sure you're prepared for all kinds of coastal adventures, keep a day pack in your car with the following essentials: water, snacks, camera and extra film, sunscreen, sunglasses, hat, comfortable walking shoes or boots, extra pair of sandals for wading through creeks or playing in the surf, rain jacket, fleece jacket or some kind of insulating layer, beach toys (Frisbee, volleyball, kite), tide table book, and towel.

CAPE BLANCO STATE PARK
(Camping and Day Use)
www.oregonstateparks.org/park_62.php
Cape Blanco State Park is host to large campsites protected from the coastal wind by sheltering trees and a thick understory of salal, salmonberry, and thimbleberry. The Oregon Coast Trail can be accessed from the south end of the campground. Additional hiking trails lead to several viewpoints and the beach. Horse owners will love exploring a series of horse trail loops that take you through coastal forest and to the beach. A 150 acre area is also designated as an open riding area. Photographers and wildlife lovers will enjoy the natural beauty of this park with its high chalky bluffs, black sand beach, and offshore sea stacks, which are home to herds of sea lions and prime nesting sites for seabirds. From this campground, you have access to the Elk and Sixes Rivers, which offer good fishing. A boat ramp is present on the Sixes River if you want to launch your boat. If you're a history buff, don't miss exploring the 59-foot Cape Blanco Lighthouse, which is the oldest lighthouse in Oregon. Another historical structure at this state park is the Hughes House Museum built in 1898 by Patrick Hughes. This 11-room, two-story Victorian-style mansion was built out of old-growth Port Orford cedar at a cost of $3,800. It's open for tours during the summer and is filled with delightful antique furniture and old photos depicting the life of the former 1,000-acre dairy ranch that the house sits on. There is no day use fee at the park.

i Visit Fish Mill Lodges & RV Park, 4844 Fish Mill Way, Westlake, (541) 997-2511, to rent a boat and stock up on fishing supplies or to rent a cottage that is close by this prime fishing scene of Siltcoos Lake. To get there from Florence, drive 5.5 miles south of Florence on US 101, turn east between milepost 196 and 197, and follow the signs a quarter of a mile to the resort.

PORT ORFORD HEADS STATE PARK
(Day Use)

www.oregonstateparks.org/park_61.php

Port Orford Heads State Park in Port Orford features a wind-sheltered picnic area adjacent to the historic Port Orford Heads United States Coast Guard Lifeboat Station that was decommissioned in 1939. You can tour the museum located in the lifeboat station. The museum is open 10 a.m. to 3:30 p.m. Thursday through Monday from April through October. A 0.3-mile path takes you to a scenic viewpoint. There is no day use fee.

HUMBUG MOUNTAIN STATE PARK
(Camping and Day Use)

www.oregonstateparks.org/park_56.php

The centerpiece of Humbug Mountain State Park, located 6 miles south of Port Orford, is 1,761-foot Humbug Mountain, which is the highest point on the Coast. A 5.5-mile strenuous loop hike takes you to the summit of this mountain from the campground. To reach the trailhead from the campground, cross a bridge over Brush Creek and then proceed through the tunnel under US 101. The trail passes through maple and myrtle trees and then leads you through sections of old-growth Douglas fir. You'll come to a junction in about a mile that is the start of the loop portion of the trail. If you go to the right, you'll come to a viewpoint. Looking north you'll see Redfish Rocks, Port Orford, and Cape Blanco. Keep following the trail as it loops back around to rejoin the main trail. At this junction, you can hike up a short, steep trail that leads to a viewpoint looking south toward Gold Beach. Another hiking trail worth exploring is part of the Oregon Coast Trail. Start on this section of the Oregon Coast Trail by walking east in the campground and watching for the 2.5-mile signed Recreation Trail. The trail follows the old highway to where it ends at US 101 just south of Rocky Point. You can reach the beach by walking on a trail that begins near campsite C7. On the beach you may see windsurfers braving the offshore break. There is no day use fee at the park.

GEISEL MONUMENT STATE HERITAGE SITE
(Day Use)

www.oregonstateparks.org/park_55.php

This historic site, located 7 miles north of Gold Beach, has interpretive signs that give details about the Rogue Indian war skirmish that took place here. If you are traveling along the South Coast, this is a perfect spot to take a break, have a picnic, and learn about this area's colorful history. There is no day use fee.

OTTER POINT STATE RECREATION SITE
(Day Use)

www.oregonstateparks.org/park_58.php

At this recreation site, 4 miles north of Gold Beach, you'll have the opportunity to hike on different trails that have spectacular views of sandstone rock formations. You'll also have access to the beach where you can enjoy all kinds of beach activities. There is no day use fee.

CAPE SEBASTIAN STATE SCENIC CORRIDOR
(Day Use)

www.oregonstateparks.org/park_73.php

Located 7 miles south of Gold Beach, this recreation area has two parking areas with scenic viewpoints that are located on bluffs 200 feet above the ocean. From the south parking area you can see Humbug Mountain 43 miles to the north and Crescent City 50 miles to the south. A hiking trail leads you 1.5 miles out to the tip of Cape Sebastian through a thick Sitka spruce forest. From the tip of the cape you'll have a good chance at spotting migrating gray whales from December through June. Beach access and fishing are also available. There is no day use fee.

PISTOL RIVER STATE SCENIC VIEWPOINT
(Day Use)

www.oregonstateparks.org/park_76.php

Pistol River is located 11 miles south of Gold Beach on US 101. At the north parking area you'll have access to Myers Beach, which is strewn with huge boulders, making it a very scenic spot. From the south parking area, you'll see the Pistol River carving its way to the Pacific through a series of

Close-up

Western Snowy Plovers

The Pacific Coast breeding colonies of western snowy plovers can be found from southern Washington to Baja California. Snowy plovers are sparrow-sized birds with a dusty, sand-colored back and a white underside with a black chest band. They like to nest in open, sandy areas next to the water, where they usually lay two to three greenish brown eggs in a sandy depression above the beach. The nesting season is from mid-March through mid-September. In 2001, 110 nesting adults were counted along the southern Oregon Coast. Out of 110 nests, only 34 were successful, producing 94 hatchlings. Sturdy areas include Necanicum Spit, Bayocean Spit, Sutton Beach, Siltcoos, Dunes Overlook, Takenitch, Tenmile, Coos Bay North Spit, Bandon State Natural Area, New River, and Floras Lake.

The snowy plover's rapid decline is due to several factors. The encroachment of European beach grass has caused a large amount of habitat loss. The grass stabilizes dunes and reduces the amount of unvegetated area above the tide line, making the sandy beach narrower and steeper and ultimately rendering the nesting area less suitable for the birds. Predators are one of the main reasons for the decline in snowy plover populations. Major predators include gulls, crows, ravens, skunks, dogs, cats, coyotes, foxes, opossums, raccoons, hawks, and owls. The most controllable factor is human impact on nesting habitat. Off-road vehicle use, loose dogs, walking and running on the beach, and beach raking have all taken their toll.

Unfortunately, the nesting season for the snowy plover coincides with the highest traffic of beachgoers. Measures have been introduced to help protect this tiny bird. Nesting sites are now fenced off, thereby minimizing human impact, and nest enclosures have been introduced to protect the birds from predators. After you reach the beach, keep a lookout for these quick birds as they run up and down the beach feeding on crabs, marine worms, beetles, sand hoppers, shore flies, and other insects.

sand dunes. Bring your binoculars to spot birds in the estuary. Windsurfing is very popular in this park and the conditions are so good that national championships have been held here. Horseback riders will love riding on the beach. There is no day use fee.

i The following state parks have horse camping sites: Nehalem Bay, Bullards Beach, and Cape Blanco.

SAMUEL H. BOARDMAN STATE SCENIC CORRIDOR

(Day Use)

www.oregonstateparks.org/park_77.php

This scenic corridor covers 1,471 acres and stretches from Burnt Hill Creek 11 miles south.

The coastline here is rugged and wild and filled with offshore rocks and sea stacks, secluded sandy beaches, and wild coastal headlands. The first access point is Lone Ranch, located 4 miles north of Brookings. Lone Ranch has scenic picnic sites and restrooms adjacent to the beach. A hike that should not be missed is a 7-mile section of the Oregon Coast Trail that begins at the Cape Ferrelo parking area just north of Lone Ranch off US 101. The trail begins in the northwest corner of the parking area and takes you 1.5 miles through a coastal forest to the House Rock Viewpoint, which can also be accessed from US 101. From this point you'll have a good chance of spotting migrating whales and a variety of seabirds. Continue walking north on the trail through a spruce-filled forest. The trail eventually begins a steep descent through an open, grassy area to the sandy beach. You'll walk 1.5 miles on the beach to Whalehead Cove, which is the next developed access point off US 101. From here you'll be able to see Whalehead Island, which is just offshore. This area has picnic sites and restrooms. As you continue walking, look for the Oregon Coast Trail marker that is located off a side road leading toward US 101. On this section of the trail you'll hike up a headland to a scenic viewpoint. After a mile you'll reach Indian Sands, another access viewpoint off US 101. Shore pines dominate the scene in this area. You can also see a Native American midden (a pile of shells and bones leftover from meals) at this spot. If you continue north on the trail, you'll wind around headlands that offer more outstanding vistas. After Indian Sands there are many more viewpoints off US 101 as you continue north. Plan on spending the day exploring this park—you won't be disappointed. There is no day use fee.

ALFRED A. LOEB STATE PARK
(Camping and Day Use)
www.oregonstateparks.org/park_72.php
This park is located adjacent to the salmon-rich Chetco River, 7.5 miles east of Brookings, and is the starting point for two self-guided nature walks. The 0.7-mile River View Trail takes you along the banks of the scenic Chetco River through an old grove of myrtle trees, and the 1.2-mile Redwood Nature Trail loops you through a grove of immense 300- to 800-year-old coastal redwood trees. The River View Trail can be accessed from the picnic area adjacent to the campground. Be sure to pick up an interpretive brochure that corresponds to numbered trail markers along this nature trail. You'll hike on this trail for 0.7 mile and cross a paved road where you'll begin the 1.2-mile Redwood Nature Trail. If you are visiting this area for a few days, you can camp at this state park (see the South Coast section in the Camping chapter for more information). There are also excellent swimming holes on the Chetco River, and great fishing opportunities abound in Chetco River and ocean fishing is available out of Brookings Harbor (see the Fishing, Clamming, and Crabbing sections, in the Sports and Activities chapter for recommended outfitters in the Brookings area). There is no day use fee at the park.

HARRIS BEACH STATE PARK
(Camping and Day Use)
www.oregonstateparks.org/park_79.php
The campground in this state park is located in a wooded area bordered with bright azaleas 2 miles north of Brookings. Wildlife watching and beachcombing are favorite activities at this state park. You can look for seabirds nesting on Bird Island and also watch for whales offshore during their semiannual migration. Walk along the sandy beach and admire the rocky coastline and look for sea lions and harbor seals on the offshore rocks. If you have a bicycle, you'll want to try the park's scenic bike path. There is no day use fee.

i **To find out the latest information on surfing on the Oregon Coast, such as the forecast, popular breaks, current conditions, surf shops, classifieds, photos, and chat sessions, visit the Oregon Surf Page at www.oregonsurf.com.**

SPORTS AND ACTIVITIES

This chapter covers a variety of activities that you can enjoy on the Oregon Coast. You can cycle on the Oregon Coast Route; hike on shady forest trails to view scenic waterfalls; kayak quiet creeks, bays, and lakes; and go horseback riding on the beach. It also lists surfing and windsurfing hot spots; fishing, clamming, and crabbing opportunities; and outfitters that offer whale-watching and fishing trips, jet boat tours, and dune buggy rides.

ATV AND DUNE BUGGY RENTALS AND TOURS

SANDLAND ADVENTURES
85366 US 101, Florence
(541) 759-3313
www.sandland.com
Located 1 mile south of Florence on US 101, Sandland Adventures offers all kinds of family fun including go-karts, bumper boats, miniature golf, and dune tours. Up to five people can take a sand rail tour for a 30-minute tour. A sand rail tour is like taking a ride in a tour bus but instead it is a dune buggy outfitted with seats for several people—a tour leader takes a large group on a scenic tour of the dunes and beach. All you have to do is sit back, relax, and enjoy the scenery. Call or visit their Web site for current fees and hours.

SPINREEL DUNEBUGGY RENTALS, INC.
67045 Spinreel Rd., North Bend
(541) 759-3313
www.ridetheoregondunes.com
Located next to the Oregon Dunes National Recreational Area, Spinreel Dunebuggy Rentals offers ATV rentals for $40 for one hour, $125 for a half day, and $200 for a full day. Call or visit their Web site for current fees and hours.

BICYCLING

THE OREGON COAST BIKE ROUTE
355 Capitol St. NE, Room 210, Salem
(503) 986-3556
www.oregon.gov/ODOT/HWY/BIKEPED/maps.shtml
Traveling from north to south, the Oregon Coast Bike Route covers 368 miles (378 miles if you opt to ride on the Three Capes Scenic Loop) following US 101 beginning in Astoria and ending in Brookings. Most cyclists can complete the route in six to eight days by cycling 50 to 65 miles per day. The Oregon Department of Transportation recommends that you travel the route from north to south from May through October due to prevailing winds that blow from the northwest. This ride offers stunning ocean views, scenic beaches, and great camping facilities. However, it also has heavy car and truck traffic during the summer season, steep ascents and descents, and many narrow, dangerous sections. You can obtain a free map of the Oregon Coast Bike Route by downloading it from their Web site. If you would like to take day trips along this route, here are some suggestions:

- Astoria Bridge to Nehalem Bay State Park (44 miles)
- Nehalem Bay State Park to Cape Lookout State Park (48 miles)

- Cape Lookout State Park to Beverly Beach State Park (57.5 miles)
- Beverly Beach State Park to Jessie M. Honeyman Memorial State Park (60.3 miles)
- Jessie M. Honeyman Memorial State Park to Sunset Bay State Park (54.9 miles)
- Sunset Bay State Park to Humbug Mountain State Park (57 miles)
- Humbug Mountain State Park to the California border (56 miles)

Bike Shops

BICYCLES 101
1537 8th St., Florence
(541) 997-5717
http://bicycles101.net
This friendly shop will help you find some of the best biking routes on the South Coast. They rent and sell road and mountain bikes.

BIKES AND BEYOND
1089 Marine Dr., Astoria
(503) 325-2961
You can find the gear you need at this fully stocked bike shop. Call for store hours.

BIKE NEWPORT
150 Northwest 6th St., Newport
(541) 265-9917
www.bikenewport.net
This bike shop sells and rents mountain bikes and also carries cycling accessories and equipment. Open 10 a.m. to 6 p.m. Monday through Saturday.

MIKE'S BIKE SHOP
248 North Spruce St., Cannon Beach
(503) 436-1266
Mike's Bike Shop offers bike rentals for those wanting to ride on the beach and trails around Cannon Beach. You can rent a three-wheel recumbent bike popular for beach cruising, a one-speed beach cruiser, or a mountain bike. The shop is open from 10 a.m. to 6 p.m. Thursday through Monday.

ℹ The following state parks have paved bike paths: Fort Stevens State Park, Nehalem Bay State Park, and South Beach State Park.

PROM BIKE SHOP
622 12th Ave., Seaside
(503) 738-8251
You can rent a variety of bikes from the Prom Bike Shop, including surreys that two to four people can ride. A variety of other fun beach mobiles are also available. The bike shop is open from 10 a.m. to 6 p.m. daily.

Mountain Bike Trails

NEAHKAHNIE MOUNTAIN (MODERATE)
Getting There: Drive 9 miles south of Cannon Beach on US 101 to Oswald West State Park campground located on the right side of the road.
Length: 8.6 miles (out and back). Ride south out of the parking lot on US 101. Ride 2.7 miles on the highway and then turn left onto Road 38555 and begin a steep climb up a double-track dirt road. Ride 1.6 miles on this road to where the road intersects with a hiking trail. This is where the bike ride ends and you can opt to hike 0.4 mile to the summit of 1,631-foot Neahkahnie Mountain.

CUMMINS CREEK LOOP (DIFFICULT)
Getting There: Drive 28 miles south of Newport on US 101. Turn left and drive to the Cape Perpetua Visitor's Center parking area.
Length: 10.4-mile loop. From the parking area ride back out to US 101 and turn right (north). Ride 0.5 mile on US 101 to the intersection with Forest Service Road 55. Take a right onto Forest Service Road 55 and ascend steeply for 4 miles to a gravel parking area on the right side of the road at the Cooks Ridge Trailhead. Turn onto this trail and ride for 0.2 mile to a trail junction. Turn left at this junction onto the Cummins Creek Trail. Ride about 0.5 mile and turn left at the next trail junction. At the next junction stay to the right and continue to follow the Cummins Creek Trail. After approximately 8.5 miles the trail intersects with a paved road. Follow the paved road back to US

Bicycling the State Parks

These state park campgrounds have hiker/biker campsites, which charge $4 a night for you and your two-wheel steed. We've listed the state parks from north to south and also directions on how to get there:

Fort Stevens—From US 101/Highway 30 in Astoria drive south on US 101 for approximately 2.5 miles and turn right (west) onto East Harbor Drive. Proceed about 4.5 miles on East Harbor to Hammond. From Hammond drive south about a mile on Lake Drive to the state park.

Nehalem Bay—From Manzanita go 3 miles south on US 101 to Carey Street. Turn west onto Carey Street and head 1.5 miles to the park.

Cape Lookout—From Tillamook go 12 miles southwest on Netarts Highway (Three Capes Scenic Loop) to the entrance to the state park.

Devils Lake—You can access Devils Lake State Park by turning east from US 101 in Lincoln City onto Northeast 6th St. and proceeding 0.1 mile to the campground.

Beverly Beach—From Newport go 7 miles north on US 101 to the park entrance.

South Beach—From Newport go 2 miles south on US 101 to the park entrance.

Beachside—Go 4 miles south of Waldport on US 101 to the park entrance.

Carl G. Washburne—From Florence go 12.5 miles north on US 101 to the park entrance.

Jessie M. Honeyman—From Florence go 3 miles south on US 101 to the park entrance.

William M. Tugman—From Reedsport go 8 miles south on US 101 to the park entrance.

Bullards Beach—From Coos Bay drive approximately 22 miles south on US 101 to the park entrance located on the west (right) side of the road. If you are in Bandon, the park is 2 miles north on the left (west) side of US 101.

Sunset Bay—From US 101 in Coos Bay, follow the signs to Charleston Harbor and Ocean Beaches and drive on the Cape Arago Highway 12 miles southwest to Sunset Bay State Park.

Cape Blanco—To reach Cape Blanco State Park, go 46 miles south of Coos Bay or 4 miles north of Port Orford on US 101 to the junction with Cape Blanco Road. Turn west and go 5 miles on Cape Blanco Road to Cape Blanco State Park.

Humbug Mountain—From Port Orford go 6 miles south on US 101 to the park entrance on the left (east) side of the highway.

Harris Beach—From Brookings go 2 miles north on US 101 to the park entrance located on the left (west) side of the highway.

---

101 where you'll turn right (north) and head back to your car at the visitor center.

SILTCOOS LAKE TRAIL (MODERATE)

Getting There: Drive 7 miles south of Florence on US 101 and turn left at the Siltcoos Lake Trail sign. If you are coming from Reedsport, drive 13 miles north on US 101 to the Siltcoos Lake Trail sign.

Length: 4.5-mile loop This short, fun loop trail takes you by the shore of Siltcoos Lake and has short, intense hills. The trail starts at the SILTCOOS LAKE TRAILHEAD sign adjacent to the parking lot.

CANOEING AND KAYAKING

Many coastal bays and rivers offer great kayaking and canoeing opportunities. We recommend calling one of the outfitters listed below to rent gear and get advice on where to spend the day on the water.

BLUE HERON LANDING
4006 West Devils Lake Rd., Lincoln City
(541) 994-4708
You can rent a canoe from Blue Heron Landing and paddle around scenic Devils Lake. Canoe rentals are available March through September.

CENTRAL COAST WATER SPORTS
1901 US 101, Florence
(541) 997-1812
www.centralcoastwatersports.com
Central Coast Water Sports rents all kinds of water gear to maximize your fun. Scuba equipment, canoes, kayaks, ocean kayaks (sit on top style), wet suits, surfboards, and boogie boards. Call for hours and rental information.

THE KAYAK SHACK
850 Hwy. 34, Waldport
(541) 563-4445
www.whskayakshack.com
The Kayak Shack offers lessons and kayak rentals in the Waldport area. Call or visit the Web site for current hours, rental rates, and lesson fees. Open mid-June through Labor Day. Reservations are highly recommended.

FISHING

Fresh coastal lakes interspersed amongst sand dunes and burgeoning coastal forest produce prize-winning largemouth bass, bluegill, black crappie, and yellow perch. Coffenbury Lake, located at Fort Stevens State Park, is stocked with rainbow trout and steelhead. Other species that are fun to catch are the brown bullhead and panfish that thrive in Cullaby Lake, located 4 miles north of Gearhart. Siltcoos, Takenitch, Sutton, and Woahink Lakes are only a small sample of the freshwater lakes that offer dozens of angling opportunities. See the Freshwater Lakes sections in this chapter for information about these lakes and many more.

More than a dozen coastal rivers rush to the Pacific Ocean from the Coast Range and each has its own secret fishing holes and runs of wild and hatchery-raised salmon and steelhead. Even though wild salmon and steelhead runs in coastal rivers and streams have been on a rapid decline for many years, you can still find some good salmon, steelhead, and trout fishing holes. See the Bays, Rivers, and Streams sections for detailed information about individual rivers and streams.

Sturgeon is a good catch in coastal bays and rivers. This ancient fish species is caught from an anchored boat with bait cast to the bottom of the river. Strong sturgeon fisheries can be found in the Lower Columbia River and Winchester Bay. Spring and summer are the best seasons to catch these fish, although the season is open year-round.

If you like to surf fish, you can catch perch, rockfish, and greenling off many coastal beaches and jetties. See the Bays, Rivers, and Streams sections of this chapter for information about jetty fishing hot spots.

Bottom fishing on the Oregon Coast produces healthy catches of halibut, cabezon, lingcod, red snapper, and sea bass. Late summer is also the time albacore tuna are running offshore and you can catch these feisty fish by renting a charter boat (see the Ocean Charter Services and River Outfitters section). Also keep in mind that most fishing charters also offer whale-watching tours. See the Ocean Charter Services and River Outfitters section for details on individual outfitters and guide services in each area. Popular bottom fishing and deep-sea fishing hot spots along the coastline include the Lower Columbia River, Nehalem Bay, Garibaldi, Netarts Bay, Nestucca Bay, Depoe Bay, Newport Harbor, Waldport, Florence, Winchester Bay, Charleston, Bandon, and Brookings Harbor.

North Coast
Freshwater Lakes
CAPE MEARES LAKE

Cape Meares Lake covers 90 acres and is known for its fun catches of rainbow trout, bass, bluegill, and an occasional steelhead. The lake has an average depth of about 10 feet and can be filled with an excess of aquatic plants, especially around its perimeter, in the warmer months of the year. The lake is located approximately 10 miles northwest of Tillamook off of Bay-Ocean Road.

COFFENBURY LAKE

Covering 50 acres, Coffenbury Lake in Fort Stevens State Park is a popular freshwater lake that has good stocks of brown bullhead, rainbow trout, steelhead, and yellow perch. There is good road access near the north end of the lake, and a trail circles the perimeter of the lake. Fun family camping is available in the state park. Coffenbury Lake is located 2 miles west of Warrenton in Fort Stevens State Park. For more information about Fort Stevens State Park, see the Coastal Parks section of The Great Outdoors chapter.

COLUMBIA RIVER

The Columbia River ends its mighty 1,200-mile journey west of Astoria where it meets the ocean. The Columbia is home to large runs of migratory coho, chinook, and steelhead salmon and sea-run cutthroat trout. Some of the best salmon fishing in the river occurs at Buoy 10 from early August through Labor Day. You can fish off the bank for salmon at Clatsop Spit. The Columbia River also has a strong white and green sturgeon fishery with white sturgeon dominating. Sturgeon fishing is open all year but spring and summer are the best seasons to try your luck. Desdemona Sands to Grays Bay Point are sturgeon hot spots. If you like to surf fish, you can try your luck at the north or south jetties for lingcod, greenling, rockfish, or perch.

CULLABY LAKE

Cullaby Lake covers 200 acres and has an average depth of 6 to 12 feet. This lake is well known for its excellent panfish stock as well as bluegill, brown bullhead, black crappie, largemouth bass, and perch. You'll have the best luck at landing these fish from early spring through the late fall. The lake is located 4 miles north of Gearhart on the east side of US 101 via Cullaby Lake Road or about 12 miles south of Astoria off US 101.

HEBO LAKE

If you like to catch cutthroat trout, you may want to take a trip to Hebo Lake, which is stocked with cutthroat trout every spring. There is a campground at the lake and there are wheelchair-accessible fishing spots. The lake is located approximately 20 miles southeast of Tillamook off of Highway 22. From the intersection of Hebo and US 101, drive east on Highway 22 for 0.1 mile, and turn left onto Mt. Hebo Road (Forest Service Road 14). You'll reach the lake in approximately 4.5 miles.

SAND LAKE

Sand Lake is a tidal basin that has formed at the mouth of Sand Creek. During July and August you can try your chances at catching some sea-run cutthroat trout, or go for steelhead during February and March. In rare cases you may be able to catch flounder using mud shrimp or night crawlers—the hot spots are near the outlet. There are also good opportunities to do some surf fishing for perch on either side of the outlet. You can reach Sand Lake by driving approximately 11 miles south on US 101 from Tillamook to the junction with Sand Lake Road. Turn west on Sand Lake Road and follow this road for 4 miles to the junction with Cape Lookout Road. Turn south onto Sand Lake Road and you'll reach the lake in about 2 more miles.

SMITH LAKE (CLATSOP COUNTY)

Largemouth bass, yellow perch, bluegill, white crappie, and black crappie are present in decent numbers in 41-acre Smith Lake. You'll have the best luck fishing from a boat early in the spring. The lake is located 2 miles south of Warrenton off of Ridge Road. Warrenton is located approximately 8 miles southwest of Astoria via the Warrenton-Astoria Highway. This highway can be accessed by following US 101 south from Astoria.

SMITH LAKE (TILLAMOOK COUNTY)

You may want to try your luck at landing some rainbow trout at 35-acre Smith Lake. The water in this lake averages 8 to 12 feet in depth and provides good bait and lure angling. Brown bullheads thrive in this lake, and largemouth bass can be found in small numbers. The lake is located less than a mile north of Barview on the west side of US 101. Barview is located 12 miles north of Tillamook on US 101.

i **Bring along a pair of binoculars or a spotting scope to get a close-up view of wildlife. Remember that some of the best times to view wildlife are dawn and dusk.**

SPRING LAKE

Spring Lake is a small 13-acre lake that supports fair numbers of largemouth bass, rainbow trout, and cutthroat trout. The lake is located about a mile north of Barview on the east side of US 101. Barview is located 12 miles north of Tillamook on US 101.

SUNSET LAKE

Good trout, largemouth bass, black crappie, brown bullhead, and yellow perch can be found at Sunset Lake. Also known as Neacoxie Lake, this pencil-thin lake is only 500 feet wide and 2 miles long and covers approximately 107 acres. You can reach the lake by driving 4 miles north of Gearhart on US 101. Turn west onto Sunset Beach Road and drive 0.25 mile to the lake.

Bays, Rivers, and Streams
THE BIG NESTUCCA RIVER

Sea-run cutthroat trout are present on the Nestucca River and August is the peak month to catch these fish. Spring and fall chinook runs are also strong, with June and July being the peak months for the spring chinook and September and October for the fall chinook. Most anglers find the best salmon fishing on the river below Hebo. Steelhead also have a strong presence in the river year-round. The river can be accessed at Beaver off US 101. The community of Beaver is located approximately 15 miles south of Tillamook and about 30 miles north of Lincoln City.

DEPOE BAY

Good chinook fishing can be found near the buoys marking the entrance to Depoe Bay. This scenic bay is located right in the heart of the community of Depoe Bay, 12 miles south of Lincoln City and 10 miles north of Newport on US 101. Trolling with herring or spinners often works well. Bottom fishing is also good off the reefs to the north of Depoe Bay. Use jigs or herring to catch rockfish, lingcod, red snapper, perch, and other common bottom fish. The entrance to the ocean is one of the most dangerous on the Oregon Coast and it is recommended that you hire a charter boat to take you ocean fishing. See the Ocean Charter Services and River Outfitters section in this chapter for recommendations for finding a guide in the area.

ECOLA CREEK

This little stream has good catches of steelhead and cutthroat trout, with January and February being the best times to catch steelhead. The stream empties into the ocean at Cannon Beach.

FOGARTY CREEK

This small stream produces some good catches of hatchery steelhead and small numbers of cutthroat trout. The creek meets the ocean at Fogarty State Park located approximately 2 miles north of Depoe Bay and 8 miles south of Lincoln City.

KILCHIS RIVER

Fall chinook fishing in November is popular on the Kilchis River. Winter steelhead are also strong in this 20-mile-long river, with the peak runs occurring November through March. This river can be accessed via Alderbrook Road north of Tillamook off US 101.

NECANICUM RIVER

Try fishing the Necanicum for winter steelhead from November through January. The Necanicum River parallels US 26 and some of its best access points are on the river's upper stretches. To reach some of these access points, drive east from Cannon Beach on US 26 toward Portland.

NEHALEM BAY

If you like to bottom-fish and surf fish, Nehalem Bay is a good fishing destination. Try casting for greenling, perch, or rockfish off the south jetty or the beaches located north and south of the bar. Nehalem Bay is located approximately 15 miles south of Cannon Beach off US 101.

NEHALEM RIVER

The Nehalem River stretches for more than 100 miles from its origin near the town of Timber off US 26 to where it meets the ocean at Nehalem Bay and the community of Nehalem. This fun fishing river has good runs of steelhead, cutthroat trout, and salmon. The best time to try for steelhead is December through March, with the lower section being the most productive. The Nehalem River is located approximately 15 miles south of Cannon Beach off US 101.

NESTUCCA BAY

Fall chinook have a strong presence in Nestucca Bay during August and September. Sea-run cutthroat also make their way into the bay near the end of the summer. Surf fishing for perch and greenling is recommended at the beach located in Robert Straub State Park. Nestucca Bay is located south of Pacific City off Brooten Road.

SALMON RIVER

The Salmon River has a strong fall chinook run and fair runs of winter steelhead, coho, and sea-run cutthroat. Your best bet for bank angling is at the US 101 bridge located a few miles north of Lincoln City.

WILSON RIVER

The Wilson River empties into Tillamook Bay and produces large runs of steelhead that are at their prime from December through March. Spring chinook runs peak in June and July and the peak of the fall run is November. Sea-run cutthroat are also present in this award-winning stream. The Wilson River can be accessed via Highway 6, which heads east from Tillamook.

Central Coast
Freshwater Lakes
ALDER LAKE

You can find good rainbow trout fishing in three-acre Alder Lake. Alder Lake is a part of a unique system of freshwater lakes around the Florence area. If you want to stay and fish for a while, there is a campground at the north end of the lake. To reach the lake, drive 4.1 miles north of Florence on US 101 to the Alder Dune Campground turn-off. Turn west and you'll reach the lake in about 0.5 mile.

CLEAWOX LAKE

Cleawox Lake is a best bet to catch rainbow trout and you might also reel in some largemouth bass, black crappie, brown bullhead, bluegill, or yellow perch. This 82-acre lake tends to get crowded during the height of the summer because it is located in the popular Jessie M. Honeyman State Park. The park is located 3 miles south of Florence off US 101. See the Coastal Parks section of The Great Outdoors chapter for more information about this state park.

DEVILS LAKE

Devils Lake provides some good opportunities to reel in rainbow trout, brown bullhead, black crappie, panfish, and yellow perch. A camp-ground and a boat ramp are on the west side of the lake. The campground can be found by turning east on to Northeast 6th Street from US 101 in Lincoln City and driving 0.1 mile to the campground entrance. The day use area and boat ramp can be accessed by turning east on to Northeast 1st Street from US 101 in Lincoln City and driving to the end of the road.

Elbow Lake

Rainbow trout and yellow perch are good catches at 13-acre Elbow Lake. The lake is located on the west side of US 101 about 4 miles north of Reedsport.

Erhart Lake

Erhart is a small gem of a lake that provides excel-lent rainbow trout fishing. The lake is located approximately 8 miles south of Florence on the east side of US 101.

Mercer Lake

Largemouth bass prove a challenging catch on the 340-acre Mercer Lake. Other fish that may bite your line include bluegill, panfish, rainbow trout, and yellow perch. You can rent a boat from the resort that is located on the lake. Mercer Lake is located about 5 miles north of Florence on the east side of US 101 via Mercer Lake Road.

Munsel Lake

Munsel Lake is a good trolling lake where you may get bites from rainbow or brook trout. Other likely catches are bluegill, brown bullhead, yellow perch, and largemouth bass. To get there, drive approximately 2.5 miles north of Florence on US 101. Turn east onto Munsel Lake Road North and you'll reach the lake in about a mile.

Siltcoos Lake

Siltcoos Lake is bursting at the seams with brown bullhead, bass, bluegill, black crappie, yellow perch, trout, steelhead, and salmon. This 3,500-acre lake is the largest lake on the Oregon Coast and offers some of the best wild cutthroat trout fishing around this area. Native steelhead can be caught as they migrate to their spawn-ing grounds on the Siltcoos River. All steelhead fishing is catch-and release only, with the best times to catch the feisty fish during the months of December and January. To get there, drive 6 miles south of Florence on US 101. The lake is located on the east side of the highway.

Sutton Lake

Sutton Lake has a good stock of rainbow trout, largemouth bass, bluegill, panfish, and yellow perch. At 100 acres in size, there is plenty of room for everyone to try their luck. The lake is located approximately 6 miles north of Florence via US 101.

Takenitch Lake

Covering more than 1,600 acres, Takenitch Lake is a good family fishing spot. You'll need to fish from a boat because the shore is not very acces-sible due to thick brush. The boat ramp is located about 9 miles north of Reedsport at the north end of the lake. Best catches on this lake are yellow perch, crappie, and bluegill. Small numbers of largemouth bass can also be found in this lake, as well as wild cutthroat trout and rainbow trout. The lake is located approximately 13 miles south of Florence on the east side of US 101.

Woahink Lake

Woahink Lake provides fair fishing opportunities for largemouth bass, brown bullhead, black crap-pie, bluegill, rainbow trout, wild cutthroat trout, and yellow perch. The lake is most well known for its yellow perch fishing and 15-inch fish are usually caught in water depths over 30 feet. This lake is located in Jessie M. Honeyman State Park, 3 miles south of Florence off US 101. Camping facilities are available in this popular state park. See the Coastal Parks section of The Great Out-doors chapter for more information.

Bays, Rivers, and Streams

ALSEA BAY

Alsea Bay offers a strong fall chinook run during September and October. Hot spots for these lively catches are at the mouth of the Alsea River and the lower main channel of the bay. Coho may also be caught but this fishery is subject to closure and you should always check the most current regulations to see if it is open. Trolling with feather spinners and herring works well for adult salmon. Perch are also abundant in the bay and can be caught using kelp worms and sand crabs. Alsea Bay can be accessed via US 101 at Waldport. Waldport is located 17 miles south of Newport and 8 miles north of Yachats on US 101.

ALSEA RIVER

Good steelhead fishing can be found on the Alsea River beginning in November and running through the end of March. The rule is that they can only be caught using barbless hooks. The peak time to catch fall chinook is late September. The Alsea River can be accessed via US 101 at Waldport. Waldport is located 17 miles south of Newport and 8 miles north of Yachats on US 101.

SILETZ BAY

During early spring and summer, anglers use sand shrimp, kelp worms, and clam pieces to catch bottom fish in Siletz Bay. Fall chinook fishing begins in late September and October with a large majority of fish caught in the upper bay. Spinners with feathered hooks work well. Siletz Bay is located 5 miles south of Lincoln City via US 101.

SILETZ RIVER

Good runs of fall chinook and summer and winter steelhead can be found on the Siletz River. The river meets Siletz Bay at Kernville, which is 5 miles south of Lincoln City via US 101.

SIUSLAW RIVER

The Siuslaw River offers strong fall chinook and winter steelhead fishing. The fall chinook hit their highest numbers September through December and the winter steelhead runs begin in late November and last through February. Other good catches on this river are hatchery-raised cutthroat trout in the early spring. The Siuslaw runs into Siuslaw Bay at Florence.

YAQUINA BAY

Good bottom fishing is present in Yaquina Bay. Cabezon, striped perch, rockfish, and greenling are landed from the north and south jetties. South Beach Marina offers good opportunities to jig for herring with the best catches landed during February and March. Fall chinook also enter the bay from September through November. Fair numbers of sturgeon are also available in the bay during the winter and spring. Yaquina Bay is located in the community of Newport.

South Coast

Freshwater Lakes

CLEAR LAKE

This small 15-acre lake is a local's favorite for cutthroat trout and yellow perch. The lake is located approximately 5 miles south of Reedsport on the east side of US 101.

EEL LAKE

Eel Lake covers 350 acres and supports healthy populations of black crappie, cutthroat trout, rainbow trout, and largemouth bass. It also has a smaller population of brown bullhead. The southwest section of this lake is part of William M. Tugman State Park, which has camping facilities. This lake is located approximately 7 miles south of Reedsport on the east side US 101.

FLORAS LAKE

Floras Lake is a popular 250-acre lake that is well stocked with rainbow trout. You may also reel in some largemouth bass, chinook, or steelhead. You can reach this lake by driving 17 miles south of Bandon, turning west on Floras Lake Loop Road, and then continuing west on Floras Lake Road to the lake.

ⓘ Fishing regulations vary depending on the region and species of fish. To help you sort through all the regulations, it is highly recommended that you pick up a copy of Oregon Sport Fishing Regulations, which is available at local outdoor stores or tackle shops where tags and licenses are sold. You can also view the regulations online at www .dfw.state.or.us or call (503) 947-6000.

GARRISON LAKE

Largemouth bass, rainbow trout, wild cutthroat trout, and good stocks of yellow perch can be found at 134-acre Garrison Lake. This lake follows the lead of many other coastal lakes that tend to be weedy, so it is recommended that you fish from a boat. There are boat ramps at the north and south ends of the lake. The lake is just west of Port Orford off US 101.

SAUNDERS LAKE

Saunders Lake covers 55 acres and boasts prime fishing for bluegill, crappie, yellow perch, rainbow trout, largemouth bass, and panfish. Your best bet for catching rainbows is in early spring when the lake has been freshly stocked. A boat ramp and park are located at the south end of the lake. To get to the lake, drive approximately 15 miles south of Reedsport on US 101. The lake is located on the west side of US 101.

TENMILE LAKES (NORTH AND SOUTH)

You can catch your limit of largemouth bass, brown bullhead, rainbow trout, cutthroat trout, and bluegill at Tenmile Lakes, which cover over 1,700 acres. You may also land some hybrid bass (a cross between white and striped bass) that are great fighters and can weigh up to 15 pounds. If you don't have a boat, you can fish off the dock at the county park located in Lakeside. In late May there are also good opportunities to try your luck at catching trout and bass in the Tenmile Creek outlet. The lakes are located 12 miles north of Coos Bay on US 101 at the community of Lakeside.

Bays, Rivers, and Streams

CHETCO RIVER

The Chetco River produces good runs of fall chinook that can be landed from September through December. Winter steelhead are another favorite catch on the Chetco River, with the peak season happening in January. The Chetco meets the ocean at Brookings, and several boat launches are present along the North Bank Chetco River Road, which follows the river east from Brookings. Camping is available at Alfred A. Loeb State Park, 7.5 miles east of Brookings off the North Bank Chetco River Road.

COQUILLE RIVER

This river features spring chinook, fall chinook, and winter steelhead runs. Coho are also present in this river. Fall chinook begin running in September and coho begin running in October. Winter steelhead runs peak in January. Boat ramps are available at Bullards Beach State Park, located 2 miles north of Bandon off US 101, and at the Bandon Boat Basin.

COOS BAY

Try catching lingcod, perch, and greenling off the south jetty in Coos Bay. You can reach the south jetty by turning west from US 101 in Coos Bay on to Newmark Street, which turns into the Cape Arago Highway. Follow the Cape Arago Highway southwest for approximately 8 miles to the community of Charleston. Drive through Charleston and in 2 miles watch for a sign indicating the turnoff to Bastendorff Beach Park located on the north side of the highway. Turn north and proceed to Bastendorff Beach Park. The south jetty can be accessed from this county park. Fishing for perch is also popular from the docks and bridges at downtown Charleston's waterfront.

COOS RIVER

If you want to have some fun fishing for shad, you can try using small spinners or wobblers to catch these feisty fighting fish during May and June. Fair winter steelhead runs are also present on the

Fishing Guides and Bait Shops

Fishing Guides

Tiki Charters, Astoria; (503) 325-7818, www.tikicharter.com

Charleton Deep Sea Charters, Warrenton; (503) 861-2429

J. R. Amicks Guide Service, Tillamook; (503) 842-3775

Haystack Fishing Club, Pacific City; (888) 965-7555, www.haystackfishing.com

Tradewinds Charters, Depoe Bay; (800) 445-8730, www.tradewindcharters.com

Newport Sport Fishing, Newport; (800) 828-8777

Newport Tradewinds, Newport; (800) 676-7819

Betty Kay Charters, Charleston; (541) 888-9021, www.bettykaycharters.com

Strike Zone Marine & Charters, Winchester Bay; (541) 271-9706, www.strikezonecharters.com

Mark Van Hook Guide Service, Gold Beach; (541) 247-6702, (877) 247-6702 www.markvanhookguideservice.com

Prowler Charters, Bandon; (541) 347-1901

Critters Sporthaven Charters, Brookings; (888) 754-9990, www.prowlercharters.com

Tidewind Sportfishing, Brookings; (541) 469-0337, www.tidewindsportfishing.com

Tackle and Bait Shops

Tackle Time Bait Shop, Warrenton; (503) 861-3693, www.tackletime.net

Wheeler Marina, Wheeler; (503) 368-5780, www.neahkahnie.net/wheelermarina

The Guide Shop, Tillamook; (503) 842-3474, www.guideshop.com

Lyster Bait & Tackle, Garibaldi; (503) 322-3242

Garibaldi Marina, Garibaldi; (503) 322-3312, www.garibaldimarina.com

Bayshore RV Park & Marina, Netarts; (503) 842-7774, www.netartsbay.com

Rose Lodge Park Store & Feed Store, Lincoln City; (541) 994-2415

Newport Marina Store and Charters, Newport; (541) 867-4470, www.nmscharters.com

Hillco Bait, Waldport; (541) 563-6730

The Dock of the Bay Marina, Waldport; (541) 563-2003

The Sportsman, Florence; (541) 997-3336

The Reedsport Outdoor Store, Reedsport; (541) 271-2311

Winchester Bay Market, Winchester Bay; (541) 271-2632

Basin Tackle Shop, Coos Bay; (541) 888-3881

Bandon Bait, Bandon; (541) 347-3905

The Dock Tackle, Port Orford; (541) 332-8985

Rogue Outdoor Store, Gold Beach; (541) 247-7142

Sporthaven Marina, Brookings; (541) 469-3301

Coos River during December and January. The Coos River empties into Coos Bay and only runs for 5 miles from its origin at the convergence of the South Fork of the Coos River and the Milla-coma River.

ELK RIVER

Fall chinook runs are popular on the Elk River and good bank access can be found by heading south on the beach from Cape Blanco State Park to the mouth of the river. Winter steelhead fishing is also present during January and February. You can reach Cape Blanco State Park by driving 46 miles south of Coos Bay or 4 miles north of Port Orford on US 101 to the junction with Cape Blanco Road. Turn west and drive 5 miles on Cape Blanco Road to Cape Blanco State Park.

ROGUE RIVER

The Rogue is a very productive river with quality runs of spring and fall chinook and summer and winter steelhead. September through February are the prime months to fish for steelhead, and August and September are the peak months for chinook. The Rogue meets the ocean just north of Gold Beach. The Sand Spit offers good bank fishing for fall chinook July through September. The Sand Spit can be accessed via Gold Beach Airport Road in Gold Beach.

SIXES RIVER

Wild trout can be landed in the Sixes River in the early spring, and steelhead and chinook runs hold their own in this 36-mile-long river. You can fish for steelhead from November through March and for fall chinook from October through December. Access the river via Cape Blanco State Park. To reach Cape Blanco State Park, drive 46 miles south of Coos Bay or 4 miles north of Port Orford on US 101 to the junction with Cape Blanco Road. Turn west and drive 5 miles on Cape Blanco Road to Cape Blanco State Park.

UMPQUA RIVER

The Umpqua River provides bountiful fishing for spring chinook, coho, white and green sturgeon, winter and summer steelhead, and shad. Good shad fishing can be found at Sawyers Rapids, which can be reached by driving 27 miles east of Reedsport on Highway 38. Winter steelhead fishing is good at Scottsburg, located about 17 miles east of Reedsport on Highway 38. During the winter and spring months, good sturgeon fishing can be found between Reedsport and Winchester Bay. Fair numbers of white and green sturgeon are usually caught using sand shrimp, smelt, anchovies, or herring. Striped bass are another likely catch on the river between Gardiner and Scottsburg, with the best season beginning in the late spring and lasting through the fall months. Good chinook fishing can be found in the river above Winchester Bay, with July and August being peak months. Good spots for bank fishing for chinook salmon include South Jetty, Half Moon Bay, Osprey Point, and Orca Point, which are located near the mouth of the Umpqua River south of Winchester Bay on Salmon Harbor Drive, which is accessed off US 101.

WINCHESTER BAY

Winchester Bay offers the best sturgeon fishing on the Oregon Coast. Striped bass, perch, and spring and fall chinook are other prime catches in this productive bay. Peak times to catch white sturgeon are in mid-March and green sturgeon are present in midsummer. Winchester Bay is located 4 miles south of Reedsport via US 101. See the Ocean Charter Services and River Outfitters section in this chapter for recommendations for finding a guide for this area.

CLAMMING

You can clam anywhere on the Oregon Coast for free, and the only gear you need is a pair of rubber boots, a bucket, and a clam gun or shovel. You need to dig clams at a minus tide; tide tables are published in local newspapers and most tackle shops have yearly tide tables available for free. Razor clams are abundant on the sandy beaches starting at the mouth of the Columbia River and stretching south to Seaside. Cockle, littleneck, butter, and gaper clams can be caught in Nehalem and Tillamook Bays. Netarts Bay is another excellent place to have fun clamming. Gaper, razor, and softshell clams can be harvested in Winchester Bay, and Umpqua Bay is thought to have the largest population of softshell clams on the Oregon Coast. Favorite places to clam in and around Winchester Bay are 1 mile upriver from Winchester Bay and approximately a mile north of Gardiner. You can also try the mud flats at the mouth of the Smith River. See the Boat and Equipment Rental section for places to rent clam guns.

North Coast
COLUMBIA RIVER

Dig for razor clams on the flat sandy beaches starting at the south jetty at the mouth of the Columbia River stretching south to Seaside.

FORT STEVENS STATE PARK

At low tide the beaches in Fort Stevens State Park are home to fast-digging razor clams. You can rent clam guns from many gas stations along US 101. The park is located 10 miles west of Astoria off US 101. Follow the signs to the park. For more information on Fort Stevens State Park see the Coastal Parks section of The Great Outdoors chapter.

NEHALEM BAY

Try your luck at digging for softshell clams in the mud flats about 3 miles above the mouth of Nehalem Bay off Bayside Gardens Road. Nehalem Bay is located approximately 15 miles south of Cannon Beach off US 101.

NETARTS BAY

Netarts Bay is a prime clamming area, and you can find good numbers of butter, cockle, gaper, and littleneck clams via the spit at Cape Lookout State Park, on the north part of the bay near the mouth, Wilson Beach, and Whiskey Creek Flats. Smaller numbers of razor clams can also be found here. Netarts Bay is located approximately 5 miles south of Tillamook via the Netarts Highway.

NESTUCCA BAY

Nestucca Bay produces healthy numbers of softshell clams that can be found in the mud flats off of Brooten Road located approximately 2 miles south of Pacific City.

SILETZ BAY

During a zero tide, Siletz Bay offers good softshell clam harvesting on the tidal flats between Cutler City and Kernville. Siletz Bay is located 5 miles south of Lincoln City via US 101.

TILLAMOOK BAY

This bay is one of the top-producing clamming spots on the coast. Cockles, gaper, softshells, and razor clams can be found in tidal flats along the perimeter of the bay. Butter clams and littleneck clams are more prevalent in the northern part of the bay. US 101 skirts the east part of the bay at Bay City and Garibaldi, and Bay-Ocean Road parallels the south and west sides of the bay.

Central Coast
ALSEA BAY

Dig up some cockle clams on the south shore of Alsea Bay along Lower Bay Flats. Along the north shore Lower Bay Flats, you'll discover cockles and gaper clams. Softshell clams can be found in the mud flats above Eckman Slough. Alsea Bay can be accessed via US 101 at Waldport. Waldport is located 17 miles south of Newport and 8 miles north of Yachats on US 101.

SIUSLAW BAY

Softshell clams thrive in Siuslaw Bay. The mud flats on the east and west sides of the mouth of the bay are good digging sites. Siuslaw Bay is located at Florence.

i Be sure to pack a large cooking pot to cook the crabs or clams you may catch, as well as a small ice chest packed with ice where you can store your clams and crabs before you cook them.

WINCHESTER BAY

Softshell clams can be found in many of the mud flats and coves surrounding Winchester Bay. Winchester Bay is located 4 miles south of Reedsport via US 101.

CRABBING

Crabbing season is open year-round on the lower Columbia River and no license is required. Boats, crab pots, and rings can be rented from local marinas. Tillamook Bay, Netarts Bay, Alsea Bay, Winchester Bay, and Coos Bay are excellent destinations to try your luck at catching tasty Dungeness crabs. Dungeness crabs are in peak quality in the winter months beginning in December. You should be aware that there are regulations on which crabs you can keep. You can only keep male crabs that have a minimum shell width, between points, of 5.75 inches. You can identify male crabs by the elongated flap on their underside, while the female crabs have a rounded flap. For more information on where you can rent a boat or crab rings and purchase bait, see the Boat and Equipment Rental section in this chapter.

North Coast

NEHALEM BAY

Nehalem Bay offers prime crabbing in the lower channel during the summer and fall. Nehalem Bay is located approximately 15 miles south of Cannon Beach off US 101.

NETARTS BAY

Netarts Bay is one of the most productive crabbing bays on the Oregon Coast. Peak months to catch tasty Dungeness and red rock crab are September through November. Netarts Bay is located 5 miles southwest of Tillamook via the Netarts Highway.

SILETZ BAY

Excellent crabbing opportunities exist in Siletz Bay and popular crabbing spots are off the public fishing docks in the bay. Siletz Bay is located 5 miles south of Lincoln City via US 101.

TILLAMOOK BAY

Try your luck at catching some crabs from the refurbished wheelchair-accessible pier located west of Garibaldi off US 101. If you have a boat, you can try your luck at Crab Harbor located east of Bayocean Peninsula.

YAQUINA BAY

Dungeness crab can be taken year-round in Yaquina Bay. Crab pots are favored over crab rings in the bay due to hungry seals that will steal your bait. You can also try your luck from the shore on either side of the Yaquina Bay channel to the east of the Yaquina Bay Bridge. Yaquina Bay is located in the community of Newport.

Central Coast

ALSEA BAY

A hot spot for crabbing in Alsea Bay is in the main channel below Lint Slough. You can rent boats and supplies in Waldport. Waldport is located 17 miles south of Newport and 8 miles north of Yachats on US 101.

SIUSLAW BAY

Prime crabbing sites in Siuslaw Bay are in the lower channel of the bay and at the "Rock Dock," a wheelchair-accessible pier located east of the south jetty. Siuslaw Bay is located at Florence.

WINCHESTER BAY

You're more than likely to bag your limit of crabs in Winchester Bay. The best season to catch crabs in this productive bay is in the spring off Winchester Point. Winchester Bay is located 4 miles south of Reedsport via US 101.

BOAT AND EQUIPMENT RENTAL

North Coast

BAYSHORE RV PARK AND MARINA
2260 Bilyeu St., Tillamook
(503) 842-7774
www.netartsbay.com
If you want to go crabbing in Netarts Bay, Bayshore RV Park and Marina offers boat rentals, crab ring rentals, and bait for sale. A crabbing package is available that includes a boat and motor, bait, and three crab rings for two hours for $45. They also have crab cooking facilities and charge $7 a dozen to cook your crabs. The crabbing season in this area is late September through December. Visa and MasterCard are accepted.

i If you plan on crabbing for the day, call ahead to reserve a boat and crabbing equipment, rain gear, rope, etc. Call for the most current rental rates. The marina is open 6:30 a.m. to dark seven days a week from May through mid-November. They are open from 7 a.m. to dark on the weekends from mid-November through May 1. Visa, MasterCard, and American Express are accepted.

GARIBALDI MARINA
302 Mooring Basin Rd., Garibaldi
(800) 383-3828, (503) 322-3312
www.garibaldimarina.com
You can rent boats to go crabbing in Tillamook Bay from Garibaldi Marina. The marina also has a crab cooker and they will cook your crabs for you. The marina also stocks bait and tackle, rain gear, crabbing equipment, clam shovels, and other marine supplies. The marina is open from 6 a.m. to 6 p.m. seven days a week from March through November, and Friday, Saturday, and Sunday from 7 a.m. to 4 p.m. December through February. Visa and MasterCard are accepted.

WHEELER MARINA
278 Marine Dr., Wheeler
(503) 368-5780,
www.neahkahnie.net/wheelermarina
If you want to try catching some delicious Dungeness crab in Nehalem Bay, you can rent a boat and gear from Wheeler Maria. The marina also has a full line of fishing poles and tackle, and life jackets. They also rent sea kayaks if you want to go on a tour of the bay.

Central Coast

THE DOCK OF THE BAY MARINA
1245 Mill St., Waldport
(541) 563-2003
Discover the bounty of clamming and crabbing in Alsea Bay by renting a boat and crabbing or clamming gear from the Dock of the Bay Marina. This marina offers a crabbing special that includes a boat, crab rings, life jackets, and bait for three hours. The peak crabbing season in this area is August through November. Visa and MasterCard are accepted. Call ahead for current rental rates.

NEWPORT MARINA STORE & CHARTERS
2122 Southeast Marine Science Dr., Newport
(541) 867-4470, (877) 867-4470
www.nmscharters.com
Newport Marina Store & Charters has a diverse set of charters that are sure to please just about anyone. This outfitter's most popular charter is a six-hour trip that combines bottom fishing with crabbing. Other charters offered include a spring chinook salmon trip, silver salmon trip, and albacore tuna trips beginning in late July. Whale-watching trips are also offered. To catch some tasty Dungeness crab, you can rent a boat with three crab rings and bait. A crab cooker is also available and you can cook your crab catch. The recommended season for crabbing is December through February. This store also has groceries, ice, and other marine supplies. The marina is open from dawn to dusk May through October and from 8 a.m. to 5 p.m. November through April. Visa and MasterCard are accepted.

i To find information on the statewide effort to restore salmon and trout in the watersheds, visit The Oregon Plan for Salmon and Watersheds home page at www .oregon-plan.org.

REEDSPORT OUTDOOR STORE
2049 Winchester Ave., Reedsport
(541) 271-2311
The Reedsport Outdoor Store offers a full line of fishing tackle, bait, and marine supplies. They also stock camping, crabbing, and clamming supplies and equipment. You can also obtain hunting and fishing licenses from this friendly outdoor store.

WINCHESTER BAY MARKET
8th St. and US 101 Winchester Bay
(541) 271-2632
Winchester Bay Market has a smorgasbord of supplies that will meet the needs of just about anyone who walks in their door, including bait and tackle supplies, crab ring sales and rental, groceries, espresso, video rental, and a post office.

South Coast
SPORTHAVEN MARINA
16374 Lower Harbor Rd., Brookings
(541) 469-3301
This full service marina offers tackle, licenses and bait, deep-sea fishing charters, local salmon and steelhead river guides, and other marine supplies. Call for rates and reservations.

OCEAN CHARTER SERVICES AND RIVER OUTFITTERS

There are hundreds of ocean charter and river outfitters on the coastline and it would be impossible to list them all. In this section, we have listed ocean charter and river outfitters from some of the best ocean and river fishing hot spots along the Coast. If you don't see an outfitter listed in the area you are visiting, we recommend that you visit the local chamber of commerce and ask for a list of quality outfitters for you to contact.

North Coast
CHARLETON DEEP SEA CHARTERS
P.O. Box 637, Warrenton 97121
(503) 861-2429, (503) 338-0569
www.charltoncharters.com
Charleton Deep Sea Charters offers full-day ocean charters for bottom fish (red snapper, lingcod, halibut, flounder) during May and June. They also offer day trip ocean charters for silver and chinook salmon in late July. During the month of May, river charters are available to catch sturgeon and salmon in the Columbia River. All bait and tackle is included and the crew can also fillet your fish for you. Crabbing trips are also offered. The best time to catch crabs is October through December. Whale-watching trips are offered during late December and January. Call for current rates and to make a reservation.

THE HAYSTACK FISHING CLUB
P.O. Box 935, Pacific City 97135
(888) 965-7555
www.haystackfishing.com
Take a unique fishing charter in one of Pacific City's famous dory boats. These boats are launched from the beach right into the surf and can accommodate up to six people. This outfitter offers fishing trips for salmon, halibut, lingcod, sturgeon, and bottom fish. If you would like your fish cleaned, this outfitter will clean and vacuum seal your fish for an additional fee. The main ocean-fishing season is May through October and guided river trips are offered beginning in October for fall chinook. Exciting whale-watching tours are also offered as are guided river trips for chinook salmon and sturgeon. This outfitter recommends that you make a reservation at least a month ahead for summer weekends and one to two weeks in advance for summer weekday trips. Gift certificates are also offered. Call for visit the Web site for current trips, times and rates.

SALMON MASTERS GUIDE SERVICE
1135 Ave. F, Seaside
(503) 717-9901
www.salmonmaster.net

Dennis Steward is a local expert guide who offers salmon and sturgeon guided trips on the Lower Columbia near Astoria and Nehalem Bay. You can fish for chinook and coho salmon on the Lower Columbia from the beginning of August through mid-September. The cost of the trip includes bait and tackle and cleaning fish. He can take up to four people at a time in his boat. The busiest time of the year is March through August. He also recommends that you bring rain gear, sunglasses, sunscreen, and a sack lunch. Call to make a reservation and to find current trip rates.

TRADEWINDS CHARTERS
US 101, Depoe Bay
(800) 445-8730
www.tradewindscharters.com
This outfitter has been in business since 1938 and offers bottom fishing trips, coho salmon excursions, and halibut and tuna trips. They also offer one- to two-hour whale-watching tours. Call for visit the Web site for current trips, times, and rates.

Central Coast
NEWPORT TRADEWINDS
653 Southwest Bay Blvd., Newport
(800) 676-7819
www.newporttradewinds.com
This full-service ocean charter service offers bottom fishing, halibut and tuna fishing, crabbing, and whale-watching trips. Tuna season is mid-August through October 1. Peak whale-watching months are December and January and March and April. Call for visit the Web site for current trips, times and rates.

STRIKE ZONE MARINE & CHARTERS
465 Beach Blvd., Winchester Bay
(800) 230-5350
www.strikezonecharters.com
This U.S. Coast Guard-approved charter service offers fun fishing charters for salmon, halibut, and bottom fish. They also offer scenic whale-watching tours and specialty trips to suit your needs. Call for visit the Web site for current trips, times and rates.

South Coast
BETTY KAY CHARTERS
P.O. Box 5020, Charleston 97420
(800) 752-6303
www.bettykaycharters.com
Betty Kay Charters offers several different charter fishing trips where you may catch blue rockfish, black sea bass, cabezon, yellow tail, rose thorn, turkey rock, vermilion, or china rock. Bait and tackle are included, and you also have the option of purchasing a one-day license from this outfitter. They also offer whale-watching trips. A 50 percent deposit is required with your reservation and group discounts are offered. Call for visit the Web site for current trips, times, and rates.

TIDE WIND SPORTFISHING
16368 Lower Harbor Rd., Brookings
www.tidewindsportfishing.com
Owned by Jim and Jan Pearce, Tide Wind Sportfishing has three vessels in its charter fleet and offers charters for bottom fishing, salmon, and albacore tuna. Bait and tackle are included as well as coffee, hot chocolate, and tea. In addition to fishing charters, Tide Wind Sportfishing offers whale-watching trips, day trips to view the historic St. George lighthouse, and other sightseeing trips. This outfitter recommends that you dress warmly and bring sunglasses, a camera, and snacks along with you. Call ahead to make a reservation and to find out current rates.

HIKING

Hikes are listed geographically from north to south.

CATHEDRAL TREE TO ASTORIA COLUMN, ASTORIA
The moderate 3-mile out-and-back route explores a unique coastal forest right in the heart of Astoria. On this tour you'll get to view a 300-year-old Sitka spruce and climb to the top of the historic, 125-foot Astoria Column. From the top of the column, you'll have gorgeous views of downtown Astoria and the Columbia River.

To get there from US 101 in Astoria, turn south onto 16th Street toward the Astoria Column. Travel 0.3 mile and turn left on Irving Street. Continue 0.8 mile and park in a small, gravel parking area on the right side of the road. Start walking on the wide gravel path. At 0.4 mile turn right and begin walking on a wooden ramp. Turn left at the next trail junction and continue a short distance to the Cathedral Tree. After viewing this impressive tree, go back to the last trail junction and continue straight up a series of stairs. Watch for blue and white circular trail markers placed on trees marking the route. After 1.1 miles turn right and continue toward the signed Astoria Column. At 1.5 miles you'll arrive at the historic Astoria Column. Climb the narrow, spiral staircase to the top of the 125-foot tower. Enjoy the spectacular views from the top and then retrace the same route to your starting point.

For more information, contact Astoria/Warrenton Chamber of Commerce, (800) 875-6807.

HAYSTACK ROCK AT CANNON BEACH

Haystack Rock is a well-known landmark in the small, artsy coastal community of Cannon Beach. This 235-foot rock is situated 1.1 miles south of downtown on a scenic stretch on flat, sandy beach. Part of the Oregon Islands Wildlife Refuge, it is home to nesting pigeon guillemots, pelagic cormorants, tufted puffins, and western gulls. The rocky tide pools at the base of the landmark are filled with colorful creatures such as sea-green anemones, bright orange starfish, and prickly purple sea urchins. To explore this scenic landmark, take the easy 2.2-mile out-and-back beach walk from downtown Cannon Beach.

To get to Cannon Beach and Haystack Rock, drive 90 minutes west of Portland on US 26 to US 101 South. Take the Ecola State Park/Cannon Beach exit off US 101. Head into downtown Cannon Beach to the intersection with Second Street and park in the public parking area. From the parking area, head west on Second Street to the beach. Walk south along the beach about a mile to Haystack Rock. Before you head out be sure to grab lunch to go at Osburne's Grocery Store & Delicatessen on Hemlock Street just north of Second Street.

For more information, contact the Cannon Beach Chamber of Commerce and Information Center, (503) 436-2623; www.cannonbeach.org.

NEAHKAHNIE MOUNTAIN, CANNON BEACH

This difficult, 3.2-mile out-and-back trail climbs through forests of Sitka spruce and open meadows to the 1,631-foot summit of Neahkahnie Mountain, where you'll have far-reaching views of the scenic Oregon coastline. Start hiking on the single-track trail marked with a brown trail sign. You'll immediately begin climbing steeply. After 1.5 miles you'll round a sharp bend to the right (before emerging from the trees). Look for a rough trail that heads steeply uphill to the right. Turn right and ascend on this rough, rocky trail to the summit viewpoint. Return to the trailhead on the same route.

To get there from the junction of US 26 and US 101 (just north of Cannon Beach), travel 17.2 miles south on US 101 (or 28 miles north of Tillamook) to the junction with gravel Road 38555 marked by a brown hiker sign (this turn is difficult to see). Turn left (east) and continue on Road 38555 for 0.6 mile and park in a pullout on the left.

For more information, contact Oregon State Parks and Recreation, (800) 551-6949; www.oregon.gov/OPRD/PARKS/index.shtml.

CASCADE HEAD, LINCOLN CITY

This 4.2-mile moderate route takes you on a trek through the Cascade Head National Scenic Research Area that harbors rare wildflowers and one of the six remaining populations of the threatened Oregon silverspot butterfly. You'll take a journey through coastal forest where you may see Roosevelt elk or black-tailed deer and then arrive on the top of the open, windy summit of Cascade Head.

To get there from the junction of Highway 18 and US 101, travel north on US 101 for 1.3 miles to the junction with Three Rocks Road. Turn left and continue 2.5 miles to a parking area on the left side of the road at Knight County Park.

For more information, contact Cascade Head Scenic Research Area, The Nature Conservancy of Oregon, 821 Southeast 14th Ave., Portland; (503) 230-1221; www.nature.org.

DRIFT CREEK FALLS, LINCOLN CITY

This easy 3-mile out-and-back forest path descends 340 feet for a fun tour through a thick coastal forest and across a magnificent suspension bridge over Drift Creek. From the bridge you'll have a grand view of the shimmering cascade of Drift Creek Falls.

To get there from US 101 just past milepost 119 in Lincoln City, turn left (east) on Drift Creek Road. Go 1.6 miles on Drift Creek Road to the junction with South Drift Creek Road and turn right. Go 0.4 mile and turn left onto Drift Creek Camp Road. Continue 0.9 mile to another road junction signed DRIFT CREEK FALLS TRAIL and turn left. Continue about 9.8 miles (following signs to the Drift Creek Falls Trail) to a parking area on the right side of the road. A $5 Northwest Forest Pass is required for this hike. You can purchase a pass online at www.fs.fed.us/r6/feedemo or by calling (800) 270-7504.

For more information, contact Siuslaw National Forest, Hebo Ranger District, 31525 Hwy. 22, Hebo; (503) 392-5143; www.fs.fed.us/r6/siuslaw/contact/index.shtml.

MIKE MILLER EDUCATIONAL TRAIL, NEWPORT

This 1-mile interpretive trail explores a unique coastal forest ecosystem in the Mike Miller Educational Area. The tour takes you past old-growth Sitka spruce trees and huge rhododendrons and over a small creek where you may see blue herons, ducks, and geese feeding.

To get there from the junction of US 101 and US 20, travel 2.8 miles south on US 101 and turn left (east) at the Mike Miller Educational Area sign. Continue on a gravel road for 0.2 mile to the signed trailhead on the left side of the road.

For more information, contact the Lincoln County Public Works office, 880 Northeast 7th St., (541) 265-5747; www.co.lincoln.or.us/lcparks.

ALSEA FALLS AND GREEN PEAK FALLS, WALDPORT

Waterfall lovers will enjoy this 5-mile out-and-back tour of Alsea Falls and Green Peak Falls in the Alsea Falls Recreation Area. The route travels next to the South Fork of the Alsea River to Alsea Falls and then leads you through a cool forest corridor along the banks of smooth-flowing Peak Creek to Green Peak Falls. There is a picnic area at the trailhead and the campground is just down the road if you want to stay overnight.

To get there from US 101 in Waldport, turn east onto Highway 34 and travel 39.5 miles and enter the small town of Alsea. At an unnamed road turn right where a sign states LOBSTER VALLEY and cross the North Fork of the Alsea River. Continue to the junction with South Fork Road and turn left where a sign indicates ALSEA FALLS 9/ MONROE. Go 8.7 miles (the pavement ends after 1.8 miles) and turn left at a sign for the Alsea Falls Recreation Area. Continue 0.2 mile and park in a large parking area adjacent to the trailhead.

For more information, contact the Bureau of Land Management, (503) 375–5646; www.blm .gov/or/index.htm.

i You can buy an annual day use permit for $25 that is good for all Oregon state parks for a year. The permit is pasted to the inside of your windshield. If you don't have an annual pass, getting into a day use fee park costs $3 per vehicle per day (state park campers get in at no charge on the day they're camping). Most state parks that require a day use permit also have self-pay stations where you can purchase a permit. Call (800) 551-6949 or visit www.oregon.gov/OPRD/PARKS/dayuse_ permit.shtml to view a list of vendors where you can purchase a pass.

CAPE PERPETUA TRAILS, YACHATS

Take your pick of 10 trails that wind through the 2,700-acre Cape Perpetua Scenic Area. Depending on the trails you select, you can experience

🔍 Close-up

Take a Walk through Time

Walking and viewing the geologic features on the Oregon Coast gives you a snapshot of the area's rich geologic history. Rocky headlands, sea stacks, and eroding high cliff walls all provide clues to a time long ago when hot lava rushed toward the sea. Here we've listed some locations you may want to visit to view some unique geologic formations.

Devil's Churn Parking Area at Cape Perpetua

The Devil's Churn parking area is located a few miles south of Yachats off US 101. Note there is a $5 day use fee to park here. You can purchase a day use permit at the Cape Perpetua Visitor Center located about a mile south of the Devil's Churn parking area off US 101.

The Devil's Churn area is an exposed volcanic shoreline that is a slice in geologic time. Forty million years ago hot lava originating from a string of offshore volcanoes intruded the softer sedimentary rock. As the hot lava cooled, hot gases escaped into the atmosphere and formed air spaces in the rock, leaving behind the rough, porous texture that you see today. Over millions of years, waves crashing into the lava rock created a sea cave. Eventually, the roof of the cave collapsed, leaving the wide rocky channel of Devil's Churn open to the sky. As waves crash into this wide channel, you'll be able to see spectacular displays of frothy ocean spray shoot dozens of feet into the air.

Quarry Cove at Yaquina Head Outstanding Natural Scenic Area

From Newport drive 3 miles north on US 101 and turn left at the Yaquina Head Outstanding Natural Scenic Area sign. Drive 0.5 mile to the Quarry Cove parking area. (You'll have to pay a $7 fee at the entrance station.)

The shape and texture of rocky headlands differs depending on how the lava cooled and solidified. The curved and creviced cliff walls in Quarry Cove are made of crystalline basalt, breccia basalt, and columnar basalt. Crystalline basalt has a felt-like surface and is made of fine-grained crystals of pyroxene, feldspar, and magnetite, mixed with a dash of volcanic glass. Breccia basalt is formed from an age-old recipe of volcanic glass, and the variously shaped pieces have a broken glass or fragmented appearance. As the name implies, the straight vertical columns of basalt that form along the cliff walls can be recognized as columnar basalt. The symmetrical columns were created when the basalt cooled very slowly and cracks formed in the solidifying rock perpendicular to the cooling surfaces. Look at cliff faces in Quarry Cove and see if you can recognize any of these forms of basalt.

Sunset Bay to Cape Arago

From US 101 in Coos Bay, follow the signs to Charleston Harbor and Ocean Beaches and drive on the Cape Arago Highway 12 miles southwest to Sunset Bay State Park. Park in the day use picnic area located on the west side of the highway. Look for the Oregon Coast Trail marker located on the right side of the restrooms.

The Oregon Coast Trail takes you on a tour of the rocky coastline between Sunset Bay State Park and Cape Arago. The intricately carved cliffs are composed of sandstones that were deposited here over 45 million years ago when this area was a shallow sea. Over millions of years these sandstone layers have eroded away uncovering layer upon layer of gold-colored sandstone with detailed designs. Many of these layers are tilted and bent—while others are curvy where ancient ocean currents left their mark as soft swirls in the layers of sandstone.

a botanical wonderland of coastal forest, rocky tide pools, and other ocean spectacles such as the geyserlike spouting horn and the narrow rock channel of Devil's Churn. While you're here, plan on spending a few hours at the Cape Perpetua Interpretive Center. The center provides a good introduction to the plants and animals that live here as well as a look into the area's rich history.

To get there from Yachats, travel 3 miles south (or 22 miles north of Florence) on US 101 to the Cape Perpetua Interpretive Center located on the east side of the highway. A $5 day use fee is required to park here.

For more information, contact the Cape Perpetua Interpretive Center, (541) 547–3289; www.fs.fed.us/r6/siuslaw/recreation/tripplanning/capeperpetua/index.shtml.

SWEET CREEK FALLS, FLORENCE

This easy 2.2-mile out-and-back route takes you along the banks of bouldery Sweet Creek to a viewpoint of Sweet Creek Falls. To get there from Florence, head 15 miles east (or 46 miles west of Eugene) on Highway 126 to Mapleton and the junction with Sweet Creek Road. Turn south onto Sweet Creek Road and travel 10.2 miles to the Homestead Trailhead on the right. From the Homestead Trailhead, start walking upstream. You'll pass small waterfalls, and after 1.1 miles you'll reach 20-foot Sweet Creek Falls (your turn-around point). Head up a short side trail to a fantastic view of the upper falls. This trail requires a $5 Northwest Forest Pass. For more information, contact Siuslaw National Forest, (541) 902-8526; www.fs.fed.us/r6/siuslaw.

KENTUCKY FALLS, REEDSPORT

This moderate 4-mile out-and-back route descends 760 feet through a mossy forest of western hemlock and Douglas fir dotted with trillium, sword fern, and oxalis. After about 0.5 mile you'll arrive at the shimmering double cascade of Upper Kentucky Falls. Continue about another 1.5 miles to a viewpoint of Lower Kentucky Falls and North Fork Falls (your turnaround point). To get there from Reedsport, head north on US 101.

Cross a bridge over the Umpqua River, and turn right (northeast) onto Smith River Road (Forest Road 48). Go approximately 14.5 miles on Smith River Road and turn left (north) on North Fork Road. Go about 10 miles on North Fork Road to its intersection with Forest Road 23. Turn right onto Forest Road 23 and follow signs to Kentucky Falls. After another 9.8 miles you'll arrive at a T intersection. Turn left on Forest Road 919 and continue 2.6 miles to the trailhead. For more information, contact the Mapleton Ranger District, (541) 902-8526; www.fs.fed.us/r6/siuslaw.

NORTH FORK SMITH RIVER, REEDSPORT

This difficult, 17.4-mile out-and-back route travels along the banks of the North Fork Smith River, which is filled with many great swimming spots. You'll hike through a jungle coastal forest where you can admire huge old-growth Douglas firs. You are treated at the trail's turnaround point with a great view of Kentucky Falls. To get there from Reedsport, head north on US 101, cross a bridge over the Umpqua River, and then turn right (northeast) on Smith River Road (Forest Road 48). After about 15 miles, turn left (north) onto North Fork Road 48A. Continue about 9.5 miles to a road junction and go right toward Mapleton. Go 0.5 mile to another road junction and turn right on Forest Road 23. Continue 4 miles to the trailhead parking area on the left side of the road. For more information, contact the Mapleton Ranger District, (541) 902-8526; www.fs.fed.us/r6/siuslaw.

SOUTH SLOUGH ESTUARINE PRESERVE, COOS BAY

You can explore a series of trails through a wetland ecosystem at this 4,700-acre Coos Bay estuary. Paths lead through fresh and saltwater marshes, mudflats, and floodplains. The visitor center is open from 8:30 a.m. to 4:30 p.m. Monday through Friday during winter and from 8:30 a.m. to 4:30 p.m. daily during summer. To get there from Coos Bay or North Bend, follow signs to Charleston, Shore Acres State Park, and Ocean Beaches. From Charleston, head west on Cape Arago Highway and in 0.1 mile turn left (south) onto Seven Devils Road. Follow signs to South Slough Sanctuary and Ban-don. Drive 4.5 miles, turn left at the interpretive center, and continue to a parking area. The trailhead is past the interpretive center to the left of a panel entitled JOURNEY TO THE SEA. For more information, contact South Slough National Estuarine Research Reserve, (541) 888-5558, www.oregon.gov/DSL/SSNERR/index.shtml.

GOLDEN AND SILVER FALLS STATE NATURAL AREA, COOS BAY

This spectacular trail takes you on a tour of the shimmering cascades of Golden Falls and Silver Falls. To get there from US 101 in Coos Bay, head east on the Coos River Highway, following signs to Allegany. Travel 13.5 miles east on the north side of the Coos River to the town of Allegany. From here, follow state park signs another 9.5 miles to the Golden and Silver Falls State Natural Area. Start by crossing a bridge over Silver Creek. At the junction, head left and enjoy the shady canopy of old-growth Douglas fir trees. At 0.4 mile turn left to view the billowing 160-foot cascade of Silver Falls. After viewing the falls, head back to the main trail and turn left. Continue uphill as the trail follows the edge of a steep cliff to the viewpoint of Golden Falls at 0.9 mile (your turnaround point). For a less precipitous view of Golden Falls, take the right fork at the beginning of the hike and walk 0.3 mile to the viewpoint. For more information, contact Oregon State Parks and Recreation, (800) 551-6949; www.oregonstateparks.org/park _96.php.

NEW RIVER, COOS BAY

Several different trails explore the New River area, which is haven to an abundance of wildlife including mallard ducks, northern pintails, green-winged teal, bufflehead, hooded mergansers, and tundra swans. Raptors you may see include peregrine falcons, northern harriers, and bald eagles. Trails lead through coastal forest and open meadows to viewpoints of the New River, which is an outlet stream of Floras Lake. To get there from Bandon, travel 9 miles south (or 18 miles north of Port Orford) on US 101 to the junction with Croft Lake Road. Turn west onto Croft Lake Road and go 1.5 miles to a road fork. Turn right and continue to the first trailhead adjacent to a small group of buildings. For more information, contact Bureau of Land Management, (541) 751-4303.

HORSEBACK RIDING

Riding on the beach or through a scenic coastal forest on horseback is a fun afternoon's adventure on the Oregon Coast. In this section, we've listed some outfitters that offer guided trips in geographical order from north to south.

NORTHWEST EQUINE OUTFITTERS
Manzanita
(503) 801-RIDE (801-7433)
This outfitter offers hourly and half-day rides for spectacular views of Nehalem Bay. Call for rates and times.

C&M STABLES
90241 US 101 North, Florence
(541) 997-7540
www.oregonhorsebackriding.com
The experienced wranglers at C&M Stables will take you on guided trips through a scenic forest to the beach. Rides are scheduled at 12:30 p.m. and 3:30 p.m. daily. The facility is open from 10 a.m. to dusk daily.

BANDON BEACH RIDING STABLES
2640 Beach Loop Dr., Bandon
(541) 347-3423
Have fun riding on the beach on your trusty steed from Bandon Beach Riding Stables. You can rent a horse by the hour or choose scenic sunset rides, buggy rides, or pack trips. All ages are welcome as well as handicapped riders. Call ahead for trip schedules and reservations.

JET BOAT TOURS

JERRY'S ROGUE JETS
P.O. Box 1011, Gold Beach 97444
(800) 451-3645
www.roguejets.com

Jerry's Rogue Jets, gift shop, and museum, is located at the mouth of the Rogue River in Gold Beach. This guide service offers world-class educational river tours for all ages. On each tour you'll be able to view a variety of wildlife on this National Wild and Scenic River. You can take a 64-mile, 80-mile, or 104-mile trip up the Rogue River, which varies between six and eight hours. Overnight trip packages are also available. Call ahead to find out trip rates and departure times. Reservations are recommended.

SURFING HOT SPOTS

Surfing on the Coast is cold, clean fun. Huge and small breaks can be found along the entire Coast. Beware that the locals can sometimes be territorial and unfriendly to out-of-towners but don't let this deter your adventurous surfing spirit. There are plenty of waves and plenty of awesome rides for everyone. Note that when you surf off the Oregon Coast you'll need a full 5mm wet suit, booties, and gloves. In this section we've listed some recommended surf spots from north to south. We've also included information about local surf shops so you can rent gear in case you don't have your own.

The Point

If you are an experienced surfer and don't mind braving the mad rush of a strong rip tide boulder-strewn beach, you can ride a huge left-handed break off The Point located off Sunset Avenue in Seaside. You can also surf the less radical cove that can be accessed off the sandy beach. Be forewarned—the locals are a tight-knit group that doesn't always appreciate outsiders. You can rent wet suits, surfboards, and boogie boards from Cleanline Surf Company, 2970 US 101 North, Seaside, (503) 738-2061.

Indian Beach and Haystack Rock

Indian Beach, a pretty little cobble beach located in Ecola State Park located off US 101 2 miles

north of Cannon Beach on Tillamook Head, has some great right-handed wave action. You'll have to pay a $3 day use fee to enter this state park. Another popular spot is "The Needles" break just south of Haystack Rock. You can rent gear from Cleanline Surf Company, 171 Sunset Blvd., Cannon Beach, (503) 436-9726.

Short Sands Beach

Short Sands Beach is thought to be one of the best surfing spots on the Coast. This secluded, scenic beach can be reached by driving to Oswald West State Park, located 10 miles south of Cannon Beach off US 101. You'll have to hike in about a mile to the beach through an old-growth Sitka spruce forest. This beach is also popular with kayakers and boogie boarders. Expect crowds during the summer months. You can rent gear from Cleanline Surf Company, 171 Sunset Blvd., Cannon Beach, (503) 436-9726.

Cape Kiwanda Beach in Pacific City

Protected by Cape Kiwanda, Cape Kiwanda Beach in Pacific City is an ideal spot for catching a good break. Pacific City is located 25 miles south of Tillamook and 20 miles north of Lincoln City off US 101 on the Three Capes Scenic Loop.

SURF SPOTS AROUND NEWPORT

Some good waves can be found at **Beverly Beach** located 7 miles north of Newport off US 101, and some good breaks can also be found at **Agate Beach** just south of Yaquina Head. Agate Beach is located 1 mile north of Newport off US 101. **South Beach State Park** will also not disappoint you. Check out the waves around the south jetty. South Beach State Park is located 2 miles south of Newport. Get local advice and gear from Ocean Pulse Surfboards located at 429 Southwest Coast Hwy., Newport, (541) 265-7745.

GOLF

Sweeping dunes, spectacular ocean views, bubbling creeks, and coastal forest are the primary backdrop to the golf courses on the Oregon Coast that allow public play. All the courses in this chapter have their own set of unique and challenging holes that will give all levels of players a fun golfing experience. Along with spectacular scenery, you'll find that the majority of the courses have a pro shop, snack bar, and putting area, and offer lessons and club rentals. Most of the courses listed are open year-round but can close due to wet and windy conditions, and we recommend that you always call ahead to find out what the current weather conditions are.

We've listed the course descriptions for each course by region—North Coast, Central Coast, and South Coast—and then by city from north to south. The yardages given are for men's white tees, and we've listed cart rentals separately. All the courses listed accept Visa and Master-Card. If you would like to check out golf resort packages, you should contact Salishan Golf Links or Sandpines on the Central Coast or Bandon Dunes located on the South Coast. These premier resorts offer world-class courses, fine dining, and excellent accommodations.

NORTH COAST

Gearhart

GEARHART GOLF LINKS
1300 North Marion Ave.
(503) 717-9243 (office)
(503) 738-3538 (pro shop)
www.gearhartgolflinks.com
Wide fairways with a good mix of rolling hills, mounds, and bunkers will challenge you at the Gearhart Golf Links course. Established in 1892, this 5,922-yard par 72 classic seaside links course is open year-round. Gearhart Golf Links is the only 18 hole course in Clatsop County and is geared toward all levels of players. If you need to rent clubs or fine-tune your game, rentals and lessons are offered. Other amenities include a driving range, snack bar, and the Gearhart Club House, which includes the Pro Golf Shop, the McMenamins Sandtrap Bar and Grill. If you feel your game is especially good, see if you can beat the course record of 63. Soft spikes are required. Reservations are recommended starting in June. Call for current greens fees.

THE HIGHLANDS AT GEARHART
1 Highlands Rd.
(503) 738-5248
www.oregongolf.com/highlands
If you like to golf nine holes with an ocean view, The Highlands at Gearhart may be the course for you. This 2,000-yard par 30 course is built on sand dunes and stays in immaculate condition year-round. Spectacular ocean views and narrow rolling fairways that are well bunkered add to your golfing fun at this well-managed facility.

If you want to warm up before you play a round, you can do so in an area with a putting green and a chipping green with a sand bunker. The pro shop boasts the lowest prices in the country on all major brands of equipment and offers free shipping anywhere in the U.S. The operating goal at this course is "Offering value for dollar every day" and has reasonable greens fees. You'll get plenty of exercise when you play here because power carts are not available. However, you can rent a pull cart. Call ahead for current greens fees.

Seaside

SEASIDE GOLF COURSE
451 Ave. U
(503) 738-5261
www.oregongolf.com/seaside

The scenic Necanicum River runs through the 2,593-yard par 35 Seaside Golf Course, which is a popular nine-hole course in the Seaside area. Seaside is open year-round though it has a tendency to get wet during the winter months. Besides seeing other players on this course, you may also see some local wildlife such as blue herons, beavers, and elk. This 80-year-old course is an easy walking course and is a favorite for novice players. The top-rated No. 4, a 485-yard par 5, splashes widely to the left, bending with the turns of Necanicum River to a small, tree-lined green. The Necanicum River also comes into play on the No. 8 and No. 9 holes. Amenities at this course include a snack bar, restaurant and lounge, and pro shop. Call for current greens fees for this course. Reservations are not required.

Manzanita

MANZANITA GOLF COURSE
908 Lakeview Dr.
(503) 368-5744
www.oregongolf.com/manzanita

The Manzanita Golf Course is a picture-perfect nine-hole course that has a fast driving range and a well-manicured putting green. This 2,100-yard par 33 course is fairly flat and has a sprinkling of hills with narrow fairways. The highly rated No. 4, a 320-yard par 4, has some sweeping views of the Pacific Ocean and is characterized by its thin uphill sweep to a well-manicured green. The No. 9, a 225-yard par 3, has a challenging approach due to the pond that sits just to the right of the hole. This course is open year-round and metal spikes are permitted. Call for current greens fees. Manzanita does not have power carts. If you want to take a break from the sometimes damp and windy weather, check out the pro shop or grab a quick bite to eat in the snack bar. Be sure to call ahead for reservations during the summer.

Tillamook

ALDERBROOK GOLF COURSE
7300 Alderbrook Rd.
(503) 842-6413
www.oregongolf.com/alderbrook

The 18-hole Alderbrook Golf Course is a beautiful well-established 5,692-yard par 69 course with rolling terrain, crowned greens, and nice views from the holes. This course is open year-round and challenges all levels of players with its short and long holes that dogleg left and right and its numerous bunkers, streams, and ponds. Bright evergreens accentuate this 100-acre facility, and deer, elk, rabbits, and a variety of birds can often be seen here. The No. 13, a 373-yard par 4, will test your skills, as a creek and thick trees line the left side of this shot. The No. 15, a 128-yard par 3, strikes a short, steep pitch that has earned respect from those who play here often. PGA pro Jon Kukula oversees day-to-day course activities and the pro shop offers lessons and carries signature apparel, gloves, hats, balls, shoes, bags, and clubs. Alderbrook also features a snack bar with a high-quality menu. Call for current greens fees. Pull carts are available. No reservations are required.

BAY BREEZE GOLF AND DRIVING RANGE
2325 Latimer Rd.
(503) 842-1166
www.exploreoregongolf.com/oregon-golf-association-course-detail.php?cnum=2

Built in 1993, this nine-hole course was designed and built by Bud Gienger and Mike Lehman. A creative water hazard named "Bud's Bay" will test your skills on the No. 6 and No. 7 holes. Bentgrass greens and sand are also present on this fun 1,061-yard par 27 course. At the handy, covered driving range you can practice your power strokes, and a smooth putting green is available where you can practice your softer strokes. Greens fees are $15 for 9 holes and $27 for 18 holes. Additional facilities at this course include a deli, clubhouse, and pro shop. Keep in mind that this course is closed from November through mid-February. Reservations are not required.

Neskowin

NESKOWIN MARSH GOLF COURSE
48405 Hawk Creek Ave.
(503) 392-3377
www.exploreoregongolf.com/oregon-golf-association-course-detail.php?cnum=233
Kiwanda and Butte Creeks wind their way through the 2,616-yard par 35 links-style Neskowin Beach Golf Course. This pretty seaside nine-hole course is flat and easy to walk and is home to abundant wildlife, such as bald eagles, blue herons, swans, beavers, elk, and deer. Situated at sea level, Neskowin Beach can be wet during periods of high rain or high tides. An unusual approach has been used to combat this problem: Nicknamed "The Jewel," this course features 13 greens and has three different course layouts (white, red, and green) sloped and rated by the Oregon Golf Association. This unique plan allows players to avoid wet areas and still provides an interesting and challenging golf experience. In early May, golfers play the white course and then transition to the red course as summer approaches. During July, August, and September, golfers can play the green course. When the wet fall weather begins, players switch back to the white course before the course is closed for the winter from November 1 through May 15. Good holes on this course are the No. 1, a 287-yard par 4, that wanders over rolling terrain to a smooth green, and the 311-yard, par 4 No. 5 that is intersected by Kiwanda and Butte Creeks, offering a unique water-hazard challenge. Greens fees for the different courses range from $12.50 to $17.50 for nine holes and $20 to $30 for 18 holes. This golf course offers discounts to seniors and junior players during the week. A snack bar and pro shop are available when you want to take a break from playing.

i If you want to find out more about golfing in Oregon Coast and the rest of Oregon, you can request the free *Official Golf Directory Oregon* from the Oregon Tourism Commission, 775 Summer St. NE, Salem, OR 97310, (800) 547-7842, www.traveloregon.com.

CENTRAL COAST

Lincoln City

CHINOOK WINDS RESORT GOLF COURSE
3245 Northeast 50th St.
(541) 994-8442
www.chinookwindscasino.com/golf_home_northwest_resort
The 18-hole Lakeside course has a reputation of being tough and tricky. With some parts of the course situated on a hillside with narrow rolling fairways filled with bunkers and water hazards, this 4,310-yard par 65 course will test your skills. Before you begin your round, you may want to practice on the well-maintained putting or chipping green. In addition to a pro shop and snack bar, this facility also has a health and fitness center, racquetball courts, and tennis courts. Greens fees at this challenging course are $25 for nine holes and $40 for 18 holes. Power carts rent for $18 for 9 holes and $30 for 18 holes. It is highly recommended that you call ahead for tee times.

Gleneden Beach

SALISHAN GOLF LINKS
7760 US 101 North
(800) 452-2300
(800) 890-0387 pro shop
www.salishan.com
The Salishan Golf Links is a classic 18-hole Scottish links-style course that was designed by Fred Federspiel and renovated in 1996 by Bill Robinson. Named by *Links* magazine in 1997 as one of the top 100 resort courses in the United States, this premier 6,390-yard, par 73 course challenges you with water hazards, elevated greens, and steep slopes. The course weaves through a forest-strewn hillside and offers spectacular views of Siletz Bay and the Pacific Ocean. The course is open year-round but expect windy, wet weather in the winter months. This beautiful and well-designed course is designated as a Certified Audubon Cooperative Sanctuary and was the first Oregon course to receive this designation. The facilities at Salishan are hard to beat.

The pro shop offers club rentals and lessons and hosts tournaments. There is also an 18-hole putting green and a driving range to practice your strokes. Call ahead for current greens fees. Greens fees include golf cart rental and a basket of balls for the driving range. These rates are discounted if you are a Salishan Lodge guest. It is recommended that you call two weeks in advance for tee times. You can also reserve tee times online. When you're finished with your game, you can catch a quick bite in the coffee shop or head to one of Salishan's three restaurants. If you want to stay a few days, you can stay in one of the lodge's 205 guest rooms that are fully equipped with a fireplace, balcony, and covered carport. Other activities you can enjoy at this resort are hiking, tennis, and walking on miles of sandy beach.

Newport

AGATE BEACH GOLF COURSE
4100 North Coast Hwy.
(541) 265-7331
www.exploreoregongolf.com
The 3,000-yard par 36 Agate Beach Golf Course offers excellent year-round play and excellent ocean views. Located on an easy-sloping hill, this nine-hole course has a wide track with some fun holes. The tree-lined No. 6, a 501-yard par 5, will test your swing and a water hazard comes into play on the No. 7. Equipped with a pro shop, restaurant, and clubhouse, this is a favorite nine-hole course for all levels of players. Greens fees are $18 for 9 holes and $36 for 18 holes.

Toledo

OLALLA VALLEY GOLF COURSE
1022 Olalla Rd.
(541) 336-2121
www.exploreoregongolf.com
The Olalla Valley Golf Course will challenge you with hilly, wooded terrain and water hazards on seven of its nine holes. Olalla Creek meanders through this challenging 3,078-yard par 36 course and provides a pretty distraction as well as a water hazard. A driving range, pro shop, and

full-service restaurant are some of the additional services offered at this fun course. Call for current greens fees and to reserve a tee time.

Waldport

CRESTVIEW HILLS GOLF CLUB
1680 Southwest Crestline Dr.
(541) 563-3020
www.crestviewgolfclub.com
The nine-hole Crestview Hills Golf Course is open year-round and is to many golfers a best-kept secret. This 50-acre, 2,881-yard par 36 course is fairly flat and is host to a dual-tee track that offers a good round for intermediate players. Trees and a pond await you at the top-rated No. 5 and the same landscape hazards are present on the No. 6. Crestview Hills has a friendly, family atmosphere and has many tournaments during the summer months where they invite anyone passing through to stop by and join the fun. Reservations are recommended up to a week in advance during the summer months. Call for current greens fees.

Florence

OCEAN DUNES GOLF LINKS
3345 Munsel Lake Rd.
(541) 997-3232
www.oceandunesgolf.com
The 5,613-yard par 71 Ocean Dunes Golf Links is a sweeping 18-hole course that is located on rolling sand dunes and resembles a true links course. Wind, sand, and sun will challenge you on this carefully constructed course, which has narrow fairways and water hazards. One of the toughest holes on this course is the No. 16, which is surrounded by dunes on a sloping green. Every amenity you could ever want is offered at this course, including a pro shop, restaurant, driving range, putting green, club rentals, lessons, and banquet and tournament facilities. Discounts are offered to juniors and seniors. Call ahead for tee times and current greens fees.

SANDPINES

1201 35th St.
(800) 917-4653
www.sandpines.com

The award-winning Sand Pines 18-hole course captures the natural surroundings of dunes, forest, and lakes. Well-known golf course architect Rees Jones designed this 7,190-yard par 72 course that tracks through wind-swept dunes on the inward nine and takes you among pine forest and small lakes on the outward nine. This course was rated by *Golf Magazine* as one of the top 50 courses for women in 1998, and the May 1999 edition of *Golf Digest* rated Sandpines as a "4-star rated Places to Play in the USA." Living up to its award-winning reputation, the facilities at this course include a well-stocked pro shop, snack bar, a driving range, and a beautifully manicured putting green. In addition, you can take a break in the Tavolo Restaurant & Lounge located in the spacious club house. Greens fees for 18 holes are $79 during May, $89 June through September, and $79 during October and $69 the rest of the year. Carts are $32. To find out about golf packages, contact Driftwood Shores Resort at (800) 422-5091. Driftwood Shores Resort has spectacular ocean-view rooms, fine dining at the Surfside restaurant, indoor pool and Jacuzzi, and 10 miles of sandy beach for you to explore.

i **If you plan on spending a summer weekend playing golf on a scenic course, be sure to call ahead and ask if a tournament is being held on the weekend you are planning to visit. Tournaments are often fun to watch, but they can bring large crowds and close the course to public play.**

Reedsport

FOREST HILLS COUNTRY CLUB

1 Country Club Dr.
(541) 271-2626
www.golfreedsport.com

You can play nine challenging holes at the Forest Hills Country Club, a 3,086-yard par 36 course that is host to wide, flat fairways and fast, well-bunkered greens. This facility is semiprivate but allows unlimited public play. Forest Hills is host to different tournaments in the summer and fall months that offer couples play, four-man team play, senior play, and ladies-only play. A fully stocked pro shop is also available, as well as a restaurant that is well known for its Peppered New York Steak. Other offerings include a driving range, clubhouse with storage, locker rooms, and club repair. Greens fees are $18 for 9 holes and $30 for 18 holes. Power carts are always available for $14 for 9 holes and $25 for 18 holes. If you prefer to walk the course, pull carts rent for $3 for 9 holes and $5 for 18 holes and discounts are offered to students and military personnel. During the summer months, it is recommended that you call two weeks in advance to reserve a tee time.

SOUTH COAST

North Bend

KENTUCK GOLF COURSE

680 Golf Course Rd.
(541) 756-4464
www.exploreoregongolf.com

Water comes into play at almost every hole on the 18-hole Kentuck Golf Course. This easy-to-walk 5,394-yard par 70 course is open all year long but has a reputation for being wet during the winter months because it lies in a flood plain. A pro shop, snack bar, and club rentals are added pluses at this course. Call for current greens fees and to reserve a tee time.

Coos Bay

SUNSET BAY GOLF COURSE

11001 Cape Arago Hwy.
(541) 888-9301
www.sunsetbaygolf.com

Sunset Bay Golf Course is adjacent to Sunset Bay State Park and is a popular golfing destination for RVers who stay at the state park. This nine-hole course is in a picturesque setting of hemlock and spruce near the pounding Pacific Ocean. The 2,609-yard par 36 course is impeccably maintained and is quite challenging due to Big Creek, which comes into play on eight out of nine holes. You can warm up on the putting or chipping green or have a refreshing drink at the snack bar. If you need balls or want to rent clubs, you should check out the pro shop. Greens fees for this architecturally sound course are $15 for 9 holes and $18 for 18 holes on the weekdays, and $25 for 9 holes and $28 for 18 holes on weekends. You can enjoy the view from a power cart for $16 for 9 holes and $30 for 18 holes.

Bandon

BANDON DUNES
57744 Round Lake Dr.
(888) 345-6008
www.bandondunesgolf.com
Opened in May 1999, the 6,112-yard par 72 Bandon Dunes course designed by David McLay Kidd sits atop a scenic stretch of sand dunes 100 feet above the sandy shoreline. This 18-hole course is fairly flat with some hills and has sweeping ocean views from every hole. Greens fees for this world-class course are $275 May through October. A replay fee of $110 is charged if you want to play another round in the same day. Bandon Dunes is a walking only course, and professional caddies are available. Single-rider carts are available for the physically challenged. A chipping area, putting green, and driving range are available for warming up. When you are finished with your round, the Clubhouse at Bandon Dunes offers every amenity under the sun, including a pro shop, spa and sauna, hot tub, exercise and locker rooms, a restaurant and bar, rooms in the lodge and several other cottages that can be rented for larger groups.

OLD BANDON GOLF LINKS
3235 Beach Loop Dr.
(541) 329-1927
www.oldbandongolflinks.com
Old Bandon Golf Links sits right next to the frothy

Pacific Ocean and is a great place to bring the family for a fun nine-hole round. Johnson Creek meanders through the 2,201-yard 9 hole course and serves as a water hazard for many holes. Keep in mind that the conditions here can be very windy due to its location. This course is open year-round and lessons and club rentals are available. A covered driving range will let you try out your strokes even if the weather is wet. You'll enjoy an ocean view from the clubhouse as well as fine dining. The greens fees are $28 for 18 holes and $18 for 9 holes. You can gaze at the course.

Gold Beach

CEDAR BEND GOLF CLUB
34391 Squaw Valley Rd.
(541) 247-6911
http://cedarbendgolf.com/
Cedar Bend Golf Course is a nine-hole course located in a quiet forested setting in Squaw Valley located 14 miles south of Port Orford and 12 miles north of Gold Beach. This 3,000-yard par 36 course is open year-round and is a good walking course due to the mostly flat terrain. Fun holes are No. 8, a 320-yard par 4, which has a large pond as a water hazard, and the No. 9, a 405-yard par 4, that has a fast right hooking fairway that leads to a sloping green. An RV park and a driving range are added bonuses in addition to the clubhouse, lounge, snack bar, and pro shop. You'll appreciate the reasonable greens fees at this facility: $25 for nine holes and $30 for 18 holes. If you want to play with a power cart, the rates are $37.50 for nine holes and $47.50 for 18 holes. Senior discounts are offered.

i Plan to golf in the morning to avoid the often-windy conditions that are common in the afternoon. Family discounts are offered. Call ahead to reserve tee times.

DAY TRIPS

Nothing is more fun than taking off for a day or a weekend to a destination you've not visited before, and the fun of driving to a new place and stopping at different points along the way is just as much fun as arriving. While the scenery and activities on the Oregon Coast are hard to beat, you may want to try heading east and checking out some of Oregon's world-class wineries; Portland, the largest city in Oregon; or the impressive cave formations at Oregon Caves National Monument located in the Siskiyou National Forest in southern Oregon.

WINERY TOURS

Oregon has three distinct appellations (wine-growing regions) that are accessible from the Oregon Coast: the Willamette Valley, Umpqua Valley, and Rogue Valley. The wineries listed below are in alphabetical order by region.

The **Willamette Valley** is an easy day trip from the North and Central Coast and is the largest source for wine grapes in the state, with Pinot Noir and Chardonnay being the most planted grape varieties. The Willamette Valley stretches approximately 100 miles from north to south from Portland to Eugene and is approximately 60 miles wide at its broadest point. You can access the Willamette Valley via US 26 just north of Cannon Beach; Highway 6 from Tillamook; Highway 18 just north of Lincoln City; US 20 at Newport; and Highway 126 at Florence. Most wineries in this region are located in the lower hills on the western edge of the Willamette Valley in distinct regions. These regions include the region west of Eugene close to the town of Veneta, the South Salem Hills, the Eola Hills located northwest of Salem, and the Red Hills of Dundee located southwest of Portland.

The **Umpqua Valley** is easily accessible from the Central and South Coast via Highway 38 at Reedsport or Highway 42 at Coos Bay and is located in the Coast Range between Roseburg and the coast. This region is higher and drier than the Willamette Valley and is host to a rich diversity of soils that produce excellent varieties of Chardonnay, Sauvignon Blanc, Cabernet Sauvignon, Pinot Noir, and Riesling.

The **Rogue Valley** located in southern Oregon stretches from Ashland westward to the Illinois Valley, and south to the wild, rugged Siskiyou Mountains. This appellation is at the highest elevation of all Oregon wine appellations and is the most accessible. You can get there by traveling east from Coos Bay on Highway 42 toward Roseburg and then traveling south on I–5 to Grants Pass, Medford, or Ashland. This appellation consists of three subregions: the Bear Creek Valley, Apple-gate Valley, and the Illinois Valley. The warmer eastern side of the Rogue appellation features Cabernet Sauvignon, Merlot, Cabernet Franc, Sauvignon Blanc, and Syrah; and the cooler, western side of this appellation produces Pinot Noir, Pinot Gris, Pinot Blanc, Chardonnay, and Gewürztraminer.

All three of these appellations have moderate temperatures and long growing cycles. Two significant geographic factors that affect the climatic conditions for winegrowers in the western half of Oregon are the Pacific Ocean and the north-south Cascade mountain range. Moist marine air flows in from the coast and the Cascade Mountains form a barrier that keeps most of the moisture on the west side of the mountains, creating rainfall that averages between 40 and 80 inches a year. This moisture results in a moderate temperature zone and, when combined with

Wine Tasting Tips

Wine tasting is a fun way to learn about different types of wine, and we thought we would help you in your wine tasting tour by providing you with a few wine tasting tips. When you are served a glass of wine, pay attention to the winery that produced the wine and the type of grape. Swirl the wine in your glass and notice its color and clarity. Wines that display brown characteristics have become oxidized or stale. The wine should be clear and not cloudy, although some older wines may leave sediment at the bottom of the glass. After you swirl the wine in the glass, hold the glass close to your nose and smell the aroma of the wine.

Many wines have aromas that are very distinctive, and, with practice, you will learn the nuances of a fine wine's scents. Next, take a small sip of wine, slowly swallow, and concentrate on the different flavors of the wine as you swallow. Fine wines have a complex range of tastes that you'll learn to distinguish.

warm sunlight and cool nights, the perfect environment for grapes to ripen is created.

Oregon is home to many world-class wineries, and before you plan your winery tour, we thought it would be helpful to introduce you to the different varieties of wines produced in Oregon and also give you some wine tasting tips.

Willamette Valley Wineries

AMITY VINEYARDS
18150 Amity Vineyards Rd. Southeast, Amity
(888) 264-8966
www.amityvineyards.com

Well known for its Pinot Noir, the vineyards also feature Gewürztraminer and Riesling, Gamay Noir, and Oregon Blush. A newer addition to this winery's outstanding selections is Pinot Blanc. This vineyard is open June through September 11 a.m. to 6 p.m. and noon to 5 p.m. October through May. They are closed Thanksgiving Day, Christmas Day, and New Years Day. Other locations where you can sample Amity's outstanding wines are The Oregon Wine Tasting Room and The Lawrence Gallery, located 9 miles southwest of McMinnville on Highway 18, (503) 843-3633; and the Oregon Wine Tasting Room Too with the Nestucca Bay Trading Company, located in Pacific City (2.5 miles west of US 101), (503) 965-7369.

ARCHERY SUMMIT WINERY
18599 Northeast Archery Summit Rd., Dayton
(503) 864-4300, (800) 732-8822
www.archerysummit.com
The Archery Summit Winery produces premium Pinot Noir wine that is harvested from more than 100 acres of vines and is aged in French oak barrels. You can taste four of their select Pinot Noir wines for $15. Open daily 10 a.m. to 4 p.m.

ARGYLE WINERY
691 Hwy. 99 West, Dundee
(503) 538-8520 Ext. 233
(888) 427-4953 Ext. 233
www.argylewinery.com
You can enjoy tasting Chardonnay, Pinot Noir, and Dry Riesling in a quaint Victorian farmhouse at Argyle Winery. Argyle produces grapes on more than 235 acres of premium vineyards and is well known for its New World sparkling wines. Visitors are welcome 11 a.m. to 5 p.m. daily. The winery is closed Easter, Thanksgiving, Christmas, and New Year's Day.

DUCK POND CELLARS
23145 Hwy. 99 West, Dundee
(503) 538-3199, (800) 437-3213 ext. 13
www.duckpondcellars.com
Duck Pond Cellars in Dundee produces award-winning wines at affordable prices. Some featured

varieties include golden, buttery Chardonnays; Pinot Noirs that have the rich essence of black cherries and cedar; and spicy, velvety Merlots. Another favorite is Semillon Ice Wine—a rich dessert wine that has splashes of apricot and pineapple. Visitors are welcome 10 a.m. to 5 p.m. daily (May through September) and 11 a.m. to 5 p.m. daily (October through April). The winery is closed New Year's Day, Easter, Thanksgiving, and Christmas Day.

ELK COVE
27751 Northwest Olson Rd., Gaston
(877) 355-2683
www.elkcove.com
Elk Cove is well known for its dessert wines as well as Chardonnay, Cabernet Sauvignon, Pinot Gris, Pinot Noir, and Riesling. Visitors are welcome from 10 a.m. to 5 p.m. daily. Elk Cove is closed Thanksgiving, Christmas Eve, Christmas, and New Year's Day.

i Turn your day trip wine tour into a weekend wine tour. Plan on enjoying the wine country longer by staying at a bed-and-breakfast. Wine Country Farm, 6855 Breyman Orchards Rd. near Dayton, is at the center of several different wineries including Archery Summit, Erath Vineyards, and Sokol Blosser. Contact them at (503) 864-3446, (800) 261-3446, or www.wine countryfarm.com. Another wonderful bed-and-breakfast is the Baker Street Bed and Breakfast, 129 Southeast Baker St., McMinnville, (800) 870-5575, www.bakerstreetinn .com, which is conveniently located near Amity Vineyards and Chateau Benoit.

EOLA HILLS WINE CELLARS
501 South Pacific Hwy. (99 West), Rickreall
(800) 291-6730
www.eolahillswinery.com
Eola Hills has an award-winning late-harvest Gewürztraminer named "Vin d'Epice" that is part of its vast line of wines produced at four differ-

ent vineyards that include Visconti, Rivenwood, Oak Grove, and Illahe Hills. Other surprises you'll find at this winery are luscious berry Cabernet and herby Sauvignon Blanc. Fabulous Sunday brunches are also featured at this winery. Visiting hours are 10 a.m. to 5 p.m. daily. Eola Hills is closed Thanksgiving and Christmas Day.

ERATH VINEYARDS WINERY
9409 Northeast Worden Hill Rd., Dundee
(503) 538-3318, (800) 539-9463
www.erath.com
Located in the picturesque Dundee Hills, Erath Vineyards produces excellent Pinot Gris, Pinot Noir, Pinot Blanc, Riesling, Gewürztraminer, and Dolcetto. More than two-thirds of the wine production at Erath Vineyards is dedicated to Pinot Noir. The red clay soil of the Dundee Hills is ideal for growing Pinot Noir and four different types of Pinot Noir are offered at the winery. The least expensive is the Vintage Pinot Noir, which displays fruity characteristics and is easy drinking. The Vintage Select Pinot Noir is rich and complex and is made from only select grapes. The Reserve Pinot Noir and Single Vineyard Pinot Noir are very special batches that are made in small quantities and only come from the rare and special vineyard sites. Visiting hours for this winery are 11 a.m. to 5 p.m. daily. Closed Easter, Thanksgiving, Christmas, and New Year's Day.

KING ESTATE WINERY
80854 Territorial Rd., Eugene
(800) 884-4441
www.kingestate.com
King Estate lives up to its name by producing top-quality Pinot Noir, Pinot Gris, and Chardonnay on more than 465 certified organic acres in the southern Willamette Valley. Everything about this winery breathes success, starting with its 110,000-square-foot European chateau wine-making facility to its carefully managed nursery and orchards. This estate features a premier restaurant and wine bar that is open 11 a.m. to 8 p.m. daily.

Oregon Grapes

The Reds

Cabernet Sauvignon takes on the flavors of berries and herbs when grown in cooler regions of Oregon and spicier flavors of mushroom and dark chocolate in warmer regions. When aged in oak barrels, these flavors blend into a more sophisticated, softer wine.

Merlot is a rich wine that has distinctive fruity flavors of cherry and plum. This wine is a favorite across the country and is grown mainly in the southern and eastern parts of the state. Over time, this wine combines flavors of mushroom, toasted nut, and tobacco.

Pinot Noir is the most common variety produced in Oregon and grows well in Oregon's cool climate. This variety is complex and when still young captures the flavors of black cherry, currants, and plum. As the wine ages and grows in complexity, flavors can become a mix of earth, leather, mushroom, spice, and tobacco.

Zinfandel is grown in warm regions and, when young, blends flavors of berry, cherry, and plum. This wine becomes very strong and can develop flavors that resemble roasted coffee.

Other Reds: Wineries throughout Oregon are beginning to produce other red varietals such as Dolcetto, Gamay Noir, Maréchal Foch, Nebbiolo, Syrah, and Tempranillo.

The Whites

Chardonnay is crisp and complex and comes in second behind Pinot Noir as the most-planted grape in the state. Chardonnays have an acidic profile and can range in flavor from green apple, banana, and citrus to caramel, herbs, and toasted hazelnuts.

Gewürztraminer is a pungent grape that produces flavors of cinnamon, ginger, and honey and is a good match for spicy cuisine.

Müller-Thurgau is mild and low in acidity and complements spicy dishes.

Pinot Blanc is a dry, crisp wine. It captures the essence of apples, pears, almonds, and a touch of lavender, with a buttery finish.

Pinot Gris is a crisp, fruity wine with floral aromas that is emerging as a popular varietal for Oregon growers.

Sauvignon Blanc can have traits of citrus or herbs with strong varietal aromas. These vibrant tastes and aromas soften as the wine ages.

White Riesling is produced in the cooler wine-growing regions in Oregon and can be made into a dry, crisp wine or a sweeter wine.

Other Whites: Wineries throughout Oregon are beginning to produce other white varietals such as Muscat, Viognier, and Semillon.

---

i If you want to find out more about Oregon's wine industry you can contact: Oregon Wine Advisory Board, www.oregonwine.org; Wines Northwest, www.winesnw.com; Yamhill County Wineries Association, www.willamettewines.com.

OAK KNOLL WINERY
29700 Southwest Burkhalter Rd., Hillsboro
(503) 648-8198, (800) 625-5665
www.oakknollwinery.com
Oak Knoll Winery gained its early success from producing berry wines at an affordable price. Star

varieties from this winery include Pinot Gris, Pinot Noir, Chardonnay, Riesling, and a scrumptious raspberry wine labeled as Frambrosia. Oak Knoll is also proud to sell Niagara, which is produced from a grape varietal called Niagara, a member of the Vitus Labrusca family of vines. This wine is the color of pale straw and has a slightly sweet grape flavor that is long lasting. Visiting hours are 11 a.m. to 6 Monday through Friday and from 11 a.m. to 5 p.m. Saturday and Sunday from May through September. They are open daily from 11 a.m. to 5 p.m. October through April. The winery is closed major holidays.

PONZI VINEYARDS
14665 Southwest Winery Lane, Beaverton
(503) 628-1227
www.ponziwines.com
Ponzi Vineyards is one of the oldest wineries in Oregon and has Pinot Noir, Chardonnay, Riesling, and Pinot Gris vines that were planted in the 1970s. This winery makes one of the most well loved Pinot Gris in Oregon. Another favorite is the Pinot Noir, which is smoky and complex The tasting room for the winery is open 10 a.m. to 5 p.m. daily. Ponzi also runs the Dundee Bistro, 100-A Southwest 7th St., (503) 554-1650, which serves delicious Northwest cuisine featuring local wines, and the Ponzi Wine Bar, 100 Southwest 7th St., Dundee, (503) 554-1500. The Ponzi Wine Bar is open 11 a.m. to 5 p.m. daily.

REDHAWK VINEYARD
2995 Michigan City Ave. Northwest, Salem
(503) 362-1596
www.redhawkwine.com
Redhawk Vineyard produces French oakbarrel-aged estate Pinot Noir, Pinot Gris, and Chardonnay. Cabernet Sauvignon and Merlot are also favorites from this winery. Visiting hours are 11 a.m. to 5 p.m. daily. They are closed Thanksgiving Day, Christmas Day, New Years Day, Easter, and Super Bowl Sunday.

REX HILL VINEYARDS
30835 North Oregon Hwy. 99 West, Newberg
(800) 739-4455
www.rexhill.com
Rex Hill Vineyards boasts a warmly furnished tasting room with a huge fireplace, antiques, and an interesting collection of modern art. Winemaker Lynn Penner-Ash produces wonderful Pinot Blanc, Pinot Noir, Pinot Gris, Chardonnay, Sauvignon Blanc, and White Riesling on more than 225 acres of vineyards. Visiting hours are from 11 a.m. to 5 p.m. daily. The winery is closed Thanksgiving, Christmas Day, and New Year's Day.

SOKOL BLOSSER WINERY
5000 Northeast Sokol Blosser Lane, Dundee
(800) 582-6668
www.sokolblosser.com
Susan and Bill Blosser started Sokol Blosser Winery in 1971. The grapes at this winery are harvested by hand and Pinot Noir and Chardonnay are aged in French oak casks to produce full-flavored wines. In addition to a fine tasting room with grand views of the Willamette Valley, this winery also features a walk-through showcase vineyard that is designed as a self-guided tour where you can learn about the different grape varieties and seasons at the vineyard. Visiting hours are 10 a.m. to 5 p.m. daily. The winery is closed Thanksgiving, Christmas, and New Year's Day.

TUALATIN ESTATE VINEYARDS
10850 Northwest Seavey Rd., Forest Grove
(503) 357-5005
www.tualatinestate.com
Tualatin Estate Vineyards produces Chardonnay, Gewürztraminer, Pinot Noir, Pinot Blanc, Riesling, and Semi-Sparkling Muscat on 145 acres of vineyards. Established in 1973, this winery is one of the oldest in the Willamette Valley. Visiting hours are noon to 5 p.m. Saturday and Sunday (March 1 through December 31). The winery is closed Is closed January and February and major holidays.

Umpqua Valley Wineries

ABACELA VINEYARDS & WINERY
12500 Lookingglass Rd., Roseburg
(541) 679-6642
www.abacela.com
Abacela produces handcrafted Dolcetto, Grenache, Malbec, Syrah, and Tempranillo varietals that are aged in oak casks. You can visit the wine tasting room 11 a.m. to 5 p.m. daily. The winery is closed New Year's Day, Mother's Day, Thanksgiving, and Christmas.

CALLAHAN RIDGE WINERY
340 Busenbark Lane, Roseburg
(541) 673-7901
(888) WINE-4US (946-3487)
The Callahan Ridge Estate produces Chardonnay, Cabernet Sauvignon, and Pinot Noir, as well as Zinfandel, Riesling, Merlot, Grenache, and Syrah. The wine-tasting and production facility is housed in a historic 1878 restored hay barn. You can visit the tasting room from 11 a.m. to 6 p.m. daily. The winery is closed from November through March.

GIRARDET WINE CELLARS
895 Reston Rd., Roseburg
(541) 679-7252
www.girardetwine.com
Girardet Wine Cellars was established in 1971 by Philippe Girardet and is one of the few wineries in the West producing Baco Noir and Seyval Blanc. Wines produced here are grown on 25 acres of carefully cultivated vineyards. The winery also produces Cabernet Sauvignon, Chardonnay, Pinot Noir, Riesling, White Zinfandel, Country Rosé, Vin Rouge, and Maréchal Foch. Visitors are welcome 11 a.m. to 5 p.m. daily. The winery is closed major holidays.

HENRY ESTATE WINERY
687 Hubbard Creek Rd., Umpqua
(541) 459-5120
(800) 782-2686 (tasting room)
www.henryestate.com
Chardonnay, Pinot Noir, Pinot Gris, Gewürztraminer, Müller-Thurgau, and White Riesling are specialties of the Henry Estate Winery, which was established in 1972. Located next to the scenic Umpqua River, this winery has a pretty picnic area and flower gardens and welcomes visitors 11 a.m. to 5 p.m. daily. The winery is closed major holidays and Super Bowl Sunday.

SPANGLER VINEYARDS
491 Winery Lane, Roseburg
(541) 679-9654
www.spanglervineyards.com
Spangler Vineyards features Cabernet Sauvignon, Merlot, Dry Riesling, Pinot Gris, and a dry, white cabernet called "Rosado de la Casa." Visiting hours for the winery are 11 a.m. to 5 p.m. daily.

Rogue Valley Wineries

ASHLAND VINEYARDS
2775 East Main St., Ashland
(541) 488-0088
www.winenet.com
Ashland Vineyards is located in the heart of Ashland and produces top-quality Cabernet, Merlot, Chardonnay, Sauvignon Blanc, Cabernet-Merlot Blend, Pinot Gris, and Müller-Thurgau. You can taste these fine wines in a friendly, country cottage tasting room. Visiting hours are: January and February by appointment only; 11 a.m. to 5 p.m. Tuesday through Saturday during November, December, and March; and 11 a.m. to 5 p.m. Tuesday through Sunday (April 1 through October 31); closed December 24 through January 1.

BEAR CREEK WINERY
6220 Caves Hwy., Cave Junction
(541) 592-3977
Bear Creek Winery makes Pinot Noir, Cabernet Sauvignon, Merlot, Sauvignon Blanc, and Gewürztraminer from some of the oldest vineyards in Oregon. The winery features a picnic area with grand views of the Siskiyou Mountains. Visiting hours are noon to 5 p.m. daily Memorial Day through Labor Day. By appointment only from September through March.

Touring Wine Country Right

Keep these thoughts in mind before you begin your wine tour:

Always call a winery ahead of time to verify the times they are open. Make sure you have a designated driver.

Allow enough time for your planned route; the distances between some wineries can be deceiving.

If it's during dry weather, bring a blanket and pack a picnic lunch. Most wineries have picnic facilities.

Always be prepared for wet weather by packing an umbrella, rain gear, and warm clothing.

BRIDGEVIEW VINEYARDS
4210 Holland Loop Rd., Cave Junction
(877) 273-4843
www.bridgeviewwine.com
Bridgeview is located in the sunny coastal mountains of Southern Oregon and produces award-winning Pinot Noir, Chardonnay, Merlot, Pinot Gris, Gewürztraminer, and Riesling. The winery has two vineyards covering 165 acres and boasts state-of-the-art equipment and a unique tasting room surrounded by beautiful landscaping and panoramic views. Visiting hours are 11 a.m. to 5 p.m. daily.

FORIS VINEYARDS WINERY
654 Kendall Rd., Cave Junction
(800) 84-FORIS (843-6747)
www.foriswine.com
Foris Vineyards is located in the Siskiyou Mountains and is a leader in making Chardonnay, Gewürztraminer, Early Muscat, Pinot Blanc, Pinot Gris, Pinot Noir, and Ruby (Pinot Port)—a unique variety that exhibits juicy cherry character and earthy chocolate. Visiting hours are

11 a.m. to 5 p.m. daily. Call ahead if you plan to visit on a holiday.

VALLEY VIEW WINERY
1000 Upper Applegate Rd., Jacksonville
(800) 781-9463
Anna Maria's Tasting Room
125 West California St., Jacksonville
(800) 781-9463
www.valleyviewwinery.com
Valley View Winery makes Cabernet Sauvignon, Merlot, Chardonnay, Syrah, and Cabernet Franc, which thrive in the sunny, warm climate of the Applegate Valley. Valley View's premium wines are marketed under the "Anna Maria" label and their more affordable wines are labeled "Valley View." Visiting hours are 11 a.m. to 5 p.m. daily.

i If you want to spend the weekend exploring the Rogue Valley wineries, you can stay at the Kerbyville Inn located at 24304 Redwood Hwy., Kerby, (541) 592-4689.

WEISINGER'S OF ASHLAND
3150 Siskiyou Blvd., Ashland
(541) 488-5989, (800) 551-9463
www.weisingers.com
Weisinger's is located just off I-5 in Ashland and features a deli, gift shop, and tasting room. Weisinger's makes Chardonnay, Cabernet Blanc, Pinot Noir, Merlot, and Gewürztraminer. They also feature red and white blends such as 50 percent Chardonnay and 50 percent Semillon. The picnic area has outstanding views of the Rogue Valley. Visiting hours are 10 a.m. to 6 p.m. during the spring and summer months and 11 a.m. to 5 p.m. during the fall and winter months.

PORTLAND

Portland is a beautiful city that is only a couple hours drive from the Central and North Coasts. Portland covers 130 square miles and is filled with over 37,000 acres of parks, historic bridges, unique shopping districts, art museums, funky bookstores, cream-of-the-crop coffeehouses, boisterous brewpubs, unique restaurants, and fun nightlife. Portland is separated into east and west sides by the Willamette River. US 26 is the main arterial highway leading into downtown Portland from the west; I–5 leads into the city from the south and north; and I–84 comes in from the east. The city is separated into the Northwest, Southwest, Northeast, and Southeast districts by the east-west running Burnside Street and the Willamette.

A good place to start exploring Portland is the downtown core area, which is made up of the Southwest District and part of the Northwest District. Be sure to stop by the **Portland Visitors Association,** 701 Southwest Sixth Ave., (503) 275-8355, where you can find a free copy of the *Official Visitors Guide, Portland, Oregon* that contains detailed maps and descriptions about Portland and the surrounding area. Or pick up a copy of the *Insiders' Guide to Portland* at local bookstores. If you look at a map of the downtown area, you'll see that Broadway and 6th Street run right through the heart of the downtown. Front Avenue runs north-south along the edge of the Willamette River and parallels **Tom McCall Waterfront Park,** which runs for 2 miles along Front Avenue. The vast lawns and jogging paths of this park are a favorite for walkers, joggers, and Rollerbladers. RiverPlace is located on the south end of the park and features a hotel, restaurant, shops, and marina. The **Japanese-American Historical Plaza** is located on the north end of the grassy park and is a memorial to the Japanese-Americans who were interned by the U.S. government during World War II.

Book lovers need to be sure to stop by **Powell's City of Books** located at 1005 West Burnside St., (503) 228-4651. Powell's City of Books is a Portland landmark and is the largest independent bookstore in the United States. The one-of-a-kind bookstore covers an entire city block and features over a million new and used books. **Powell's Travel Store,** 701 Southwest 6th Ave., (503) 228-1108, is another great bookstore where you can find numerous guidebooks on Oregon and the Northwest as well as other travel destinations. This bookstore is located in **Pioneer Courthouse Square,** a redbrick square that is host to numerous concerts, festivals, and exhibits throughout the year. Pioneer Courthouse Square is at the heart of downtown and is close to some of Portland's major shopping venues such as **Pioneer Place,** Southwest 5th Ave. and Morrison; **Nordstrom,** 701 Southwest Broadway; **Meier & Frank,** 621 Southwest 5th Ave.; and **Niketown,** 930 Southwest 6th Ave. Another unique shopping district worth visiting is the **Pearl District,** which stretches from Northwest 10th to Northwest 14th Avenues between Everett and Glisan. This unique shopping district contains galleries, boutiques, and fun restaurants in an area of renovated industrial sites and hip new buildings. A fun event in this district is the first Thursday **art walk,** when galleries stay open late the first Thursday of each month and admission is free. If you are in the mood for more art, you should visit the **Portland Art Museum,** 1219 Southwest Park Ave., (503) 226-2811, or catch a play or symphony concert at the **Portland Center for Performing Arts,** 1111 Southwest Broadway, (503) 248-4335. If you are a movie buff, visit the **Northwest Film Center,** 1219 Southwest Park Ave., (503) 221-1156.

From the downtown area you can catch a ride on **MAX (Metropolitan Area Express)** light rail that heads east toward Gresham crossing over the Steel Bridge and passing through the **Lloyd District.** The Lloyd District includes the massive **Rose Garden Arena,** home to the Portland Trail Blazers, and the **Lloyd Center,** with more than 200 stores and a large ice rink that is a popular hangout for kids. MAX also heads west and stops right at the **Oregon Zoo,** (503) 226-1561, and **World Forestry Center,** (503) 228-1367, before continuing toward Beaverton and Hillsboro. You can also catch a ride on Tri-Met transit, (503) 238-RIDE (238-7433). Rides on Tri-Met and MAX are free in the 300-block downtown area known as "Fareless Square." To pick up schedules and find out more information, visit the **Tri-Met office** located on Southwest 6th Ave. between Morrison and Yamhill at Pioneer Courthouse Square.

The **Heathman Hotel,** 1001 Southwest Broadway, a classy club that plays cool jazz with no cover. Good blues music can be enjoyed at the **Candlelight Cafe & Bar,** 2032 Southwest 5th Ave., seven nights a week. If you just want to check out the Portland night scene, stop by **Hubers,** 411 Southwest 3rd Ave., which is famous for its flaming Spanish coffees served with style and flair, or you can try blending into the hip, late-night scene at the trendy **Montage** located at 301 Southeast Morrison.

The **Southeast District** is filled with unique antiques shops, bookstores, secondhand stores, and brewpubs. It is also home to **Oregon Museum of Science and Industry (OMSI),** 1945 Southeast Water Ave., which contains interesting exhibits on science and technology and also shows movies in its state-of-the-art Omnimax Theater. If you're in the mood for a movie and a brew, mosey on over to the **Bagdad Theatre and Pub,** 3702 Southeast Hawthorne Blvd., (503) 236-9234, where you can see a movie and taste some local McMenamin's brewed beers. Hammerhead and Terminator are two favorite brews at this pub. A favorite locals' hangout is **The Lucky Labrador Brew Pub,** 915 Southeast Hawthorne Blvd., which serves great local brews and bentos (a bowl of rice topped with veggies or meat with a special sauce, such as curry sauce) in a warehouse-style atmosphere. Recommended brews are the Lucky Dog IPA or Hawthorne Bitter. If you don't mind hanging out in the outside eating area, you can bring your canine pal along to keep you company as you sip your brew. Unique restaurants are sprinkled throughout this district, such as **Esparza's Tex-Mex Cafe,** 2725 Southeast Ankeny St., which serves dishes in true Texas tradition including fried cactus and buffalo briskets, outlandish ostrich dishes, and cheesy, jalapeño enchiladas; **Greek Cusina,** 404 Southwest Washington St., serves delicious Greek food, which should always be accompanied by nourishing hummus and fresh, hot pita bread; **Noho's Hawaiian Cafe,** 2525 Southeast Clinton St., makes a mean bowl of yakisoba noodles and vegetables as well as other outlandish ethnic

dishes that will tantalize your palate; **Caprial's Bistro,** 7015 Southeast Milwaukee Avenue, serves wonderful Northwest dishes such as salmon with white truffles. Great Mexican food can be found at the **Iron Horse Restaurant,** 6034 Southeast Milwaukee Avenue.

The trendy **Northwest District** has two popular avenues (Northwest 21st and Northwest 23rd) that are filled with trendy coffeehouses, treasure-filled shops, and unique restaurants. This area of Portland also has some magnificently restored Victorian houses gracing its side streets. Parking is tight and walking is the recommended method for getting around this area. If you are looking for a perfect cup of coffee or some scrumptious ice cream, be sure to stop by **Coffee People** located at 533 Northwest 23rd Ave.. For a fun place to sip on a brew and eat some tasty Mexican food, go to **Santa Fe Tacqueria,** 831 Northwest 23rd Ave., where you can order a huge plateful of Chicken Mole nachos that won't break your pocketbook. Other notable restaurants in this district include **Wildwood,** 1221 Northwest 21st Ave., which serves innovative Northwest cuisine.

i If you want to taste some locally produced wines on the way to the Oregon Caves National Monument, be sure to stop by Bridgeview Vineyards, 4210 Holland Loop Rd., and Foris Vineyards, 654 Kendall Rd., both located off Highway 46. For more information about these two wineries, see the "Winery Tours" section of this chapter.

MacTarnahan's Taproom, 2730 Northwest 31st Ave., which serves delectable German sausages, delicious rosemary fries, and other German-style fare and homemade local brews. Artsy film flicks can be seen at **Cinema 21,** 616 Northwest 21st Ave., (503) 223-4515. Northwest Portland is also the gateway into the green expanse of 5,000-acre **Forest Park.** A good place to start exploring this forest-filled park is at **Lower McCleay Park,** which can be accessed at the end of Northwest Upshur or via stairs at the Northwest Thurman Street Bridge. A well-maintained hiking trail leads you next to tumbling Balch Creek and eventually leads you to the **Audubon Society, Pittock Mansion,** and **Washington Park.** If you feel like cycling through the park, you can rent a mountain bike at **Fat Tire Farm,** 2714 Northwest Thurman St., (503) 222-3276, and ride up to the end of Northwest Thurman and hook up with **Leif Erikson Drive** that winds through a forest landscape filled with big-leaf maple and evergreens. There are several fire lanes that also lead off Leif Erikson Drive where you can use up some calories on thigh-burning ascents. Be sure to pick up a free **Forest Park Trail map** at Fat Tire Farm to help you plan a route that will fit your mood and skills.

OREGON CAVES NATIONAL MONUMENT

Established in 1909, the Oregon Caves National Monument is located in the rugged Siskiyou Mountains of southern Oregon. The 480-acre monument is an easy two-hour drive from Brookings and can be accessed by driving 20 miles south on US 101 to Crescent City, California. From Crescent City, drive 46 miles north on US 199 and then turn east on Highway 46 at the town of Cave Junction and travel 20 miles east to the park entrance. (Note that the last 8 miles to the park entrance are narrow and windy and trailers are not recommended. You have to enter California to reach this Oregon site.)

The main attraction at this national monument is a large, intricately carved cave that contains 3 miles of chambers and the fast-flowing River Styx, which runs through the entire length of the cave. This cave began as limestone deposits in a shallow sea about 200 million years ago. As the continental crust shifted, the limestone layers were lifted up and molten lava protruded into rock faults and formed marble. As the Siskiyou Mountains continued to rumble and shake, the marble formations were exposed and water began to erode the soft rock, creating tunnels and caves. You can explore this magnificent cave by taking a 90-minute guided cave tour through more than a half mile of the gleaming marble passageways. Cave tours are given year-round except Thanksgiving and Christmas. Fees for the cave tour are $8 for adults, $5.50 for juniors age 16 and younger. Children under 42 inches tall are not allowed on standard cave tours but can participate in a five- to ten-minute free tour given by the park staff. Dress warmly for the tour because the cave has a constant temperature of 41 degrees Fahrenheit year-round and can be wet and slippery. The tour takes you through passages filled with stalactites, columns, cave popcorn, pearls, and moon milk. For more information, call Oregon Caves National Monument at (541) 592-2100 ext. 262; www.nps.gov/orca.

Other activities at the monument include 5 miles of trails that wind through a predominantly Douglas fir forest that is home to 80 species of birds, 35 species of mammals, and more than 110 unique species of plants. The **Cliff Nature Trail** is a 0.75-mile loop with informative signs that describe the geology, plants, and trees of the wild and beautiful Siskiyou Mountains. The **Big Tree Trail** is a 3.3-mile loop that takes you on a tour of a magnificent old-growth forest whose shining star is a 1,200-year-old Douglas fir. Unfortunately, dogs are not allowed on any of the trails in the monument.

Another attraction that should not be missed is the **Oregon Caves Chateau,** (541) 592-3400. The chateau is an attractive six-story wooden lodge and restaurant that boasts a magnificent fireplace and numerous windows with a spectacular view. The lodge is open Memorial Day through the last weekend of September. A snack bar in the lower part of the lodge is open year-round. This is the only overnight accommodation in the monument. If you want to camp, you can drive to **Cave Creek Campground** located 4 miles from the monument or **Greyback Campground** located 8 miles from the monument. For more information on these campgrounds, you can contact the **Siskiyou National Forest,** (541) 471-6500, www.fs.fed.us/r6/rogue-siskiyou.

RELOCATION

According to our unscientific survey, most people who move to the Oregon Coast are seduced by the beauty of the ocean. And when they arrive, they are thrilled to find charming towns that have robust cultural scenes, wonderful restaurants, and interesting museums; and they are enchanted to discover that the Coast also has lovely rivers and lush forests to explore. Then there are the hikes, bike trails, surfing, games of golf, and other outdoor activities that demand attention. And that is before they realize that there are so many absorbing classes at the local community college and opportunities to volunteer. They find themselves busier than ever, even before they find a job. Or maybe not. That's the wonderful thing about the Oregon Coast. You can be as busy or as idle as you wish.

LIFE AT THE COAST

Before moving to the Oregon Coast, you will have to decide where you want to live. Do you want the forests of the North Coast? Do you long for the dunes of the Central Coast? Or the windswept solitude of the South Coast? Not only must you choose a geographical area, but you must also choose whether you want to live in town or out, in a planned community or independently, in a golf course condominium or on a lonely bluff overlooking the ocean. Plan carefully: When US 101 washes out and you have to take a two-hour detour to the grocery store, the house on the bluff that seemed like the perfect antidote to civilization can feel pretty forlorn. You may wish you lived closer to town.

When deciding where to live, you should think about how you like to spend your time in the rain. Oregonians are used to the rain. We don't see it as a deterrent to many activities we wish to pursue; we'd never go anywhere or do anything if we waited for the sun. Some waterproof shoes and a Gore-Tex jacket or a couple of sweaters will see us through all but the very worst weather. We have other ways of managing the weather, too. In the winter months, when the Oregon Coast has the wettest and windiest weather in the state and a foot of rain in one

month is no surprise, we entertain ourselves by watching the storms from comfortable indoor spots. And these theatrical storms leave behind many beachcombing prizes. Of course, it is not all rain here on the Oregon Coast. We also have fog. But the sun shines too; typically, the driest months are July and August and the hottest is September. These months, with their splendid evening light and plentiful stars, are the due reward for all the months of rain.

Work may be another factor in your decision about where to live. If you don't have a job before you move and you're planning to get one, do some research before you decide. The cost of living can be a little higher here than in other parts of Oregon. Goods have to travel farther to get to the stores and so do you. Moreover, while renting houses or apartments can be less expensive than in the city, wages are also proportionately less. And although there are many jobs in this 400-mile stretch of country, unemployment rates on the coast of Oregon are uneven and vary wildly within the region. That's because many of the coastal towns rely on fishing, timber, and tourism, all seasonal and unpredictable.

Nevertheless, you can find good work on the Coast. In an effort to make economic life more stable, many communities have encouraged businesses that are less seasonal.

People move to the Oregon Coast for many reasons—to be closer to the ocean, to live a simpler life, to play more golf. Some seek solitude, others desire the intimacy of small-town life where everyone knows the neighbors. Sometimes work brings people; sometimes it's retirement.

With 400 miles of real estate to choose from, you are bound to find something to suit your taste. Following are brief descriptions of coastal towns to help you form an impression about where you'd like to live, and the overall real estate picture. The best way to find the perfect place to live, of course, is to go exploring for yourself (taking this book with you).

North Coast
Astoria/Warrenton

These unpretentious, hardworking towns near the camp of the Lewis and Clark Expedition have a relatively long history. They began as early settlements—Astoria gives 1811, when John Jacob Astor set up a trading post out here, as its official birth date, though it was held by the British for a few years after that. Still, it retained its pioneer spirit: It became the first post office west of the Rocky Mountains in 1847. And it preserves its historical air, with lovingly maintained Victorian houses and buildings adding appeal and character to the town. However, Astoria and Warrenton do not look back on a glorious past—the people here are too busy with the fishing fleet and the salmon charters and the tourists and with piloting huge oceangoing ships up and down the Columbia River. Warrenton has a big shopping center right on the highway; Astoria has an old-fashioned main street to explore. The Astoria/Warrenton area is one of the few on the Coast to have a comprehensive public transportation system. Houses here tend to top out at about $350,000, but many are priced much lower; you can get a lot of house for your money, especially compared with other North Coast locales.

Gearhart

Even though there is a resort here, many of the houses are actually owned by people who live in them. Gearhart is a peaceful little town with many weathered houses and a nice beach renowned for its clamming. Small shops and offices line the main street. It also has the second-oldest golf course in the west, built in 1892. (See the Golf chapter for more details.) Nice houses line the golf course in addition to those that overlook the sea. The resort, Gearhart by the Sea, is thriving. Houses here tend to be expensive. Condominiums in the resort complex can run more than $340,000 and beachfront houses can cost more than $600,000.

Seaside

Seaside was the favored resort community for Portlanders at the turn of the 19th century, and the beachfront houses built then can now fetch millions of dollars. In early 2009, the average house price in Seaside is $170,000 and the average listing price is $442,000. Between the houses and hotels and the beach grass is a long walkway called "the Prom"; residents and tourists alike love to amble along its 2-mile length. And there are many tourists: Seaside has a brand new convention center, an outlet mall, a number of large hotels, bumper cars, candy shops, gift stores, and a really big, popular, sandy beach filled with admirers.

Cannon Beach

What can we say about Cannon Beach? If you are a Microsoft executive with a suitcase full of cash, this is the town for you. The North Coast, especially the Cannon Beach area, is not only the hottest market on the Coast, it may be the hottest market in the state. You can still find nice houses in the Cannon Beach area for $400,000 and up, they just won't be right on the water. Property seekers in Cannon Beach usually start out wanting a house right on the beach, but now that beachfront properties sell in the $850,000 to $1 million range, they are looking around at other possibilities.

And why does everyone want to come to Cannon Beach? Besides the lovely beach with the visual interest of Haystack Rock; besides the cohesive feel of the community; besides the local ambience of artist and intelligentsia and gallery and bookshop; besides the imaginative chamber of commerce that has developed interesting festivals, celebrations, and ceremonies throughout the year; besides all these, there is planning. Cannon Beach thus far has been careful and thoughtful about its building and architecture, so it has retained an attractive character. And in addition, it is right at the end of US 26, which is the principal route from the Coast to Portland.

Manzanita/Neah Kah Nie
Manzanita is a peaceful town off the highway that is mostly residential with some tourist business. We can't say enough good things about this friendly, quiet community. The beach stretches from the base of Neahkahnie Mountain to Nehalem Bay State Park to the south; if you walk all the way to the south end, you'll find a jetty where seals and sea lions like to play. Manzanita also has some excellent restaurants and shops, a fine bed-and-breakfast, and possibly the best periodical selection of the entire Oregon Coast. In early 2009, the average listing price for a house in Manzanita is $590, 500 and the median sales price is $480,000.

Tillamook
Tillamook is a quaint hamlet with old-fashioned stores, a wonderful natural history museum, and, of course, a big cheese manufacturing plant just to the north of town. Though floods did a lot of damage a few years ago, this dairy farming community seems to be recovering. Tillamook, and the fishing towns to the north like Garibaldi, Wheeler, and Nehalem, are residential, working places; the properties here tend to be houses that people live in instead of simply visit. You can get some very good value for your money here. In early 2009, the average listing price for a house in Tillamook is $327,000 and the average sales price is $187,250.

Central Coast
The Central Coast has a lot of great properties for sale; it's a popular weekend spot for people who live in Corvallis and Eugene. Realtors here say that compared with pricier communities farther north, you can get a lot of house for your money.

Lincoln City
Once this area was five independent towns; they joined together to form the "20 Miracle Miles," and the rest is development history. This congested bit of highway is busy all year long; that means, however, that the economy is relatively healthy. Lincoln City itself has about 8,000 people, employed mostly in tourism, with retirement-related industries and services rounding out the economic picture. Though the highway is crowded, the area itself has some remarkable landscapes and a beautiful 7.5-mile beach. The town is surrounded by water—not just the ocean, but also Devils Lake to the east, the Salmon River to the north, and Siletz Bay to the south. Like many places on the Coast, the median price of a house in early 2009 is about $193,500.

Newport
An active center on the Central Coast, Newport is an exemplar of farsighted planning. An economic development committee made up of local businesspersons realized in the mid-1980s that the economy of Newport had to diversify if the town was going to survive the continual crises in fishing, tourism, and timber. It is now a year-round destination, with attractions that include not only the Oregon Coast Aquarium but also a beautiful performing arts center, an active community theater, and a flourishing arts scene. Newport boasts one of the few real airports on the Coast, as well, so it is easier to get to than some places; moreover, it has a brand-new, modern instrument landing system to help navigate the marine air stew. This is all in addition to the busy fishing fleet that you can watch from the appealing waterfront on Yaquina Bay. In early 2009, the median sales price for a home in Newport is $242,000 and the average sales price is $435,000.

Florence
Florence is a charming city at the edge of the dunes; it is poised to take advantage of all the beauty and recreation activities therein. The landscape changes dramatically here—miles of sand between you and the ocean. The Siuslaw River lends its green grace to the area too, making it

one of the most interesting spots on the Coast. Florence has a prosperous Old Town shopping district that draws both tourists and locals, as well as a large events center that is host to a variety of concerts and plays throughout the year. Average house prices in Florence run a little less than those of Newport.

Also look at Florence's northern neighbors—Yachats (that's ya-HOTS) and Waldport. Both of these quiet communities offer great fishing, clamming, some charming hotels and restaurants, and great, if more expensive, real estate. You can find more luxury houses in these areas than in some of the surrounding ones; the average price for a house in Yachats is about $400,000.

Reedsport/Winchester Bay
Winchester Bay is a little fishing town built where the Umpqua River spills into the sea. Upstream, Reedsport is a quiet community that attracts retirees (see the Retirement section) with its temperate weather, its mix of activity and leisure, and its natural beauty. The headquarters for the Oregon Dunes National Recreational Area are here, and an elk preserve attracts drivers to the side of US 38. Many little cottages and mobile homes can be purchased here for less than $150,000 and properties don't seem to go much higher than $250,000.

South Coast
The South Coast has many good properties for sale—it's a buyers' market here. Its location—it takes awhile to get there—means that the property prices have not appreciated as fast as they have in the north. Sometimes you can find amazing bargains: fixers for $100,000, for instance. Keep in mind, though, that the economy is not quite as vigorous as it is in the north either.

Coos Bay/North Bend
Coos Bay has had it rough for a while as the timber market and fishing industries have morphed into tourism. Unemployment tends to be higher in Coos County than in other coastal areas. But development officials are making the best of it, emphasizing their assets—a rich history, one of the few airports on the Coast that connect to

PDX in Portland, and the largest coastal harbor between Puget Sound and San Francisco, with a refurbished boardwalk that's nice for hanging out. You won't see them from US 101, but Coos Bay has some beautiful old houses that are restored and well maintained. Go up the hill, away from the waterfront and you'll see what we mean. These houses are more expensive than the average. Average prices for a three-bedroom, two-bath house in the area are in the $170,000 range, though, like anywhere, you pay more for a good view.

Bandon
Bandon is an enchanting town—some folks say it actually is enchanted—with a handsome lighthouse (Coquille River Lighthouse), unusual rock formations, and an attractive Old Town district with art galleries and cafes. The town's key industries are dairy products and cranberries, and tourists and residents alike take advantage of excellent golf, fishing, windsurfing, and beachcombing. Contractors are being kept busy on Beach Loop Drive, with its dramatic views of Bandon's rock formations and its beach access. Overall, you may find many properties listed for under $200,000 and the most expensive and elegant beachfront houses can be had for under $600,000.

Gold Beach
The Rogue River meets the ocean here, and it makes for some dramatic scenery. If we say that Gold Beach offers the usual assortment of recreational activities associated with the Coast—beachcombing, fishing, horseback riding, golf, hiking, and so on—it is merely that we are suffering from an embarrassment of riches. And that's even before we get to talking about the recreational opportunities on the Rogue River. Housing prices in this area, about 40 miles north of the California border, tend to be similar to those found in Brookings or maybe a little less.

Brookings-Harbor
Practically as far south as you can get and still be in Oregon, the Brookings-Harbor area offers natural beauty, a busy harbor, and charm. The surrounding beaches are uncrowded and the surf pounds

them smooth; spectacular bluffs with meadows of profuse wildflowers drop dramatically to the frothy blue-green water below. And that doesn't include the great fishing on the Chetco River or the redwood groves nearby. Brookings is a wonderful place that inspires great devotion in residents and visitors alike. Many of these are retirees attracted by the beauty of the area and the weather: It tends to be warmer here than anywhere else on the Coast. Brookings is a little larger than many of the boroughs on the Coast, with 13,500 residents. The real estate scene is varied; everything from manufactured homes for under $100,000 to luxury houses at $600,000. The high-end houses are not as expensive as they are in, say, Cannon Beach; correspondingly, the average house price is lower—it is about $250,000.

i **Never buy property while you are actually on vacation and suffering from buyer's fever. If it's worth buying, it's worth making a special trip for.**

REAL ESTATE

There are two strong markets for houses on the Coast: residential properties and vacation properties. The economic boom that urban areas like Seattle and Portland have enjoyed is trickling down to some communities on the Coast. The demand is strong for vacation properties and for middle-income year-round houses, but the money involved with the first group puts pressure on the second, especially in the North, where beachfront houses may now sell in the $850,000 to $1,500,000 range. All along the Coast, properties are selling well; they seem, however, to move faster and have appreciated more in the North. If you are a middle-income person thinking of relocating to the Oregon Coast, you might try some of the areas that have fewer vacation houses. And whatever your budget and location, expect to pay a lot more for houses that are on the water. These properties will occasionally skew the curve—an average house in a town might

i **Buying a vacation property? Thinking of renting it out to defray costs? Consult your tax advisor for the latest information about how much time you can spend there and how much time other people can before the tax picture gets complicated.**

cost $250,000 but a fancy one on the beach could be four or five times that.

If you're interested in buying a vacation property, be sure to cover the same steps that you would if you were buying a residential property: study the markets, comparison shop, hire an inspector, and so on. Some additional factors, however, will be important in your vacation house purchase. Consult property management companies in the area about vacancy and rental rates. Experts say that the most important factor in vacation house purchasing is the accessibility of recreational activities. So be sure that there are enough recreational activities in the area for the house to maintain its value. And develop an accurate picture of the expenses of maintaining a second house. Will you be maintaining it yourself, or will you hire someone to do it? If you're considering the purchase of a condominium in a resort complex, for example, find out the cost of fees and maintenance. Finally, make sure you understand the tax rules: If you rent out the house, you may not be able to take a mortgage-interest deduction on it. Ask your tax advisor.

Building a house is another alternative. Some developers will build to suit you or modify their designs. Whether you go it alone or go with a developer, make sure you fully comprehend any development restrictions. And you might consider hiring an engineer: Sands have been known to shift and threaten even expensive developments with irreparable erosion. The Oregon Coast has quite a few builders associations that can help you sort through the hundreds of contractors and subcontractors waiting to help you break ground. Most chambers of commerce can help you find the one for your area, or you can look at a list of a number of Oregon builders associations at www.contractorfind.com/assoc/

RELOCATION

or.htm. Once you have a contractor, you should check that the contractor has a current registration number with the State of Oregon; this registration can offer you some (but not comprehensive) financial protection if something goes wrong.

Building permits have held fairly steady in recent years after an upward trend early in the 1990s. As with other aspects of real estate on the Coast, the hot building spots vary from county to county, with the North Coast seeing the most activity.

Whether or not you are planning to purchase a house, renting can be a fine way to get to know an area. Realtors can often help you find rental houses; many of the companies listed below have property management divisions. Apartments on the Oregon Coast seem to all be in the $500 to $800 range, with occasional cheaper studios and more expensive condominiums. Some property management companies can help you find an apartment, and these companies can sometimes put you in touch with long-term leases of vacation properties too. And finding employment as an on-site property manager can procure rental rates that are excellently low, enabling you to move to the Oregon Coast sooner than you might have otherwise.

The beauty of the Oregon Coast brings people here and therefore, paradoxically, contains the seeds of its own destruction. One of the most pressing difficulties facing coastal residents is to maintain the aesthetic quality of the Coast and to preserve the environment while at the same time encouraging business. The pace and manner of growth is a subject of much debate at town meetings all up and down the Coast, and you should be aware of this debate if you are planning to buy or build on the Coast.

i Owners of vacation properties sometimes look for long-term leasers and offer their houses at significantly cheaper prices per month than they would be if you were just renting the house for a week. Ask your vacation rental agency.

OREGON ASSOCIATION OF REALTORS
P.O. Box 351, Salem 97308
(800) 252-9115
www.oregonrealtors.org

The Oregon Association of Realtors is the professional organization for Oregon Realtors and it tries to ensure its members follow strict ethical practices. While they won't recommend a particular realtor, they can give you comprehensive information about locating realtors in the areas where you want to look for property or about simply finding properties. And they can give you information about local Associations of Realtors. Their Web site is useful for information about legislation that affects real estate and for obtaining publications that can help make your real estate transactions simpler.

North Coast

COLDWELL BANKER KENT PRICE REALTY, INC.
Seaside: 2367 South Roosevelt
(503) 738-5558, (800) 829-0419
Cannon Beach: (503) 436-1171
Manzanita: (503) 368-5179
www.coldwellbanker.com

In business since 1941, this company has 20 agents and three offices. The Realtors in this firm handle every type of property in Tillamook and Clatsop Counties, and their long history in the area makes them extremely knowledgeable.

DUANE JOHNSON REAL ESTATE
296 North Spruce, Cannon Beach
(503) 436-0451
www.duanejohnson.com

This firm sells more real estate in the Cannon Beach area than anyone else. Duane Johnson has been in the real estate business for over 20 years himself, and his firm has been in operation for more than 10 years. Johnson attributes their success to their low-key approach and complete devotion to the area—they handle properties that are in Cannon Beach and Arch Cape, and that's it.

PETE ANDERSON REALTY, INC.
Better Homes and Gardens Main office:
2480 South Holladay Dr., Seaside
(503) 738-9531, (800) 800-2998
www.peteandersonrealty.com
Eight offices on the Coast from Astoria to Newport, and more in Portland, make this large company a leader in North and Central Coast realty. With about 60 agents on the Oregon Coast, they live up to their motto, "We move the most on the Oregon Coast," and the agents are among the top producers each year.

WINDERMERE/MANZANITA
467 Laneda Ave., Manzanita 97130
(503) 368-6609, (888) 741-9329
www.manzanitarealestate.com
www.windermere.com
Kay and Walt Covert affiliated with Windermere in the mid-1990s. Their office, with five agents total, specializes in the Manzanita, Wheeler, and Nehalem Valley regions and also has many listings at the Neah Kah Nie and Pine Ridge developments. Their love for the area makes them good matchmakers for prospective buyers and properties.

Central Coast
COLDWELL BANKER GESIK REALTY, INC
1815 Northwest US 101, Lincoln City
(541) 994-7760, (800) 959-7760
www.newportnet.com/cbg
A big player in the resort market on the Central Coast, Gesik lists properties for Salishan, Searidge, Waters Edge, and other condominium communities. And that doesn't even count the beachfront properties. This firm has excellent resources for finding you a vacation house. Bernice Gesik, the Designated Broker-Owner, has agents who specialize not just in resort properties but also in lakefront and other exotically located houses.

COLDWELL BANKER 1ST NEWPORT REALTY
306 East Olive (US 20), Newport
(541) 265-2345, (800) 866-2988
www.central-oregon-coast-real-estate.com
Over 25 years of experience make this firm one

ℹ Buying a piece of rural property can be more involved than buying a piece of property in the city. Be sure you have accurate information about access, utilities and water, and the true boundaries of the property.

of the top sellers in the area. Broker-owner Jon Lynch's expertise extends from beach property to commercial property, and his agents list everything from cute condominiums to spectacular view lots.

OREGON COAST PROPERTIES, INC.
415 Northwest Coast St., Newport
(541) 265-8531, (800) 234-7485
www.newportnet.com/ocp
This eclectic firm is the source for a number of lower-priced properties, including fixers. But they don't stop there—they list a number of commercial and multiunit investment properties, as well as view lots, development sites, and coastal retreats. Oregon Coast Properties is an independently run office.

South Coast
BLUE PACIFIC REALTY
16289 US 101 South, Suite A, Brookings
(541) 412-8424, (888) 412-8424
www.blupac.com
The staff has had an average of 20 years of experience selling real estate, and they commit themselves to the area they know best, from the California border north to Pistol River and no farther. The hardworking team of six will not rest until they find the right house for you. They also have a very active Web site, meticulously updated every single day.

CENTURY 21 AGATE REALTY
29642 Ellensburg Ave., Gold Beach
(541) 247-6612, (800) 421-8553
Brookings: (800) 637-4682
www.goldbeachproperties.net
Century 21 Agate Realty has been in business since 1978 with two offices in Brookings and one

Finding Your Home

While the best way to find a house on the Coast is to do some legwork, there are a number of resources that can help you do it more efficiently. Kiosks up and down the Coast have brochures, guides, pamphlets, and books full of properties for sale on the Oregon Coast. Some of these include *The Real Estate Book: North and Central Oregon Coast,* the *Southern Oregon Real Estate Guide,* and the *Oregon Coast Real Estate Guide,* the latter covering properties on the Central Coast. You can also, of course, look at classified ads and supplements in all the local papers for a wealth of information (see the Media chapter).

in Gold Beach. The Gold Beach office has seven full-time agents whose combined experience totals over 50 years. The agents in these offices handle every kind of property in the areas of Brookings, Carpenterville, Gold Beach, Harbor, Hunter Creek, Nesika Beach, and Pistol River and have behind them the considerable resources of the Century 21 network.

DAVID L. DAVIS REAL ESTATE
1110 Alabama St., Bandon
(541) 347-9444, (800) 835-9444
www.bandonhomes.com
Want to buy a cranberry farm? David Davis can find one for you. In business since 1970, this firm lists an impressive array of commercial properties in the Bandon area from picturesque farms to multiplex dwellings to sites on US 101 ready to be transformed into your dream business. The firm also handles residential properties including beachfront mansions and cute little cabins, and everything in between.

GOLD COAST PROPERTIES, INC
125 Baltimore Ave. Southeast, Bandon
(541) 347-4533
www.coastproperties.com
This firm covers the entire area of Coos and Curry Counties and has a proven track record.

EDUCATION AND CHILD CARE

The Oregon Coast is lucky to have 15 school districts and four community colleges that offer state-of-the-art technology and a variety of educational opportunities for children and adults. Known for its innovative, pioneering spirit Oregon has embarked on a mission to require higher educational standards for its children.

Four community colleges, Clatsop, Tillamook Bay, Oregon Coast, and Southwestern, offer a variety of programs that will meet the needs of those who want to obtain a one-year certificate, a two-year associate degree, a four-year bachelor's degree, or even a master's degree in a variety of disciplines. In addition, all four community colleges offer courses that are transferable to four-year colleges and universities, and they also offer distance education classes that are given via the Internet or a two-way interactive video conferencing system. See the Colleges section in this chapter for more detailed information on each of these community colleges.

A difficult challenge parents must face is finding affordable, safe, and stimulating child care for their children. In the state of Oregon, there are generally three types of certified child care providers that are available to you: a group child care home that is located in a single family dwelling, has a certified provider who can care for up to 12 children, and can hire additional employees; family child care where one person is certified and responsible for caring for up to 10 children in the home without additional help; and child care centers that are located in a commercial building, are inspected and certified by the state, and have a number of employees. Child care providers that are certified by the state are inspected and must abide by a comprehensive list of regulations that are designed to provide a safe environment for your child. In this chapter, we've listed child care referral services for each county on the Oregon Coast.

North Coast
Public Schools
ASTORIA SCHOOL DISTRICT
785 Alameda Ave., Astoria
(503) 325-6441
www.astoriaschools.org
The Astoria School District is represented by Astor Elementary, Gray Elementary, Lewis & Clark Elementary, Olney Elementary, Astoria Middle School, and Astoria High School. All elementary schools in this district enroll students in grades K through 5. Astoria Middle School teaches grades 6 through 8 with the high school handling 9 through 12.

KNAPPA SCHOOL DISTRICT
41535 Old Hwy. 30, Astoria
(503) 458-5993
www.knappa.k12.or.us
The Knappa school district is represented by Knappa High and Hilda Lahti Elementary, Knappa School District. Hilda Lahti Elementary enrolls students in kindergarten through 8th grade and Knappa High serves grades 9 through 12.

WARRENTON/HAMMOND SCHOOL DISTRICT
820 Southwest Cedar St., Warrenton
(503) 861-2281
www.gowarrenton.com
The Warrenton/Hammond School District serves students who live in Warrenton, Hammond, Sunset Beach, and outlying areas. The district has a high-quality staff of more than 50 teachers and 60 support staff. Bus transportation is available for more than 90 percent of the students who attend Warrenton Grade School and Warrenton High School. The goals of the district are to educate and prepare students to attend college, enter a professional technical program, or to enter the workforce.

i Visit the Oregon Department of Education Web site at www.ode.state.or.us for comprehensive information on school performance reports, performance requirements, and school listings and Web sites.

JEWELL SCHOOL DISTRICT
83874 Hwy. 103, Seaside
(503) 755-2451
www.jewell.k12.or.us
Jewell School District Has an elementary school and a high school that offers classes for children starting in kindergarten through 12 grade. For more information about the current curriculum offered visit the district Web site.

SEASIDE SCHOOL DISTRICT
1801 South Franklin St., Seaside
(503) 738-5591
www.seaside.k12.or.us
The Seaside School District has a healthy enrollment of more than 1,760 students and serves the educational needs of Cannon Beach, Gearhart, Seaside, and rural Clatsop County. The students in this school district in grades K through 5 attend one of three elementary schools depending on where they live: Cannon Beach Elementary, Gearhart Elementary, or Seaside Heights Elementary. Students in grades 6 through 8 attend Broadway Middle School in Seaside and those in grades 9 through 12 go to Seaside High School also located in Seaside.

NEAH-KAH-NIE SCHOOL DISTRICT
504 North 3rd Ave., Rockaway Beach
(503) 355-2222
www.neahkahnie.k12.or.us
With one combined junior and senior high school and two elementary schools, the Neah-Kah-Nie School District serves more than 800 students. The Neah-Kah-Nie Junior/Senior High School offers classes to about 385 students in grades 7 through 12. Garibaldi Elementary School serves 215 children in kindergarten through 6th grade who live in the Garibaldi area. Approxi-

mately 212 children living in the Nehalem area attend Nehalem Elementary School, which also offers classes to children attending kindergarten through 6th grade.

TILLAMOOK SCHOOL DISTRICT
6825 Officers' Row, Tillamook
(503) 842-4414
www.tillamook.k12.or.us

Covering 404 square miles, the Tillamook School District has four elementary schools, a junior high school, and a senior high school that serve more than 2,000 students with a staff of more than 250.

NESTUCCA VALLEY SCHOOL DISTRICT
36925 US 101 South, Cloverdale
(503) 392-4892
www.nestucca.k12.or.us

Nestucca Valley School District is made up of Nestucca High School (located in Cloverdale), which serves more than 250 kids attending grades 9 through 12; Nestucca Middle School (located in Beaver) offers classes to more than 152 children in grades 6 through 8; and Nestucca Elementary School (located in Beaver) gives instruction to more than 280 children in grades K through 5.

Child Care Referral Services
CARING OPTIONS
#10 6th St., Suite 205b, Astoria
(503) 325-1053

Caring Options is a tri-county child care referral service for Clatsop, Columbia, and Tillamook Counties that serves the community under the umbrella organization of Community Action Resource Enterprises, Inc. (CARE). The Caring Options staff will listen to your child care needs and then provide you with a list of child care options including state registered in-home day-care providers and day-care centers. For short-term care, the staff can put you in touch with evening and weekend babysitters who can come to your home or hotel fully prepared to provide high-quality care to your child.

CHILD CARE RESOURCE & REFERRAL
2211 11th St., Tillamook
(503) 842-5261

Child Care Resource and Referral provides child care options for family child care, group home child care, and child care centers in Tillamook County. The staff will assess your child's needs and provide you with a list of certified or registered providers over the phone, and they will also mail you a list. This office also has a list of short-term babysitters who can watch your child during evenings, weekends, or weekdays. They cannot give you the list of babysitters' names over the phone but they are happy to let you look at the list if you visit their office.

Central Coast
Public Schools
LINCOLN COUNTY SCHOOL DISTRICT
459 Southwest Coast Hwy., Newport
(541) 265-9211
www.lincoln.k12.or.us

Lincoln County School District is the largest district on the Oregon Coast and serves 5,400 students living in the following communities: Newport, Lincoln City, Waldport, Eddyville, Siletz, and Toledo.

MAPLETON SCHOOL DISTRICT
10868 East Mapleton Rd., Mapleton
(541) 268-4312
www.mapleton.k12.or.us

The Mapleton School District serves just over 275 students who live in the communities of Deadwood, Mapleton, and Swisshome, and is made up of an elementary school (K through 5), middle school (6 through 8), and high school (9 through 12). The district is one of five in the state of Oregon that has been recognized by the Oregon Department of Education as a High Performance Learning Center.

SIUSLAW SCHOOL DISTRICT
21111 Oak St., Florence
(541) 997-2651
www.siuslaw.k12.or.us

The Siuslaw School District is composed of Siuslaw

High School, Siuslaw Middle School, Rhododendron Elementary School, and Rhododendron Primary School. More than 1,675 students live in the district, which encompasses 210 square miles of the city of Florence and surrounding areas.

Child Care Referral Services
LANE FAMILY CONNECTIONS
Lane Community College
4000 East 30th, Building 24, Eugene
(800) 222-3290
www.lanecc.edu/lfc/index.htm
The staff at Lane Family Connections can provide you with resources and referrals for registered and exempt family care providers, group home providers, and registered child care centers in the Florence and Mapleton areas. Registered family care providers are registered with the Oregon Child Care Division to provide child care at their residence. The state requires that family child care providers be registered if they are caring for three or more children or children from more than one family (other than their own children) at any given time. If these conditions do not apply, then the family care provider is not required to registered with the state and is exempt. The center can also provide you with short-term care referrals and support materials to answer your child care questions. This service is provided on a sliding scale basis based on income. If you are traveling through the Florence or Mapleton area and need to find out about short-term care, you can also call the center and the staff can provide you with a list of short-term care providers. They accept payment in the form of Visa or MasterCard, so you can obtain the information over the phone.

South Coast
Public Schools
COOS BAY PUBLIC SCHOOL DISTRICT
1330 Teakwood Ave., Coos Bay
(541) 267-3104
www.coos-bay.k12.or.us
The Coos Bay Public School District enrolls more than 3,500 students who live in Coos Bay and surrounding unincorporated areas. The district has six elementary schools that teach grades K through

5. Middle school students (grades 6 through 8) attend one of two middle schools in the district: Millacoma and Sunset. More than 1,250 high school students in grades 9 through 12 attend Marshfield High School, which is the largest high school on the Oregon Coast. An integrated curriculum is used in the elementary schools in the district and instruction is offered in traditional classrooms as well as classrooms that have children of different ages. Middle school students are on a trimester schedule so they can take advantage of taking a wide variety of elective courses.

BANDON SCHOOL DISTRICT
455 9th St. Southwest, Bandon
(541) 347-4411
www.bandon.k12.or.us
The Bandon School District is composed of Ocean Crest Elementary, Harbor Lights Middle School, and Bandon Senior High School, which enroll just over 800 students.

CENTRAL CURRY SCHOOL DISTRICT
29516 Ellensburg Ave., Gold Beach
(541) 247-2003
www.ccsd.k12.or.us
More than 850 students who live in Gold Beach and the surrounding areas are enrolled in the Central Curry School District. This school district is made up of Riley Creek Elementary, Agness Elementary, and Gold Beach High School. Riley Creek Elementary enrolls more than 570 students in grades K through 8; Agness Elementary has a very small enrollment of students in grades K through 6; and about 260 students attend Gold Beach High School in grades 9 through 12. Students who attend Gold Beach High School are required to take courses in English, mathematics, science, health, fine/applied arts, foreign language, social studies, physical education, economics, career development, technical applications, and electives.

BROOKINGS-HARBOR SCHOOL DISTRICT
629 Easy St., Brookings
(541) 469-7443
www.brookings.k12.or.us

More than 1,800 students make up the Brookings-Harbor School District, which is composed of two elementary schools, one middle school, and one high school.

Child Care Referral Services
COOS/CURRY RESOURCE & REFERRAL AGENCY
Southwestern Oregon Community College
1988 Newmark, Coos Bay
(541) 888-7096
www.socc.edu

This agency provides child care referrals for exempt and registered providers in Coos and Curry Counties. Parents can call in and explain their short- or long-term child care needs, and the staff at this friendly agency will provide the parents with a list of providers that should fit their needs. Brochures and other literature are also available that educate parents on what to look for when seeking child care. The agency also has a lending library for registered providers that contains brochures and books on state regulations, child education programs, and tips for running a child care facility, etc.

Colleges
CLATSOP COMMUNITY COLLEGE
1653 Jerome Ave., Astoria
(503) 325-0910
www.clatsopcc.edu

Established in 1958, Clatsop Community College's main campus is located in the hills above downtown Astoria and enrolls about 10,000 students. The school offers three types of two-year degree programs in more than 30 disciplines: Associate in Arts—Oregon Transfer, Associate of Applied Science, and Associate in General Studies. Students can also earn a bachelor's degree in association with Linfield College, Oregon State University, and Oregon Health Sciences University.

TILLAMOOK BAY COMMUNITY COLLEGE
2510 1st St., Tillamook
(503) 842-8222, (888) 306-8222
www.tbcc.cc.or.us

Tillamook Bay Community College offers a variety of courses. Degree programs include two-year Oregon Transfer Associate of Arts, Associate of General Studies, and Associate of Science Transfer. Students can also earn one-year certificates or a two-year Associate of Science degree in multiple disciplines. The college also offers classes in adult basic education, English as a second language, high school equivalency (GED), and personal enrichment. Other courses, such as drawing, modern art history, anatomy and physiology, microbiology, accounting, and many others, are also available.

OREGON COAST COMMUNITY COLLEGE
332 Southwest Coast Hwy., Newport
(541) 265-2283
North County Center
3788 SE High School Dr., Lincoln City
(541) 996-4958
South County Center
265 Bay St., Waldport
(541) 563-4502
www.occc.cc.or.us

Established in 1987, Oregon Coast Community College has three centers located in Newport, Lincoln City, and Waldport and offers courses to more than 3,000 students. Programs offered include adult basic education, community education, college transfer, profession/technical, and small business assistance. The college is accredited with the Northwest Association of Schools and Colleges and has a close partnership with Chemeketa Community College in Salem.

SOUTHWESTERN OREGON COMMUNITY COLLEGE
1988 Newmark, Coos Bay
(800) 962-2838
www.socc.edu

Formed in 1961, Southwestern Oregon Community College is accredited by the Northwest Association of Schools and Colleges and by the Commission on Colleges and offers a variety of programs to meet the needs of more than 11,000 students. The college offers two-year associate degree programs in the arts and sciences, two-year associate transfer programs, certificate programs, a high school diploma program, and adult education and enrichment courses. The college also offers upper division and master's degree classes through its partnership with Oregon Health Sciences University, Linfield College, Oregon Institute of Technology, Portland State University, Southern Oregon University, and Oregon State University.

HEALTH CARE

There are hospitals and dozens of medical clinics spanning the coastline that provide high-quality health care to the coastal communities. Many hospitals offer a wide variety of services such as emergency and surgical care, obstetrics, radiology, rehabilitation, community education classes, home health, and hospice services. All hospitals offer 24-hour emergency care and can be reached by dialing 911.

North Coast

Hospitals

COLUMBIA MEMORIAL HOSPITAL
2111 Exchange St., Astoria
(503) 325-4321
www.columbiamemorial.org
Established in 1870, Columbia Memorial Hospital is an independent, nonprofit 49-bed hospital that offers a comprehensive list of health care services to the residents of Clatsop County and the Lower Columbia River region of western Washington. This hospital has a level-three trauma center and offers high-quality emergency services from physicians and nurses who are ACLS (Advanced Cardiac Life Support) certified.

This hospital is the second-largest employer in Clatsop County and has a staff of physicians and health professionals who offer services in allergy/dermatology; ear/nose/throat; family/general practice; gerontology; internal medicine; midwifery; nephrology; primary care; obstetrics; orthopedics; pediatrics; plastic surgery; psychiatry; radiology; and urology. The hospital has a high-quality rehabilitation department staffed by licensed physical therapists and physical therapy assistants who provide services in speech therapy, pediatric therapy, and occupational therapy.

The hospital has a state-of-the-art imaging center with CT scanning, an accredited mammography facility, ultrasound (including non-invasive vascular ultrasound), nuclear medicine imaging, and clinical radiographic and fluoroscopy studies and is staffed by board-certified radiologists and registered technologists.

Columbia Memorial offers monthly health insurance assistance classes to seniors and diabetes education classes. They also have a monthly newsletter called Vital Signs that features articles on health and wellness and keeps residents up to date on services offered by the hospital.

PROVIDENCE SEASIDE HOSPITAL
725 South Wahanna Rd., Seaside
(503) 717-7000
www.providence.org/northcoast
Providence Seaside Hospital is a 32-bed acute-care facility serving the residents and visitors in the Seaside area. As part of the Providence Health System, this hospital offers a variety of health care services including a birthing center, chemotherapy, echocardiography, day surgery, emergency services, imaging services, intensive care, coronary care, mammography, ultrasound, physical therapy, occupational therapy, and home health.

A 22-bed Extended Care facility located in the hospital helps elderly patients transition from the hospital setting back to their home. Additional programs and services include a low-cost community health clinic staffed by volunteers, the Health and Lifestyle Center, a diabetes education program, and occupational health services that provide safety education, vaccinations, and health screenings for local businesses.

Providence Seaside Hospital has an informative Web site where you can view the most up-to-date class schedule for the Health and Lifestyle Center. Classes offered cover a wide variety of health issues such as childbirth and infant care, how to stop smoking, grief management, nutrition, and weight management. Classes are open to Providence members at a discounted price and also to the general public.

Other helpful links on this Web site make it easy for you to find the nearest medical clinic and information on home health care, extended care, and health plans.

TILLAMOOK COUNTY GENERAL HOSPITAL
1000 3rd St., Tillamook
(503) 842-4444
www.tcgh.com

Tillamook County General Hospital is part of the Adventist Health System, which includes 70 hospitals nationwide. It features a modern birthing center, emergency, surgery, recovery, and laboratory facility.

Tillamook County General Hospital's Emergency Department is a level-three trauma center and is staffed twenty-four hours a day. The Medical/Surgical unit offers services that include immunization evaluation, diabetic management, spiritual care, social services, and rehabilitation. This facility also has hospice care for assistance with patients in their home and at the hospital. A unique service the hospital oversees is called Lifeline. Those who sign up for this service receive a small communication device that is placed in their home. At the press of a button there is someone available to help them twenty-four hours a day, seven days a week. This service allows patients with special needs to live in their own home but also have the assurance that there is someone there if they need help.

Classes offered to the community may include diabetes education, wellness screening, and CPR and first aid. The hospital has an informative Web site that allows you to find a doctor online. Physicians affiliated with the hospital specialize in general surgery, occupational health, radiology, family practice, podiatry, internal medicine, obstetrics, and midwifery.

A patient library is available online that has information on topics such as nutrition, parenting and child health, asthma, allergies and respiratory conditions, medications and drugs, cancer, and dieting and weight loss.

Clinics

PROVIDENCE NORTH COAST CLINIC
727 South Wahanna Rd., Seaside
(503) 717-7556
www.providence.org/northcoast

This clinic is affiliated with Providence Seaside Hospital and has seven physicians and a nurse practitioner on staff. Office hours for this clinic are Monday through Friday 8:30 a.m. to 5 p.m. Insurance plans accepted include Providence Health Plan, Providence PPO, ODS, Blue Cross—Indemnity and PPO, QualMed (formerly PACC), and other insurance plans.

THE O'DONOVAN MINOR EMERGENCY CLINIC
580 U Ave., Seaside
(503) 738-5571

The O'Donovan clinic has a staff of physicians specializing in family practice, gastroenterology, internal medicine, neurology, orthopedic surgery, pulmonary medicine, urology, and vascular surgery. This clinic has a doctor on call twenty-four hours a day, seven days a week. The clinic accepts walk-in patients and minor emergencies. The clinic is open 8:30 a.m. to 4:30 p.m. Monday through Thursday and 9 a.m. to noon on Friday, and accepts most major insurance plans.

PROVIDENCE NORTH COAST CLINIC
171 North Larch, Suite 16 (Sandpiper Sq.), Cannon Beach
(503) 717-7556
www.providence.org/northcoast

This clinic has a family practice physician and a family nurse practitioner on staff. The clinic accepts walk-in appointments. Office hours are Monday, Tuesday, Thursday, and Friday 8:30 a.m. to 5 p.m. Insurance coverage accepted includes

i If you are relocating to a coastal city, many hospitals with a Web site have a physician referral page where they list the name, location, and contact information for physicians who have been accredited by the participating hospital.

Providence Health Plan, Providence PPO, ODS, Blue Cross—Indemnity and PPO, QualMed (formerly PACC), and other insurance plans.

TILLAMOOK COUNTY GENERAL HOSPITAL PHYSICIANS
1000 3rd St., Tillamook
(503) 842-4444
www.tcgh.com
Tillamook County General Hospital has a group of family practice physicians and other specialists who have received credentials from the hospital. Most major medical insurance is accepted.

Central Coast
Hospitals
SAMARITAN NORTH LINCOLN HOSPITAL
3043 Northeast 28th St., Lincoln City
(541) 994-3661
www.samhealth.org/shs_facilities/snlh
Samaritan North Lincoln Hospital offers inpatient and outpatient services to the residents of Lincoln City. The hospital features an emergency department that is level-four certified; surgery; diagnostic imaging including CT scans, MRI, nuclear medicine, mammography, and ultrasound; dialysis; respiratory therapy; laboratory; nutrition services; rehabilitation therapy; and home health care.

The rehabilitation department uses conventional and holistic approaches to help patients who need physical therapy, occupational therapy, or speech therapy. A Lifeline service is offered to those patients who want to live at home but have someone to call if they need help. Social services, a wellness program, and hospice care are also offered.

Samaritan North Lincoln Hospital has a family-centered approach to childbirth. Using this philosophy, family members are part of the birth experience and new mothers can experience the joy of motherhood in a private birth suite. The birth suite is a fully equipped birthing room that gives the new mother privacy but has the resources the staff may need to ensure mothers have a safe and comfortable childbirth. Birth suites are also available for women who need to have a cesarean. The hospital teaches classes designed especially for new parents on topics such as "Overview of Birth and Delivery," "The Labor Process," "Comfort Measures," "Medications and Anesthesia," "Breathing Techniques," and "Birth Plans and Options."

SAMARITAN PACIFIC COMMUNITIES HOSPITAL
930 Southwest Abbey St., Newport
(541) 265-2244
www.samhealth.org/shs_facilities/pch
Serving the Newport community, Samaritan Pacific Communities Hospital is a 48-bed hospital that was established in 1946 as a privately owned health care facility called Pacific View Hospital. Over the years, several expansion projects have occurred at the hospital. In 1964 20 more beds were added, and in 1968 intensive care, laboratory, and radiology departments were added. The hospital has a Clinical Services Center. Other services include a birthing center, diagnostic imaging, critical and intensive care, in-home care, and hospice care.

PEACE HARBOR HOSPITAL
400 9th St., Florence
(541) 997-8412
www.peacehealth.org/siuslaw
Peace Harbor Hospital is an acute-care hospital with a staff of 60 physicians and more than 300 employees who provide care to more than 17,000 patients a year. Peace Harbor Hospital is part of a large health care system that encompasses home health, hospice services, and counseling services and is also affiliated with Health Associates of Peace Harbor, a multispecialty medical group. The hospital offers services in labor and delivery care; emergency medicine; intensive care and post-cardiac care; inpatient medical and surgical services; and diagnostic and therapeutic services.

LOWER UMPQUA HOSPITAL
600 Ranch Rd., Reedsport
(541) 271-2171
www.lowerumpquahospital.com
Lower Umpqua Hospital is a full-service hospital

serving the Reedsport community. This hospital has twenty-four-hour emergency service that includes ambulance service and acute care, a family birthing center, rehabilitation therapy, imaging services (CT scan, MRI, mammography), general surgery, day surgery, hospice services, and a long-term nursing facility.

Clinics

The following clinics all have licensed family practice physicians who have obtained their credentials from Samaritan Pacific Communities Hospital in Newport:

SAMARITAN DEPOE BAY CLINIC
539 North US 101, Suite A, Depoe Bay
(541) 765-3265

The Depoe Bay Clinic is staffed with one family practice physician and a physician's assistant. This clinic is open for appointments 9 a.m. to 3 p.m. Monday through Friday and accepts most major medical plans.

JOHN LEHRER, M.D.
775 Southwest 9th St. Suite G, Newport
(541) 265-3772

This is a single-doctor family practice staffed by John Lehrer, M.D. The office is open 8:30 a.m. to 4:30 p.m. Monday, Tuesday, Thursday, and Friday and 8:30 a.m. to 11:30 a.m. on Wednesday. This medical office accepts most major medical plans.

TOLEDO CLINIC
1744 Northwest Business Hwy. 20, Toledo
(541) 336-5181

Two family practice physicians staff the Toledo Clinic. The clinic is open 8:30 a.m. to 4:30 p.m. Monday through Friday and accepts most major medical plans.

WALDPORT CLINIC
150 Southwest Arrow, Waldport
(541) 563-3197

The Waldport clinic is staffed with two family practice physicians. Open 8:30 a.m. to 5 p.m. Monday through Friday and accepts most major medical plans.

South Coast
Hospitals
BAY AREA HOSPITAL
1775 Thompson Rd., Coos Bay
(541) 269-8111
www.bayareahospital.org

Bay Area Hospital is the largest publicly owned acute-care facility on the Oregon Coast and provides high-quality health care to Coos County residents. This 172-bed facility was built in 1970 at a cost of $6.75 million. Diagnostic and therapeutic inpatient and outpatient services include critical care, home health, oncology, obstetrical, pediatric, psychiatric, surgical, and other specialties. Patients at Bay Area Hospital can also take advantage of imaging services that include MRI, CT scan, and mammography.

The hospital is well known for its accredited cancer program, where cancer patients receive treatment in a modern radiation therapy center that was opened in 1990. The hospital also has a housing facility for the families of cancer patients so they can be close by to offer much-needed support. This facility also teaches patient and community health care classes.

COQUILLE VALLEY HOSPITAL
940 East 5th, Coquille
(541) 396-3101
www.cvhospital.org

Coquille Valley Hospital is a 30-bed hospital that serves the community of Coquille. This community hospital offers a fully staffed twenty-four-hour emergency department and services in respiratory therapy, radiology, general and orthopedic surgery, laboratory services, and a birthing suite. In addition, this hospital offers diabetes and childbirth education classes and home health services and has a physician's referral line.

i When you call a clinic listed in this section, be sure to ask what type of health insurance the clinic accepts. If you are relocating to a coastal city, your health plan may not be accepted and you may need to switch plans.

SOUTHERN COOS HOSPITAL AND HEALTH CENTER
900 Southeast 11th St., Bandon
(541) 329-1031
www.southerncoos.org

The community of Bandon has a full-service 20-bed general, acute-care hospital. This hospital features a twenty-four-hour staffed emergency department and imaging services including CT scan, mammography, and MRI. The hospital also owns and manages the Ocean View Care Center that offers long-term care for elderly patients.

CURRY GENERAL HOSPITAL
l 94220 4th St., Gold Beach
(541) 247-6621, (800) 445-8085
www.currygeneralhospital.com

Curry General Hospital is a full-service hospital offering quality health care to Gold Beach residents. This hospital offers emergency, surgery, imaging, laboratory, and other community health care services.

Clinics
NORTH BEND MEDICAL CENTER
1900 Woodland Dr., Coos Bay
(541) 267-5151

This clinic is fully staffed with physicians who specialize in audiology, family practice, gynecology, hematology, internal medicine, occupational medicine, oncology, orthopedic surgery, pediatrics, plastic reconstructive surgery, radiology, surgery, and urology. This clinic also has a licensed nurse practitioner on staff and a licensed acupuncturist. The clinic has a health resource center, gives vaccinations for those traveling abroad, and has a licensed midwife on staff. This medical center has affiliated clinics in the following cities: **Bandon** (541) 347-5191 and **Coquille** (541) 396-3111.

ALTERNATIVE CARE

Many coastal communities offer alternative health care options including acupuncture, herbal medicine, homeopathy, massage, and aromatherapy. Health food stores are an excellent resource for finding alternative care providers. Ask for referrals from the owner or other workers in the store and be sure to check to see if they have a bulletin board where business cards and flyers are often posted. *Hipfish*, a monthly alternative publication (see the Media chapter), also contains a business listing for alternative health care providers for the North Coast.

COLUMBIA RIVER DAY SPA
1215 Duane St., Astoria
(503) 325-7721
www.columbiariverdayspa.com

The friendly day spa offers massage therapy, hydrotherapy and sauna, body wraps, facials, aromatherapy, and hand and foot treatments. Open Tuesday through Sunday 10 a.m. to 6 p.m.

SEASIDE SPA & WELLNESS CENTER
2647 US 101 North, Seaside
(503) 717-1770
www.seasidespaandwellness.com

The Seaside Spa & Wellness Center offers acupuncture, massage, facials, pedicures, and hair-care services from a staff of licensed professionals. This full-care spa also has a licensed naturopathic physician who specializes in women's and children's health care. The spa stocks massage oils, bath products, and other self-care products. The spa is open 9 a.m. to 5 p.m. Monday through Saturday.

REJUVENATION MASSAGE & SPA
4783 Southwest US 101, Lincoln City
(541) 994-1819
www.rejuvenationmassageandspa.com

Rejuvenation Massage & Spa is owned by Carol Ritzert and Donna King and has licensed massage therapists on staff. This spa offers several different services that will relax the mind and spirit including body treatments, facials, massage, hydrotherapy, aromatherapy, and reflexology (the zones of the feet are massaged). This spa also has a small retail shop that stocks scented candles, natural soaps, skin products, massage tools, and much more. The spa is open 10 a.m. to 5 p.m. Monday through Saturday and it is recommended that you call ahead to schedule an appointment.

WELLNESS MASSAGE CENTER
530 Northwest 3rd St. Suite B, Newport
(541) 265-8468

The Wellness Massage Center has a staff of four licensed massage therapists and is open Monday through Saturday from 10 a.m. to 7 p.m. by appointment only. Techniques offered at this facility include Swedish massage, lymphatic drainage, and deep tissue massage.

BANDON MASSAGE
190 2nd St., Bandon
(541) 347-9877

This office offers a full range of massage services.

SENIOR SERVICES

Seniors make up a large sector of the economy and the services for seniors are relatively plentiful. But all counties can provide some kind of advice and assistance, notably in the population centers of Astoria, Seaside, Tillamook, Lincoln City, Newport, Florence, Coos Bay, and North Bend. Furthermore, senior centers, community colleges, houses of worship, arts guilds, historical societies, and many other organizations supply fellowship, education, and entertainment. Wherever you decide to go, retiring to the Oregon Coast will put you in good company.

Oregon Senior & Disabled Services Division

The Senior & Disabled Services Division (SDSD), (500 Summer St. Northeast E12, Salem; (503) 945-5921; www.oregon.gov/DHS/spwpd/index.shtml), part of the Oregon Department of Human Services, is the state agency that provides assistance to older adults, persons with disabilities, and caregivers, and they are dedicated to helping people live dignified and independent lives.

The following numbers are for branch offices of SDSD and related agencies on the Coast. The staff at these offices will help you find local options for transportation, meal services, shopping, housekeeping, medical care and supplies, employment or volunteer opportunities, and many other services and possibilities in which you may be interested. They will do whatever they can to help you stay in your own house. They can also help you evaluate whether residential or nursing home care is appropriate and help you find the right facility.

GEARHART AGING AND DISABILITY SERVICES
3523 US 101 North, Gearhart
(503) 738-5191, (800) 442-8614

NORTH COAST SENIOR SERVICES
278 Rowe St., Wheeler
(503) 368-4200

TILLAMOOK AGING NORTHWEST SENIOR AND DISABILITY SERVICES
4670 East Third St., Tillamook
(503) 842-2770, (800) 584-9712

NEWPORT AREA AGENCY ON AGING
111 Southeast Douglas, Suite F, Newport
(541) 265-7719

LANE COUNTY SENIOR AND DISABLED SERVICES
3180 US 101, Florence
(541) 902-9430

REEDSPORT AREA AGENCY ON AGING
680 Fir Ave., Reedsport
(541) 271-4835

AREA AGENCY ON AGING
93781 Newport Lane, Coos Bay
(541) 269-2013, (800) 858-5777

GOLD BEACH MULTIPLE SERVICES OFFICE (INCLUDING SDSD)
94145 5th Place, Gold Beach
(541) 247-4515, (800) 257-1385

BROOKINGS/HARBOR MULTIPLE SERVICES OFFICE (INCLUDING SDSD)
97829 Shopping Center Ave. Suite F,
Brookings
(541) 469-0481, (541) 469-9299

Senior Centers

Senior centers on the Coast often provide the central locations for the outreach services arranged by SDSD; they may coordinate the dial-a-ride service; they may provide meals there or in your home; they may help you with Medicare and taxes; and that's just the beginning. In addition, they usually sponsor a smorgasbord of special events and social activities, from bingo to samba lessons and everything in between. Even if you're just traveling through, many senior centers will welcome your participation.

ASTORIA SENIOR CENTER
1111 Exchange, Astoria
(503) 325-3231

SEASIDE SENIOR CENTER
1225 Ave. A, Seaside
(503) 738-7393

SENIOR CENTER DROP-IN CENTER
316 Stillwell, Tillamook
(503) 842-9660

NEWPORT SENIOR CENTER
20 Southeast 2nd, Newport
(541) 265-9617

FLORENCE BOOSTERS SENIOR CENTER
1424 West 15th, Florence
(541) 997-8844

LOWER UMPQUA SENIOR CENTER
460 Winchester Ave., Reedsport
(541) 271-4884

BAY AREA SENIOR ACTIVITY CENTER
886 South 4th, Coos Bay
(541) 269-2626

NORTH BEND SENIOR RECREATION AND ACTIVITY CENTER
1470 Outpost Lane, North Bend
(541) 756-7622

BANDON SENIOR ACTIVITY CENTER
1100 Southwest 10th, Bandon
(541) 347-4131

PORT ORFORD SENIOR CENTER
1536 Jackson, Port Orford
(541) 332-5771

GOLD BEACH SENIOR CENTER
29841 Airport Way, Gold Beach
(541) 247-7506

CHETCO SENIOR CENTER
550 Chetco Lane, Brookings
(541) 469-6822

RESIDENTIAL CARE AND NURSING HOMES

ASTOR HOUSE
999 Klaskanine Ave., Astoria
(503) 325-6970

HILLSIDE HOUSE
1400 Southeast 19th St., Lincoln City
(541) 994-8028

Part of the Assisted Living Concepts network of facilities, which specializes in rural senior care, Astor House and Hillside House are dedicated to providing their residents with an atmosphere that is as uninstitutional as possible. Hence, apartments have small kitchens; residents can bring their pets and cars with them; there are plenty of social activities and ample, pleasant common spaces; and home cooked meals are served. But in addition to the comforts of home, Astor House and Hillside House provide the extra services that their clients need: assistance with the administration of medication; with bathing, dressing, or grooming; with medical or physical conditions such as incontinence or dementia. Best of all, services are adaptable as a resident's needs change.

NEAWANNA BY THE SEA
20 North Wahanna Rd., Seaside
(503) 738-5526

Neawanna by the Sea has nearly 60 units, 40 of them assisted-living units and the remainder duplexes for those who are more independent. The tidy facility was built in 1990 within walking distance of the ocean and overlooking Neawanna Creek in Seaside. The duplexes each have two bedrooms and two baths, full kitchens, washers, and dryers; moreover, they offer yard care, housekeeping and building maintenance, and a twenty-four-hour emergency call system. Plus, those living in duplexes have access to the amenities of the main building, which include a dining room, a beauty salon, transportation services, and social activities. The assisted-living apartments in the main building, which are private apartments of one or two bedrooms or studios, include all the same amenities. In addition, they provide kitchenettes, housekeeping and linen services, three daily meals, and the security of an emergency call system, a twenty-four-hour staff, and people trained to look out for the well-being and health of their clients.

SUZANNE ELISE ASSISTED LIVING
101 Forest Dr., Seaside
(503) 738-0307

Suzanne Elise Assisted Living is a large, immaculate facility in Seaside with well-trimmed grounds and a large, sunny patio. Residents live in private apartments with attentive housekeeping, laundry, and linen services; transportation is provided or coordinated for clients (including a luxurious bus with a wheelchair lift); and a 24-hour emergency alert system is also offered. Three meals a day are included. Suzanne Elise's philosophy is to keep residents in their homes as long as possible, and it's a close community with many activities featured and a lot of interactivity with the larger community. Schoolchildren trick or treat; the high school students might put on a play; local artists visit. It's also a good place just to hang out. The library is especially nice.

NEHALEM VALLEY CARE CENTER
280 Rowe St., Wheeler
(503) 368-5171

Right next to the noted Rinehart Clinic in the charming village of Wheeler, you'll find the Nehalem Valley Care Center. This Medicare-contracted nursing facility offers both ongoing nursing care and rehabilitative services. In addition to a special Alzheimer's and dementia program, the 50-bed center provides teams of caregivers in order to give the most comprehensive care possible—their goal is always to get the patient back home and, once there, to enable him or her to live as independently as possible. Rooms are private. The Agency on Aging office is next door so social service outreach programs are coordinated here—especially useful after a person is discharged.

THE DORCHESTER HOUSE
2701 Northwest US 101, Lincoln City
(541) 994-7175
www.thedorchesterhouseret.com

The Dorchester House offers studio or one-bedroom apartments in an old-fashioned house with a big stone fireplace in the living room and other lovely common room areas like a library and gar-

---

Senior Friendly Site

The Web site for the Senior and Disabled Services Division, www.oregon.gov/DHS/spwpd/index.shtml, is user friendly and comprehensive. In addition to its own well-organized material about programs and services for seniors, it features many links to local, state, and national organizations providing information on everything from how to look for residential care to legal advocacy for seniors. This excellent resource should not be missed.

den. This spot is for the relatively independent—there's not a medical staff. But there are services to make life more comfortable and easy. In addition to housekeeping and linen service, two meals are served each day, a security and emergency alert system gives you peace of mind, and a management staff will be there to keep an eye on you and your place.

OCEAN CREST RETIREMENT
192 Norman Ave., Coos Bay
(541) 888-2255
An attractive building with nicely landscaped grounds, Ocean Crest is both a retirement home and a licensed assisted-living facility with several levels of personal care. They'll develop a plan to fit your own assistance requirements. Their basic plan provides three daily meals and scheduled transportation, as well as cleaning and maintenance of your apartment, laundry areas, and beauty and barber shops on the premises. They'll help plan the social calendar too, with a number of recreational activities scheduled weekly.

OCEAN VIEW CARE CENTER OF BANDON
2790 Beach Loop Rd., Bandon
(541) 347-4402
This facility overlooks the sea in Bandon, is the setting of the Ocean View Care Center. It is an exquisite place in which to receive nursing care. For those clients who can manage to tear themselves away from the window, there are four scheduled activities each day, including such activities as visits with pets, Golden Age Radio, and trivia games. At least one outing is scheduled per week; this may be a scenic drive, a bus tour, or a special shopping trip.

ELDER HOME ADULT FOSTER CARE
903 Lakeshore Dr., Port Orford
(541) 332-1007
For some people, a small homelike care facility is best and that's just what Elder Home provides. This licensed facility in a nice house has just five bedrooms. They'll provide either short- or long-term care. They can also help you set up a program for day care or respite care.

CHETCO INN RESIDENTIAL CARE FACILITY
417 Fern St., Brookings
(541) 469-5347
Brookings is a favorite with retirees and so is the Chetco Inn, which sits on a hill above town. The building used to be a hotel; it was built in 1915 and retains many of its lovely original furnishings and features, including the fireplace in the living room and a staircase that sweeps up to the second floor (there's also an elevator). The Chetco Inn has 35 private or partially private units; they will provide you housekeeping and linen services, three meals each day, emergency phones by the bed and in the bathroom, and private telephones. You will also receive twenty-four-hour medical supervision, with a medical director, two RNs, and a LVN on staff. The backyard is a favorite gathering place for horseshoes and croquet or just for chatting peacefully in the sun.

MACKLYN HOUSE
755 Elk Dr., Brookings
(541) 469-7182
The maintenance of independence is the mission of the folks at Macklyn House, a licensed assisted-living facility. Macklyn house provides basic assisted-living services, but it also has a twenty-four-hour staff trained to provide nursing, personal, and other care for more complex problems such as confusion. The studio and one-bedroom apartments are private (you can lock the doors), but they have emergency call systems for extra security. Three meals are served each day; laundry facilities are provided; and transportation can be arranged. Pets are welcomed, too.

MEDIA

The media scene on the Oregon Coast reflects the rich history of the area, has a commitment to providing news coverage that informs residents of local issues, and celebrates the individuality of the people that live in coastal communities. The majority of these communities have a weekly or biweekly paper that has kept residents well informed for more than half a century. Two daily papers, the *Daily Astorian* and the *World*, provide local as well as international news. A large majority of the newspapers also have Web sites that provide easy access for those who like to read about local news and events online. In the Television section, we've provided you with a listing of the local TV channels available, and there are a rich variety of radio stations that play a broad range of music with Adult Contemporary and Country-Western dominating the radio airwaves.

NEWSPAPERS

North Coast

Dailies

THE DAILY ASTORIAN
949 Exchange St., Astoria
(503) 325-3211, (800) 781-3210 ext. 233
www.dailyastorian.com
Established in 1873 by DeWitt Clinton Ireland, the *Daily Astorian* keeps readers up to date on the local happenings in Astoria and surrounding areas. It is published five days a week Monday through Friday. Subscription rates are $31.20 for 13 weeks—local or mail subscription. The paper's circulation area includes Clatsop County, northern Tillamook County, and Washington's Pacific and Wahkiakum Counties.

Weeklies and Biweeklies

THE COLUMBIA PRESS
P.O. Box 130, Warrenton
(503) 861-3331
www.thecolumbiapress.com
Established in 1922, this community publication is distributed every Friday and provides news on local events. An annual subscription is $24 for residents of Clatsop County. For residents living outside the county an annual subscription is $28.

SEASIDE SIGNAL
730 Broadway, Seaside
(503) 738-5561
www.seasidesignal.com
The Seaside Signal is published every Thursday and serves the communities of Seaside, Gearhart, Cannon Beach, and South Clatsop County.

CANNON BEACH GAZETTE
P.O. Box 888, Cannon Beach
(503) 436-2812
www.cannonbeachgazette.com
Published every Thursday, the *Cannon Beach Gazette* is a strictly community newspaper distributed to subscribers who live in Cannon Beach, Tolovana, and Arch Cape. It also has an informative Web site for those readers who prefer to read their local news online.

HEADLIGHT-HERALD
1908 2nd St., Tillamook
(800) 275-7799
www.tillamookheadlightherald.com
A community newspaper that was established in 1888, this publication spotlights news, sports, community issues, and classified ads.

ℹ️ Be sure to visit the Web sites listed for each newspaper. Many of these Web sites provide links to local businesses, weather and tide information, activities, arts and entertainment, cultural events, and real estate.

Central Coast
Weeklies and Biweeklies
THE NEWS GUARD
930 Southeast US 101, Lincoln City
(541) 994-2178
www.thenewsguard.com
This insightful paper, covering the Lincoln City news beat, is published every Wednesday and features news, announcements, beach life, business, legal notices, obituaries, classifieds, weather, sports, tide charts, and letters/opinions.

NEWS-TIMES
831 Northeast Avery, Newport
(541) 265-8571
www.newportnewstimes.com
Established in 1882, the *News-Times* keeps subscribers in touch with local issues in Newport and surrounding areas every Wednesday and Friday. The "Travel & Leisure" section gives you ideas for your next weekend getaway as well as other outdoor and travel-related topics.

SIUSLAW NEWS
148 Maple St., Florence
(541) 997-3441
www.thesiuslawnews.com/v2_main_page.php
Every Wednesday the *Siuslaw News* highlights local news, weather, sports, tides, court reports, opinions, and classifieds. The weekly insert "Soundings" covers the local arts and entertainment scene, contains TV and movie listings, and has a restaurant directory.

South Coast
Dailies
THE WORLD
350 Commercial Ave., Coos Bay
(541) 269-1222
www.theworldlink.com
Established in 1878, *The World* is the largest daily paper on the South Oregon Coast. This paper is distributed to readers in Coos County, Curry County, and selected areas in Douglas and Lane Counties. It offers a robust coverage of local and international news.

Weeklies and Biweeklies
BANDON WESTERN WORLD
1185 Baltimore Ave., Bandon
(541) 347-2424
www.bandonwesternworld.com
Solid reporting focusing on community issues makes this award-winning weekly paper a local favorite. Published on Wednesdays. This paper is also available online and features daily events in and around Bandon, job listings, stories on the local arts scene, and a message board where Bandon readers can communicate their opinions in cyberspace.

CURRY COASTAL PILOT
507 Chetco Ave., Brookings
(541) 469-3123
www.currypilot.com
Established in 1946 by Dewey Akers and Dave Homan, the Curry Coastal Pilot is published every Wednesday and Saturday morning and focuses solely on community news. This paper is distributed to customers in the Brookings-Harbor area and Curry County.

Magazines and Other Print Media
HIPFISH
1355 Exchange St., Astoria
(503) 325-0227
www.hipfishmonthly.com
Hipfish is a monthly alternative paper that is distributed in the Lower Columbia Pacific region that

includes the lower Washington State peninsula, Astoria, and coastal communities as far south as Newport. It is also distributed in the Portland and Seattle metropolitan areas. This lively and off-beat publication features local commentary on social and community issues, a monthly calendar of cultural events, a guide to gallery openings, "North Coast Eatery Guide," and classifieds for local businesses.

LOWER COLUMBIA BUSINESS
P.O. Box 1088, Seaside 97138
(503) 738-3398
www.lcbiz.com
This monthly is distributed free of charge to local business owners and community leaders. It focuses on business issues on the North Coast and includes stories on new businesses, prominent business leaders, and updates on the retail, hospitality, and construction industries.

OREGON COAST
4969 US 101 North, Suite 2, Florence
(541) 997-8401
www.northwestmagazines.com
This photo-packed, regional bimonthly magazine includes feature articles about the many things to see and do on the Oregon Coast. It features stories on subjects such as exploring the Coast with your kids, whale-watching spots, music festivals, and favorite hiking trails.

LOCAL TELEVISION

KCBY-TV CHANNEL 11 (CBS)
3451 Broadway, North Bend
(541) 269-1111
www.kcby.com

KBSC-TV CHANNEL 49
Oregon Coast Television Network, Inc.
613 "A" Chetco Ave., Brookings
(541) 469-4999
www.kbsctv.com

RADIO

Adult Contemporary
KACW 107.3 FM, Coos Bay/North Bend
KAST 92.9 FM, Astoria
KCBZ 96.5 FM, Reedsport
KORC 820 AM, Waldport
KSND 95.1 FM, Tillamook
KYTE 102.7 FM, Newport

Christian
KYTT 98.7 FM, Coos Bay/North Bend

Country-Western
KCST 1250 AM, Florence
KCST 106.9 FM, Florence
KCYS 98.1 FM, Seaside
KDUN 1030 AM, Reedsport
KOOS 94.9 FM Coos Bay
KSHL 97.5 FM, Newport
KSHR 97.3 FM, Coquille
KVAS 1230 AM, Astoria

News, Talk, Sports
KAST 1370 AM, Astoria
KBBR 1340 AM, Coos Bay/North Bend, Newport
KTBR 94.1 FM, Myrtle Point
KWRO 630 AM, Coquille

Nostalgia/Oldies
KDCQ 93.5 FM, Coos Bay/North Bend
KHSN 1230 AM,

Public Radio Stations
KLCO 90.5 FM, Newport
KMUN 91.9 FM, Astoria
KSYD 92.1 FM, Reedsport

Rock
KBDN 96.5 FM, Bandon

INDEX

ABOUT THE AUTHOR

Lizann Dunegan has spent the last 25 years living in and exploring Oregon, and the Oregon Coast is one of her favorite destinations. She grew up on a cattle ranch in Central Oregon, where she developed her love of the Oregon outdoors. In 1983, she moved to Portland to attend Portland State University. Since that time, Lizann has worked as a freelance writer and photographer and has published several outdoor and travel guidebooks about Oregon including: *Canine Oregon, Trail Running Oregon, Road Biking Oregon, Hiking Oregon, Mountain Biking Oregon, Hiking the Oregon Coast, Best Easy Day Hikes Bend and Central Oregon, Best Easy Day Hikes Portland Oregon,* and *Best Easy Day Hikes North Oregon Coast.*

When Lizann isn't busy writing, she spends almost all of her free time in the outdoors hiking, camping, mountain biking, trail running, and cross-country skiing. She is often accompanied by her two fun-loving Border Collies, Bear and Sage, and her equally energetic and enthusiastic partner, Ken Skeen. Lizann currently resides in Portland and spends many weekends exploring the beaches, forests, and communities on the Oregon Coast.